SCOTLAND
IN THE
SEVENTIES

SCOTLAND
IN THE
SEVENTIES

THE DEFINITIVE ACCOUNT OF THE
SCOTLAND FOOTBALL TEAM
1970-79

RONNIE McDEVITT

First published by Pitch Publishing, 2019

Pitch Publishing
A2 Yeoman Gate
Yeoman Way
Worthing
Sussex
BN13 3QZ
www.pitchpublishing.co.uk
info@pitchpublishing.co.uk

A CIP catalogue record is available for this book
from the British Library.

ISBN 978-1-78531-439-1

Typesetting and origination by Pitch Publishing
Printed and bound in India by Replika Press Pvt. Ltd.

Contents

FOR BRIAN McKECHNIE

A true Scotland fan from the 1970s
onwards and an all-round decent bloke
who sadly passed away just as this book
was nearing completion

Author's Introduction

Whilst researching *Scotland in the Sixties* I had an inkling I would like to do a follow-up on the 1970s, a decade I was more familiar with.

It is fair to say that the only two World Cups discussed at any great length in Scotland are those in the 1970s and for differing reasons.

I was 13 at the time of the 1974 World Cup and was one of the few boys in my class who had a dislike of football. That changed when it became impossible to ignore Scotland's participation in West Germany. Curious, I watched my first ever football match, the opening game between Yugoslavia and Brazil on television. I may even have fallen asleep during the goalless draw but it didn't put me off watching Scotland vs Zaire the following evening. I was entertained enough to go out of my way to watch the Brazil game who, I was informed, were apparently better than the Africans.

By the time of the Yugoslavia match I was hooked and recall the disappointment watching with my father that Saturday afternoon. He was less enthralled than Arthur Montford who spoke of "Brave brave Scotland" at Joe Jordan's late equaliser. Dad's response was one of "Too bloody late!", words which have come back to me many times since when watching Scotland.

Scotland's 1974 squad has been referred to as a Golden Generation. A few months later a missed penalty kick in the opening European Championship qualifier denied Willie Ormond's side the opportunity to progress and do well in that tournament.

Aged 17 it was awful not being able to go to the 1978 World Cup and I collected all the newspaper accounts of the fans alongside the match reports for my Argentina scrapbook.

I envied the supporters who travelled overland and lived out my dream. In later years many of them became personal friends although

I never felt their equal regardless of how many Scotland games I attended. How I must have bored them with my constant questions about '78.

One whom I had never met but knew of was Robbie Sterry and I was delighted to track him down to Canada whilst researching the book. I knew his tale would be good but had no idea just how enthralling his trip to South America and back would be and his is a story which deserves to be in print. The thought of two Scotland fans clinging to a freight train crossing the Alps, in conditions so cold their hands were stuck to the rungs of a ladder, after watching Scotland draw with Iran is astonishing.

It is also fair to say that the supporters who went on organised trips to Argentina gave up an awful lot to finance the trip. As Robbie Jenkins says, 'So many sacrificed so much.'

I have experienced great hospitality in a number of locations watching Scotland overseas but have no doubt that the warmth extended by the people of Cordoba to Ally's Army surpassed any of these and I hope this is reflected in the text. William McIlvanney recorded of the fans in Cordoba, 'They are left with a deep affection for the spontaneous generosity and kindness of the Argentine people and a sense that nevertheless they have been cheated of their true purpose in coming here.'

What went wrong in Argentina? is a question still posed 40 years after the event partly because there is no easy answer, there were so many events which turned out badly. Youngers fans may be baffled at how those of my age look back on that period nostalgically. The most obvious explanation for me is that the good times arguably outweighed the bad.

Like John Grigor, my biggest regret is not making it to the 1978 World Cup and Robbie Jenkins, the only supporter I know who has watched Scotland play in eight tournaments, still considers 1978 to be his favourite. I have always intended to visit Cordoba and a trip there is on my bucket list for the near future.

Based solely on World Cup results Ally MacLeod's record is no worse than subsequent Scotland managers but his reign in charge still provokes debate and disagreement with the jury still split. One consistent theme was that everyone I spoke to liked Ally regardless of their views on his abilities.

Scotland have fared no better in any tournament since Argentina and I have always been of the opinion that losing to Costa Rica in 1990 was worse than the defeat to Peru but that never seems to get mentioned.

The 1970s was a period when there was so much talent around that no one could take their place in the Scotland side for granted. Joe Jordan is on record as saying he played every international as though it was his last.

Retrospectively, the importance that the Scottish public attached to the result of the annual Scotland v England match does seem ridiculous and this started to change as the 1970s gave way to the 80s with regular World Cup participation.

As with my previous publication, I have included the League Internationals and Under-23/21 matches which were seen as a stepping stone to the full side. Certainly the players I spoke with remember them and I wanted to be consistent with the 1960s volume. One glance at the Appendix will see that the line-ups for those fixtures against the Football League or England's Under-23 side invariably included members of England's World Cup-winning team, an indication of how important they were.

Although I attended most Scotland internationals from the middle of 1977 I have not included my own experiences in the text. I felt it would have been rather self-indulgent to suddenly change to the first person so I continued to feature other fans' reminiscences.

It really was quite fascinating to revisit the period and I hope you gain some of the enjoyment from reading the book that I did when working on it.

I have no plans for a third volume on the 1980s, but I guess you never say never.

Ronnie McDevitt
November 2018

Acknowledgements

As with my look at the 1960s I was rather flattered by the calibre of people who chose to share their memories with me for this volume.

At the age of 95 Bobby Brown's recollections were as good as anyone's I interviewed and I always enjoy our conversations.

John Blackley and Lou Macari spoke passionately about just being part of the Scotland squad even if they did not make the starting XI. On both occasions it was me who ended the conversation, so generous were they with their time.

Bobby Clark has amazing recall of events and was most accommodating with my numerous queries. I don't think there was one of his internationals that he had no memory of.

Like Bobby, Asa Hartford was around the Scotland set-up for most of the decade and clearly enjoyed his days with the squad. Again Asa was very helpful in answering my many questions. I have always considered Asa something of an unsung hero who played in many big matches without perhaps gaining the recognition of some of his team-mates. An entry into the Scottish Football Hall of Fame is surely overdue.

I am also indebted to Asa's nephew and Scotland fan Chris Norton for arranging the contact.

It is always interesting chatting with Willie Johnston, who Jimmy Bone considers 'the most underrated player ever'. Bud laughs quite a lot when looking back and again his memories are always detailed.

Likewise, Willie Morgan was full of enthusiasm for the subject and to his credit was able to comment on Tommy Docherty's time at the SFA without influence from a later disagreement.

Eddie Gray was able to more than adequately fill in some of the blanks during the mid-70s whilst Jimmy Bone spoke with great enthusiasm of his time with the Doc in Brazil.

Jimmy Millar also deserves a mention for clearing the way for me to contact his namesake.

Gary Keown of the Scottish *Daily Mail* was, as always most helpful, as was Matthew Lindsay at the *Herald*. Gary's assistance in speaking with Archie Macpherson and Rodger Baillie was invaluable. These two gentlemen were very much there at the time and it is fascinating to converse with people who knew many of the big names like Stein and Bremner personally.

Rodger always ended my calls with 'anything else I can help with just call me'. I thoroughly recommend Archie's recently published *Adventures in the Golden Age* for anyone with an interest in the Scotland side.

The supporters' input is crucial to a book like this and I am indebted to Robbie Jenkins, Andy McArthur, John Grigor, Stuart Borrowman, Tommy Collin, David Stephen and Stevie Newlands for giving their time to discuss a period I think we all look back on fondly.

Robbie Sterry's travels to and from the 1978 World Cup could fill a book on their own. He was so detailed with his input it was difficult to leave much of it out and his contribution is probably my favourite part of the book. I was delighted to be able to meet up with Robbie on a rare return visit to Perth in October 2018 and found him to be a most entertaining chap whose entire life could be described as an adventure.

I have credited all the journals and productions sourced for quotes. I always think it is quite poor to read elsewhere, for example, '*Smith later said...*' followed by a quote I recognise from a documentary with no credit given to the production. The journals and broadcasts consulted are all acknowledged although if I have come by the same quote twice it will be listed as '*Smith told the press...*' or '*during the press conference Smith said...*'

Thanks also to Andy Cameron for permission to reproduce the lyric from one of his lesser-known Argentina songs in Chapter 9 and to John Smith for his assistance in reaching Andy.

Also to John Lister for offering his views on early drafts of the opening two chapters.

When compiling the statistics section two reference books were particularly useful: *Scotland The Team* by Andrew Ward and Richard Keir's Scotland – *The Complete International Record*. The details for the Under-23/21 and League Internationals were quite challenging and are almost comprehensive. I was unable to locate the clubs of just two opposition players, one each from the Under-23s/21s, and a small number of times substitutes were introduced. I won't bore you with how many libraries I visited and the number of newspapers I consulted in pursuit of the sub times for an Under-21 game against Norway but let's just say it was the last available newspaper I checked which provided the information. That was a good moment!

Sandy Riddoch was able to fill in most of the opposition clubs for the 1977 Toulon tournament and Andy Mitchell was helpful with those players Sandy did not have a record of so a big thank you to both of them.

And of course many thanks to Paul and Jane at Pitch Publishing for their faith and support in the project, not forgetting Duncan Olner for another excellent cover design which should sit nicely on the bookshelf alongside the 1960s title.

1970

*"Bestie picked the mud up to throw
at him, but Ronnie ducked and it
hit the referee and he sent him off!"*
Willie Johnston

The Swinging Sixties had ended in disappointment for the Scottish national side, with a gallant display in West Germany deserving more than the narrow 3-2 defeat that ended qualification hopes for the 1970 World Cup. This was on top of the failed attempts to reach the 1962 and 1966 tournaments.

A host of naturally gifted players had worn the dark blue, some of whom, such as Baxter and Mackay, had been replaced by players from the seemingly endless conveyor belt of Scottish football talent.

There was still room for optimism in a new decade, which would see the introduction of colour television to Scotland, the first North Sea oil pumped to the mainland, a referendum on devolution, the restructuring of the Scottish League and the punk rock phenomenon.

Scotland's first international fixture of the 1970s took place on 14 January, with Pittodrie Stadium hosting the annual Under-23 match against Wales. Scotland's last outing at this level had been an impressive 4-0 win over France in the previous December.

Manager Bobby Brown made five changes from the French match, explaining his intention to assess as many potential full internationals as possible. Along with the Inter League fixtures the under-23 games were still considered an important part of the international calendar, offering players the opportunity to progress to a full cap. The selections generally contained a mix of youngsters and established internationals – a blend of youth and experience.

"They were big games for me because I had never had any international recognition at all until the Under-23s," recalls Hibs defender John Blackley, who had debuted against the French. "I'd gone through school trials and never got picked at Under-18s. I never even got sent for a trial with the club and I was thinking, 'I am way behind here.' Then all of a sudden the Under-23 squad gets picked and it was great for me as it was my first recognition. The next stepping stone was if you got picked for the League side." The Dons' new floodlights were switched on for the first time watched by a crowd of 15,349, which would have been larger but for the stormy conditions that did not encourage skilful football.

Brown gave the captaincy to Blackley who rather modestly plays down the award. "To be fair I did get the captaincy but Tam McNiven was the Hibs physio and also the Scotland physio and I think Tam would have a wee input when the question came up. I always think that he put my name forward. That's my belief anyway."

Wales took an 11th-minute lead through a Dick Krzywicki glancing header and the West Brom midfielder almost scored again when another effort rebounded from Stewart's crossbar. His goal looked to have won the contest until John O'Hare levelled when he shot home following a corner kick taken by Harper with four minutes remaining. The Scots then almost won the match with the very last kick – Peter Lorimer's shot against the goalpost.

Norman MacDonald wrote in the Aberdeen *Press and Journal* that: "Despite the fact the game was played in a wind and rainstorm the switch-on of the new floodlighting system at Pittodrie was an instant success. But sadly the play of Scotland's youngsters failed to match the brilliance of the illuminations. John Blackley, the Scottish captain, guessed the spin of the coin correctly and then inexplicably decided to play against the elements. The end product was that Scotland came within an ace of losing the match." In the same paper Bobby Brown defended his captain: "John Blackley and I went on to the pitch and decided to take advantage of the wind if we won the toss. At that time the wind appeared to be blowing from the west. By the time the game started, however, it had veered and was blowing in exactly the opposite direction."

An 18-year-old Kenny Dalglish spent the entire match on the bench, just as he had done against France. It was a frustrating 90 minutes for the Celtic forward, as he recalled in his autobiography, *Dalglish*, published in 1996. "I thought my whole world had collapsed," was his reaction to not playing.

Aberdeen FC received ground rental of £903.13s.7d. from the evening, which was 25 per cent of the gate receipts of £3,614.14s.6d. After the Scottish Football Association's (SFA) hotel bill of £1,081.9s.9d. and other expenditure was taken into account the SFA made a profit of £55.4s.4d. on the evening.

Two days after the match the *Press and Journal's* Norman MacDonald called for the city to be given a greater share of international action. "The time is opportune for the SFA or the Scottish League officials to end the Glasgow monopoly and stage one of the Inter League fixtures or a full international against Wales or Ireland in the provinces. Considering the appalling weather conditions," he continued, "Scotland's football legislators could not but have been impressed with the attendance. The crowd was almost 6,000 in excess of the combined attendances of the recent Inter League and Under-23 fixtures staged in Glasgow. Glasgow enthusiasts simply don't want to know about minor representative games," MacDonald concluded.

With no full internationals scheduled until the British Championship series in April, the next fixture was also at under-23 level, when a party of 15 players headed to Sunderland to face the Auld Enemy England on 4 March. On the eve of the game the manager stressed to his players that every one of them had the opportunity to progress to the full side for the European Championship qualifiers starting in the autumn.

Again there were changes, with three players making their debuts: Billy Dickson of Kilmarnock, Celtic's George Connelly and Archie Gemmill of Preston North End. Unlike Connelly, Dalglish was not released by Celtic who had a European Cup quarter-final against Fiorentina the same night.

The young Scots started well but fell behind to a Peter Osgood strike after 24 minutes, which altered the pattern of the game. Again the weather spoiled the spectacle for the 12,885 crowd, with a snowstorm creating near-impossible conditions. Osgood scored again before Brian Kidd gave England a three-goal lead after almost an hour of play. Colin Todd then reduced the margin by heading into his own net from a Munro free kick, before the relentless snow forced Welsh referee Clive Thomas to take the teams from the pitch on 62 minutes.

A ten-minute interlude was planned in the hope that the match could restart but the players failed to reappear and the game was abandoned. There would have been little complaint from the Scottish camp whose reaction was later summed up in the SFA's Annual Report: "Mercifully, from our point of view, a heavy fall of snow during the second half, caused the game to be abandoned, at a time when we were lagging by 3-1."

Of equal value, but not under the jurisdiction of the SFA, were the Scottish League internationals. Since the early 1960s the Scotland team manager had traditionally taken charge of the League side, providing continuity and experience. This also meant, of course, an additional payment to the manager. The Scottish League's first fixture of the decade came just two weeks after the Under-23 match against the Football League at Coventry City's Highfield Road.

There was some good news for Scotland with Osgood withdrawing due to a heavy cold. Sir Alf Ramsey traditionally took charge of the Football League side and he was keen to assess his players ahead of their defence of the World Cup in the summer.

No Celtic players were available for the Coventry game due to the second leg of their European Cup tie and Brown chose a 4-3-3 formation, with Tommy McLean, Henry Hall and Willie Johnston playing up front.

The home side established a two-goal lead after 24 minutes through Astle and Rogers but Ramsey's replacement of two Manchester United players at half-time affected the flow of the game. "The Football League's rhythm vanished in the second half when Kidd and Stepney were taken off," noted Desmond Hackett in his *Daily Express* report. Peter Cormack, taking advantage of a defensive mix-up, brought the Scots back into the match before Astle restored England's two-goal lead in the 72nd minute.

Hibs' Johnny Graham, who had replaced Hall, made the final score a more respectable 3-2 following good work by Johnston on the left. The scoreline was considered "ridiculous" in Hackett's view, considering the gulf between the teams in the first half.

Bobby Brown released a list of 17 names for the opening Home International in Northern Ireland on 18 April. When appointed team manager in 1967 Bobby had been granted complete control over team selection. There was still a Selection Committee, which continued to travel the length and breadth of the UK monitoring the form of players before submitting its reports to the manager. After deciding on his team Bobby Brown would go through the formality of handing his list to the committee, which rubber-stamped it without interference.

The manager did not place too much emphasis on the findings of the Selection Committee, having a good relationship with many club managers whose views he considered more relevant.

"They were only there in name anyway," Bobby reflects. "It was said sometimes that they went and looked at players. That was up to them but I never took their word. I took Jock Stein's or Don Revie's or Bertie Mee's at Arsenal, people I could rely on."

Following Celtic's victory over Leeds in the semi-final of the European Cup, full-back Davie Hay was added to the squad and was personally driven by Jock Stein to Glasgow Airport to join up with the squad the morning after the Leeds game. Also called in were Arsenal duo George Graham and Frank McLintock, who had both played in Amsterdam in another European semi-final – that of the Fairs Cup.

Bobby had a long-standing friendship with Arsenal manager Bertie Mee whom he praised in the *Evening Times*, saying: "It says a lot for Arsenal that they have done this for Scotland at such short notice." John O'Hare was chosen to play up front alongside Alan Gilzean, with the captaincy awarded to McLintock, who was making a return to international football after a three-year gap. Four players represented Scotland for the first time – O'Hare, Hay, Billy Dickson and Willie Carr.

As a one-off experiment the 1969 Home Internationals had been played within an eight-day period at the end of the season with each game televised live.

The four home nations decided to continue with the format into the new decade but without any live TV coverage. The SFA was particularly opposed to over-exposure of the game on television and its Annual Report contained the following in reference to the paltry attendance of 7,483 at Hampden for the Northern Ireland game. "If vindication were needed of the Association's attitude towards television down the years, this was it."

The television coverage of the 1970 series saw the matches screened either in full or as edited highlights later in the evening, and the game in Belfast was the first Scotland international to be televised in colour.

There was a full league programme in Scotland the same afternoon with the final round of matches in the First Division taking place. By this time Celtic had already secured their fifth successive title with Rangers assured of second place.

For the second consecutive year the Scotland v Ireland fixture went ahead on a waterlogged pitch.

George Best and Gilzean were both guilty of poor finishing in the first half with Gilzean's effort so far off target that it almost struck the corner flag.

Early in the second period Bobby Clark saved well to deny Best before the only goal of the game after 58 minutes, scored when a cross from McLean was headed past Jennings by O'Hare. This ensured that the Derby County striker has the distinction of scoring Scotland's first goal on colour television.

Five minutes later Best appeared to be fouled in a crowded goalmouth only for English referee Eric Jennings, possibly unsighted, to award a free kick to Scotland! After retaliating Best then threw a handful of mud in the direction of Jennings which earned him an early dismissal. Willie Johnston is unable to supress his laughter looking back on the incident. "Big Ronnie McKinnon had tackled or fouled him and Bestie picked the mud up to throw at him, but Ronnie ducked and it hit the referee and he sent him off!"

Bobby Clark, who had gathered the ball, also remembers the event. "I feel confident that the referee was only going to book Best but the way he reacted by throwing mud was what advanced the booking to being sent off." The seeds of Best's frustrations had been sown early in the match when McKinnon had brought him down and he had aimed a kick in retaliation, which the referee had viewed leniently.

Stein replaced O'Hare for the last 20 minutes against the ten men but there were no further goals and Scotland recorded their first win in Belfast since 1961. Most observers considered the game unmemorable with the *Sunday Post* match report suggesting that Best's antics had diverted attention from the game. "A lot of players in this international match had much to thank George Best for," wrote Jack Harkness. "This saved quite a bit of embarrassment for many players." The following day eight players were added to the pool for the games against Wales and England, five of them from Celtic – Gemmell, McNeill, Lennox, Johnstone and Hughes. McLintock and Graham left the squad to join their Arsenal team-mates for the first leg of their Fairs Cup Final against Anderlecht on the same night as the Welsh game.

The starting XI against Wales on the Wednesday had four changes including Hearts goalkeeper Jim Cruickshank who replaced Clark, with Stein partnering O'Hare in the attack.

John Greig, another addition, was made captain – a position he had previously held until Billy Bremner had taken on the role in 1968.

A determined Welsh defence thwarted almost every Scottish attempt to breach it. Greig twice threatened with free kicks but it was Hay who came closest to grabbing a winner when Swansea keeper Tony Millington saved his deflected shot in the dying seconds.

The 0-0 result ensured that the visitors left with a point to supplement that gained in the 1-1 draw with England on the Saturday. In his summary for the *Press and Journal* Norman MacDonald was in no doubt about who ought to have won the game: "On play and creative ability Scotland should have won handsomely and how the Welshmen survived despite all their courage and tenacity is something of a mystery." Despite the lack of goals there was praise from supporters with Jack Kelly of Dorchester Avenue in Glasgow writing a letter to the *Evening Citizen*: "Our team against Wales was like a breath of fresh air with the successful introduction of new faces like Moncur, O'Hare, Dickson, Carr and Hay. At long last we have the feeling that Scotland is going places from now on with such young stars available." With the manager's contract due to expire on 31 December, the SFA International and Selection Committee met that week to discuss Bobby Brown's future. After the Wales game Bobby announced to the press that he had agreed to remain in charge for a further four years with the extension due to expire after the 1974 World Cup.

The prices for the 134,000 tickets for the home game against England ranged from seven shillings and sixpence for a place on the uncovered East Terracing to 50 shillings (£2.50) for the best seats in the South Stand.

There was annual discontent over the demand and distribution of Scotland v England tickets, whether the game was in Glasgow or London. The only public sale was a limited number, which had to be applied for through a postal ballot for which the number of requests always far outweighed availability. After the clubs and various associations had received their allocation the number left for the ballot was a mere 12,572, less than ten per cent of the total number of tickets printed.

Scotland v England fixtures at Hampden Park had been televised live north of the border since 1956 but the contract with the television companies had been agreed some months ahead of the 1970 game, which allowed for delayed coverage only. With all tickets sold, there had been an indication from the SFA secretary Willie Allan a few weeks before the 25 April fixture that the match might be available for a live screening. He later claimed that there had been no approach from either of the broadcasters.

The *Daily Record* dated 7 April highlighted the situation and quoted an unnamed "top TV official in the south" saying: "It was made clear to us that only recordings would be considered. It was on this basis that the contract was agreed." A spokesman for Scottish Television (STV) told the same newspaper: "We are under contract to show the Scotland–England game in the evening. There are no signs that we will be changing our plans." Peter Thompson, head of BBC Sport in Scotland, did, however, appear to have a more conciliatory stance and advised the *Record*: "We have had no contact with the SFA on this subject, but would be interested if the question of a live showing cropped up."

Coupled with Willie Allan's comments there appears to have been a stalemate which was never broken, and those unable to get their hands on a ticket had to listen to the radio commentary until 7.15pm when STV showed a recording of the entire game, just as it had done with the Wales match. The BBC screened extended highlights at 9.15pm in a 90-minute version of *International Match of the Day*, which also featured the Wales v Northern Ireland game. It was the first Scotland v England international to be televised in colour and the four home associations each received £20,000 for the television coverage of the series, which was £10,000 down on the previous year's agreement when all the action had been shown live.

Brown made two alterations from the Wales game with Tommy Gemmell, having served his three-match suspension from a sending off in Germany, replacing Willie Callaghan whilst Jimmy Johnstone was preferred to Tommy McLean.

Bobby Brown recalls the team doctor, Archie Downie, giving the winger a sleeping tablet on the eve of the game. "I remember asking Jock Stein about Jimmy Johnstone," says Brown. "I said: 'Jock, how do you train wee Jimmy, how do you coach him?' And Jock's answer was 'Aw him, his brains are brand new!' In other words he meant that he was such a natural player that you didn't need to coach him."

With the World Cup in mind England chose not to risk Bobby Charlton who had broken a bone in his right hand during training. It was Everton's Brian Labone whose name was destined to be the most talked about following the game, and to those old enough to remember is still synonymous with the match today. The British Championship trophy was at stake for three of the four competing nations with Scotland and England level on three points each and the Welsh on two points, ahead of their game with Northern Ireland. Since the first Scotland v England fixture in 1872 the Scots had won 35 times and the English 30 times. There had been 21 draws.

The first cheer of the day greeted the Ayr Majorettes as the tartan-bedecked girls accompanied a pipe band before the teams came out. It was noticeable that there were fewer England fans inside the ground than in previous years, indicating that much of the FA's allocation had fallen into the hands of exiled Scots.

Scotland took the game to England from the outset and a shot from Greig flashed past Gordon Banks's right-hand post. Then, in the 19th minute, as Stein dashed into the box, he was sent crashing to the turf by Labone only for the West German referee to indicate that the striker had dived. This decision infuriated both the home players and spectators and has never been forgotten by Bobby Brown, as he recently confirmed: "I remember quite clearly that Colin Stein was my centre-forward and Labone brought him down in the box when we were very much on top."

Scotland's superiority, despite the lack of goals, was recognised when the crowd broke into a chant of "Easy! Easy!" after half an hour, with keeper Cruickshank at this point a bystander. Johnstone was having a great game despite being continually fouled, whilst Moncur and Hay were in sparkling form. The goalless scoreline at the interval did little to reflect the gulf between the sides.

"Jimmy Johnstone played on the wing," Bobby Brown recalls, "and I had said to him before the match, 'Now listen, a lot depends on you, son.' 'Right, right,' he said, and he would take the full-back Emlyn Hughes on and he played his heart out that day beating him this way, that way and putting balls across."

Johnstone and Stein both had shots saved as the game wore on, with the massive crowd sensing that time was running out. With quarter of an hour left Gemmell fired a piledriver towards goal which looked to have struck Bobby Moore's hand but again claims for a penalty were ignored.

A third penalty claim came in the 85th minute when O'Hare was felled inside the area by Nobby Stiles but again Herr Schulenberg was not impressed.

The crowd was silenced for the only time late in the match when Hurst headed beyond Cruickshank from a great Peters cross, but the referee adjudged the striker to have been offside. Again this was a contentious decision from the referee who had been praised for his handling of both the Celtic–Leeds semi-final and Scotland's last win against England three years earlier. But it would have been cruel had Scotland lost a match they had deserved more from. It was the first time that the annual fixture had failed to produce a goal since the inaugural meeting 98 years earlier.

"We should have won the match and we should have had two penalty kicks, but we came out with a lot of credit," Bobby Brown remembers.

The Labone–Stein incident occupied much of the Sunday journals' sports columns. Jim Parkinson of *The Herald* had the referee in his sights, referring to, "His adamant refusal to recognise one of the most blatant penalty fouls seen at Hampden for many years, and later he rejected two other lesser claims ... A goalless draw did the Scots no justice and made a mockery of their overwhelming superiority." "If that wasn't a penalty then I've never seen one!" was Harry Andrews's assessment of the Labone–Stein controversy in the Scottish *Sunday Express*. In the same publication the referee responded to persistent journalists with: "The Scots player had pushed the ball well in front of him. It was not a scoring chance and the player seemed to throw himself down."

Alan Hoby offered "The English View" to Scottish readers of the *Express*, which included the following: "I thought it was most emphatically a penalty. But then I also thought that England's 'goal' two minutes from the end was perfectly valid. But it would have been outright robbery if Sir Alf Ramsey's men had come away with the Championship after this in-and-out show." Even Sir Alf conceded in the *Express* that his team were "more than a little fortunate to get away with it", referring to the match as a whole rather than the Labone incident.

After Wales's defeat of Northern Ireland, England, Scotland and the Welsh all finished the tournament on four points with the Irish having lost all three of their games.

Newspapers speculated over the official attendance figure of 137,438, which was well in excess of the 134,000 tickets printed. SFA investigations found that a number of what were described as "high-quality forgeries" had been accepted and planned to meet with the police to discuss the matter.

Secretary Willie Allan later advised that he had been shown two forgeries, made with photocopying equipment, which were difficult to distinguish. An officer at Glasgow Southern Police Headquarters told *The Herald* that inquiries were continuing to identify the source of the counterfeits.

After spending four days sifting through the thousands of tickets, rather embarrassingly for the SFA, police officers found spectators had gained entry with, amongst other objects, a plain piece of card, a discotheque ticket and a hospital visiting card! It would, of course, be naive to think that the England match was the first occasion that cunning fans had entered the stadium by similar means.

There was no shortage of ticketless supporters who found alternative ways of entering the ground. Stuart Borrowman recollects standing outside Hampden before the previous England game in 1968 when an elegantly dressed supporter had the confidence to blag his way in. "We were standing outside the schoolboys' enclosure and this guy appeared in a smart raincoat and says, 'Watch this, guys.' Then he just went up to the policeman at a gate and said, 'Good afternoon officer,' and he opened the gate and he just walked in! A superb bit of skill!"

There was a stark contrast in the final balances for the two Home Internationals played at Hampden Park, which illustrated the financial benefits of the Scotland v England fixture. The profit for the Wales match was a total of £6,388.7s.5d. whereas the figure for the England game was £54,786.7s.8d.

During England's reign as world champions Scotland had lost the annual fixture just once and recorded one victory themselves with the other two meetings drawn.

Scotland's international season had concluded with what most considered a disappointing result but a "moral victory". The Celtic players still had the small matter of a European Cup Final to deal with in May. In his capacity as Scotland manager Bobby Brown travelled to Milan as a guest of Celtic Football Club, where Feyenoord triumphed 2-1 after extra time.

Bobby remembers good times in the company of Jock Stein. "Big Jock and I were always very friendly; I got on well with him. The first match we attended together was down in Leeds when we went to see Leeds playing Ferencváros." Their friendship later extended beyond the assessment of players. "Quite often he would phone me for the Ayr races where he always got the red-carpet treatment. The routine was that I'd go up to Parkhead and Sean Fallon would drive the Mercedes and Jock always sat in the back of the car with a wee fellow called Solly. That's where they counted the spoils on the way back."

Following the Mexico World Cup Scotland were under consideration for an invitation to take part in a "Mini World Cup" in Brazil that the newly crowned world champions were hosting as part of their 150th Independence Day celebrations in 1972. The event was originally conceived as a competition between all the previous winners of the World Cup but the criteria had to be altered because the matches were scheduled for the end of June and beginning of July, which was unsuitable for some of the Europeans including England. This led to the Brazilians considering other nations, with Scotland one of the names on the shortlist.

Bobby Brown had the Inter League International with the League of Ireland to assess his players early in September, ahead of Scotland's opening European Championship qualifier against Denmark in November.

It would be an understatement to say that the Irish record in the fixture was poor with just one victory in the 20 matches played. The last three home games in the series had ended 5-1, 11-0 and 6-0 and, not surprisingly, the Scots were expected to win convincingly at Celtic Park.

The evening did not go to plan with only 7,654 restless spectators present to see a single second-half George Connelly goal separate the sides. "The pitch was invaded by hundreds of youngsters when Connelly, at long last, put the Scots ahead on 62 minutes," reported the *Press and Journal*.

"A LOAD OF OLD RUBBISH" was the headline of Malcom Munro's report for the *Evening Times*, which criticised Bobby Brown's tactic of playing out of defence rather than going all out for goals.

The manager was realistic when interviewed by *The Herald*'s Jim Parkinson. "It is a well-worn cliché but I did learn several things from this game. For instance, some players there didn't fit into my future team plans." He did praise Pat Stanton's performance with the forthcoming visit of the Danes in mind. "He could be a most useful player for the future, especially against teams who employ packed defences."

During an SFA Council meeting the following week there were strong pleas, by the Aberdeen representative George Rattray and the North of Scotland's Fred Newton of Ross County, for Pittodrie to be allocated the Denmark match. But there was a unanimous decision in favour of Hampden Park and the two most northern members of the Council had to be content with the award to Aberdeen of the under-23 meeting with England early in 1971.

Brown attended the Dunfermline v Rangers First Division match at East End Park on the Saturday before the Denmark game. Davie Hay missed Celtic's game with Cowdenbeath the same afternoon due to flu and was not expected to join up with the squad. This resulted in Sandy Jardine being added to the pool.

Hay surprised everyone by joining the players in Glasgow on the Sunday before they set off for their base at the Queens Hotel in Largs. Bobby Moncur, winning his sixth cap, was chosen as captain for the night.

Scotland were expected to attack from the kick-off. They had overlapping full-backs Hay and Greig, Stanton and Moncur in midfield and Willie Johnston and Jimmy Johnstone on the wings to feed forwards O'Hare and Stein.

The game began well with a 13th-minute O'Hare header from a Johnston cross slipping from Poulsen's hands then through his legs and over the line for what proved to be the only goal of the match. Johnston then went close with a swerving shot but a second goal never really looked likely. Although the Danes rarely threatened, Cruickshank safeguarded the points with his only real save close to the end, diving to keep out a shot from Benny Neilsen. At the final whistle there was a strange anti-climactic feeling, with even the goal considered sloppy.

A disappointing 24,618 had turned up on an awful night but there had been enough present to soil the evening. Jimmy Johnstone, who had been so effective in the England game, had been jeered against Wales three years earlier when he had been chosen ahead of Old Firm rival Willie Henderson. The boo boys had returned for the Denmark match and both Johnstone and Hay were barracked from the traditional "Rangers End" of the ground before Hay was replaced by Jardine for his first cap. Clearly Hay had not been fully fit but the substitution led to accusations that the manager, a former Rangers goalkeeper, had bowed to the demands of the crowd, ignoring the fact Hay had been first choice.

Four years later, in the *Glasgow Herald*, as Jardine was about to captain his country for the first time, he praised the more unified crowd. When reminded by Ian Archer of his Scotland debut, Jardine, clearly, had not forgotten the circumstances: "Put it this way, it wasn't the nicest way to start an international career."

The abuse which descended from the West Terracing that evening was not prevalent in every international but there was always an uneasy feeling that it could surface at any time. "Night of Shame – for fans" was the headline in the next edition of the *Evening Times* with the match itself given less importance than the crowd's behaviour. It was an issue the manager could well have done without.

Historically Celtic supporters were not entirely innocent in these matters. During an Inter League match between the Scottish League and the League of Ireland four years earlier at Celtic Park the abuse directed at Ronnie McKinnon was considered unpleasant enough for the club newspaper, the *Celtic View*, to comment on its front page: "The management were extremely disappointed with the attitude of some sections of the crowd last Wednesday. There was no excuse for the booing and baiting of the sole Rangers player in the Scottish League side." A letter to the same publication the following week from Airdrie reader Joseph McLaughlin expressed similar sentiments, describing the treatment of McKinnon as "unbelievable". The letter went on: "I am as ardent a Celtic supporter as anyone but when a player is good enough to be chosen for a place in a Scottish team it is the duty of the fans to give him and his team-mates the support they deserve." But when it came to Hampden internationals it was undeniably only a problem for Celtic players. Following the vitriol levelled at Hay and Johnstone, the *Celtic View* highlighted the issue in its editorial which advised that the club's players were "unhappy at this treatment". Reader David Crotty of Glasgow wrote to the newspaper thus: "I was disgusted by the attitude of the so-called Scotland fans towards the Celtic players in the team. Before and during the match most of the scarves I saw were Rangers and it seems Scotland is becoming more like Rangers every game. David Hay being taken off was the last straw. I don't think I'll be back at any more internationals." Fellow Glaswegian Philip Keane used his letter to appeal to the players, "I implore all Celtic players to reject all offers to play for Scotland."

On the match itself Norman MacDonald labelled it an "exercise in boredom" in his *Press and Journal* report, summarising with: "It was an untidy and unsatisfactory 90 minutes. The Scots lacked the inspiration and imagination to demolish an unimpressive, all-amateur Danish team." John MacKenzie was just as critical in the Scottish *Daily Express,* describing a "rock bottom performance" and reporting: "With the derisive whistles of an impatient, bitterly disappointed crowd ringing in their ears, they crept from Hampden with a solitary, lucky goal to show for 90 minutes of unimpressive endeavour."

Scotland contested only four full internationals throughout the calendar year of 1970, three of those in the British Championship. Two of the four games had been won and the other two certainly ought to have been. There had been many positives including the emergence of Hay, O'Hare and Moncur and, although the victory over the Danes had been unimpressive, the qualifying campaign had at least got off the ground with the desired two points. Tougher times lay ahead in the New Year with six away matches from seven games in the first six months of 1971 including trips to Belgium and Portugal.

During a meeting with the Selection Committee in December Bobby Brown expressed his desire for more international matches to aid the qualifying campaign. The offer of a match against Australia in November had been turned down as was an invitation to Hungary the following June. The manager had held a number of squad get-togethers in the latter part of the 1960s to try to build a club spirit within the camp but these had been hindered by midweek fixtures and call-offs and were reluctantly discontinued, much to his frustration.

1971

"It is the greatest honour ever given to me."
Tommy Docherty

Aberdeen's position at the top of Division One merited the inclusion of Jim Hermiston, Martin Buchan and Joe Harper in Bobby Brown's starting XI for the Under-23 match in Swansea on 13 January. Bobby had long been an admirer of Harper who had been his joint top scorer during the ten-match, unofficial world tour in the summer of 1967.

A crowd of 9,037, which included around 2,000 noisy Scots who were employed on a nearby oil refinery, watched the match. After an Asa Hartford "goal" was ruled out for a marginal offside decision in the first half, Keith MacRae kept Scotland in the game with a number of saves. But the Motherwell goalkeeper looked suspect when he misjudged a corner, allowing Peter Price to head into the net for the only goal midway through the second half to give the Welsh a deserved win.

The result of the next match in the SFA diary was of less importance. A charity event was held at Hampden Park on 27 January to raise money for the Ibrox Disaster Fund, after 66 fans – many of them youngsters – had been crushed to death on a stairway at the end of the traditional New Year Old Firm match.

A Scotland team lined up against a Select side made up of players from both Old Firm clubs plus three guests from English teams. Bobby Brown took charge of the Scotland XI whilst his old Ibrox team-mate and Rangers manager Willie Waddell looked after the Select XI assisted by Jock Stein. Brown included four Old Firm players in his starting XI, two from either side.

The match was widely praised for its entertainment value with a large crowd of 81,405 watching. The Select XI played in a Real Madrid-inspired all-white strip and started with Chelsea's Peter Bonetti in goal with Best and Charlton of Manchester United the other guest players. "No finer display of football could have been provided than that last night," was the *Daily Record*'s view.

Scotland struck first blood when Colin Stein fed Gemmill who found the net from some distance before Best, who seemed to be enjoying the occasion, equalised just before the half-hour mark.

Peter Lorimer headed past when a goal seemed certain and a Charlton effort was adjudged offside in the second half before Lorimer made amends by shooting the winner with six minutes left.

Both ends of the ground stayed to applaud the players in what was widely reported as being an entertaining spectacle. However, J. Duffy of Glasgow's Logan Street penned a letter to the *Evening Times*'s Sportsbag which claimed the match had been "too friendly", commenting that "there was hardly a real tackle in the whole game". The event generated £38,414 and 14 shillings for the Disaster Fund.

For the European Championship match in Belgium the following week Scotland had to make do without Lorimer, McLintock and Harper. The increasing number of withdrawals was becoming the most frustrating aspect of the manager's job.

After assembling at Glasgow Airport Jim Cruickshank realised that he had left his passport at home but there was enough time for an emergency document to be issued which allowed the goalkeeper to board the flight.

The home association took the match away from the capital to Liege where the tight pitch of the Stade Sclessin and a partisan crowd were expected to give the Belgians further advantage.

There were grumbles over the standard of accommodation and rumours of player indiscipline on the trip. The hotel in Liege required that all public room lights be switched off at 6pm as an economy measure. With little else to occupy them the players then played cards in their rooms with one of them said to have lost £60 to a team-mate.

Brown chose a 4-3-3 formation, intimating that circumstances had changed since the attacking display in West Germany and suggesting that a draw would not be a bad result.

The Belgians included six players from local side Standard but awful conditions meant the pitch resembled a swamp. Large pools of water were visible which aided neither side in what was a disastrous night for Scotland who were rarely seen in attack.

In the 36th minute McKinnon went to deal with a high ball whilst Cruickshank hesitated. As he went to clear, the defender slipped on the surface and toed the ball out of the goalkeeper's reach and into his own net to give the hosts the lead.

Scotland failed to force a single save from the Belgian goalkeeper in the first period and the loss of the goal necessitated personnel changes, with Stanton and Stein replaced by Jim Forrest and Tony Green. A spectacular free kick from Van Himst, which flew high into Cruickshank's top right-hand corner ten minutes into the second half all but killed Scotland off, but there was worse to come when Moncur was adjudged to have brought down Van Moer for a penalty.

The decision looked harsh and Greig kicked the ball off the spot in disgust as Gemmell indicated a dive whilst arguing with the referee. Van Himst netted to complete the 3-0 scoreline with a few minutes left. The deficit might have been worse, as on two occasions Moncur cleared from the goal line and it was all of 81 minutes before Brown's men earned their first corner kick.

There was no sympathy from Scottish reporters with the pressure beginning to mount on the manager. The *Daily Record*'s veteran reporter Hugh Taylor considered: "I have never seen a worse Scottish international team than that which fell 3-0 in the swamp fields of Liege." In the same newspaper Alex Cameron believed that the issue lay deeper than the players and posed the question: "What is wrong with Scotland? It has been proved conclusively that the set-up is neither professional nor authoritative."

Although there is no reference to player misbehaviour in the minutes of SFA meetings during the period, the association's 1970/71 Annual Report contained the following intriguing entry: "To those who cared to see, it has been plain for some time, that there were certain players who had ceased to take pride in playing for their country; that other considerations weighed more heavily with them;

that they were not amenable to discipline; that they were not prepared to discipline themselves. Nowhere was this more evident than in Liege, where we suffered a humiliating and disastrous 3-0 defeat at the hands of the Belgian national team."

The next match was at least at Hampden – the Under-23 clash with England on 24 February. A fire in the Pittodrie Stand just a few days after the game in Liege had damaged 1,500 seats and part of a dressing room, and the game had been hastily rescheduled. It was the first international to be staged in Scotland under the new decimal currency system, with prices ranging from 80 new pence for a South Stand seat to 30 new pence for a standing place.

A disappointing crowd of 13,839 saw the Scots restore some pride in a drawn match they ought to have won convincingly. The manager responded to criticism of his tactics by fielding two wingers, Arthur Duncan and Quinton Young, who repeatedly tormented the English defence.

Scotland almost got off to a perfect start inside the fifth minute as a pass-back from Derek Parkin beat his own goalkeeper with Drew Jarvie in pursuit. Ray Clemence halted the Aberdeen striker but conceded a penalty kick, with which John Blackley struck the junction of post and crossbar.

John remembers the incident as if it were yesterday. "It was after five minutes and nobody had said if there was a penalty who would be taking it, and I was the captain and they all just looked towards me. So I said, 'Oh go on then, I'll go up and take it.' So I put the ball down, never confident like, rattled the crossbar and the post right in the corner!"

Scotland did take the lead in the 28th minute when a low Eddie Kelly cross struck Clemence on the chest and went into the goal. There was more joy for the small but vociferous crowd when Davie Robb stabbed in a second eight minutes later.

Young shot well wide of an open net shortly after the interval, a miss that later proved more costly than Blackley's penalty. Lloyd rose to power in a header from a Hudson corner for 2-1 in an isolated attack and the home side continued to press, but a blunder ended in disaster late in the game.

This from Bob Driscoll's *Sun* match report: "Robb stunned his team-mates by sending a long pass back to the feet of Tony

Currie who tapped the ball in for an embarrassing equaliser for England."

Sir Alf Ramsey conceded that the Scots had deserved more when addressing the press. "They were the better team and deserved to win," he told reporters. The English press, too, were generous towards the young Scots. Driscoll's *Sun* report was headlined: "England Kids So Lucky", and Norman Giller wrote in the *Daily Express*: "Young England were torn to tartan tatters at Hampden Park last night ... The pride and passion that has been missing from recent Scottish performances in the international arena pumped back." A letter from Airdrie resident Frank Cussack featured in the *Daily Record*'s Sportsbag and claimed: "The Great Train Robbers would have been proud of the way the English team stole a point at Hampden. What a performance by wingers Duncan and Young. I only hope that Brown keeps these boys together as they are our World Cup hopes of tomorrow."

Both BBC1 and STV featured highlights of the match which showcased the captain's penalty miss to a far greater audience, as he was to find out. "The people that pulled me up about that – it was unbelievable!" says John Blackley, able to laugh off the reaction today. "I didn't think that many people watched the Under-23s. I used to get pelters for that miss, deservedly mind, but we should have beaten them, I remember that."

For the second time in less than a year Scotland had dominated a match against England at Hampden but had to be content with a draw. But the performance had lifted some of the gloom after the loss in Belgium.

The poor attendance along with the recent crowds for the League International with Ireland and the Denmark game gave an aggregate spectator total of 46,099 for the three Glasgow matches. Aberdeen chairman Dick Donald was quick to claim that had the original venue of Pittodrie been available the attendance at the Under-23 fixture would have been around 25,000.

The manager included nine of the Under-23 side in his pool of 15 for the Inter League fixture against England at Hampden just three weeks later on 17 March.

A low-key approach was adopted for this game with the players meeting for a light training session at Firhill only four hours ahead of kick-off, before crossing the city to Hampden.

With Aberdeen still perched at the top of Division One, Brown selected Bobby Clark as his goalkeeper. Just weeks earlier Clark had established a world record of 1,155 minutes without conceding a goal – a period which spanned more than 12 consecutive matches.

The Scots fell behind to a Ralph Coates goal after only six minutes. Moore sent a cross into the goalmouth from which two Geoff Hurst efforts were blocked before the ball landed at the feet of Coates who could barely miss from five yards. Hearts striker Donald Ford almost equalised with a spectacular overhead kick which Jackson pushed behind in the second period, and the same player later rounded the keeper but shot wide of an empty net. World Cup hat-trick hero Hurst missed the game's best opportunity before the end, shooting wide from eight yards with the goal at his mercy. The English side had made the better chances with most of the Scots' efforts coming from long range. Coates's early goal proved to be the match winner.

"I remember that as a fairly uneventful game," says Bobby Clark of his only appearance for the League Select XI. "The League Internationals were losing their popularity but they were quite good platforms to look at the home-based talent and nice introductions to the full squads."

The race for the First Division title between Leeds and Arsenal hindered Bobby Brown's selection for the European qualifier in Portugal in April. Leeds led the Gunners by six points but the London side had three matches in hand. Don Revie had advised that his Leeds trio of Lorimer, Gray and Bremner would be unavailable whilst Arsenal would not release McLintock but allowed Eddie Kelly's selection. Four Leeds players were included for England's game with Greece but two later withdrew. To be fair to the Yorkshire club they were forbidden from withholding players from their own association but the Scottish and Welsh FAs had no power over player availability.

Although Leeds did not actually have a fixture during the week of the international they did have three vital matches in a four-day period from the following Saturday, including a crucial meeting with Arsenal on the Monday. Six of the side who lost in Liege – Cruickshank, Greig, Stein, Gemmell, Gemmill and Cooke – were dropped from the pool. There was a surprise recall for Alan Gilzean and a number of players who had performed well in the Under-23 and League Internationals were brought in including Buchan, Robb, Clark and Jarvie.

"I'm fed up with all the call-offs we have had in the past," the manager told Malcolm Munro of the *Evening Times*. But he did sympathise with club managers: "I'm not blaming the clubs. They've got to look after their own interests first."

The party flew on the Monday and based themselves in the coastal town of Estoril, west of Lisbon. Stanton was instructed to mark Eusebio, one of six Benfica players playing on their home pitch, whilst Gilzean and Robb played up front. Scotland played in a white strip to aid television viewers, as the local channel could only broadcast in black and white.

"I remember the stadium, as it was the best [pitch] I had ever played on," says Bobby Clark. "It was amazing with not a blade of grass out of place and seemed more suited to lawn bowls than football."

Just as in Liege things were fine until an own goal changed the course of the game. Stanton diverted the ball into his own net midway through the first half with Clark stranded. Scotland did create chances – McCalliog and Gilzean were both off target – but they were always second best. Clark performed heroics particularly with one spectacular stop from Pereas. The same player came close again just before an hour had been played, when a powerful shot cannoned off the face of the crossbar before curling ten feet into the air.

It took until the 82nd minute before Clark was beaten again, as Eusebio, who had had a comparatively quiet match, hit the ball into an empty net after the keeper had once again thwarted Pereas. Eusebio was full of praise for Clark's heroics and was quoted in *The Herald*: "This was a world-class performance," predicting, "This is a player we will hear more of in the future."

Bobby himself has good recall of the evening. "The game itself was a good contest. There was an early own goal but we stayed in the game right up until a late goal. They were an excellent team, especially on their own home turf. It was disappointing as this result was very important with regards to qualifying in a very tough group. The two away losses at both Belgium and Portugal were two tough nails in our coffin."

Having signed a new contract Bobby Brown felt the pressure increase with each defeat. His record since taking over in 1967 until the end of 1970 had been good but there was no denying that results had been poor in the first half of 1971 although at least some of this could be attributed to player withdrawals and bad luck on the park such as own goals. The manager was still hopeful of turning things around as he knew one good result changed everything but Bobby had a hunch that his long-term future may lie away from football. He had kept his options open and had become a partner in a restaurant due to open next door to the gift shop run by his wife Ruth in Helensburgh.

The SFA chose Swansea as a base for the opening Home International in Cardiff on Saturday, 15 May. Heavy rain, a regular occurrence at Scotland matches, had begun around three hours ahead of the kick-off. As in Liege, pools of water made the conditions farcical with passes halting in the mud. English referee Jack Taylor later conceded that had the occasion been a league match a postponement would have been more likely but the tight schedule of the recently restructured British Championship left little room for the rearranging of fixtures.

"As an international spectacle this was rubbish, with no reflection on the players of either side. The game just should not have been played," was Malcolm Munro's view in the *Evening Times*.

Goalkeepers kept the score level in an even first half when Sprake turned over a 20-yard strike from Robb before Davies forced an excellent save from Bobby Clark.

Speaking recently the goalkeeper relates how his defence dealt with the attacking threat posed by the Welsh. "The Welsh air force was Mike England and the two Davies lads, Wyn and Ron, three big men who were all excellent in the air. It was the first time I learned from Billy Bremner that when Leeds played against teams with very big aerial threats they put small players on them to break their runs and left our tall defenders in the key scoring zones. We used this and it worked well."

The players adapted a little better to the conditions after the break and Toshack had the ball in the net after an hour, but his header was considered offside by the nearby Taylor.

The Scots found themselves under pressure as the game wore on and Gray hacked a Yorath shot from the line, although Scotland did create some chances. The game ended goalless with Brown probably the happiest of the managers. Eddie Gray was considered Scotland's best player but the worrying statistic of one goal in the last six internationals was concerning.

With Bremner and Robb both out Greig, Hugh Curran and Tony Green came in for the Northern Ireland game in Glasgow on the Tuesday. But the match did not go well and Scotland lost to the Ulstermen at Hampden for the first time since the war – to yet another own goal. Derek Dougan connected with a corner in the 14th minute only for the ball to cannon off Greig and beyond Clark. Scotland had most of the ball in the second half but again failed to find the net. George Best came closest to scoring with an effort which hit the post. Curran was praised for his performance but it was all doom and gloom ahead of the trip south to Wembley. England's goalless draw with the Welsh on the Wednesday gave a glimmer of hope, however.

As usual tens of thousands of Scots converged on the English capital in the days leading up to the match. For those at home both ITV and the BBC had been given permission to screen the game live in colour, although at this time many viewers still owned black and white sets.

Brown surprisingly replaced Hay with Greig explaining to reporters that he considered Greig was more experienced for the occasion and that Hay had accepted this explanation. Six of the Scottish players would be taking part in a game against England for the first time and eight, including Jimmy Johnstone, would be making their Wembley debuts.

Wembley's pitch looked immaculate as the teams took to the field with a red ball which had probably been selected with the colour TV cameras in mind.

Bobby Clark was playing at the stadium for the first time and remembers the walk from the tunnel. "Playing at Wembley was special. Walking out was moving as it seemed that there were no England supporters with all the Scottish flags, and all the chanting seemed to be coming from the thousands of Scots who had made the trip."

The red ball lasted less than 60 seconds before Bobby Moore picked it up indicating a puncture. It was replaced by a more traditional white one.

England led after just nine minutes when Chivers nodded on a Ball corner to Martin Peters, whose powerful header went in via the underside of Clark's crossbar. Greig had tried to punch the ball out but the Dutch referee ruled that it had crossed the line.

Scotland fought back bravely and Curran reacted quickly to sweep home a loose ball following a Johnstone cross just two minutes after going behind. There followed a lot of tough tackling with Bremner squaring up to Peters, followed by an incident between Robb and Storey.

The Scots went behind again when the normally cool Brogan was harried into a rash clearance across his own penalty area which Chivers gratefully intercepted and fired beyond Clark from 20 yards.

Scotland's defence looked vulnerable and conceded again just before the break when Moncur misjudged a lob by Lawler and, as Clark came out, Chivers kept his head and coolly chipped over the goalkeeper and into the net.

Bobby Clark remembers: "Martin Chivers then came alive and scored two very good goals. One, the shot from just on the edge of the box, was a great shot."

The clinical finishing of the home side left the Scots with a mountain to climb and goalscorer Curran was replaced by Frank Munro. Chivers found the net again after an hour but was adjudged offside, meaning all the goals had been scored in the first half.

At the end Bobby Brown was consoled by Sir Alf Ramsey who put his arm around him and offered words of comfort as they began the long walk up the Wembley tunnel.

This was welcome but unusual behaviour from the England manager. Bobby has memories of "a man of few words – you were lucky to get two from him. He would maybe say 'good luck' and that were all. We never exchanged many words I must admit."

Following Ireland's win against the Welsh, the Scots finished bottom of the table with one solitary point and one goal from their three matches.

The qualifying match in Denmark on 9 June was now a must-win game and was closely followed by a friendly in Moscow five days later which repaid the debt for the Soviets' visit to Glasgow in 1967. The SFA had received invitations from East Germany and Brazil with a view to also playing in Peru and Argentina. Due to the world champions' choice of dates – 11 or 18 July – the association reluctantly declined the offer as it would have been impossible to extend the season beyond June. Conscious that the participants for their Independence Day tournament the following summer had still to be finalised, the SFA did, however, make it clear that they would welcome an invitation to Brazil in the future.

Following Leeds' Fairs Cup Final against Juventus both Lorimer and Bremner pulled out of the trip and Blackpool refused to release Tony Green due to their involvement in the Anglo-Italian Cup Final.

Motherwell's Bobby Watson, Hibs' John Brownlie and John "Jocky" Scott of Dundee were drafted into the party with no guarantee that they would be granted visas for the match in Russia at short notice.

A further distraction for the manager was the protracted transfer negotiations between Rangers and Kilmarnock for Tommy McLean. Ibrox manager Willie Waddell and Rugby Park boss Walter McCrae even flew to Denmark to complete the deal, with the winger signing for £60,000 in the Vedbaek hotel where the SFA was based.

Just when it seemed things could hardly get any worse for Scotland, a Finn Laudrup free kick seconds ahead of the break resulted in a shock defeat which killed off any lingering qualification hopes. "The free kick deflected of the wall ... another own goal!" rued Bobby Clark.

The scoreline might have been even more embarrassing as Clark made four outstanding saves in the last quarter of an hour. A McKinnon header, cleared from the goal line just after the restart, was the closest Scotland came in the Idraetsparken.

The following day's report in the *Record* was scathing and included the following: "You weep tartan tears when you see Denmark, once the country cousins of global football, taking the mickey out of a once-proud Scotland."

Some sympathy was later expressed in the SFA Annual Report: "Rarely can Scotland have embarked on an international venture less well prepared than it was for the European Championship match with Denmark. The party of players which finally set out was but a shadow of our full strength."

The demoralised party now had the inconvenience of the Russian game to contend with before they could enjoy the close-season break, and further injuries to Moncur and McLean threatened to leave the manager with fewer than 11 fit men.

News that Peter Lorimer had played in an exhibition match in South Africa did not go down well with the SFA following the player's withdrawal. The Leeds man had been under contract to spend six weeks as a guest player for Frank Lord's Cape Town City with the emphasis of the trip on coaching and he felt he would be unable to go back on the commitment having signed some time earlier.

With the visa situation rectified the SFA party did not leave Denmark until the Saturday morning, two days ahead of the game which many speculated may be Brown's last in charge. There was a touch of mystery on board the Soviet airliner with not even Willie Allan aware of where the party would be accommodated or the kick-off time for the match.

The players' training session in the Lenin stadium on the Sunday was affected by a piece of gamesmanship by the hosts. The manager requested Scotland be given the type of ball to be used in the game but was told this would not be possible. The explanation given was that as Sunday was a state holiday for elections there was no one in the stadium who had a key for the equipment room. Training then took place with the SFA's own ball before the Russian under-23 side, preparing for a match with Bulgaria, arrived. They observed the Scots going through their paces then took to the pitch themselves with several of the polka-dot-style balls which Bobby Brown had been told were not available.

Speaking just after his 95th birthday in 2018, Bobby Brown remembers the regimental routines that had to be adhered to in their accommodation. "There was a bit of a mystique about the Russians in those days. The cold war was on and I remember they came and asked you how many would it be for breakfast and you would tell them and if a couple of the players didn't want to go for their breakfast in the morning the Russians would come and tell you two players were not there. I remember they asked me how long the training would last and I said probably an hour and a half and the snow came on abandoning the workout but they wouldn't let us back in because we had said it was a certain time we were out there. You had to stay outside until your time was up.

"You were controlled by the Russians. Even at the end after the game there was no fraternisation, no sort of mutual celebration at night. They were on the one side and the Scotland team were on the other and they gave us little Sputniks which was a lovely souvenir and we gave them a tartan rug."

The differences between Russia and Demark were vast as Bobby Clark explains. "One of the hard things about the Russia trip was that we had been in Denmark where the hotel and food was first rate and then we went to Russia where the hotel was rather dingy and the food was different. The good thing about the hotel was it was just round from the Kremlin and we could walk round and see the Red Square and St Basil's Cathedral. We visited the Moscow State Circus the night before the game and that was quite spectacular."

The Russians were confident, having scored no fewer than 15 goals in their last three outings against Cyprus, Spain and Algeria, whilst Brown's men had netted just once in six games. The irony was that during that period three players in dark blue had scored for the opposition!

Bobby Brown remained upbeat, announcing a 4-2-4 formation with Robb and Stein up front and Bobby Watson debuting in midfield. In Moncur's absence, Stanton was appointed captain. The manager did express his regret that the order of the matches had not been reversed, i.e. with the qualifier second.

The predicted 100,000 crowd failed to show with the attendance closer to 20,000 on the day. The makeshift team surprised everyone by taking the game to the Russians, with Jim Forrest sending in a couple of dangerous crosses before a Scott effort was turned behind by the Soviet keeper Rudakov.

Despite playing well, luck deserted the Scots who fell behind after 24 minutes. There was a touch of fortune in the goal as Yevryuzhikhin's left-footed cross from near the byline flew past Clark and into the corner of his net.

Davie Robb almost levelled just a minute later but was thwarted by another outstanding save from Rudakov. Clark was also in good form and produced a couple of fine saves before the end.

Scotland's efforts were credited after the one-goal defeat and the performance had been an improvement on Copenhagen, but the worrying statistic was that single goal in a run of seven matches.

On the same day that Apollo 15 went into orbit – Monday, 26 July – Bobby Brown arrived at Park Gardens with his reports on the five matches from the Cardiff to Moscow trip. It was normal practice for the manager to deliver a written report after a match, although it was anticipated that this would be D-Day with regard to his future.

The waiting reporters in Park Gardens later commented on how untroubled Bobby seemed as he climbed the steps to the SFA offices at house number six.

As well as his reports on the two blocks of matches Bobby submitted a blueprint outlining his recommendations for the future of the Scotland team to the International and Selection Committee. Amongst his ideas was a demand for more regular international matches and squad get-togethers targeting a place at the 1974 World Cup. He was then asked to leave the room and after a lengthy delay was summoned back.

"I have been informed that I have been removed from the office of Scotland team manager," he told the attentive reporters who had been waiting outside the building for some time. There was no bitterness in his voice as he continued: "I would like to add that I would wish my successor in a job that is complex and not easy, good fortune. I hope he, more readily, is able to gain the release of players. And I hope Scotland have a good season ahead of them and qualify for the 1974 World Cup." Without taking questions he then descended the steps of Park Gardens for the last time where his daughter was waiting to drive him away.

Inwardly he felt relief and a friend of his wife threw a party that evening where he relaxed free from the pressures of worrying about what criticism the following day's sports writers might be preparing for print. His wife's gift shop had been a great success since opening the previous year and, with the restaurant, plus an option to buy further units in the same building, there was scope to expand his business interests.

Bobby recollects a cordial parting of the ways. "I never fell out with any of the Selection Committee and I got plenty of warning that they wanted to make a change. It wasn't as if immediately after the Russian game they said, 'That's it.' I think there was about six weeks and it was very diplomatically done, they were very decent about it. Jimmy Aitken was the chairman of the selectors at the time and he discussed it with me and I was very happy to have the weight taken off my shoulders. I mean I had no intention of carrying on and having all the problems that the Scottish manager had at that time. I felt I had had enough after four years, with all the frustrations, and I had made up my mind I was having another career."

Reflecting on the large number of withdrawals from his final squad, Bobby Brown bears no grudges the best part of 50 years later when asked if he felt it was the players or their clubs who were responsible. "I think the players felt that they wanted a holiday. At the end of the season players are more interested, and understandably so in my opinion, in going on their holidays. I think it's a piece of nonsense that they arrange these tours at the end of the season. The families should come first and I think they would benefit if they had two- or three-weeks' rest and refresh."

A surprise announcement from the SFA meeting was the choice of Aberdeen as the venue for Scotland's home match with Belgium in November, a few weeks after Hampden had hosted Portugal.

The draw for the 1974 World Cup qualifiers took place early in August with rather less pomp and ceremony than for later tournaments. Scotland were placed in Group 8, along with Denmark and Czechoslovakia, the winners of which would go to West Germany. A letter from FIFA advised the competing associations that they had until the end of the following March to mutually agree fixture dates.

Names immediately linked with the vacant Scotland position included Willie Ormond of St Johnstone, former Dunfermline manager George Farm, Jimmy Bonthrone of Aberdeen, Hearts' Bobby Seith and Falkirk boss Willie Cunningham. Although the next international was not due until October, Willie Allan advised of the SFA's "intention to appoint a suitable successor as soon as possible".

Written applications were invited for the £4,000 per annum position through advertisements in daily newspapers during the second week of August. A full month later it was revealed that Northern Ireland-born Willie Cunningham had been offered the job. Like his predecessor, Cunningham had not applied for the position but had been approached at a secret meeting in Perth at the beginning of September with the apparent offer of £7,500 a year – almost twice Bobby Brown's salary. The Ulsterman had overseen a successful spell at Dunfermline, reaching the Scottish Cup Final and finishing just one point behind champions Kilmarnock in the First Division in 1964/65. More recently his Falkirk side had ended the 1970/71 season in a healthy seventh place in the 18-team league table.

But the Brockville board fought hard to keep him and held a meeting on the morning of 7 September. At 6pm the press were invited into the Falkirk boardroom where a tense Cunningham read from a prepared statement the shock news that he had turned down the Scotland job.

"The position which has arisen has been an embarrassment to all concerned," he read. "After having gone through the past ten days, which have been quite a strain, and after very careful consideration, I have decided my duty is to remain with Falkirk FC."

It had seemed certain that Cunningham would be taking over for the Portugal match but the SFA was now no nearer to finding a replacement manager than on the day six weeks earlier that they dismissed Bobby Brown.

A meeting of the SFA's International and Selection Committee was arranged for three days later to discuss what was fast developing into a crisis.

The SFA took the unusual step of issuing a statement on a Sunday, 12 September, with the surprise news that Tommy Docherty would be taking charge of the Scotland team for the next two matches. The brief statement read: "Mr Tommy Docherty has been appointed interim manager of the Scottish international team for the forthcoming matches with Portugal and Belgium. Whilst it is the intention of the International Selection Committee to have a full-time manager for Scotland, no decision has been taken in this respect yet."

The appointment had been agreed during a meeting between SFA chairman Hugh Nelson and Docherty in a Bristol hotel the previous day. Docherty had been in the city in his capacity as assistant manager at Hull City, who were playing Bristol City.

Charismatic Glaswegian Docherty, then 42, had been capped 25 times for Scotland and had captained the side on 11 of those occasions. He had played at the 1958 World Cup and had managerial experience at a number of clubs including Chelsea, Porto and Aston Villa. Just a few months earlier he had held talks with a view to taking charge of Hamilton Academical before accepting the offer from Hull player-manager Terry Neill to join him early in July.

Coincidentally, Neill operated a similar role with Northern Ireland whilst playing and managing Hull, and the club were happy for Docherty to continue his duties at Boothberry Park.

It was widely believed that Docherty was essentially on trial for the two matches with a view to being offered a long-term contract; he was granted complete control of team matters.

The caretaker manager travelled north on the Wednesday for a meeting with assistant secretary Ernie Walker and Jimmy Aitken, chairman of the Selection Committee. Willie Allan was not in attendance as he was on holiday but he was kept up to date with developments. The trio then journeyed east to take in the Hearts v Newcastle Texaco Cup tie that evening.

The Doc was back in Edinburgh seven days later having travelled to watch the League Cup quarter-final between Hibs and Willie Cunningham's Falkirk, with the home side's Stanton, Blackley, Brownlie and Alex Cropley under consideration for the Portugal game.

Docherty's 16-man selection was described as a "shock squad" by Jim Blair in the *Evening Times*. Nine Anglos were included as well as what Blair termed "two Englishmen" in Cropley and Arsenal keeper Bob Wilson, who both qualified through Scottish parents.

"These are the best 16 players I have seen," the reporters at Park Gardens were informed. "Obviously in the time available it was impossible to check on every player. The Anglos I know about. If I don't know them now, I'll never know them. Now it's my job to have a look at the young home Scots like Connelly and Dalglish of Celtic. I don't want to give these boys the impression they are being ignored." As well as the two English-born players other new faces were George Graham of Arsenal and Sheffield United centre-back Eddie Colquhoun.

True to his word Docherty attended both of the midweek League Cup semi-finals, Partick v Falkirk and Celtic against St Mirren, with opportunities to attend club matches restricted by his weekend duties at Hull.

The new manager's first squad assembled in the familiar setting of Largs on Monday 11 October, two days before the Portugal game. Some light training at the Inverclyde Recreation Centre was followed by a practice match against Partick Thistle – said to be mutually beneficial to both sides with the Jags due to play in the League Cup Final later that month. Docherty had knowledge of many of the visiting players thanks to his recent managerial stint at Porto.

All four of the newcomers – Wilson, Cropley, Graham and Colquhoun – were in the starting line-up, which included six Anglos. Pat Stanton was the sole survivor from Bobby Brown's last match in Moscow although the number would probably have been higher had the Russian game had fewer withdrawals. Docherty reinstated Bremner as captain and assured the public that his side would be going for goals. Bobby Brown would have been interested to learn that Frank Munro was the sole player to pull out of the squad.

"I believe Scotland can be successful. If I didn't think so, I wouldn't have taken the job," Docherty said in the match programme, describing his appointment as "the greatest honour ever given to me".

With a crowd of 58,612 exceeding all predictions it was clear that interest in the national team had been boosted by Docherty's appointment. As promised the new-look team attacked and took a deserved lead midway through the opening half with an O'Hare header following good work by Bremner and Graham. Eusebio was substituted at half-time suffering from a pulled muscle. A Rodrigues free kick from 22 yards beat both the wall and Wilson before crashing against the stanchion for 1-1, with just under an hour on the clock. But within 60 seconds the spirited Scots fought back to regain the lead in controversial circumstances.

A Stanton free kick was headed on by Colquhoun for Gemmill to challenge Portuguese keeper Damas and the ball ended up in the net. The visitors protested vehemently that there had been a handball but the Polish referee allowed the goal. Another O'Hare header went narrowly over before the end and the crowd stayed to cheer the deserved 2-1 victory.

Docherty had perhaps enjoyed the luck denied Brown with the lack of withdrawals and good fortune over the winning goal but, nevertheless, the overall performance was a massive improvement.

The manager heaped praise on the team after the match. "I am thrilled to bits for the players. They worked from the heart," he told the pressmen inside Hampden. "I think they would have died for Scotland out there tonight," he added before also crediting the passion of the large crowd which had turned up for what was effectively a meaningless match.

Bobby Clark recalls the positive impact the new manager had on the players. "I was on the bench for that match and the Doc breezed in with total confidence. Tommy had coached in Portugal so he really gave a great debrief on them and Scotland played well."

The word from the SFA was that no decision would be taken on Docherty's future until the conclusion of the match with Belgium on 10 November. Had they been consulted it is likely that each and every one of those 58,000 fans who had watched the Portugal game would have offered the Doc a contract that very evening.

The Doc's second squad included a further four new faces: Celtic's Kenny Dalglish, Jim Steele of Dundee, Aberdeen's Steve Murray and Partick goalkeeper Alan Rough, who had recently collected a League Cup winners' medal. On that same day Docherty's club, Hull City, had a £50,000 transfer bid for Rough rejected. Missing were Wilson, Graham and Colquhoun whose clubs had a League Cup match scheduled for the Monday evening ahead of the international.

As with the Portugal match it was a youthful selection, with the manager planning for the future. On the same day as the squad was announced the SFA accepted an invitation to play in the Netherlands four weeks later.

Group leaders Belgium, two points clear of Portugal, required a solitary point for qualification with the two meeting in Lisbon in the final match later that month. The Portuguese manager Gomez Da Silva flew in to watch the Scotland game hoping for a home victory, which would keep his own side's chances alive.

Docherty was his usual confident self ahead of the match, displaying no signs that his future may depend on the evening's result. His starting XI included seven of those who had played against Portugal.

The manager's optimism was justified when Jimmy Johnstone, freed from the pressures of a Hampden crowd, beat no fewer than five Belgians before delivering a perfect cross to O'Hare, who hooked Scotland ahead, the ball going in off a post with just six minutes on the clock.

A header from Hay landed on top of the net and Clark saved well from Van Himst before the 36,500 crowd enthusiastically applauded the teams off at half-time.

Dalglish replaced Cropley for the second period to make his international debut. Jim Parkinson wrote in the following day's *Glasgow Herald*: "Intelligently he kept the Scots moving with a smooth, fluent rhythm ... and he could be around the international scene for years to come."

Eddie Gray witnessed Dalglish's debut that evening: "He had so much talent, Kenny. He was always going to be a top player, as he went on to prove."

With a steady defence and a confident goalkeeper, the Scots were comfortable 1-0 winners and might have had a second goal through Gray before the final whistle prompted even more rapturous applause.

"These kids played like a club side," the manager-in-waiting told Malcolm Munro afterwards, adding, "One for all, all for one. That's what I'm after." In just 180 minutes of football Scotland's international fortunes had been re-energised in front of over 95,000 spectators.

The *Celtic View* was happy to report that Johnstone had been "cheered every time he touched the ball", noting that "the fans gave him a standing ovation when he was substituted late in the second half". The winger himself praised the north-eastern fans who he considered, "Fabulous, absolutely fabulous."

Five days later an SFA press release advised that the job was Docherty's should he wish it, with the same £7,500 salary that had been offered to Cunningham on the table.

The Doc's guarded response to the press was that he was "thrilled and delighted" with the offer but stated that he wished to discuss "certain aspects" before committing himself.

If Aberdonians expected more regular internationals to be staged on their doorstep they were soon put in their place. The same November, an SFA meeting decided that all future full internationals would be staged at Hampden Park. Whether the Committee had considered the location of the fixture inconvenient or were perhaps eyeing a regular increase in attendances, was not clear, although it was stated that Queen's Park would not be able to afford the upkeep of Hampden Park on their own. It would be the best part of another 20 years before Aberdeen hosted another full international.

Docherty drove north for a meeting with Willie Allan and Jimmy Aitken in a restaurant in the West End of Glasgow on Tuesday 16 November. After 30 minutes of discussions Aitken emerged to address the waiting reporters: "I am happy to announce that a satisfactory conclusion has been reached by ourselves and Mr Tommy Docherty, and he will now take up his post as team manager as from Monday."

The contract was for a period of four years and included a Rover car, unlimited travel and what was referred to as "suitable office accommodation".

Having parted company with Hull City on amicable terms much of Docherty's first day in office – 22 November – was spent taking telephone calls from well-wishers. It was already clear that he was a popular choice and could count on the cooperation and goodwill of many.

Docherty recalled Wilson and Colquhoun, now free of club commitments, along with Tony Green who was by this time a Newcastle player, for Scotland's last match of 1971 – the friendly in Amsterdam on 1 December. Like Scotland, the Dutch had also failed to qualify for the European Championships but were fast establishing themselves at both club and international level.

The squad gathered in Glasgow two days before the Holland match without a single withdrawal. This was even more remarkable considering that the game was not a competitive fixture; it indicated the willingness of the players to turn out for Docherty. There was one initial absentee due to Archie Gemmill's car suffering a puncture en route to East Midlands Airport which caused him to miss his Glasgow flight. After a telephone call he was rerouted through London and actually arrived in Amsterdam slightly ahead of his team-mates.

Docherty's game plan was again positive with Dalglish starting for the first time up front with Gemmill, but the opening 45 minutes were a wake-up call with the Scots given no opportunity whatsoever to carry out their attacking instructions. The Dutch were streets ahead, moving the ball around as they sought to perfect the art which would come to be associated with their great side of 1974 – Total Football. Several of that 1974 squad played that evening including Ajax pair Cruyff and Neeskens.

The 24-year-old Cruyff gave his side a fifth-minute lead then rattled a shot off Wilson's crossbar with Docherty's men camped in their own half. The Arsenal goalkeeper was later quoted in *The Herald* saying: "In the first half the Dutch were queuing up to take shots." Changes were made during the break with O' Hare substituting for Johnstone as Scotland gradually edged their way back into the match.

Bremner sent in a free kick for Graham to equalise after 58 minutes before Gemmill found himself clean through on goal with just four minutes left. After beating the goalkeeper he looked certain to score but overran the ball which went out of play. The player later said he halted as he thought the ball was rolling into the net but claimed it must have hit a bump.

Moments later Barry Hulshoff rose to meet a corner and head beyond Wilson to win the match. Although Scotland had been outclassed in the first half they had improved vastly after the break losing only to a very late goal. The trip was considered a worthwhile exercise.

"One Step From Glory" was the headline of Hugh Taylor's match report for the *Daily Record*, highlighting the Gemmill chance. Taylor praised the change of approach in the second half with: "A fine tactical move by manager Docherty brought the Scots roaring back into the game." The manager expressed sympathy for his players in the newspaper: "When I walked into the dressing room just minutes after we had lost I could only say to the players how sorry I felt for them. What I got from this game was much more than the scoreline might suggest."

The target of the 1974 World Cup was mentioned more regularly and the quest was on to secure more fixtures ahead of the Home Internationals at the end of the season. At this point the SFA had still not received an invitation to the Brazilian tournament which was taking place after the British Championship.

1972

"In many ways I think he was suited to international football, comparing him to other managers that came and went."
Asa Hartford on Tommy Docherty

At the beginning of 1972 Tommy Docherty was still living in Birmingham, although he planned to move north of the border once the sale of his house was completed.

The Doc had three Under-23 matches to plan for in the space of 16 days in mid-January. All of these were home games, the first against the West German Olympic team at Hampden Park on 10 January. The Doc selected five players who were untried at any international level and listed a separate squad for the match against a Scottish Professional Youth Select XI the following week. Alan Rough was the only name to feature in both squads, which illustrated the manager's intention to assess as many players as possible.

Heavy rain ruined the first game as a spectacle with passes continually sticking in the Hampden mud. Willie Donachie, one of the newcomers, scored the only goal after 18 minutes, firing low into the German net from 20 yards after a Dalglish free kick had been blocked. The Germans had their opportunities and 20-year-old Uli Hoeness, bound for greater achievements, missed a sitter in the first half, but the Scots deserved their narrow win and almost doubled their lead when Ally Brown headed on to the crossbar in the final minute.

Only 5,903 spectators had turned up on that awful night with the inevitable questions posed as to whether anything had been gained from the exercise. The SFA accounts recorded a loss of £2,137.80 on the venture although it was not unusual for the balance sheet to show a deficit for this type of fixture.

The manager only met up with his players on the afternoon of the game against the Professional Youths at Partick. In an attempt to boost the crowd he promised attacking football, suggesting that Firhill could be in the running for similar fixtures if things went well. The Under-18 Pro Youth team formed part of the SFA's development policy and played matches against club sides such as Falkirk, Hearts and Clydebank during the same period, as well as against their Welsh counterparts.

Three Thistle players started on their home pitch along with future internationalists Gordon McQueen, Danny McGrain, Willie Young and Lou Macari. The opposition team included youngsters from clubs including Kilmarnock, Morton, Ayr United, Chelsea and Birmingham City.

With admission set at 60 new pence for the stand and half that for the terrace, the 2,800 crowd were treated to, as Docherty had promised, an entertaining evening with none of the treacherous conditions which had spoiled the Hampden match.

After beating three men Paul Wilson opened the scoring for the Under-23s with a fine goal, only for Ian McLaughlan to level within a minute. It remained 1-1 at the break after which Jimmy Bone replaced Macari to make it four Thistle players on the park. The substitute scored by lobbing the ball over Jim Stewart's head after 58 minutes which turned what had been an evenly matched contest into one favouring the Under-23 side. Further goals from Young, Wilson and Somner gave them a final total of five whilst Kenny Burns had grabbed a second goal for the Youths with the score at 3-1.

The association calculated a deficit of £741.56 on the night which had been reduced by a £200 payment from STV which allowed them to screen 15 minutes of highlights during *Scotsport*.

"It was a sort of trial game that Tommy Docherty had set up and it was a good idea," goalscorer Jimmy Bone recalls. "He just went and organised the two teams and he sat and had a look at it which made sense, but the clubs wouldn't condone it now. Being a new manager it let him go and have a look at what was about and it made sense at the time. It would give guys who maybe played for one of the less fashionable clubs an opportunity."

For the meeting with Wales at Pittodrie seven days later Docherty's pool more closely resembled that for the West German match than for the game at Firhill. The International and Selection Committee met in Aberdeen to discuss the recently received invitation to the Brazilian tournament, concerned that the June and July dates could have an impact on player availability. It was felt that, even if clubs agreed to their release, some players may be reluctant to travel such a distance after a long season and a decision on whether to accept the invitation was held over until the next committee meeting three weeks later.

Docherty embraced the Pittodrie fixture in the match programme. "I would stress that I consider under-23 internationals to be of great importance. In fact, in my opinion, we cannot have too many of them, because I think these games are a stepping stone for the players to a full international side."

Again the Aberdeen public responded and although a Macari shot had rebounded from the bar, a disappointing first half ended scoreless with the 15,000 present making their disapproval audible.

"The transformation was quite incredible," said *The Herald*'s "Special Correspondent", of the Scots' second-half performance. Dalglish forced a wonder save from Parton in the Welsh goal before the same player laid the ball off for skipper Jardine to score with a left-foot shot from just outside the penalty area.

Macari and Cropley brought further saves from the Burnley keeper as the Scots' confidence grew, but it took an error from Parton to secure victory. With seven minutes left Denis McQuade's corner kick was punched into his net by the goalkeeper although there was a suggestion that Macari may have supplied the final touch.

Derby on 16 February was the next port of call for Scotland's Under-23 team, before which the International and Selection Committee held a meeting in the city's Midland Hotel. After an hour of discussions it was decided to again delay the decision on whether to travel to Brazil. The situation had been hindered when five players – Hay, Dalglish, Johnstone, Gemmill and O'Hare – had advised over the weekend that they did not wish to be considered. The manager, however, was adamant that he would have sufficient numbers available and argued continually for the invitation to be accepted.

The line-ups for the game at the Baseball Ground contained a number of names who would go on to play at the highest level. England's forward line alone boasted Mick Channon, Malcolm MacDonald, Kevin Keegan and Tony Currie whilst the Scottish XI included Jardine, Dalglish, Buchan, Hartford and Macari.

Jimmy Bone, then playing for Norwich City, had no doubts over the value of the fixture. "I remember we played a front three that was Lou Macari, myself and Kenny. The bulk of the guys were regulars in their first teams. They were real serious because at that time you saw it as a stepping stone if you got into the Under-23s. You knew you had a chance if you had done well of getting into the first team, whereas I don't think the kids today feel that when they get to the Under-21s. It's a big, big gap. The couple of years does make a difference."

The government had declared a State of Emergency the previous week as a national strike by mineworkers threatened the supply of electricity. Power cuts had been introduced and floodlit football outlawed, requiring the midweek game to begin at 2.30pm. A crowd of 18,176 still turned up and were rewarded with an excellent game despite another muddy pitch. Scotland went ahead after 38 minutes when Dalglish finished off a fine move involving Macari and Bone, only for Channon to reply almost immediately.

As the match swung from end to end a defensive misunderstanding allowed Hudson to square the ball for Channon, who beat two defenders then Ally Hunter midway through the second half.

Six minutes later Macari fed Dalglish who beat Parker from 16 yards to complete the scoring at two goals apiece. It would not be the last time that the names of Channon and Dalglish featured on the scoresheet during England v Scotland clashes.

"BRAZIL – WE'RE GOING" was the *Evening Times*'s headline on 28 February after the next committee meeting confirmed that the invitation would be accepted.

"I will be taking the strongest possible side," a delighted Docherty told the press, adding, "Most of the verbal assurances I have had from players and managers have been confirmed." It was said to be the commitments of those players which had swung the committee's decision. "This is a wonderful chance to introduce some of the younger players to this level of football, the Doc continued. "If you play the best you must improve."

Jimmy Bone still remembers receiving a phone call from Docherty. "It wasn't a case of a letter coming out; he phoned and said: 'With this trip I'd like you to go.'"

Asa Hartford sacrificed more than the close-season break when accepting the call-up: "I was getting married in 1972 and put it off to go on the tour. When I found out I was being picked I changed my honeymoon so obviously I was definitely wanting to go on the trip." The manager was later accused of not adhering to protocol whilst approaching the players of at least one club.

At this point there was no indication as to who Scotland's opponents would be or even where they would be playing but they had been assured of a minimum of three matches with a pay-out to the SFA of £10,000 for each appearance in the tournament.

The next important date in the Doc's diary was 15 March when he took charge of the Scottish League XI for the first time, against Sir Alf Ramsey's Football League side in Middlesbrough.

The programme for the match contained a full-page article titled What Value Do Inter League Matches Have?" which highlighted the benefits of the fixture at a time when the demands of club football saw an increasing number of midweek matches.

"I remember that game," says John Blackley, who made his one and only appearance for the League side alongside his Hibs clubmate and good friend John Brownlie. "They had a winger called Wagstaffe and Brownlie couldn't handle him. He was away deep, taking the ball and switch plays and Brownlie didn't want to go down the line and pick him up. Honestly, Brownlie had nightmares about him!" John Blackley laughs as he reveals that the winger's name still gets brought up during player reunions. "Every time we get together we have a laugh about it when we mention David Wagstaffe!"

Brownlie's night of frustration was captured by Raymond Jacobs' report in *The Herald*, which included: "England had a left-winger of the old-fashioned mould in Wagstaffe, who gave the talented Brownlie a rough passage with his sweeping runs and crosses."

Another lively match saw the home side start strongly with goals from Currie and Mike Doyle establishing a deserved two-goal lead by the 25th minute.

The Scots fought back after the interval with good work by Colin Stein supplying McQuade, who beat Ray Clemence for 2-1. But within three minutes England had scored again when Currie took advantage of a mix-up between Hunter and Connelly. An unmarked Stein controlled a cross from Arthur Graham before shooting home to complete the scoring. The 3-2 scoreline was said to flatter the Scots.

In his *Daily Mirror* match report Ken Jones did the fixture no favours with his opening paragraph, which read: "A makeshift England team was unable to sustain any genuine enthusiasm for the job of beating Scotland in a now obsolete Inter League fixture last night." He further referred to "the overall boredom of the contest". Nevertheless, the match had attracted an attendance of just four customers short of 20,000 and had given the locals an opportunity to see some top names in action.

The following Monday the manager released the 20 names who would be making the long trip to Brazil. Most headlines featured the return of 31-year-old Denis Law who had last played for Scotland in May 1969. Following their performances in the Inter League match Donald Ford and Colin Stein were included. The SFA had reluctantly turned down the offer to play a game in the USA en route to South America.

Due to the competitive nature of his game, Law had suffered from injuries and a loss of form in the three years since his last international appearance. During season 1969/70 he had featured only 11 times for Manchester United, scoring just twice. Determined, he trained all through the close season to regain his fitness and the return for his hard work was 34 appearances and 16 goals – almost one every two games – during the 1970/71 campaign. This form continued into the following season and did not go unnoticed by the Scotland manager. Although Docherty placed a lot of importance on youth, he recognised that Denis's inclusion in the squad would be a huge benefit to the younger players. As someone who always claimed his greatest honour was representing his country, Law had no second thoughts when enquiries were made as to his availability for the Brazil trip.

After prolonged negotiations a suitable date of 26 April was agreed for a Hampden match against Peru who were undertaking a European tour at the time. The timing of the match pleased the manager as it was just ahead of the Home Internationals and the

Brazil tournament. After a schedule of three full internationals in a seven-week period following his appointment, Docherty later felt frustrated by the limited opportunities to spend time with his players. Like his predecessors it was a club spirit he sought to instil and his pleas for squad get-togethers were hindered by a lack of cooperation from some managers, just as Bobby Brown had experienced. The Inter League and Under-23 matches were useful but Docherty continually pleaded with the SFA Committee for more full internationals.

Law started in the Peru game and Docherty paid tribute to Derby County boss Brian Clough, who allowed the inclusion of O'Hare and Gemmill even though their club faced Airdrie that same evening in the second leg of the Anglo-Scottish Cup Final. There was an absence of any Hibs or Rangers players as those clubs had met in a Scottish Cup semi-final replay two days earlier and the Ibrox club also had a league match scheduled against Dunfermline the day after the international.

To his undisguised delight Law was made captain and told Malcolm Munro: "It's marvellous to be back – wonderful. Just to be in the squad was enough – but to be made captain – it's unbelievable. I've done extra training and I'm as keen as I was when I joined Huddersfield when I was 15."

Lou Macari was just as delighted to find himself included in the 19-man pool. "If you managed to get in the squad even if you didn't play, that was an achievement because there were that many players that the managers could pick, genuine contenders that could play for Scotland. So getting in the squad was the first thing I was delighted with and obviously you go along with the squad and you mix with the players and you've got to pinch yourself to believe that you are there."

Hibs' right-back John Brownlie was added immediately after his club's win over Rangers, and Kilmarnock keeper Hunter was one of three players making their full international debuts; Hartford and Donachie were the others. The visitors' line-up included one Teófilo Cubillas, an attacking midfielder whose name would haunt Scotland fans for many years after the 1978 World Cup.

Law's return did little to boost the crowd, which numbered 21,001. The following evening Rangers and Dunfermline could only attract 6,021 followers to Ibrox which suggests that the First Division game had less impact on the Hampden attendance than the semi-final replay, which came just eight days after 80,000 had watched Rangers triumph over Bayern Munich to book their place in the final of the European Cup-Winners' Cup.

The opening period was somewhat disappointing with Cubillas and Law missing the only chances of note. *The Herald's* Jim Parkinson reported that "the first half ranked as flat as any seen at Hampden". A well-organised defence was finally breached two minutes into the second half when O'Hare headed in from Morgan's indirect free kick for the last of his five international goals, four of which had come from his head.

Ten minutes later hordes of youngsters flooded on to the pitch to celebrate the return of the King as Law headed another Morgan cross into goal. After a delay it became clear that the flag of a linesman had spoiled the homecoming – but that moment was only postponed by eight minutes.

Following good work by Hartford, O'Hare fed Law who powered the ball into the roof of the net from eight yards. The goal did not trigger the traditional one-arm salute synonymous with Law. This first international goal since 1968 merited both arms being raised followed by a hug of gratitude for O'Hare. The King was well and truly back in business.

The following week the manager included Billy McNeill amongst the 22 names for the Home Internationals. In uncannily similar circumstances to Law, the 31-year-old Celtic skipper had not featured since the match in West Germany in 1969. Due to their appearance in the final of the European Cup Winners' Cup, Rangers' players were omitted as their date with Moscow Dynamo in Barcelona fell right in the middle of the series. Bremner regained the captaincy whilst his Leeds club mate Peter Lorimer returned following his exile almost 12 months earlier after his South African excursion. Docherty had insisted on Lorimer's inclusion despite initial opposition from within the SFA. The manager pointed out that he had been assured complete control over selection and eventually got his way.

Just ahead of the Home Internationals the International Committee sanctioned Docherty's request to check on training and hotel facilities in Brazil. On his return he told the *Evening Times'* Malcolm Munro that he had been given the "red-carpet treatment" throughout his stay. He said that the Brazilians had been impressed by

Scotland's last few results. "What we've got to do now to impress them even further is to win the Home Championship. Our match against Ireland at Hampden is every bit as important as the match against England. We've got to win them all." The players took up residence in the Queens Hotel in Largs on Thursday 18 May, where they would remain until after the England match on the 27th. Docherty had recently bought a house in the Ayrshire town.

A decision had been taken by the International and Selection Committee the previous November that Scotland would not be prepared to play in Belfast whilst there was a danger of being caught up in the sectarian troubles. The Irish FA then agreed that their 1972 "home match" would be played in Glasgow with the gate receipts in their favour. This to a degree suited both parties as it gave the Scots home advantage and the Irish potentially greater revenue from what was expected to be a large crowd. It also had the added bonus of allowing the Scottish party to settle in Largs for the full week.

The match pitted Docherty against his old Hull City colleague Terry Neill, who was both player and manager of the Ulster side. Neill had been deprived of his star player when George Best failed to arrive at their base in Troon but still had a number of big names in Jennings, Nelson, Rice and Dougan.

The game was considered poor with the near-40,000 crowd further frustrated when another Law effort was disallowed for offside halfway through the first period. Scotland did the bulk of the attacking although the visitors were still a threat, but a no-score-draw seemed the most likely outcome as the match entered its closing stages.

As the fans broke into slow handclaps the Lawman struck – with just four minutes left. Lorimer, who had come on for Johnstone, intercepted a pass-back and sent over a cross which Law spectacularly hooked past Jennings. Law reverted to his traditional one-arm salute, punching the air. The win was sealed when Lorimer himself scored with a powerful 25-yard strike in the closing seconds, sending the once-restless fans home, or to the soon-opening Glasgow bars, happy.

News reached Largs from Rangers' Spanish camp that Sandy Jardine had withdrawn from the Brazil trip. The defender had played around 70 matches that season and his manager Waddell insisted the decision had been a personal one and not taken by the club. Jardine's team-mate Colin Stein was, however, still expected to be available.

Controversy surrounded the Scotland v Wales game with the Rangers match also scheduled for the Wednesday evening. Because of the international the SFA had vetoed moves to televise the final live – a decision taken almost immediately after Rangers had defeated Bayern Munich in the semi-final.

An emergency board meeting was held at Ibrox on Saturday 22 April, prompting a letter to the association requesting that the Wales game be brought forward by 24 hours. The correspondence assured the SFA that the club were not attempting to devalue the British Championship, adding: "Rangers Football Club have always helped the national team in any way we can – and will continue to do so. We feel in view of the impact and interest Rangers have made in Europe this season that the fans should see the game."

A meeting of the SFA Executive and General Purposes Committee on 28 April rejected the suggestion out of hand. It was reported that the FA of Wales had no objection to a change of date but Rangers' request was nevertheless declined.

There was talk of a boycott of the Wales game by those Rangers fans not travelling to the continent. Duncan Perrett, secretary of the Rangers Supporters' association, told the *Sunday Mail*: "The mood of the fans is clearly that they will stay away if the international is not switched to accommodate the live televising of the match in Barcelona."

Seven days later an official statement was made by SFA secretary Willie Allan which stated: "The chairman of the Rangers club addressed a letter to the president of the association requesting the date of the international match to be altered in order to leave the way clear for a live television transmission of the final tie of the European Cup Winners' Cup competition. The members of the Executive and General Purposes Committee were not prepared to fall into line with the suggestion. There is no objection to a delayed televised transmission of the final tie provided it did not start before 11pm."

One concession was gained by the broadcasters with STV's *Scotsport* on air at 11.30pm, five minutes before BBC Scotland's *Sportsreel*. Both broadcasts showed the Rangers match in its entirety followed by highlights of the Scotland game, and went off air after midnight. The Spanish broadcasters failed to supply the promised colour transmission so viewers had to make do with black and white coverage.

The Doc told Lou Macari he would earn his first cap against Wales. "I think actually being picked to play in the game was pretty irrelevant, it was just the fact that I'm in the squad with 18 or 20 players who are top, top players," is Lou's memory. Even better was the fact that he would be lining up with one of his idols. "I remember I thought 'Bloody hell, I'm playing with Denis Law tonight. I can't believe it!' The team was picked on the morning of the game and I went to my bed that afternoon thinking, 'Bloody hell, I'm playing with Denis Law!'"

The Hampden gate was recorded as 21,332. Comparing like for like it was 10,000 down on the previous year's midweek Hampden Home International versus the Irish and some 18,000 short of the Irish fixture, also midweek, 12 months later. There is no doubt that some of the thousands of Rangers' supporters in Barcelona would have attended the international had there been no clash of fixtures, whilst others may very well have stayed away and listened to radio commentary from Spain.

There was no question of the Welsh being treated lightly as debutant Lou Macari explains: "Before a ball was kicked, before you played Wales, you realised it was seriously taken and it really, really mattered."

There were similarities with the Northern Ireland game and the Scots struggled to break through, with the Welsh narrowly shading the first 45 minutes.

An improved second-half performance was eventually rewarded when Lorimer finished off a move involving Bremner and Macari, powering the ball into the roof of the net after 72 minutes. Law and Lorimer continued to shoot on sight with the slender lead only threatened in the last few minutes when the Welsh ventured upfield. Lorimer's goal was enough to win the match which meant that, following Northern Ireland's shock win at Wembley, Docherty's men topped the Championship table on four points ahead of England's visit.

Scotland had not won the England fixture at home since 1964 and there was a growing belief that 1972 could be their year. A solitary point would secure the Championship but Docherty had only victory in mind. His record since taking office was exemplary – five wins out of six matches played. The one defeat was in Amsterdam, the only away match in the sequence.

In an interview with *The Herald*'s Jim Parkinson published on the morning of the game, Docherty indicated that he was looking at greater prizes than the British Championship trophy.

"I think the Home International Championship, and that includes the game with England, must be used for bigger things," he told the journalist. "Of course it is a very important match but we must have it as a lead-up to Brazil and World Cup commitments." He went on to forecast "a nice game of football", a description which would not feature in anyone's account of the game. A bad-tempered match saw four players booked, two from each side, and a total of 46 fouls committed which again were fairly evenly split with Scotland the offenders on 24 occasions compared to England's 22 fouls.

In his annual *Scottish Football Book* Hugh Taylor labelled the contest "a disgrace, a blot on football … the season ended in one of the most unpleasant matches between the two countries."

Lou Macari was again excited to be in the team: "It was the fixture that everybody was desperate to play in. You did realise that you were playing against the world champions from 1966 so playing in that game was great."

Asa Hartford made his third international appearance that afternoon. "It opened my eyes that game because Norman Hunter nearly cut his clubmate Billy Bremner in two with a tackle and I thought, 'how fierce is this?'" he said. "It was quite a tough game because they had Peter Storey in midfield and he didn't take any prisoners either." Alan Ball was booked for bringing down Bremner and McNeill then had his name taken for pushing Rodney Marsh. Some of the exchanges were so fierce that Italian referee Gonella called captains Moore and Bremner together in an effort to calm the players down, many of whom were involved in personal feuds.

Most of the attacking was by the home side and a deflected shot from Hartford deceived Banks before Storey cleared from the line. The huge crowd was silenced when England took a surprise lead just as the half-hour mark approached. A poor pass from Bremner was intercepted by Chivers, who quickly fed Ball who scored from close range. Ball then responded to earlier abusive chants by gesturing to the crowd.

Bobby Clark can still see the goal today. "I came out to block Alan Ball. He got to it first and the ball hit me but unfortunately I did not get enough on it and it crept frustratingly into the goal."

"Bally's goal didn't even hit the back of the net," says Asa Hartford. "It just seemed to crawl over the line."

The Scots then almost fell further behind when a shot from Colin Bell struck Clark's far post.

England improved in the second half, even if the standard of football did not, and Marsh and substitute MacDonald both went close. Johnstone, introduced for Gemmill, caused the visitors' defence some problems but there was to be no equaliser and no fairy-tale return to the fixture for Denis Law, with Ball's goal still separating the sides at full time.

"We must develop a Hampden mentality," the manager told reporters. "We must always go out to win on our home ground. If you talk of settling for a draw in one game here you are letting yourself down. I could have played 11 defenders to get a point, but that would not have been progress." He was responding to the suggestion that a less adventurous approach could have been enough to secure the Championship, as England had finished top of the table, level on four points with Scotland but one goal better off. He would also have been aware that no Scottish crowd would have tolerated seeing their side play for a draw against England at any time.

"It didn't matter to the supporters how you played on the day as long as you beat England," reflects Lou Macari. "The Scottish players realised what it meant to the supporters."

Following Jardine's withdrawal the lack of a right-back concerned the manager and he approached Hibs with a view to including Brownlie in the party for Brazil.

It was believed that Brownlie himself was keen to travel but the club refused his release. This begged the question: could the SFA demand a player's services?

On 2 June, assistant secretary Ernie Walker announced that "Brownlie will not be going to Brazil," adding, "The SFA will not insist on any club releasing any player." It then transpired that a letter circulated to clubs ahead of the SFA's acceptance of the Brazil invitation had enquired about their cooperation. It had been made clear that there was no compulsion.

The Edinburgh club's stance was that they had earlier agreed to releasing just one player for the trip and with Stanton set to travel they were not prepared to consider any further requests.

Relations between the club and the SFA deteriorated further the following week when a letter from Stanton was delivered to Park Gardens. The player stated that he would be unable to travel due to concerns about the health of his wife who had recently given birth.

On the same day Hibernian chairman Tom Hart released a statement following a board meeting at Easter Road. The SFA was criticised for not requesting Brownlie's release in writing, only via what it referred to as "statements and threats by the Scottish manager in the press".

Hart also condemned Docherty's initial approach for the release of players which had involved direct contact with Stanton, Cropley and Brownlie, bypassing manager Eddie Turnbull. "This invitation was highly irregular according to the code that is followed at Easter Road," read the statement. A later meeting between the club and the international manager led to the agreement that one Hibs player of Docherty's choice would be permitted to travel. The statement concluded: "Hibernian FC in the past have been generous in their attitude to the release of players for international games. They will continue to be sympathetic, other than those brought belatedly and without notice and by banner headlines in the national press." Hart also made it clear that Stanton's withdrawal would have no impact on the non-availability of Brownlie.

Docherty did not take Stanton's decision well, announcing that the player would not be picked for Scotland again as long as he was in charge. The player revealed he had enclosed his wife's medical certificate with the letter which Willie Allan had acknowledged. The manager's view was that Stanton ought to have communicated directly with him rather than with the secretary.

Chelsea then refused to release Charlie Cooke but Partick Thistle's Denis McQuade was added to the squad with his club's blessing.

The 18 players reassembled at Largs on 18 June four weeks after the England game and five days ahead of the flight to Brazil, emphasising how seriously the tournament was being taken. "The preparation at Largs was excellent," says Bobby Clark. "The Doc had even ordered the small white balls that Brazil used. They seemed more like size 4s and the lads referred to them as ping-pong balls!"

The first Scotland international side ever to travel to South America departed from Glasgow via Paris on Friday 23 June. Due to the costs involved just four sports journalists accompanied them.

"The players know it won't be a picnic," Docherty told the *Evening Times*'s Jim Blair before departure. "They're not there for a suntan and they have a job to do. I've every confidence in them ... they have shown a willingness to play for Scotland," he added, a comment which was almost certainly directed at absentees.

Two of the three Partick players included had already taken part in their club's Far East tour since the conclusion of the domestic season and Rangers' Colin Stein had scored in the European Cup-Winners' Cup Final a month earlier. The thoughts of the striker are recorded within the pages of *Rangers News*: "To go there and play in the company of big names from so many countries is the kind of chance which rarely comes along. Yes, I would call it the chance of a lifetime and for another reason too. Perhaps through it I can clinch a regular place again in the full Scottish side. I'm one of those guys who enjoys playing for his country ... the more the better."

Bobby Clark remembers an exciting but hectic period. "I had had a very busy summer as I played in all three of the Home International Championship games and then immediately flew out to Toronto where I met up with the Aberdeen team who were on their American tour. I played five games there and on returning home had a four-day break before joining Tommy Docherty's squad at Largs to prepare for the Brazil trip."

Jimmy Bone recalls the influence two of the senior players had during the trip. "Denis Law was brilliant; he was very, very good in the squad. Him and Billy Bremner were fantastic; they looked after the young players and made sure everything was fine. They were first class. They made everybody feel welcome, to feel a part of it."

"You learned a lot from people like Denis who had done it all," Lou Macari remembers. "Apart from having the ability that he had, Denis was a tough, no nonsense centre-forward. He could dish it out as well; that was part of the game."

Scotland, in Group A, faced tough opposition in Yugoslavia, Czechoslovakia and the hosts Brazil. The Slavs had already come through a tough first round undefeated in their four matches whilst the Czechs, like Scotland and Brazil, had been given a bye into the second stage. This saw eight nations split into two groups of four with the winners of each meeting in the final on 9 July.

The SFA party was accommodated in the Hotel Gloria in Rio de Janeiro. The building had been constructed 50 years earlier as part of the country's centennial celebrations and was one of the city's most recognisable landmarks.

The players flew to Belo Horizonte for their opener against Yugoslavia where only 3,500 watched a tough affair played in 80-degree temperatures. As tempers frayed Paunovic and Donachie were involved in a punch-up before Morgan fed Macari who gave Scotland a 40th-minute lead. The advantage was held for 20 minutes until a Bajević shot squared the match – but only for three minutes. Although not the tallest of players, Macari rose above the defence to head Morgan's cross into the net to give his side the lead for the second time. The Scots were visibly tired in the second half and Law was replaced by Jimmy Bone, whose first impression of football Brazilian-style has stayed with him: "The one thing I remember was the difference in the grass," he recalls. "It was really thick, quite brittle and completely different to what it was back home. The ball sort of sat on the top of it for you to go and hit it."

The small crowd jeered as Scotland kept possession before venturing upfield in the 77th minute, when a Hartford run was halted by two defenders, leading to the award of a penalty kick. Ken Gallagher's match report for the *Daily Record* adequately captured what followed: "Morgan placed the ball well but did not hit it hard enough and the lanky Slav keeper Mešković was able to dive to his left and save."

This encouraged the opposition, who drew level again in fortunate circumstances four minutes from time. Jerković hit a powerful shot which struck Buchan's shoulder before entering the net – the deflection giving Hunter no chance. A linesman had raised his flag for offside but the goal stood. The Slavs poured forward in the remaining few minutes and came close on three occasions before the game ended at 2-2, with the Scots rueing Morgan's miss from the spot. Ironically the penalty sinner had been Scotland's best player. "For the rest of the game this had been Morgan the master," Gallagher had typed.

The Czech game was in Porto Alegre three days later and the manager, popular with the local press due to his grasp of the language, announced that he planned to field an unchanged team. All four teams had a point each following Czechoslovakia's goalless draw with the hosts. The Czechs were of course in Scotland's qualifying group for the next World Cup.

Gallagher's report described "furnace-like heat" inside the stadium where the Scots, along with the Czech players, were booed for the second time by another small crowd estimated at 15,000. The locals were frustrated as Scotland kept possession in midfield seeking an opportunity for Hartford or Bremner to break.

Clark, replacing Hunter, stopped what seemed a certain goal when he took the ball from Medvid after 24 minutes. At the other end Bremner miskicked when an opportunity arose on the edge of the area, which earned him whistles from the crowd. Stein replaced Law with 12 minutes to play and it was Rangers' Barcelona hero who almost won the game after controlling a pass from Bremner, but his shot rebounded from the Czech keeper Viktor. The match finished goalless to the disapproval of those watching who were used to the silky style of their own World Cup-winning team.

Rodger Baillie was one of the quartet of Scottish reporters covering the tour and has fond memories of his dealings with the manager. "He was just the Doc!" he smiles. "Extremely ebullient and good to deal with. To eat in the headquarters of the tour in the Hotel Gloria you had to have chits and he used to hand us them willy-nilly – enough to make sure we ate rather well every day. I don't think Mr Allan was too chuffed to see us sitting there but there was nothing he could do as we had the necessary passes."

There were reports of a great spirit amongst the players but behind the scenes there was a split and a potential confrontation with the SFA. "A near revolt by Scotland's angry players was only averted by a late-night meeting in our luxury hotel," was how Ken Gallagher reported the events.

The row stemmed from the hosts' hospitality, with the Brazilian Federation inviting the Scots to remain as guests until the tournament's conclusion, should they fail to reach the final. All but five of the 18 players were in favour of staying, with three of those having to return for a Partick tour to Sweden. Following a meeting, those players chose to side with the majority to preserve the unity which had been built up on the trip. As any extra costs were being paid for by the Brazilians it seemed an easy decision. However, their own association informed the players that, should their interest in the tournament be ended, they would all be returning together as planned on Friday 7 July, two days ahead of the final. Ken Gallagher reported: "Several players have told me that they were ready to stay on in spite of any SFA ruling. Others made it plain they would be reluctant to feature for Scotland in the future if this was the treatment they could expect."

"We did hear about the opportunity to stay for the final and I suppose the camp was split on this," says Bobby Clark. "I would have loved to have seen the final and it would also have let us get some time in Rio without the pressure of a game but I also realised that we had to get back home for pre-season. So I could see both sides of this."

The manager found himself in an unenviable position between his players and employers. Docherty had, after all, negotiated with the clubs for the players' release and his, in some cases already fragile, relationship with them could be endangered if their stay was extended, with the new season fast approaching. The Doc favoured a 48-hour extension but his attempts to change the itinerary were met with the expected response from the immovable SFA Committee.

It took an intervention from the respected Denis Law to prevent a possible mutiny when he spoke up for the manager, reasoning that they should return when Docherty said so. This was accepted by the players who could, of course, have influenced the situation by gaining the required point from Brazil and winning a place in the final. Another option was to finish second in the group, which required participation in a play-off with the runners-up from Group B in Rio ahead of the final.

A confident Billy Bremner was quoted in the *Evening Times* saying: "We are going out to win. We've surprised a lot of people by our performances out here so there's no reason we shouldn't upset Brazil."

As they both hailed from Stirling, Jimmy Bone struck up a good bond with Bremner. "Wee Billy always thought that when he went on to the park he would be the best player on that park and he would tell you that. It wasn't because he was big-headed or anything, it was because, as he said, 'I've practised all my life to be the best and I've worked really hard and every time I go on the pitch I think I'm going to be at my best and if I'm at my best I'll be the best player.' It wasn't conceit or anything, it was just real belief in himself because of the hard work. When Billy was 14 he used to play Under-21 football and he was only five foot seven so he was used to looking after himself, and with all his footballing ability he could play."

With such an influential captain, Jimmy recalls there was a genuine belief that Scotland could overcome the world champions on their own pitch. "You also had Denis who was a top, top player and these guys' charisma rubbed off on everybody. And with Tommy Docherty being the kind of manager he was, we had no fear against anybody."

Lou Macari is of a similar opinion: "It wasn't a squad that was big-headed in any way but we started to grow in confidence. We started to believe that we could take on whoever we had to and give them a run for their money."

"The game in the Maracana was special," says Bobby Clark. "The Doc made sure we were there very early to beat the traffic and, if my memory serves me correctly, we arrived three hours before the game. This meant we had a lot of time to kill before kick-off. I remember being advised to take a book and that helped me forget nerves before such a big game."

With the players prepared, an official entered their dressing room to advise that the Brazilian team coach had been held up in traffic and that the kick-off would be delayed for at least half an hour. The Brazilians were, in fact, inside the stadium in plenty of time and the ruse was designed to upset Scotland's preparations. "We were there so early it didn't matter anyway," says Bobby Clark.

If there had been a lack of atmosphere at the previous two matches there were no such problems that evening with 130,000 fanatical supporters, accompanied by the constant beat of bongo drums, cheering the Brazilians. Jimmy Bone recalls a barrage of oranges pelted at the Scotland bench throughout the game.

The Maracana impressed Asa Hartford. "You knew it wasn't full, you could see that, but it did seem like well over 100,000. Not being blasé about it, but once you got going you weren't really aware of the enormous crowd." Like Jimmy Bone in Belo Horizonte, Asa was unprepared for the playing surface: "The first thing that struck us was that the grass seemed strange – it just wasn't like our grass. It was thicker and not what we were used to."

Scotland attacked and George Graham forced a save from Leao from 30 yards. Shortly afterwards an angled drive from the same player was kept out by a diving save from the keeper. The Scots, uninhibited by the reputation of the world champions, were gaining the respect of the huge crowd. Just beyond the half-hour mark Macari back-headed a Hartford free kick for Graham, whose diving header was touched over.

As the contest entered its last third, the Brazilians at last began to play. A super save by Clark thwarted Dario before Gerson missed the best chance of the game. With the hosts frustrated by a solid defence there were a few rough challenges as they displayed another side to their game; this aggressive play tended to surface when things were not going their way.

"Scotland played well and we came within minutes of putting Brazil out of their own tournament," recollects Bobby Clark. "Rivelino swung a neat cross over and Jairzinho bulleted a diving header past me. Very disappointing as, had we tied, we would have played Portugal in the final."

With ten minutes left the goal was enough for a home victory.

"Playing in the Maracana was unbelievable, against some of the greatest players," says Willie Morgan. "The only sad thing for us was that Pele wasn't playing at that time. They had Rivelino and Tostao, Jairzinho, Gerson and we gave them a bit of a fright. We could have won in the Maracana. That's what made everybody frightened of us because we had a really good team."

"Going to Brazil was a massive thing and you realised how good a team Brazil were," says Lou Macari. "It was a close game but the idea of the tour was to get used to playing against teams like that because the home nations were the only teams you would play against."

Does Lou feel he benefitted as a player from the experience? "Without a doubt because Brazil back then were really strong, they were competitive and they were just natural athletes. Apart from being really talented players they were very athletic. It was a whole new experience playing against them."

Yugoslavia defeated the Czechs the following day to finish a point clear of Docherty's men and claim a place in the play-off, ensuring that the SFA party departed as scheduled, two days before the tournament's final matches.

Gallagher was full of praise for Docherty's men in his *Record* summary: "The Scots were so good that the Brazilians, for so long the masters of world football, had to lash out – had to kick out – in an attempt to stop us," he wrote.

The *Record* also printed the manager's post-match thoughts. "I'm sick that we did not qualify but the way we played was fantastic. How can I change this team now? The Czechs are very worried about us for the World Cup game and if I was in their shoes I'd be worried, too. I always said that we had the skill and we have now proved that in the ground of the world champions. The spirit has been wonderful. All the lads on and off the park have accepted responsibility." The latter comments were echoed by skipper Bremner, with the rift with the SFA seemingly forgotten. "I have never been in a Scotland party which has such harmony on and off the field," he told Gallagher.

The reporter also spoke with the Brazilian manager Mario Zagallo, who offered consolation and praise. "We felt that we were a bit lucky to beat the Scots. The Czechs are not as good as your team and I cannot see them being a barrier to Scotland going to the World Cup finals."

There was still a little time for relaxation before flying home, as Bobby Clark fondly reminisces. "I always remember going to the Copacabana the next day. There were four of us. Not sure exactly who but I remember playing in a sand soccer game with the locals who thought we were Germans. Sand soccer has its own special set of skills and the locals were much more adept with their bare feet than the Scottish internationals.

"All in all it was a great trip, a wonderful experience, although I returned right into pre-season with Aberdeen. I think this meant that I had just a four-day close season."

With expenditure of £19,428 against income of £29,963, the SFA made a healthy profit of £10,535 from their first venture to South America.

Reflecting on the selection process for the trip, Docherty, as guest writer in the October issue of the magazine *Scottish Football*, said he would do things differently in future. "The big thing I have learned is that if you plan to take a Scottish international party abroad, you do not ask the players if they would like to go with you. At the time we got the invitation it seemed to me the fair thing to do so that if a boy had a genuine reason why he did not want to be away in midsummer he could tell me without having to pretend he was injured or something like that. In some instances my 'come if you want' offer rebounded against me, and so, on reflection, I think it was a mistake. In future when I plan a trip abroad for Scotland I will pick the players I want, tell them where to report and expect them to be there. If anything other than injury keeps them away then I doubt if I'll be asking them a second time."

Jimmy Bone can remember the standards Docherty expected of his players. "The one thing about him was if the bus was leaving at a certain time he didn't do a head count. The bus left at that time and if you weren't on it then you weren't on it. Because he was like that – there were no grey areas – everybody knew the parameters so he never had a problem discipline-wise. Everybody knew where the line was and everybody responded to that."

These thoughts are echoed by Eddie Gray. "I enjoyed playing under Tommy, and you can imagine it was always a laugh a minute with him. But he was disciplined as well; that was the thing. You couldn't step out of line with Tommy. After the game, if you wanted to have a beer he'd let you have a beer, but you wouldn't go daft."

Lou Macari plays down talk of a booze culture. "Drinking wasn't a big thing at the time in Scottish football. People might find it hard to believe but drink wasn't really acceptable."

With just two internationals in the last five months of the year – both World Cup qualifiers against Denmark and one Under-23 trial match – Tommy Docherty found he had more time on his hands than in his first few months in office.

The Doc's pool for the trip to Copenhagen in October included Aberdeen striker Joe Harper, whose impressive record of 19 goals in 18 matches up to the end of September merited his place at the expense of Colin Stein whose game-time had been limited following a transfer request. As expected Stanton was not on the list but Brownlie did return and two new faces not well known north of the border came in – Leeds goalkeeper David Harvey and Aston Villa midfielder Bruce Rioch, both of whom had been born in England to Scottish parents. Rioch, however, withdrew the following day and his place was taken by Arsenal's Peter Marinello. Several from the Brazil trip, including Ford, Law, McQuade and Hansen, were omitted, proving that loyalty alone did not guarantee a place in Docherty's squads.

"When you knew the squad was going to get announced, that particular day, until you got word through the media, it was quite tense for you," is how Lou Macari looks back on the time. "It was good days, when everyone genuinely wanted to be there and everyone wanted to be picked. But when the team was announced there were disappointed players, but you were still part of that squad and desperate for the team to do well."

If selected, Lou was conscious there was no room for complacency. "You had to be ready for each international because if you didn't do any good you would be out and somebody else equally as good as you would take your place."

Vedbaek, 30 miles from the Danish capital, was again chosen as the party's base – just as it had been for the disastrous trip which saw Scotland lose in Bobby Brown's penultimate game in charge the year before.

"If ever there was an attacking formation picked for Scotland this is it," the Doc cracked to reporters as he revealed a 4-2-4 line-up. Bremner and Graham, so effective in the Brazil tournament, were in midfield with a front four of Lorimer, Bone, Macari and Morgan.

To the displeasure of non-football fans the match was televised live in Scotland on two of the three available channels with the Danish coverage in black and white which required the Scots to wear white tops.

Just as the Doc had predicted Scotland served up a superb display of attacking football. The only surprise was that it took 17 minutes for the deadlock to be broken, when Macari stooped to head in a Lorimer corner. Two minutes later Bone scored from inside the six-yard box after a powerful Graham strike had rebounded from the goalkeeper.

But there was a wake-up call shortly afterwards, which had more than a little deja vu about it, as Finn Laudrup, just as he had done the previous year, scored directly from a free kick past Bobby Clark. "The last game saw a low strike deflected off the wall but this time it was a good shot over the wall into the top corner," the goalkeeper recollects.

Finn Laudrup's two sons, Brian and Michael, shared the goals 24 years later as Denmark defeated Scotland 2-0 in the rebuilt Parken Stadium.

Bremner was credited for rallying his team as the Danes briefly threatened to equalise, and another two strikes late in the second half settled the matter. Harper replaced Bone and marked his debut with a goal after good work by Morgan and Macari allowed him to finish with his left foot for 3-1. Morgan then headed in a Lorimer cross on 85 minutes to complete the scoring although in truth the goal total could easily have been seven or eight.

The pressures which preceded his introduction to international football almost cost Joe Harper his big chance. Aware that he would be one of the substitutes, he had been unable to sleep the night before and was similarly unable to relax on the bench. When the manager told him to warm up the player felt physically sick and left the stadium before vomiting. Harper was refused re-entry by a security guard but fortunately another official recognised his tracksuit and he was allowed back inside just as the manager was considering dispatching a search party.

"This must have been his finest hour," was Malcolm Munro's assessment of Bremner's performance. The captain himself was quoted in dramatic terms: "This is the result we have wanted for a long time. It can be the start of a new age in Scottish football."

There was an unexpected name amongst the 22 listed for the home match four weeks later – Pat Stanton was back. "I've given a lot of thought to the matter and I think mistakes were made on both sides," Docherty briefed reporters at Park Gardens. "I am only concerned with what is good for Scottish football and have asked Hibs director Tommy Younger to convey my apologies to the player and his club for any misunderstanding." The player was said to be "more than delighted" with the news of his recall.

Docherty was concerned about complacency and the expectations of the home crowd following the Copenhagen rout. "My only request is for the lads to play well and score one more goal than the opposition. I am not thinking in terms of a barrowload of goals and I hope the fans aren't either," he relayed through the *Record*'s Alex Cameron.

"Only the brave and only those with an off-licence in their hip pockets could have even considered coming to Hampden," typed Ian Archer for his *Herald* report. Despite the cold over 47,000 turned up that mid-November evening.

Scotland led after two minutes, showing a disregard for the manager's plea for patience. From a Lorimer corner, Graham played the ball in for Dalglish to score his first international goal from six yards. Lorimer, now with a reputation for the power and range of his shooting, forced a save from a 35-yard free kick. Harper forced another save from a header before the break.

The visitors chose to replace their goalkeeper for the second half but Heinz Hildebrandt was soon retrieving the ball from the net as the Scots again struck early when Graham passed accurately for Lorimer to score. Throughout, Lorimer was on the receiving end of some rough tackling and when he finally retaliated after a challenge from Ahlberg both players were ordered off five minutes from time.

As the sinners walked around the track there was some excitement to warm the crowd when Willie Carr was downed in front of goal for a penalty. After a delay Morgan missed his second penalty in five internationals, sending the ball high over the bar as the fans prepared to cheer a third goal.

After the 2-0 victory it was confirmed that Lorimer had no right of appeal and would miss the next two World Cup games – both against Czechoslovakia. "They got Lorimer sent off!" an angry Docherty told the *Record*'s Alex Cameron. "They didn't come to play ... they were jersey-pulling and kicking. I feel sorry for Lorimer."

Lorimer's dismissal and the penalty miss could not douse the flames which had been burning ever brighter since Tommy Docherty had arrived on the scene. Munich 1974 was a phrase which became uttered more frequently and the feel-good factor suggested that Scotland could make their first appearance at the World Cup since 1958.

Interviewed by Malcom Munro for the *Evening Times,* skipper Bremner insisted that all the credit was owed to the manager. "The Doc has arrogance. He thinks there's nobody better than Scotland," he told the journalist. "He puts arrogance into you and you can't help being lifted by him. He tells you the opposition aren't entitled to be on the same field as you. In a remarkably short time the boss has welded a club spirit into the international team. It's a great feeling."

Speaking recently, Jimmy Bone recalled: "The way Tommy Docherty was there was a real good atmosphere around the squads at the time. He was the boss; it was all about the players. Everything had to be right for the players and I think they responded to that. He was great to play for, one of these managers who made you feel ten feet tall when you were going out on to the park. He was really good at massaging people's egos and getting the best out of players."

Asa Hartford's recollections of Docherty are: "All good. In many ways I think he was suited to international football, comparing him to other managers that came and went. The Doc was in his element. He was a great mixer and he could move from table to table and just kept things light. I liked the Doc."

"I was in all Tommy Docherty's squads," says Bobby Clark, "and really enjoyed him. He used to take the keepers at training and gave us a very good workout. His training was good and he was very entertaining to be around and kept the entire group smiling."

Lou Macari supports those views: "The Doc was as he still is today at 90 years of age. He was funny, he was witty, he was good company, so there were never any problems with the team spirit. The Doc was a character so the minute you met up there was a laugh, every ten minutes there was a crack from him."

There was no indication that before long the Scotland bandwagon would be derailed by a bombshell of seismic proportions that no one saw coming.

A repeat of the previous season's fixture between Scotland's Under-23 side and an Under-18 Professional Youth XI was arranged for Easter Road on Monday 20 November. The game was delayed due to problems with the floodlights and eventually started with some lights still not working. Only 1,076 saw Eric Carruthers of Hearts give Docherty's side a first-half lead but the tables were turned after the break when Chelsea's Steve Finnieston and Kilmarnock's Gordon Smith, with a header seven minutes from time, earned Peter Rice's Youth side an unexpected win. Both teams had used all five of their available substitutes with the consequence that 32 potential internationalists had taken part in the trial. No one had any inkling that that evening would be Docherty's last involvement with the Scotland set-up.

That same week Willie Allan had intimated that Docherty would be asked to explain remarks made to reporters in the wake of the Denmark match at Hampden when he had questioned the ability of the Dutch referee. The manager was said to be puzzled by the secretary's comments which suggested he could be disciplined in the same way club managers were for criticising Scottish referees.

On 16 December Docherty flew to London to attend the Crystal Palace vs Manchester United match which gave him the opportunity to assess the form of six Scots.

The Eagles won convincingly, scoring five times without reply and in doing so leapfrogged the Old Trafford team, forcing them into second-bottom place in the league table, one of the two dreaded relegation slots.

After the match the Doc was advised that Matt Busby would like to speak with him before he left for his Glasgow flight. Hinting that Frank O'Farrell's days as the United manager were numbered Busby, a director of the club, casually enquired if Docherty would be interested in the role, a comment said so matter-of-factly that he could hardly take it in.

Busby urged Docherty to give the matter some consideration before they parted company.

Over the next 24 hours the Scotland manager weighed up the two jobs. Scotland had one foot in the door of the World Cup and he might regret leaving if things did not work out in Manchester. On the other hand he found he had too much time on his hands between internationals and he knew he may never get another opportunity to manage Manchester United, who were offering a salary which far outweighed his contract with the SFA.

The following day O'Farrell was relieved from his duties and a week of speculation followed linking Docherty with the position. On Friday 22 December the Doc was unveiled as O'Farrell's successor although the decision had been made a few days earlier. "I was overwhelmed with the offer and could not refuse it," he told *The Herald*'s Ian Archer.

Sir Matt had been mulling over an approach for Docherty prior to their discussion inside Selhurst Park. "I got him the job at Man U," says Willie Morgan. "I used to play a lot of golf with Matt, I was at the same club and we played twice a week. After we came back from Brazil the gaffer [Busby] said what do you think of Tommy Docherty? I said I think he's great, that he was this and that.

"Matt asked if I 'thought he could do a job for us?' I said, 'I think he'd be fabulous, gaffer.' We left the golf club and then later on that night Matt phoned me and said, 'You wouldn't happen to have his phone number, would you?' So I gave Matt his number.

"It was twofold. I wish he had stayed on as the manager of Scotland, but I was looking forward to him coming to United ..." Willie hesitates before adding, "But it didn't work out that well as we ended up in the Old Bailey!"

Docherty was prepared to continue with the Scotland team on a part-time basis and had discussed this with his new employers, as he told the *Daily Record*. "I'm prepared to do the job for nothing until the World Cup bid is finished. I just hope that the SFA allow me to finish something I have started. The Manchester United directors have agreed."

This idea was a non-starter as far as the SFA was concerned. Jock Stein had operated a dual role with both Scotland and Celtic in the mid-1960s which had not been considered a success, and they sought a full-time manager.

On 28 December the International and Selection Committee issued the following statement: "The SFA have agreed to release Mr Docherty from his contract. The matter was discussed and will be discussed again on 5 January when investigations will be continued."

"It was a blow when he did give up," Rodger Baillie recalls. "I think it's a massive regret by him now. He has told me since he regretted it although I have no doubt that the salary scale was a major factor." Rodger also remembers a less than cordial working relationship with the SFA secretary. "The *Daily Record* had signed him up for a weekly column and the SFA objected to this. I think he was actually forced to withdraw from the *Record*'s column which didn't endear relations between him and the SFA, particularly Willie Allan, and I don't think they were bosom buddies."

"Losing the Doc was a blow for sure but Manchester United was a great opportunity for him," says Bobby Clark. "There is no question that he laid the foundation for qualifying for [the 1974 World Cup] but there was still a lot of work to be done."

Many supporters felt let down by a manager who had served just 14 months of a four-year contract.

In 2011 Ernie Walker looked back on the Doc's departure for the STV documentary series *The Football Years*. "It was astonishing. The Doc had come to us professing undying love for Scotland and the job of his life. But one learns to know Tommy and it seems that Man U came along and that love for Scotland kind of disappeared overnight."

In an interview for Radio Scotland in 2014 Docherty spoke of his regret at leaving the Scotland job whilst admitting the money offered by Manchester United had played a part. "That was the biggest mistake I made," he told Chick Young. "It was partly greed and partly stupidity."

With Jock Stein ruling himself out there appeared to be no obvious replacement and speculation threw up the names of Dave MacParland, Bobby Seith, Willie Ormond and Dave Mackay as the SFA entered its centenary year.

1973

"We are telling ourselves that we are the greatest, the best, that ever was or ever will be. Did it all really happen? Was this not a dream of glory? Will we wake up and find we watched an image?"
Ian Archer, Scotland vs Czechoslovakia

An announcement came after the 5 January meeting of the International and Selection Committee. Willie Ormond, who had emerged as the front runner, was named as the Scotland manager on an identical four-year £7,500 contract as his predecessor. The initial approach had been made soon after Docherty had cleared his desk a week earlier but for once there had been no leaks to the press.

Ormond had played for Scotland six times including at the 1954 World Cup and was a member of Hibernian's legendary Famous Five forward line of the 1950s. He had succeeded Bobby Brown as manager of St Johnstone in 1967 and just two years later took the Saints to the final of the League Cup in which they lost just 1-0 to Celtic. In season 1970/71 his club finished third in Division One behind Celtic and Aberdeen and three points above Rangers. This success brought European football to Perth for the first time, with entry into the UEFA Cup where the Saints defeated Hamburg and Hungarian side Vasas before exiting in the third round to Zeljeznicar of Yugoslavia. At the time of his appointment to the Scotland job St Johnstone were eighth in the First Division but only four points off second spot amongst a tight group of clubs in the top half of the table.

There were clear parallels between the ascent of both Brown and Ormond from St Johnstone to the Scotland job. "I felt that I had achieved all that I could with St Johnstone given the limited resources there," he told Ian Archer in comments echoing those of Brown six years previously.

"I will work on the foundations that Tommy Docherty has laid. Most of my ideas would be similar but if the ship is going to go down it will go down under me – not Tommy. I can see nothing to stop us from going to Munich," he told Ian Archer.

When quizzed on STV by Alex Cameron about dealing with international players Ormond sounded confident if looking just a little uneasy. "I wouldn't like to say I'm a hard, hard man but I'd like to say I'm fair and I expect the players to be fair with me. I'll treat them as men and I expect the same respect back from them."

After taking office on 16 January the new manager did not have long to wait for his first test – and it was a big one. As part of the centenary celebrations the SFA had arranged three showcase matches at Hampden against England, Brazil and West Germany. The English would be the first visitors on 14 February with the traditional Under-23 meeting between the two taking place 24 hours earlier.

The Under-23 match had originally been allocated to Aberdeen but this was considered unsuitable for the FA, which did not wish to split the party between Glasgow and the north-east. At one point the fixture looked likely to be abandoned until Kilmarnock's Rugby Park was agreed as a venue. The SFA Annual Report later considered that Pittodrie was "regarded almost as the traditional home for matches at under-23 level."

The attendance of around 6,000 for Ormond's introduction to international management was reasonable on a night when snow would have discouraged many from venturing outside. Kilmarnock FC received a cheque for £505.80, 25 per cent of the gate receipts, for ground rental. The young Scots went ahead after 25 minutes when Bone accepted a McLuskey pass then pivoted before lashing the ball into the net. "In any conditions and at any time, it would have been a good goal. On this bitterly cold night it was magnificent," read Harry

Miller's *Daily Mirror* report. With Ayr winger John Doyle continually tormenting the English defence the score remained that way until the break.

Sir Alf's half-time words transformed his players and they were soon level when Trevor Whymark outpaced Willie Young before slotting past Rough. The winner came just five minutes later when Stewart Barrowclough scored from close range although Scotland fought to the final whistle and were considered a little unfortunate not to salvage a draw.

Despite the quality of his goal the match proved to be Jimmy Bone's final appearance in a Scotland jersey. "That was the last time I ever got picked. I was in the next Under-23 squad but Sheffield United had a game on and the club had priority. I never got picked after that as by then I would have been too old for the Under-23s."

What was intended to celebrate 100 years of Scottish football descended into a nightmare often referred to as the St Valentine's Day Massacre. Although one report suggested around 70,000 ticket sales, the weather ensured only 48,470 turned up to watch Scotland get taken apart on an ice-covered pitch.

Bobby Clark said: "The field was really unplayable. It was a pity that a centenary international was played on such a poor surface. Normally in such conditions the pitch is heavily sanded but it was uneven, frozen solid with patches of ice and very difficult to stay on your feet. I tried three different pieces of footwear and found none of them satisfactory."

It was pretty much a Docherty line-up with eight of the 11 who had featured against Denmark starting as their former manager watched from the Hampden stand.

Just six minutes had elapsed when a Channon shot struck Lorimer's foot and found its way past the stranded Clark. After a further six minutes a long free kick was headed down by Channon to Allan Clarke who scored easily as the Scottish defence remained static. The game was over as a contest when Channon volleyed a third. The crowd broke into a chant of "What a load of rubbish" and lit bonfires on the terraces.

Morgan was injured and replaced by Colin Stein, now with Coventry City. The substitution almost paid off just after the break when one of Lorimer's specialist free kicks came back off Shilton for

Stein to dispatch into the net. Thoughts of a comeback were brief as the French referee mysteriously ruled out the "goal" with Stein appearing to be onside.

Shilton saved well from another Stein shot and Graham managed to strike the underside of the bar when it seemed easier to score, before Chivers, capitalising on a miskicked back pass-from Colquhoun, grabbed a fourth for the visitors. "We want our money back," was the cry from the crowd who could not believe the number of basic errors which had contributed to their team's downfall.

Clarke scored from a tight angle five minutes from time to complete the 5-0 misery, prompting some of those remaining to strike up a chorus of 'The Sash'. After the game the Scots team failed to appear at the official banquet where the England players ate alone. Following the feel-good factor of Docherty's reign, the match could hardly have been a worse introduction for Ormond.

"Willie was the complete opposite to the Doc," considers Lou Macari. "The Doc was laugh-a-minute but Willie was quite serious about everything and it was probably quite a big change for everybody who had been involved with Tommy Docherty. I think when players get used to a relaxed atmosphere with a manager who is very funny and very witty and somebody comes in who is maybe the opposite it's a bit of a shock to the system."

"Our defenders were more like schoolboys from Glasgow Green," claimed Alex Cameron in Thursday's *Daily Record*. "True, Scotland had no luck but did they really deserve any?" he asked. In the same journal Ormond offered no excuses when talking with Ken Gallagher: "We gave away three bad goals inside 15 minutes ... Obviously this will make me think about one or two positions in the side. I'll sleep on it, if I can sleep."

Commenting on the state of the pitch, England's Peter Storey was quoted in the Dundee *Evening Telegraph* with: "If this was a league game under such conditions the match would never have been played." The *Telegraph*'s reporter rightly pointed out: "There can be no excuses whatsoever ... conditions were the same for both sides."

Interviewed by STV at his Musselburgh home the following day, Ormond was clearly an angry man. "I went to Largs to listen and to find out about each player," he told Alex Cameron. "Now I know most of what I need to and next time I'll be doing the talking. My faith in some of the top Scottish players has been shaken but I have time to think and to act and I will not be afraid to make decisions."

"Unfortunately I shouldered the blame along with several others and was not recalled back to a squad for a couple of years," says Bobby Clark.

After the euphoria of the back-to-back wins over the Danes, a sense of gloom now hung over the national side.

Four weeks after the Hampden horror show Ormond was in charge of the Under-23 side in Swansea. The semi-final of the Rugby Union Cup, played one mile away between Neath and Llanelli, did little to attract locals to the Vetch Field. A mere 2,439 trickled through the turnstiles, paying gate receipts of £1,049, whilst 15,000 watched the oval ball game.

Despite being sandwiched between two defenders, Dalglish rose to meet a Doyle cross and headed the opener after six minutes. Rangers striker Derek Parlane then headed narrowly past and Scotland looked comfortable at the break.

The Welsh equalised midway through the second period when Leighton James got the better of Jim Stewart from 20 yards. Parlane went close again but it took until the very last kick of the match before the Scots were rewarded, when Hartford stabbed a loose ball goalwards which struck a post before crossing the line. With a win under his belt, Ormond looked ahead to the Inter League match at Hampden which offered the prospect of some revenge against the English.

The squad of 16 was largely made up from the three leading clubs with an aggregate of 13 players from Hibs, Rangers and Celtic for the game on 27 March. Also included was Dundee striker John Duncan who had already amassed an astonishing 39 goals for the season. Ramsey's selection showed little mercy and included Channon and Whymark, both of whom had already damaged Scotland during Ormond's brief time in charge.

Willie Ormond managed a smile at the end of a duel in which four goals were shared by two strikers, watched by a crowd of 18,548.

Channon drew first blood after 19 minutes but two John Duncan goals turned the Scots' fortunes around before half-time. The first followed good work by Tommy McLean who also provided the cross for Duncan to head beyond Shilton for his second, close to the interval. Scotland rode their luck when both Channon and Richards failed to convert good opportunities which came their way in the second half.

With 12 minutes remaining Bell drew Peter McCloy from his line and squared the ball for Channon to equalise. There were claims for a penalty at the death when Moore appeared to control a Parlane cross with an arm but a draw was considered a fair reflection of the play.

There was just time for Willie Ormond to praise his players in the press room before he headed for Dusseldorf to spy on the Czechs' meeting with West Germany the following evening. Whilst stressing he was not contemplating an "all tartan" team he clearly had in mind some of those whom he felt had underperformed during the 5-0 defeat when he commented: "We have players up here every bit as good as the players who have moved south. This showed the Anglo-Scots they will need to be playing their best to keep these boys out."

At the beginning of May Ormond flew to Copenhagen to scrutinise the Czechs' opening match in the World Cup qualifying group. He returned a delighted man as the unexpected 1-1 draw could hardly have been a better result for his team. Victory for Scotland in one of their two games with the Czechs would be enough to qualify for West Germany.

As with Rangers' situation the previous year Leeds' participation in the European Cup-Winners' Cup Final on 16 May ruled out selection of their players for the first two matches of the Home Internationals, with the exception of Bremner who was suspended for the game with AC Milan.

Having turned out for his club three times over five days, including the FA Cup Final, Bremner was named as one of the substitutes for the opening game in Wales on 12 May with Stanton taking over the captaincy. The performances of McCloy, Hay, Derek Johnstone, Parlane and McGrain in the League International ensured their inclusion in what was a youthful selection.

Only four of those who started in Ormond's disastrous introduction to international football started in Wrexham. Lou Macari was on the bench: "I think with the result that Willie, quite rightly, decided that he wanted to develop his own team. Most of the players who played in that game played under the Doc."

After 18 minutes Sprake could only push Morgan's free kick into the path of George Graham, who opened the scoring. Parlane curled a shot against the crossbar five minutes later as Scotland closed in on a second goal.

Scotland survived a period of Welsh pressure around the hour mark before Morgan and Graham again combined to safeguard the result.

The BBC action replay from behind the goal revealed the part Dalglish had played as he cleverly back-heeled the pass from Morgan to allow Graham to score. This piece of skill was typical of the service Dalglish's clubmates anticipated but was not always appreciated by unfamiliar international players. This sometimes led to what was viewed as bad passing and accusations of poor form in a Scotland jersey when in fact Dalglish was often thinking one move ahead of his colleagues.

Ormond named an almost identical side for the midweek home game against Northern Ireland, following his first victory in a full international. The only change was forced on him by an injury sustained by Parlane, with his place again taken by Stein who had also replaced him in Wrexham.

Northern Ireland won the game early in the match. First Martin O'Neill latched on to a pass from Trevor Anderson to beat McCloy. Then Anderson, standing all alone at the near post, collected a low cross and with all the time in the world knocked the ball over the line after 17 minutes. Television viewers could have been forgiven for thinking they were watching a slow-motion replay, so casual was the finish.

Macari, who had replaced Graham, had one isolated effort cleared from the goal line but it was not until 90 seconds from the end that Dalglish scored to make it 2-1, after a large number of the crowd had already departed. The fans had been in good spirits ahead of the trip to London but their repertoire soon reverted to that old favourite "What a load of rubbish".

John MacKenzie of the Scottish *Daily Express* was scathing. "Kind words are difficult to find on such a dismal occasion. We need a miracle or two before Saturday. We need pride above all. The team that let the fans down last night owe the Wembley pilgrims that much at least."

"Wembley Day, it seems, is still something special for the Scots," wrote Bill Brown for the front page of the *Evening Times*. "If only in that it allows Jock and Mac an excuse to get away from the wife for a raucous spell." As always a figure far in excess of the 30,000 allocation to the SFA travelled to London with many of those fans seeking one of the precious tickets. British Rail ran an additional 11 trains from different parts of Scotland on the Friday alone with many other fans travelling on overnight Football Specials. Return tickets were discounted at £6.50 from Glasgow to Euston if travelling on one of the Specials, in an effort to reduce congestion on other services. BEA laid on additional flights to London and a steady stream of supporters cruised south on the motorways. For the period leading up to the game, at least, the midweek defeat was forgotten. After all, it was the England game which really mattered.

Ally Hunter started in goal with Bremner returning as captain. Ormond kept faith with Johnstone and Holton, criticised after the midweek defeat, in the centre of defence, whilst Macari and Lorimer came into the starting line-up.

The Scots started well and Macari put Lorimer through on goal after two minutes but a fine save from Shilton kept his shot out.

England enjoyed their share of possession before Morgan sent a shot just above the crossbar close to the interval in what was a fairly even contest which no one had expected after the five-goal defeat three months earlier.

Although not descending to the depths of the 1972 meeting, the match saw more than its fair share of tough challenges and after McGrain was fouled by Ball one fan entered the playing area and aimed a punch at the England captain. Dalglish restrained the intruder before he was taken away by police officers.

Playing some good football England took the lead ten minutes after the restart. Ball swung a free kick into the area where Martin Peters, living up to his "ghost" tag, sneaked in to head past Hunter after Chivers had occupied defenders with a dummy run. Hunter then saved from Peters before Joe Jordan came on for Macari to make his international debut, with Stein replacing Lorimer near the end.

Scotland gained a corner five minutes from time and their fans in the crowd sensed a dramatic finale. Bremner sent the ball to the head of Jordan who diverted its path to Dalglish. The Celtic striker connected perfectly, sending a left-foot volley towards the top corner of Shilton's net before the home goalkeeper somehow leapt, twisted and clawed it around the post with his right hand. It was a save of breathtaking skill which denied Scotland a draw and would be talked about for many years to come.

In truth Ormond's men had only really looked likely to score on two occasions, once at the start of the game and again close to the end, but the improvement in the overall performance from the centenary debacle was massive.

The Scottish press were full of praise in spite of the 1-0 defeat, with Bremner and Hay singled out and *that* save dissected time after time. "A Scottish Defeat That Brought Only Unity and Honour" was Archer's headline in Monday's *Herald*. "A repetition of the Wembley performance against the Czechs in September, on the terraces as well as on the pitch, should take us to Munich," the journalist had typed. But he did exercise a Note: of caution with the defeat to the Irish seemingly forgotten. "That will happen only if Scotland understand that the standards set in defeat on Saturday are the ones that must apply in every match." Shilton gave his account of the match-winning save in the *Daily Record*. "I don't remember making a better save for England. Dalglish shot and I had to dive early. I went for the ball with my left hand but it was going away from me ... I had to twist and get my other arm over to get a touch."

Exiled Scot David Kyle, who had attempted to assault Alan Ball, pleaded guilty to a charge of being drunk and disorderly by post to Harrow Magistrates' Court. He was fined £10 plus a further £3 in costs and in his letter apologised for his "stupidity", promising to behave in future.

When *Daily Record* journalist Duncan Lamont visited Kyle's Coventry home his wife insisted he was out. Margaret Kyle told the reporter: "He is very quick-tempered and blows up very quickly – even when he is watching a match on TV. I nearly died when I realised it was him."

The England captain could not have been more forgiving telling the same journal's Hugh Taylor: "That man would be welcome in my house for a drink at any time. If England had supporters like him we'd beat the world. I think it's fabulous to feel that strongly about your country." With regard to the punch, Ball had this to say: "He caught me with a glancing blow that did not hurt. But it did hurt to see the way the police led him away. His actions typified the tremendous support the Scots received. I wish the so-called English fans would

show a bit of patriotism ... We never had any support on Saturday."
Shortly afterwards Ball had his wish granted and the two men were
pictured in a restaurant amicably enjoying a meal together at the
expense of a newspaper.

Apart from his gesture after scoring at Hampden in 1972, Ball
had never been guilty of anti-Scottish comments and much of his
perceived dislike of the Scots was misinterpreted patriotism for his
own nation.

Asa Hartford worked with Ball as his assistant manager at
Manchester City in the mid-1990s and supports this view: "He couldn't
speak highly enough of the Scottish people; he loved their passion."

Ball was later a team-mate of Willie Johnston's during a spell
at Vancouver Whitecaps at the end of the 1970s and Bud has fond
memories of their time together. "He was a great player to have in
your team," he says. "I got to really know him and had a lot of good
times with Bally."

Other supporters who appeared in court were charged with
drunkenness and attempted theft. Some of these latter offences took
place on Wembley's Olympic Way and it is unclear if the charges
referred to stealing match tickets or money.

Glaswegian Stuart McLean was hit with the hefty penalty of £50
for stealing a 33-seater coach after his attempt to drive home had been
thwarted by police after just three miles.

Willie Ormond chose not to attend Czechoslovakia's 6-0 victory
over the Danes on 6 June, which attracted some criticism. The result
not only confirmed that Scotland required a win against the Czechs
to eliminate them but also implied that they would be no pushovers.

Scotland's international season was not over with the second
of the centenary matches due at the end of June against Brazil. A
friendly in Switzerland was scheduled to help the team prepare after
a four-week break. During that period most of the players enjoyed
family holidays before returning to Largs on Monday 19 June.

The trip to Berne ran anything but smoothly. George Connelly
vanished before the party boarded a flight to London and it was only
at Heathrow that his absence was noticed. Willie Ormond and SFA
assistant secretary Ernie Walker waited for the next flight to arrive
from Glasgow but by that time the player was in hiding at his home
refusing to speak to reporters. There was then a three-hour delay in

London because the team's aircraft failed to start. The party finally arrived in Zurich in heavy rain, which did not let up throughout their stay. They then had a three-hour coach journey before arriving tired and ready for bed at their Interlaken headquarters.

Connelly, a promising 24-year-old midfielder once described by Billy McNeill as "about as close to Franz Beckenbauer as you could have found", was continuing a pattern of mysterious disappearing acts. This had occurred at least twice with Celtic, once after being presented with a Player of the Year award that same year. Connelly was said to suffer personal problems and was uncomfortable in the limelight.

The back-page headline in the Scottish *Daily Express* summed up the game perfectly – "ALL OUT PRESSURE – THEN SWISS BREAK AWAY TO SCORE".

Ormond's men battled to break through a well-organised defensive barrier for 90 minutes. They did find the net early on from an unexpected source, but McGrain's shot was ruled offside. "Every Scot bar Holton and McCloy joined in the attack from time to time and those forward moves were direct and often penetrating," noted John MacKenzie's report. Resorting to long-range efforts, a 30-yard shot from Derek Johnstone produced what MacKenzie considered a "magnificent save" from Burgener.

The only goal came from a breakaway just after the hour, when McCloy was beaten by a 30-yard strike from Walter Mundschin which trundled over the line after striking a goalpost.

Ormond was not too despondent when conversing with journalists afterwards: "I am happy with the defence and the midfield players and maybe we would have scored ourselves if the players had been a little sharper. But it's hard to blame them when you consider that they came back from their holidays to play for their country." The manager then flew to Stockholm where he watched the Brazilians go down to a late Swedish goal on the Monday during a hectic tour which had already seen them grace the fields of Algeria, Tunisia, West Germany, Italy, Austria and Russia with Hampden Park their next stop.

A lavish function to celebrate the SFA's centenary was held on the eve of the match in Glasgow's new Albany Hotel with representatives of 44 nations totalling over 500 guests.

The Albany was also home to the Brazilians during their stay in Glasgow and a fleet of cars was on standby for the use of players training at the match venue, where schoolchildren were permitted to watch, and at Lesser Hampden.

Over 122,000 had attended the Old Firm Scottish Cup Final in May when all 134,000 tickets had been sold, after which the Hampden limit had been reduced to a figure of 100,000 for safety reasons. With the combination of a Saturday afternoon kick-off plus the opportunity to see the world champions, a full house was expected, with cash accepted at the turnstiles. At 3pm the crowd numbered 78,181.

Joe Jordan made his first start in a Scotland jersey in that game and floored the Brazilian goalkeeper Leao early in the match as they challenged for a high ball. Scotland had their share of attacks before a freak goal gave the visitors the lead when a hard cross from Valdomira struck Johnstone and ended up in his net with 33 minutes played. The dejected centre-half beat the turf with his fist but neither he nor his clubmate McCloy could be blamed for the goal.

Jordan and Rivelino clashed before the break as the Brazilians reminded those watching that, as well as being capable of great skill, they were also a physical force.

Malcolm Munro's second-half summary for the *Evening Times*'s Sports Final report contained the following: "The Brazilians, although undoubtedly clever, were doing nothing for their reputations because of their sometimes vicious tackling. It might be said in truth the big Scottish crowd had 'gone off' the champions of the world, who knew all the tricks of the trade which prevented the opposition from settling to any kind of form."

McCloy saved spectacularly to thwart Valdomira and just the own goal separated the sides at 4.45pm. Although Ormond's men had at times performed well it did not go unnoticed that Scotland had scored just three times during their last six matches – a statistic which was of concern ahead of the more serious business of when the Czechs came to town.

Accompanied by his club manager Jock Stein, George Connelly attended a special meeting of the International and Selection Committee on 16 August. The conclusion was that there would be no action taken against the player for his walkout en route to Switzerland, with the explanation that he was concerned at his expectant wife's health accepted as "one single irrational act" by the committee.

Willie Ormond's focus was now solely on Scotland's day of destiny – 26 September – and he had a meeting said to have lasted a number of hours with Sir Alf Ramsey, whose England side had drawn with the Czechs in a friendly at the end of May. "Sir Alf couldn't have been more helpful," Ormond told Shearer Borthwick of the *Evening Times*. "He has a very comprehensive dossier on their players and we went over them one by one."

In response to an SFA request the Scottish League Management Committee agreed to postpone any 22 September fixtures featuring players required for the Czechoslovakia game. Ormond's all-important pool of 22 was described by Ian Archer as a "Scottish squad short of proven quality" in *The Herald*. "Ormond's squad reveals what many have known already ... this is a non-vintage period for Scottish football." The journalist expanded: "The lingering fear that another World Cup failure is around the corner persists, as does the patriotic hope that everything will be alright on the night."

Whilst these observations may seem rather harsh or indeed foolish in retrospect, consideration of Scotland's form during the period places them within context. They were a side capable of both good and mediocre performances, lacking good results, goals and consistency and with just one victory under the new manager.

By today's standards the inclusion of seven uncapped players for such a significant match might seem ludicrous. Newcastle midfielder Jimmy Smith had impressed the watching Ormond enough in a recent game against Southampton to warrant selection, whilst Coventry's Tommy Hutchison was another called up for the first time. The 32-year-old Denis Law, by this time on the books of Manchester City, had not featured since the Brazilian trip more than a year before but made his second international comeback. There were some surprise omissions with McCloy, Parlane, Graham, Hartford, Stanton and Eddie Gray all absent whilst George Connelly was given another chance. The selection required just three league fixtures to be cancelled – Aberdeen vs Rangers, Celtic against Morton and Dundee United's game with Hibs.

With a capacity crowd anticipated an initial offer from STV to screen the game live was rejected in August and a subsequent bid to show the entire match later was also turned down. Highlights were then scheduled to be broadcast at 11pm on STV. It was not until little over 24 hours before kick-off that an agreement was reached which allowed the broadcaster permission to show the whole game live throughout Scotland. This ground-breaking move was the first time other than a Home International that a Scotland home match had been allowed live coverage and was another indication of the huge public interest in the game.

Although no one could doubt Ian Archer's patriotism when it came to the national team his confidence had not improved by the day of the match as his *Herald* preview showed: "There is no reason to believe that the Scotland of 1973 can succeed where the Scotlands of 1961, 1965 and 1969 have failed before them. My heart tells me Scotland," he continued, "my head insists that Czechoslovakia will draw this evening and kill us off in Bratislava next month." The *Evening Citizen*'s George Aitken also had reservations, commenting: "I Note: Scotland quoted on a bookie's list at 2-1 on with the Czechs at 5-1 against. Frankly I do not see ourselves in such a strong position. Indeed the tinges of doubt that are threaded through Scotland fan-talk pleases me much more than an arrogant bring-on-the-Czechs attitude."

In conference with reporters on the morning of the match Willie Ormond stressed the importance the crowd could play. "I know – and the players know – that if they're doing well the fans on the terracing will make that Hampden roar come alive again. We've got the players to do it," he insisted. "They are in the right frame of mind. They're fit, they're experienced – what more can I want?"

"Of course we'll win!" said the veteran Law to Malcolm Munro at Largs. "I never doubted it and when I see how the lads are going about it I know we'll win." Law's inclusion was still a gamble as injury had prevented him from playing for over two weeks. Coincidentally the date of the match was exactly 12 years to the day since Law, then aged 20, had scored the late winner against Czechoslovakia at the same ground in a qualifier for the 1962 World Cup.

Concerned that he might get pre-match nerves, Rod Stewart arranged for a colour television to be delivered to Law's room in the Queens Hotel to help him relax. The rooms there were far from luxurious with not so much as a kettle let alone a TV set.

The annual publication *Playing For Rangers* (number 6) devoted an entire chapter by Sandy Jardine to the match, entitled "The Night

We Beat the Czechs". In it the defender revealed how methodical Ormond's pre-match preparations had been. The manager had warned his players that the Czechs would be a very physical side who would drop into a 4-4-2 formation determined to secure the point which would, as Ian Archer had predicted, allow them to finish the job in Bratislava. "The boss warned us the central defenders might be suspect in the air," wrote Jardine. "He stressed that we would have to stick to our pattern no matter what happened and it paid off in the end." Jardine also credited the Leeds and England trainer Les Cocker, who had given Billy Bremner a dossier he had compiled on every Czech player who had faced England, which Ormond was able to scrutinise.

Bremner, Holton and Law all came through fitness scares to start, with Hutchison and Connelly making their international debuts.

"It's got experience and youth, it's got fire, imagination and courage," was how Arthur Montford set the scene for STV viewers as the teams prepared to kick off with deafening roars of "Scotland! Scotland!" audible on television sets throughout the country.

The tone of the match was established early as Hutchison was twice sent crashing to the turf by Panenka. Law, retaliating after a foul by Bendl, showed that the home side were up for the fight before Samek became the first to have his name taken after seven minutes. A chant of "Animals! Animals!" was the crowd's response. A Bremner header required a good save from Viktor on 14 minutes as Scotland settled. Czech skipper Kuna then had to be replaced following a kick from Bremner after 20 minutes before Viktor saved again, from a Morgan volley.

Shortly after half an hour Nehoda hit a speculative shot from the right, just outside the penalty area and at a comfortable height for a goalkeeper. But although Hunter touched the ball with both hands, it went through him and into the net to the horror of his team-mates, and the crowd fell silent.

It was then that Arthur Montford uttered the immortal line "Disaster for Scotland!" as the atmosphere in the ground briefly resembled a library. The silence did not last and, when on another day the goalkeeper might have found himself jeered, the crowd instead actually began to chant his name and encouraged the team with "We'll Support You Ever More".

Jardine later recalled in his *Playing For Rangers* chapter: "Funnily enough, even when we lost the goal I couldn't see us losing the game. Somehow I had a feeling deep down that we would win and we would qualify. They broke away and scored and that was when the fans really got behind us and then the players remembered what the boss had said. We just kept on playing – there was no panic."

The crowd were rewarded when Morgan powered in a corner from the left which Holton rose to head goalwards. The ball looped over a defender and dipped into the net, confirming the manager's belief about the vulnerability of the Czech defenders in the air. As the net shook the crowd exploded with joy, a roar louder than any heard at Hampden for many a year.

Willie Morgan laughs loudly at the suggestion the goal was the result of careful planning. "Nobody rehearses corners! Believe me, that's a coach's myth! A corner's a corner. You try to put it into a dangerous area and just hope that one of our players gets his head on it – and thankfully Jim did!"

Scotland found new energy and poured forward in a series of attacks. Holton again netted with a header before being given offside. The players would not have wanted the interval to break their momentum but the Norwegian referee called a halt with matters all square.

On the resumption an eager Scotland continued to deliver high balls into Viktor's territory without reward. The Czechs still posed a danger, as demonstrated when a Pivarnik cross rolled along the top of Hunter's crossbar.

Sensing the need for a greater threat in the box Ormond gambled by replacing Dalglish with Jordan after 64 minutes, a decision which almost paid immediate dividends when the Leeds forward headed narrowly over.

Scotland's destiny was sealed following the award of an indirect free kick with just over 15 minutes to play. The adrenalin was pumping in players and spectators alike as the crowd sensed something may be about to happen. Morgan touched the ball to Bremner, who eluded the wall before striking it against Viktor's right-hand post from an angle. The ball then ran agonisingly along the line before being cleared by a defender and the chance appeared to have gone. But the under-pressure Czechs lost possession and Morgan found himself with the ball again. The winger moved forward and sent a cross in from almost the corner of the box. Jordan it was who threw himself at the ball to send a header low into the net. "It's there! Jordan scores!" exclaimed the uncontrollable Montford as Hampden Park erupted in absolute bedlam and Willie Ormond banged his head on the roof of the dugout.

This time the supplier of the cross takes credit for its accuracy. "I saw where Joe was and just played it with the outside of my foot and on to his head and he did the rest! It was just a fantastic moment," smiles Willie Morgan.

With such a huge prize at stake the Czechs poured forward. Then, in a welcome counter-attack, Law found himself with only Viktor between him and the goal. He appeared to have rounded the goalkeeper before an outstretched hand knocked the ball from his feet. But precious seconds had elapsed. The Czechs were in the middle of another attack when the referee at last blew his whistle and ended Scotland's 16-year absence from the world stage. The players who had given so much throughout the 90 minutes hugged each other, with some suppressing tears as the cheers of the crowd gave way to a continued chant of "Munich, Munich, Here We Come!" A lap of honour followed with many of the players wearing the exchanged white jerseys of the Czechs. Bremner, said to be Scotland's best player in a game where no one had played badly, was lifted shoulder high in front of the cheering fans as Jardine pulled on a tam-o'-shanter someone from the ecstatic crowd had thrust in his direction. The captain then disappeared into the tunnel before re-emerging with the manager, who typically had allowed his players to enjoy the limelight. Ormond, still in his now creased suit, was hoisted up by his players to acknowledge the crowd.

"Billy's going into the dressing room to get the boss out was instinctive – but it was something we all wanted," Jardine recalled in *Playing For Rangers*, adding that the players were aware of the criticism Ormond had suffered following the loss of five goals to England in his first international.

"The last ten minutes were the longest of my life," Ormond told the *Record*'s Ken Gallagher. "I'd never want to go through that again. Still, I always felt that we would win, even when we were a goal down." The *Record* devoted almost its entire front page to the team's achievement with the headline "WE DID IT" above a photograph of Jardine and McGrain in Czech shirts with arms around each other.

Jardine shared more of his experience in the next edition of *Rangers News*. "You can imagine what the tension and nerves were like ... but once we were out on the park they more or less disappeared. Then the crowd took over. I have never heard anything like it. They were just fantastic and the encouragement they gave the team is something I will never forget."

Ally Hunter had feared a backlash from the fans in the traditional Rangers end following his error that led to the goal. But *Rangers News* paid tribute to the fans, quoting their rivals' goalkeeper saying: "I was worried about the reaction of the fans behind me. But they were really tremendous; they cheered me all the time. It did wonders for me and the rest of the side and I have never known such backing from a crowd."

Celtic supporters wrote to *Celtic View* with similar praise for the crowd, as illustrated by Shotts resident Jim McCann's letter, published in the 10 October edition: "George Connelly was right to praise the fans at the Scotland game. I have never heard a crowd so solidly behind a Scottish international side. I was very interested to hear that Ally Hunter got a lift when the crowd standing behind him started to chant his name. There have been times in the past when mistakes by Celtic players in a Scotland jersey have brought a torrent of abuse. Not this time."

There had been five Celtic players on duty during the match and Alec Irvine of Dalmuir also saw his letter printed in the *View*. "The reaction of Rangers fans to Ally Hunter after that goal is so important. It shows a real change in attitude. Celtic supporters in turn are waking up to the fact that Scotland are as much their team as anyone else's." Of course, it should not be overlooked that there would have been many thousands of non-Old Firm fans in all sections of the ground including the vast terrace behind Hunter that evening. But the Czechoslovakia match was undoubtedly a watershed moment not only for the team but also for the crowd who became unified thereafter, with the singing of club songs or criticism of Celtic players consigned to the past.

There was no mention of Ian Archer's pre-match pessimism in his *Herald* summary which captured the aftermath in an excellent piece of writing: "Strong men wept … Others just stared in disbelief. No one remained unmoved or unemotional. It was a great and glorious night. The pulse still races, the hand still shakes. Willie Ormond has just been carried shoulder high across this turf. The wall of sound beats down. We are telling ourselves that we are the greatest, the best, that ever was or ever will be. Did it all really happen? Was this not a dream of glory? Will we wake up and find we watched an image?" In his *Playing For Rangers* piece Jardine stressed the importance of both Law and Bremner's experience during the game: "I don't think anyone who played against the Czechs would underestimate the influence these two had on us. There is just something special about Denis that he communicates to other players."

The injured Eddie Gray attended the match. "Me, Gordon McQueen and Peter Lorimer all went up in Peter's car to watch the game." Lorimer was of course suspended and after visiting the dressing room the trio decided to head back south. "But Peter had lost his keys at Hampden and we couldn't open the car," Eddie recalls. The AA was summoned but had no spare keys to fit the model. "We had to get a taxi all the way back to Leeds as we were training the next day," laughs Eddie. Lorimer then caught a train to Glasgow before driving back to Leeds courtesy of a spare key supplied by a car dealer.

Now, 45 years later, Willie Morgan reflects on the lap of honour with a smile. "We were all just so happy. It was phenomenal, an unbelievable night and one of the best ever at Hampden. Just qualifying was great."

The following Saturday STV were granted permission to repeat the entire match from 11.30pm which was a real treat for fans in the days before home video recording.

The SFA later received letters from Celtic and Dundee United requesting compensation for the loss of gate receipts following their rearranged 22 September league fixtures. A meeting of the Executive and General Purposes Committee sanctioned the payments with the amounts calculated on the average gates of the corresponding matches in the previous three seasons.

As a postscript to the Czechoslovakia game, the *Evening Times*'s Jim Blair noted that a "tremendous cheer went up" from the Wembley crowd watching England's 7-0 demolition of Austria when it was announced that Scotland had gone ahead. This illustrates that at this particular time, and with the presence of Scots in many of England's top sides, fans south of the border had no particular dislike of the Scottish team.

Holton and Bremner withdrew from the trip to Bratislava for the final group game on 17 October amid talk of Czech revenge. After his dual with Kuna which had resulted in the skipper's early departure Bremner was a clear target. Previously something of an unknown, Tommy Hutchison was considered a major discovery but had also pulled out through injury before surprising everyone by joining the squad for their Monday departure from Glasgow. Hutchison received round-the-clock treatment on arrival in a bid to make the starting line-up.

In Bremner's absence Davie Hay was given the captain's armband and Tom Forsyth returned after two years for his second appearance. Hutchison pulled through with Law and Jordan the strike force, whilst David Harvey took Hunter's place in goal.

John Blackley had first been selected for the full squad by Bobby Brown three years earlier and was delighted to finally earn his first cap, a moment that has stayed with him.

"I remember the day of the game. Willie Ormond was reading out the team and handing out bibs. I had a look around and thought 'that's the team' – and I was in it! I'd been with the team quite a bit and to be fair I was kind of always picked for the squad. So it was nice to know I was going to get my first cap. It was a bit of a nothing game so that's probably how I got in."

The occasion also allowed John to team up with his boyhood hero. "I have a lasting memory of blagging school and going to an afternoon game when Denis Law scored against Czechoslovakia in 1961. He was my idol and for him to get picked in the squad was great for myself."

The match was a complete contrast to the Hampden game with just 13,668 spectators who were unable to conjure up any atmosphere. The Scots seemed comfortable going through the motions and were under instructions to avoid the type of confrontations seen at Hampden which could result in suspensions for the World Cup.

Jordan did not react when felled by Hagara shortly before the home side scored the only goal from the penalty spot in the 17th minute. The award mystified the distant pressmen after what seemed a fair tackle by Forsyth on Nehoda, who took the kick himself and beat Harvey.

The scorer was booked before half-time for grappling with Hutchison and a deflected Jordan shot which Viktor saved just after the interval was as close as Scotland came to equalising. In the STV studio Ian St John's assessment of the 90 minutes was "a non-event".

The result ensured Scotland finished on six points, one ahead of the Czechs, leaving Denmark bottom of the group with the solitary point they took from Czechoslovakia.

Tom Forsyth told *Rangers News*: "It was a difficult match to play in. Nothing was at stake and there was no real incentive. Our main advice from Willie Ormond was to stay out of trouble of any shape or form – and everybody did that." He also cleared up the confusion regarding the penalty decision: "I went into the tackle and as I fell my arm hit the ball. I suppose technically it was a penalty but it was completely accidental."

The confidence gained from World Cup qualification continued into the final match to mark the association's centenary, when European champions West Germany came to Glasgow in mid-November.

As in Bratislava Harvey was in goal ahead of Hunter, who was still part of the squad but who failed to gain another cap following his error against the Czechs.

Again the match was all-ticket with no sales allowed on the night. There were 58,235 people inside the ground to see the heroes of the Czech victory continue in exactly the same manner by attacking from the start. They played with a visible confidence which at times bordered on arrogance and a disregard for their opponents. If anything the performance that evening even surpassed that of the previous match with none of the pressures of qualification.

"We did really well that night, we were fantastic," says Willie Morgan. "We were confident anyway plus the fact the pressure was off as we had already qualified so we could go out and just play. Germany were obviously one of the best teams in the world at the time."

The confidence intensified with an early lead in circumstances similar to the recent past. Morgan took a corner after seven minutes which Law forwarded into the area for Holton to head over the line at the same end he had scored against the Czechs.

Hoeness somehow sent the ball over the bar from just three yards but Scotland dictated the pattern of play, moving forward with ease and completing some excellent moves.

After the break Maier saved well from Bremner as the Scots chased a second goal and they were given the perfect opportunity with 15 minutes remaining when Dalglish was pushed by Beckenbauer and Jack Taylor awarded a penalty kick.

Following Morgan's two misses, penalties had formed part of the training schedule at Largs and Bremner had emerged as the most accurate amongst the squad.

The captain struck the kick towards Sepp Maier's left allowing the keeper to dive and gather the ball. Bremner had not struck his shot with a great deal of power and he told those in the press room afterwards, "I was horrified at missing. I just got myself into two minds and I missed it."

Inspired by their goalkeeper, the Germans moved upfield and were level within five minutes as Flohe found Hoeness at the far post to head the equaliser.

The Scots left the pitch disappointed with the draw as their penalty jinx continued.

"The scoreline of 1-1 is nothing short of farcical," read Jim Blair's *Evening Times* report, adding that there were no failures in Ormond's XI. He reserved special praise for veteran Law. "His performance was superb. The fitness of the man is fantastic; his presence is inspiring and his enthusiasm unbelievable."

"I could not be happier with the way we played," Ormond told reporters inside Hampden. West German coach Helmut Schoen complemented his opponents. "Scotland playing good football, as they did against us, are going to be one of the big threats in the World Cup."

"It's no wonder the crowd chanted Willie Ormond's name," wrote Ian Peebles in the December issue of the magazine *Scottish Football*. "In this one game he gave us back our faith in football."

Sadly the West German match signalled the end of George Connelly's two-match international career. He failed to turn up for training with his club on the Friday and missed Celtic's Saturday fixture plus a League Cup tie with Aberdeen. He did return to Celtic after an absence of six days but this was followed by further walkouts and he quit the game in 1975 at the age of just 26.

1974

"I'll tell you something now and I can say this from the heart – these people back in Germany – they are very happy that we are out." **Willie Ormond**

Willie Ormond attended the draw for the World Cup finals in Frankfurt on Saturday, 5 January. Scotland were placed in Group 2 alongside holders Brazil, Zaire and the yet to be decided winners of a play-off between Yugoslavia and Spain. Interviewed on BBC Scotland's *Sportsreel* live broadcast, Ormond had this message for viewers: "I can see no reason at all why Scotland cannot qualify for the latter stages. I am more than happy with the way things turned out." On Brazil he commented: "They are not the team that they were."

The opener against the Africans was scheduled for Dortmund, with the other two group games taking place in Frankfurt. The second venue was ideal with Scotland due to play West Germany there in March. Ormond remained in the country for a few days to finalise accommodation and training facilities. He planned to watch Zaire ahead of the tournament and the play-off match, which would decide the opponents for his side's final group game. The manager, however, had no plans to spy on Brazil whose abilities he considered himself familiar with.

At a meeting of the SFA Executive and General Purposes Committee on 21 January, correspondence from the Lord Provost of

Glasgow was considered. The letter suggested a "distinctly Scottish tune" should be played as an anthem before international matches rather than "God Save the Queen" which was ritually booed to the embarrassment of attending dignitaries and presumably the SFA. The minutes from the meeting read: "It was decided not to take any action."

The play-off took place in Frankfurt on 12 February where an early Katalinski goal sent the Yugoslavs into the finals. The presence of an estimated 30,000 Yugoslav fans in the Waldstadion concerned Ormond. With many thousands of Slavs working in Germany they would clearly outnumber even Scotland's fanatical following. Ormond praised the victors' back four but was of the opinion that his side were better equipped in midfield.

So by a twist of fate Scotland found that the three nations they had competed against in the Brazilian Independence Day tournament were future World Cup opponents. With the Czechs already taken care of during qualification they would line up against the others on the big stage in June, the third successive year Scotland had faced Brazil.

With no possibility of additional fixtures prior to the Frankfurt friendly, Willie Ormond turned his attention to the Under-23 match with Wales on the last Wednesday of February.

As in 1972 the government had declared a State of Emergency throughout the UK following a decision by the National Union of Mineworkers to implement an overtime ban. Again floodlit matches were outlawed and clubs had to rearrange Saturday kick-off times to take account of the limited daylight, with most opting for a 2.15pm start.

The Wednesday match at Pittodrie started at 3pm which restricted the attendance to just short of 6,000.

Ormond's programme notes included the following: "I look upon today's game as an important part of the build-up to the World Cup Finals. There could be four places available in the squad I will choose prior to the Finals and any one of the Under-23 team could win a place."

Scotland almost took an early lead in comical circumstances when Joey Jones lobbed the ball back to his own goalkeeper only to watch in horror as Phillips slipped and the ball struck a post before the keeper recovered.

Derek Parlane gave the crowd something to cheer in the 33rd minute after Phil Dwyer had fouled Bobby Prentice as the Hearts man looked set to open the scoring. Parlane sent Phillips the wrong way from the spot, putting the ball to his left.

It took until the 80th minute before Scotland secured the win, when Dundee's Bobby Robinson scored from 20 yards. In the final minute Jim Pearson beat two defenders to make the score 3-0.

The two late goals were said to flatter the Scots a little with Ian Gibb writing in the *Daily Mail*: "Team boss Willie Ormond can have seen very little evidence of good World Cup material."

The manager flew to Egypt on the first day of March to assess Zaire's performance in the African Cup of Nations. Their schedule of three matches in five days was a perfect opportunity for Ormond to spy on them.

Following their 2-1 opening win against Guinea in Damanhour, Ormond told *The Herald*'s Ian Archer: "I thought Zaire were quite good in attack but at the back they were loose, marking man to man and lacking pace. I did not see anything to give me a sleepless night ... I am sure we can take them."

He was even less impressed when the Leopards went down 2-1 to Congo: "I had expected rather more of them," he told Archer. "Other coaches had told me when I attended the draw in Frankfurt that they would not care to be in my shoes playing Zaire in the opening match. I cannot accept these views. Scotland will win their first World Cup match." The Leopards did recover with a 4-1 win over Mauritius which qualified them for a semi-final where they came out on top against the host nation.

Ormond, by then back home, may have been a little surprised to learn that Zaire became African champions after a replayed final with Zambia. In a luxury no Scotland manager could ever enjoy the Zaire squad would remain together right up until their exit from the World Cup three months later.

The manager had three matches on consecutive Wednesdays to aid his World Cup preparations. The first of these, the annual Under-23 game against England, was thrown into doubt when his initial 17-man squad was reduced to just six – and that included two goalkeepers. A freak series of results ranging from 0-0 to 3-3 ensured that each of the weekend's Scottish Cup quarter-finals had ended level leading to numerous withdrawals for the replays. With two of the quarter-finals taking place on the Sunday and the Scotland party heading for Newcastle the following day this allowed even less time to call in replacements.

Ormond's request for a postponement was rejected and he managed to assemble a makeshift travelling party of 16 players, only five of whom were original choices. Tommy Craig of Sheffield Wednesday and St Johnstone's Alec MacDonald were amongst the additions.

With the recent lifting of the floodlight ban the Scottish Cup replays were able to go ahead in the evening but the schedule for the Under-23 game had been previously arranged with an afternoon start. Heavy rain and the kick-off time meant only 4,511 were inside St James' Park.

Craig was given the dubious honour of captaining the team of acquaintances with Stewart in goal. England dominated the early period as their opponents struggled to get to know one another and the opening goal through David Mills on 17 minutes was overdue. The closest Ormond's men came in the first half was a header by Alex Bruce, playing on his home pitch, which went narrowly over.

Chesterfield goalkeeper Jim Brown took over for the second half with one of his first tasks picking the ball from the net following a fine Bob Latchford strike.

A Donny Gillies shot almost reduced the deficit but rebounded into play from a goalpost midway through the second half. England comfortably saw out the remainder of the game without increasing their two-goal lead.

The manager suffered another rash of withdrawals for the following week's Inter League match at Manchester City. Even replacements were pulled out and what had seemed like an ideal period for World Cup preparation was turning into anything but. How Ormond must have envied the Zaire squad's preparation as he suffered the greatest number of call-offs since the days of Bobby Brown.

The Football League side boasted representatives of Liverpool, Manchester City, Derby, Arsenal and QPR and the gulf in quality was reflected in the final result of England 5, Scotland 0.

Floodlights were permitted but there was little brightness from the Scots as the English dominated the midfield and went ahead through a Colin Bell header after 12 minutes. Stan Bowles was the star of the show and his 25th-minute corner caused Hearts defender Jim Brown to slice the ball into his own net.

Tueart and Bowles both saw shots come back from goalposts and Stewart saved acrobatically from Kevin Hector as the English threatened to run up a cricket score. An off-target effort from Parlane was all that the Scots had to offer in the first 45.

Ayr's Rikki Fleming fouled Bowles just after the restart to allow Tueart to score from the penalty spot, and further goals from Brooking and Bowles completed Scotland's misery.

Press reports of the Football League's large victory were guarded. "All assessment of the English performance must be weighed against massive reservations about the wretched quality of the opposition," wrote Jeff Powell for the *Daily Mirror*.

The result was the highest winning margin in the 70-game series of which the Football League had now won 39. Questions persisted as to the fixture's worth, as it was regularly devalued by withdrawals.

Ormond was said to be under considerable strain following the trips to Egypt, Newcastle and Manchester with the World Cup fast approaching. On the Friday callers to his home in Musselburgh were informed by Margaret Ormond that her husband was exhausted and in bed.

Still displaying signs of fatigue, the manager was relieved to find 18 players turn up in Glasgow for the trip to West Germany. There had already been withdrawals by Blackley, McGrain and Holton and a rearranged league match meant no Leeds players were available.

Ian Archer noticed a change in the manager in Frankfurt as detailed in his *Herald* column. "He stalked about the hotel showing little of the good humour that has during this past year become infectious to players and the entire Scottish entourage. When someone asked why Francis Munro was not here to fill the problem position at centre-half he snapped back, 'Why don't you do your homework? You should know he is suspended.' Such a bark is out of character – and a sure sign of the pressure he has suffered throughout the month of March."

Ormond's mindset would not have been helped by the prospect of his weakened side lining up against six Bayern Munich players, three from Monchengladbach, one from local side Eintracht and the other from Real Madrid.

"Denis Law will be playing for his World Cup life," Archer wrote of the 33-year-old. "He needs another good performance to keep his World Cup dream intact."

Three Scots made their debuts in the Waldstadion: Dundee goalkeeper Thomson Allan, Kenny Burns and Erich Schaedler.

A full house of 62,000 watched a match which began slowly but changed in tempo once the home side found their rhythm.

The Germans took the lead just beyond the half hour when Stanton tackled Wimmer late and Breitner, showing more composure than Bremner in the previous fixture, scored easily from the penalty. The crowd were still cheering when Grabowski accepted a pass from Hoeness to shoot past Allan for a second.

Allan did well to prevent a greater deficit before Ormond replaced Law and Burns with Donald Ford and Bobby Robinson after almost an hour of play.

In the 76th minute Ford sent Dalglish through, who ignored claims of offside to beat Maier. Ford himself came close as the goal re-energised the side that at one point had looked to be heading for a heavy defeat, and the Germans had to settle for a 2-1 margin.

"Law had been so quiet that his World Cup place must now be in question," Archer wrote for *The Herald*. Once the striker had left the party in Frankfurt Airport for a direct route to Manchester the manager was asked by travelling pressmen if he had played his final match for Scotland. "I would not say that he is out of the World Cup party by any means," was Ormond's response. "It's the effect he has on other players which impresses me and with the World Cup it's important that you have a player in the team that can raise the others. Denis is such a man."

Law would have been heartened by the comments of newly appointed City manager Tony Book during a mid-April press conference. "I'm going to do my utmost to help Denis Law regain his form. It will not only be to Scotland's benefit in the World Cup but to my club's. I will be playing him in every match until the end of the season."

On April's last day Willie Ormond released his provisional list of 40 for the World Cup finals, from which 22 were named for the Home International series. Denis Law was amongst the smaller pool as was

Jimmy Johnstone, who had not featured in dark blue for two years but whose recent performances had alerted Ormond. The deadline for registering the 22 World Cup players with FIFA was eight days before the opening match so the Home Internationals gave Ormond a final opportunity to assess form.

The SFA was still unwilling to travel to Belfast for the opener and pleas from the Irish FA to consider a neutral venue in Manchester were dismissed. The Irish reluctantly again agreed to stage their "home" game in Glasgow which assured the Scots of Hampden advantage throughout the series.

A large crowd of 53,775 turned up in good spirits and sang the "Easy Easy" World Cup song, recorded by the squad, as the Ulstermen formed a guard of honour in tribute to the Scots' World Cup team ahead of the kick-off. The mood was good, the atmosphere vibrant and all seemed right ... until the game started.

Chances were scarce although Hamilton found the back of the Scottish net midway through the first half before the referee indicated an infringement. The crowd's patience was beginning to wear thin as Sammy Morgan's header bounced back from the crossbar.

On the stroke of half-time Tom Cassidy slid the ball past Harvey for a deserved lead as Buchan desperately tried to clear.

Scotland huffed and puffed in search of an equaliser in the second half but Dalglish and Jordan were both thwarted by Jennings and the players were jeered from the pitch as the "home" team celebrated their one-goal victory.

Analysis of Willie Ormond's record at this stage did not make good reading with just two wins and seven goals in 11 matches.

"Our attitude was all wrong," the manager admitted to Ian Archer. "The team were attempting exhibition stuff. If we play like that against Zaire we will be struggling. I want more professionalism. These are players from big clubs – from Manchester United, from Celtic, from Leeds United. They know what is expected of them – and must now start to show it to me."

Jimmy Johnstone returned for the Welsh match on the Tuesday, in which another failure to win would constitute a crisis ahead of the World Cup.

Following Bremner's miss from the spot against the Germans, Ormond had organised a competition during training to find a new penalty taker. It has been suggested over the years that the captain had too much influence over the manager but the decision to relinquish Bremner from penalty duties showed that Ormond was not afraid to overrule him. Sandy Jardine won the penalty contest with Tommy Hutchison a close second.

The performance against Wales suggested the players had taken the manager's criticisms on board and sent the crowd of over 40,000 home with the chant "Bring on the English!" still echoing inside their heads.

A Buchan free kick found Dalglish who opened the scoring with 24 minutes played, as Scotland dominated the first half. The lead was doubled just ahead of the break when Mahoney fouled Hay in the area allowing newly appointed penalty taker Jardine to confidently send the ball into the corner of Sprake's net.

The second 45 was rather sedate although a spectacular save by Sprake, turning over a shot from Ford, denied the crowd the third goal they yearned for.

Back at Largs a group of players were permitted to take up an invitation from a local hotelier which concluded at around 5am on the Wednesday morning. With dawn breaking they made their way along the shore to the Queens Hotel where Jimmy Johnstone made for one of two rowing boats redundant on dry land. With Jinky seated, the foot of Sandy Jardine mischievously pushed the boat into the water unaware that the consequences of his tomfoolery would make front-page news. The tide drew the boat towards the sea and panic set in as there were no oars in the vessel. Eric Schaedler and Davie Hay decided to mount a rescue mission in the second boat – until they discovered it had a leak. Johnstone himself seemed unconcerned, standing up and singing "Michael Row the Boat Ashore" at the top of his voice.

Willie Morgan had a grandstand view of the drama from his room in the Queens. "I was sharing a room with Jim Holton and we were on the front looking out on to the sea. They'd all gone out to one of the pubs and I had gone back to bed at two in the morning or so and next thing I know Jim was waking me up at five o'clock or something with 'Hey look out the windae!' It was Jinky in the boat and it was drifting away. You could see it and he didn't have any oars. It was a bit of fun, a prank that obviously went wrong because Jinky couldn't swim."

As he drifted further out Jinky's team-mates had become concerned and a 999 call from the Queens summoned the coastguard.

"We were getting ready to head back down the road to the hotel and I think it was Eric Schaedler who came in and said, 'You'll no' believe it, Jimmy's away out in a boat!'" says John Blackley. "So we had a walk back to the hotel and we could see the boats going out to see if they could save him and we all just stayed by the quay."

When the rescue party reached the shore around 6am they were greeted by the sight of several Scotland players in fits of laughter next to a stern-faced Willie Ormond.

The drunken sailor was no longer singing when his boat was brought ashore as John Blackley's memory confirms: "When they brought him in Jimmy was absolutely frozen, shaking like a leaf because it was that cold." The players were ordered to attend a meeting at 10am with some of them probably still feeling the effects of alcohol. The discussions at the Queens remained private with Willie Ormond refusing to comment to prying pressmen.

John Blackley said: "We were all in at the meeting and the door opened. Where Jimmy was sitting, as the door opened, he faced Willie Ormond. So the eyes met and wee Jimmy goes, 'That's some fucking look you've gave me sir!' And we all just burst out laughing at the fact that Jimmy said this."

"It was nothing really," insists Willie Morgan. "It was people having a good time and Willie Ormond handled it well."

Blackley is in full agreement: "It was wrong but it was a funny moment that could have gone horribly wrong actually. Willie treated it in a manner that he was seen to be angry kind of thing and put it to the papers that was the road he was taking. But I think he handled it quite well and with the press reaction I think he was on Jimmy's side at the end of the day."

Due to the timing of the drama the only column space the players occupied in the Wednesday newspapers was in reports of the Wales game. The incident may even have been hushed up had the *Express*'s chief football writer John MacKenzie not been a Largs resident. Alerted by the commotion, the journalist had made his way to the shore in time to witness the arrival of the coastguard. The story, which has gone down in Scottish football folklore as "the rowing-boat incident", was splashed all over the front page of Thursday's Scottish *Daily Express*.

The other journals soon followed up with the general tone that the players had disgraced the team and ought to be disciplined.

This did not go down well within the Queens Hotel whose residents felt that certain Scottish reporters were attempting to undermine the players at a crucial time. If anything, the press reaction galvanised the squad as the players developed a siege mentality.

The bookmakers had England as 6-4 favourites and offered odds of 2-1 for the first Scottish win over England since 1967. The *Evening Times*'s Jim Blair pinpointed the recent poor scoring record when he typed: "For the first time ever I can honestly say I don't fancy Scotland's chances."

Following Sir Alf Ramsey's dismissal a few weeks earlier Joe Mercer had been given temporary charge of the England side and he insisted the match meant as much to his players as to the Scots.

With Hutchison injured Lorimer came into the side with Jordan and Dalglish retained as the strikers. John Blackley collected his second cap and has never forgotten the moment he learned he would play against England.

"I was going upstairs to my room after breakfast and Willie Ormond called me. 'Hey! You will be playing today,' he said. It was through an injury to Martin Buchan who had pulled out of training on the Friday and failed the fitness test. I would have got told about half ten or 11 o'clock and probably that was a good thing as you had no time to worry.

"Then it was a case of having to phone my wife and my dad to see if they wanted tickets for the game so I had to get all that arranged." John had always envied his elder brothers travelling to Wembley internationals and was grateful for the programmes they always brought back. "The England game was such a big thing in my life and in my family's lives and it was great to get the opportunity."

Again the all-ticket crowd was limited to 100,000 with the official attendance later given as 94,487. Thousands of yellow and red flags stapled on to sticks with "World Cup" above the Lion Rampant and "Munich 74" beneath had been snapped up outside and were waved fervently as the World Cup bus completed a circuit of the ground before the teams appeared from the tunnel.

Partly because the Olympic Games had been branded as Munich 72, much of the marketing for the World Cup was accompanied by a

Munich 74 logo, whilst subsequent tournaments were promoted by the name of the country rather than a city. Munich almost became a byword for World Cup or West Germany, and Sydney Devine released a novelty disc which was a reworking of "We Shall Not Be Moved" entitled "On Our Way To Munich". The Olympic Stadium in Munich was one of the match venues and would stage the final itself, but reference to the Bavarian capital should not necessarily be interpreted as an assumption that Scotland would be taking part in the World Cup Final.

It was clear from the start that the Scottish players, fired up by what they felt was a press campaign against them, were fully motivated for the game. Jordan fired a shot over in the second minute and the same player was instrumental as Scotland took a sensational lead with just four minutes on the clock. When Shilton blocked a Lorimer shot the ball fell into Jordan's territory and he instinctively stabbed a left-foot shot towards the empty goal with Shilton stranded. Attempting to clear, Stoke full-back Mike Pejic diverted the ball's path enough to ensure it ended up in the corner of the net. The identity of the scorer is still disputed to this day with the majority of newspapers crediting Pejic with an own goal and others Jordan. The striker has always claimed the goal as his own and some record books agree.

Much of the confusion concerns whether or not Jordan's shot would have entered the net without Pejic's intervention and the television evidence is inconclusive. As the ball rolls towards the goal it is impossible to say with any certainty whether it would have gone in, wide or even back into play from a post. Even an ITV Sports replay camera behind that goal was unable to clarify the situation. The *Sunday Post* report described Doug Baillie's view from the press box: "Joe's shot looked as though it was going just wide of the near post when Pejic, sliding on his back, stuck out his foot and diverted the ball into the net." What there was no doubt about was that Scotland had taken the lead as the roar of the crowd confirmed.

The loss of the early goal clearly rattled England whose players lacked Ramsey's methodical advice. Shilton, who had broken Scottish hearts with that save from Dalglish 12 months earlier, was again in inspired form, saving first from Hay and then Johnstone inside the first 20 minutes.

The crowd erupted again after half an hour when Johnstone, possibly playing his best match for Scotland, took the ball from a Lorimer throw-in before returning it with a back-heel. Lorimer then crossed for Dalglish who hit the ball goalwards. Colin Todd then stabbed it beyond Shilton. Arthur Montford described the incident to STV viewers with: "The ball's in the net and that's a crazy goal!" Lorimer and Bremner hugged each other, the winger's right arm punching the air before three of their colleagues joined in a larger celebration. This time there was no debate that it was an own goal.

The England players would have been glad to hear the half-time whistle as Scotland were so much on top at this stage and a reverse of the 5-0 result in the centenary game could not be ruled out.

Shilton saved well from Jordan soon after the restart and the elusive third goal almost arrived when a Lorimer free kick bounced from the goalkeeper and Jordan only just failed to apply the lethal touch. In the end the fans had to settle for the two-goal victory as the Scottish players ran to the crowd just as they had done after the Czech game. Johnstone, wearing Shilton's large jersey, had played the game of his life although there were no underperformers on the day. It was one of those occasions when everything seemed to click into place.

The manager joined the celebrating players on the pitch. At one point during the ITV Sport footage Ormond and Johnstone can be seen in conversation in the middle of the park. Ormond, with a scowl on his face, points towards the Hampden press box above the main stand and utters something in Jinky's ear. The winger's response was to gesture with two figures in the direction of the reporters who had both vilified and, ironically, motivated the players. As the manager headed for the tunnel he fixed a long, deliberate, lingering hard stare in the direction of the journalists above.

Willie Ormond's anger had not dissipated when he re-emerged from the tunnel for a television interview in front of the main stand. ITV Sports' Hugh Johns asked: "Willie, what was the most satisfying factor about this victory this afternoon?" The manager's rant was not quite what Johns was expecting. "Well first of all the most satisfying thing today as far as I was concerned is we've shut a few mouths up the top there." At this point Ormond again gazed angrily and deliberately towards the press box. "They do all the criticising before a match and ruled us out of the game completely. This is the main factor we've had a bit of slating this week, the players and I. We had no chance this morning. Now we'll start talking about a game." Thereafter Ormond calmly discussed the match with Johns.

John Blackley plays down the press fall-out: "It was an England v Scotland game so I don't think there was anything, certainly in my mind, that we were against the press kind of thing, but it was nice for Jimmy to get that wee bit of reaction, so good on him."

It had been Scotland's most convincing performance against England for years. But they had won only by virtue of two own goals although Shilton had prevented a greater margin. "If I were Willie Ormond I would make sure there was a boating lake near the team's headquarters," joked Doug Baillie in the *Sunday Post*. "A trip in a wee boat seems to work wonders for the unusual temperament of Jimmy Johnstone."

"I watched the game back years later and I thought I was minging!" laughs John Blackley. "Looking at the game I thought Jesus – and I thought I had played well!"

The resulting two points ensured Ormond's men finished above England in the Home International table on goal difference.

Johnstone, once jeered at Hampden, praised the supporters to *The Herald*'s Jim Reynolds. "They were magnificent," he said of the crowd, "and I am only too happy that I helped in some way to make it a great day for them. Before we went out we were all determined to put on a show for Willie Ormond. The boss has stood by us all during the past couple of weeks and I suppose our performance was our way of saying thanks to him."

Looking back, Rodger Baillie reflects on the manager: "He would hardly have been the people's choice but he was a very nice wee man. He certainly came good and belied all the doubts that were surrounding him after that awful five-nothing defeat at Hampden."

"Willie Ormond's role was underplayed a lot with the press but he had his way and he was quite knowledgeable about things," says John Blackley. "He had a nice manner and was not a dour fellow, well-mannered with a nice sense of humour."

"I liked the wee man," smiles Willie Morgan. "He was a lovely guy and I have just fond memories of him. The fact that Willie was nice, you didn't abuse the privilege of him being nice. He maybe wasn't the strongest but he'd come into the job in charge of a lot of big names and he handled it his way."

The 22 names for the World Cup were released on the Monday and, not surprisingly, the 11 who had played so well against England were all included. Denis Law, who must have been concerned about Jordan's form, was also on the list.

The players themselves were excused for a week before they returned to Largs the following Monday. Martin Buchan was absent when the squad assembled. The player had gone to Majorca on holiday and, after arriving over 24 hours after everyone else, a face-to-face meeting with a reportedly angry Ormond was said to have resolved the matter. When asked about the meeting Ormond stuck to the same line he had taken after the rowing-boat incident with: "There will be no statement. The matter is between the player and myself."

The party set off for Belgium on the Friday for the first of two preparation games ahead of the World Cup, with rumours of a rift over bonuses. A posse of photographers were refused a group photograph during their last day at Largs as they were not prepared to meet the asking price of £5,000. Ormond confessed to feeling the tension even though his team's opener against Zaire was still two weeks away.

Ormond named the same 11 players as had performed so well in the England game for the match in Bruges but was forced to make a change when Holton picked up an injury during training. Gordon McQueen deputised to win his first cap which increased the number of Leeds representatives to five. The manager had made it clear he wanted to maintain the momentum of the last two matches by winning both warm-up games before facing Zaire.

The Belgians had only missed out on World Cup qualification themselves by goal difference to one of the favourites, Holland, with whom they had drawn twice.

The players were unable to replicate their England form and Archie Macpherson's recollection is that "the players looked hungover", which may have been an accurate assessment. The home side took the lead at the midpoint of the first half following a lapse by Johnstone although McQueen almost stopped Henrotay's effort on the goal line.

Johnstone did make amends shortly before half-time when he hit a right-foot shot into the net after goalkeeper Piot had failed to deal with a McQueen free kick.

Scotland's efforts were frustrated when the number of marginal offside decisions given against them rose into double figures.

"The Scots found it hard to settle with a whistle-happy referee and two flag-happy linesmen constantly stopping play," sympathised Baillie in his *Sunday Post* report. A trademark Lorimer pile-driver was as close as they came in the second period and the winner was controversial with Dalglish deemed to have committed a foul on Van Moer after which Lambert beat Harvey from the spot. The penalty, seven minutes from time, was considered soft and a draw would have been an acceptable result but Scotland had looked jaded throughout, a fact no number of offside decisions could disguise.

The hotel in nearby Ghent had been adjacent to a busy motorway intersection which did little to quash the simmering dissatisfaction amongst the players over the bonuses. On arrival in Oslo, the venue of their final preparation match, there were further grumbles when they checked into the student campus arranged by the SFA. The complex consisted of a number of tower blocks and was described by Ian Archer as "not unlike Barlinnie [prison] with rooms to match".

The manager had allowed the players to have a drink on the flight from Belgium and this continued on arrival with some of the group breaking into duty free purchases whilst others rested in their tiny rooms. Bremner and Johnstone failed to appear at meal time and turned up later in the bar of the complex the worse for wear. Members of the Scottish press were also present and witnessed the pair singing loudly before Bremner taunted some objecting locals about his club's 10-0 defeat of Lyn Oslo in the Fairs Cup a few years earlier.

After an appearance by the manager and team doctor the pair returned to their rooms – but only temporarily. They re-emerged with their belongings and announced that they had had enough and were heading home. They were talked out of leaving but an emergency meeting of the SFA International Committee was called for the morning.

Due to the journalists' presence in the bar there was little chance of a lid being kept on the matter and again player indiscipline filled front pages back home.

Privately Ormond felt let down but it was believed that a plea by him and profuse apologies from the culprits themselves prevented the pair being sent home. The SFA meeting had been lengthy and during discussions committee members were said to be divided with some in favour of immediate expulsion.

Calls for Bremner to be relieved of the captaincy were dismissed by Ormond at a meeting with reporters whom he told: "I want to make it plain – Bremner will still captain the side. He is a very good leader."

Bremner had his frailties off the field where he was not everyone's cup of tea. "The man was an enigma," his long-term club mate Peter Lorimer says of Billy in his autobiography.

But Ormond was aware of his value as skipper of the side and his influence was vital going into the World Cup.

Having admitted to feeling the pressure before leaving Scotland, the tension intensified for the manager who responded to the latest events by excluding all press from the players' scheduled training session at the Ulleval Stadium on the Tuesday.

This was out of character for Ormond as Rodger Baillie confirms. "It was the only time I think that he lost his cool and fell out with the press. I remember the training session where he banned us from watching. In those days it was more or less open door and it was changed. It was a combination of various escapades, and he was unhappy and got very uppity. At a conference following the session in the Ulleval Stadium there were very heated exchanges, but it didn't last."

The following day John MacKenzie was summoned by Willie Allan and informed he would not be permitted to travel to Germany on the SFA's chartered aircraft due to what was considered to be inaccurate reporting of player behaviour in the *Express*.

Archie Macpherson had witnessed the drunken antics in Oslo and views the combination of Largs and Norway as a turning point in relations between the media and the SFA. "There was hostility thereafter all the way through – a three-way hostility. It was the whole of the SFA against the press, it was the footballers against the press and the footballers against the hierarchy – the SFA themselves. So there was all of that intertwined."

Both Bremner and Johnstone retained their places for the Norway game, with Hutchison replacing Dalglish who until then had started in every game since Ormond took charge.

Scotland played in an all-white strip and were in trouble early in the match with Thomson Allan required to make three saves within the first 15 minutes. The overdue opening goal came when a long clearance from Norway's Dunfermline goalkeeper Geir Karlsen eluded both Buchan and Holton, allowing Lund to beat Allan and send the home fans into a frenzy.

Norway had embarrassed Scotland before by winning 4-3 eleven years earlier and it was beginning to look as though history was repeating itself. Lorimer managed to force a couple of saves out of Karlsen before the break but the performance was scrappy as the locals greeted the half-time whistle rapturously.

With 20 minutes remaining Ormond sent on Dalglish for Johnstone. The impact was almost immediate as the substitute fed Lorimer who headed into the net. But offside had been given. Perhaps it was to be Norway's night after all.

The Scots gained a free kick with around 15 minutes left to save the match and Bremner sent the ball into the area where Jordan made the task of heading into the net look simple.

The formula was repeated a few minutes from time with another Bremner free kick. Again Jordan connected for Dalglish, almost on the goal line, to finish the job with his head. The win was almost denied when a poor back-pass from Holton, who had limped through the game, was picked up by Thunberg whose shot went narrowly wide.

The Scots had struggled for long periods but had come up with a 2-1 win to boost their morale at the right time. When all was said and done they had won three of their last four matches but no one was fooling themselves that the Oslo display would be acceptable at the World Cup.

John MacKenzie's *Daily Express* report pulled no punches: "Two late goals saved Scotland's blushes when Willie Ormond's men were struggling badly and heading for humiliation. The Scots had been given a football lesson from the talented amateurs of Norway and that elusive World Cup form looks as far away as ever." That analysis may just of course have been influenced by the author's expulsion from the SFA travelling party.

The players were permitted a celebratory drink in the bar of their accommodation with the 11pm curfew observed by all as they looked ahead to the serious business of the World Cup.

Their charter flight touched down on German soil a full seven days before the Zaire game. Coaches then took the party 35 miles from Frankfurt Airport to their base at Erbismule in the Taunus Mountains, a former hunting lodge.

After the tragic events at the Olympic Games two years earlier when Palestinian terrorists had entered the athletes' village leading to the subsequent deaths of 11 Israeli team members, the West German authorities were determined that the World Cup would be free of any such problems.

Each room in the players' hotel had been searched for explosive devices ahead of their arrival with armed security guards constantly patrolling the complex. A helicopter hovered above the team coach each time it transported the players outside the perimeter.

Excitement was mounting in Scotland with supporters preparing to travel to Germany whilst those staying at home stocked up from off-licences; some had taken advantage of special offers from television rental companies to upgrade their old sets to colour models.

On the eve of the Zaire match the Scotland party temporarily vacated Erbismule for a Dortmund hotel rather than make the 130-mile trip on matchday. They arrived in plenty of time to watch the opening ceremony on television followed by the tournament's first match.

As the holders traditionally took part in the opener, Brazil's encounter with the Yugoslavs was of more than passing interest to the Scottish party. The goalless draw was a drab affair but unquestionably a good result for the watching players who knew that two points against Zaire would see them top the section. Later events would indicate that Scotland would have benefitted more if someone had lost that opening fixture.

Although much would later be made of margins of victory there is evidence that the importance of goals had been discussed before Scotland's first match. On the morning of the Zaire game Ormond offered these words in Jim Blair's *Evening Times* piece: "We will be committed to attack from the kick-off. The more goals we score the better, because goal difference could decide this section at the end of the day."

Archie Macpherson was in the company of Jock Stein, also with the BBC in West Germany, in the lobby of the team's hotel hours ahead of the match. Billy Bremner joined them whilst launching into a tirade about the Scottish press. Archie has never forgotten Stein's reaction as he clenched his angry fist close to the Scotland captain's face. "He told him to stick it right up the press and to think of everybody who had upset him – to get out there and show us all!"

Bremner acknowledged the importance of this advice and was quoted in Bernard Bales's 1998 biography *Bremner!* saying: "He said that I should stop moaning and get on with proving the press boys to be exactly what I thought they were. He told me to take the players out there and show everyone what we were made of. It was probably the best team talk I had had in years."

Four changes were made to the line-up from Oslo with Harvey, Blackley, Dalglish and Law coming in for Allan, Buchan, Johnstone and Hutchison. "Many people thought Denis was just here for the ride," Ormond told Blair, "but I knew he could do a job for me – and I'll be looking for goals from him tonight."

A glance at Scotland's starting line-up suggested a very experienced side but it has to be remembered that the players were all *inexperienced* as far as the World Cup was concerned and they were noticeably nervous in the dressing room of the Westfalen Stadium ahead of the game.

John Blackley recalls that even the elder members of the group felt the pressure. "I must say there was a lot of tension, a real lot of tension. I couldn't believe how Denis Law and Billy Bremner were just going about with stares on their faces, and you're looking at them.

"There was a belief that 'we are here and we have got to get a result, we've got to beat Zaire' and I think everybody felt it in the dressing room that particular day."

This was the big time. This was the World Cup. This was IT.

Stuart Borrowman from West Lothian was 21 when he travelled to the World Cup by train and remembers the pre-match excitement in Dortmund. "There was an element of being proud and just happy to be there. This was something that had never happened and that must have been true for players like Denis Law as well."

As expected Scotland attacked from the kick-off and Jordan headed narrowly past inside two minutes. A long-range strike from Hay hit a post before the opening goal came after 26 minutes when Jordan nodded a Hay cross on for Lorimer to net with a powerful volley.

The lead was doubled several minutes later when Jordan, who initially looked offside, headed a Bremner free kick with such power that the African goalkeeper Kazadi let the ball slip from his grasp before it bounced over the line in comical fashion.

There was a second farcical episode when some of the floodlights failed early in the second half and play was halted for five minutes before the game continued under reduced but adequate lighting.

Zaire threatened occasionally in the second half with Harvey twice called into action as Bremner appeared to alter the tempo in midfield. Lorimer and Law, the latter desperate to justify his inclusion, were both foiled by Kazadi who produced something of a Jekyll and Hyde performance. At one stage the Germans in the crowd jeered as Ormond's men kept possession and played the ball to each other in the middle of the park.

It has been claimed that the captain instructed his players to slow things down with the forthcoming match against Brazil in mind. John Blackley dismisses this suggestion. "No, there was nothing said about taking things easy. It wasn't Billy Bremner's fault; it was just that's how the team played on the day. We weren't asked to play slow, passing football. That's how it was played out. Billy got wronged through a hard time in the press for playing too slow and not getting forward enough but we won two nothing."

Surrounded by the world's media the Scotland manager's comments were guarded: "We tired a bit towards the end of the game and Zaire surprised us with their second-half performance. I thought we should have won the match by a bigger margin but 2-0 is better than nothing."

A 19-year-old Rangers fan, Robbie Jenkins, had hitch-hiked from his Elgin home to London from where he travelled to Dortmund by coach. After celebrating the victory Robbie headed to the railway station hoping to catch a few hours' sleep before boarding an early morning train to Frankfurt. He was unprepared for a scene resembling the aftermath of Culloden when he entered the Hauptbanhof.

"When I got to the station it was absolutely jam-packed with fans with so much noise you couldn't sleep," he recollects. "You ended up talking to people and I noticed this guy was wearing slippers. So I said, 'What the hell are you wearing slippers for?' His wife wouldn't let him go to Germany so he told her he was popping out for something. He did say he would get round to buying a pair of shoes at some point."

There was a feeling within the camp that the toughest opponents could be Yugoslavia in the final game, therefore a win against Brazil could prove crucial. Ormond was expected to recall Johnstone for the match and omit Law. In the event Johnstone again had to make do with a place on the bench whilst Law took the news badly when informed he was being replaced by the recovered Morgan.

"When I joined the squad at the end of our season I had a bad groin injury," says Willie Morgan. "It took me about three weeks to get back and I was still unfit for the Zaire match. I was on the treatment table all the time and they were great. To be honest I should have called off because I was in such a bad way."

The other change in personnel was Buchan in for Blackley who, like Law, was shattered.

"Willie didn't pull me in and say 'I'm going to be playing Martin Buchan,' he just named his team. I was just shocked and I had no reason to be because Martin was such a good player anyway and with more caps than I had ever had. But it was just the fact that I was looking forward to playing against Brazil so much.

"All my life there was two teams I always wanted to play against and that was England and Brazil and here was my chance. We had won 2-0 and were on the front foot and he names his team and I was in tears. His thing was that Martin Buchan had a lot more pace than I did and Brazil would be quick, so I think that's why I was binned.

"I just really wanted to play and say I had played against Brazil. I was in tears and I was even contemplating coming home but my wife said just you sit where you are."

Prime Minister Harold Wilson, Billy Connolly, Ayr United manager Ally MacLeod and Jackie Stewart were amongst the crowd in the Waldstadion where Scotland had lost to the host nation three months earlier. Having observed that the German spectators in Dortmund had favoured the underdogs, the Scottish players unfurled a West German flag ahead of the kick-off in an unashamed public relations exercise.

Again Scotland started nervously and a Lorimer free kick which Leao saved competently was their only effort on goal in the early stages. Leivinha volleyed against Harvey's bar before the expected physical aspect crept into the game as Rivelino was booked for flooring Bremner. Bremner it has to be said gave as good as he received and as the first half progressed the Scots began to believe in themselves, with Lorimer again trying his luck, this time his shot going over.

Whatever Ormond's instructions were between the two halves it inspired the Scots to take the game to the world champions, with Bremner playing the game of his life with tough tackling and excellent forward passing.

Hay tried a shot from long range which Leao fumbled over for a corner as the Scots played with an increasing belief, troubling the Brazilian defence time after time.

"After the game we gave them in 1972 Brazil were frightened of us," says Willie Morgan, "and we should have won."

The game's defining moment came 20 minutes from time when Jordan headed a Lorimer corner down and against Leao. The ball broke back into play and hit Bremner on the shin inside the six-yard box. As the world watched he was unable to control the ball and a split second later it rolled agonisingly wide with the goal gaping. Briefly the captain held his head in his hands before returning to rally his troops. Another long-range effort from Lorimer was kept out by Leao as the final whistle left the Scottish players bitterly disappointed from a game they ought to have won. Willie Morgan: "We had a couple of chances and didn't take them, but we could have won the match. We played to win the game; we never played for a draw, ever."

Stuart Borrowman watched Bremner's effort go the wrong side of the post from behind the goal. "I was at that end and couldn't believe it at the time. With hindsight if that had gone in we would probably have beaten them and qualified. Brazil are the greatest football nation on the planet but we should have beaten them that day."

"Against Brazil in all honesty I thought we were the better side," says supporter Robbie Jenkins. "You say that to people now and they think it's a wind-up because people think of Brazil 1970 and their brilliant players but in 1974 Brazil were not great."

Ormond told the press that he felt luck had not been with his team whilst Bremner, acknowledging the difficulty of the task ahead, insisted Scotland could defeat Yugoslavia to reach the second round. "It will be very, very difficult," he told Jim Blair, "but I am confident we can win. We will never be beaten until the last whistle."

"Billy was a winner," is John Blackley's lasting memory of the captain. "He was just an out and out winner and he would go about geeing us up and getting players going. He was a good motivator in the dressing room for that particular group of players. He would certainly put his shift in before the game and at half-time making sure that we were in the right frame of mind. There was always a wee edge to the training with Billy and he put his lot in throughout. He controlled the midfield and was a good reader of the game and a real good captain."

Following Yugoslavia's 9-0 demolition of Zaire nothing less than a win would guarantee Scotland's progression with a draw enough for the Slavs. A point would only be acceptable for the Scots in the unlikely event that Brazil failed to put three past a Zaire side who would clearly be demoralised.

On the Thursday, midway between Scotland's last two group matches, there was a surprise visitor to the Scots' Erbismule base. Former England manager Sir Alf Ramsey was part of ITV Sports' World Cup team and he was interviewed alongside Willie Ormond about their views on the Yugoslavians. Other visitors included Rod Stewart and some lucky supporters who were part of a package deal organised by Cross Travel.

"Billy Connolly and Bill Martin the songwriter were about the hotel all the time and they were brilliant. They played skittles and had a drink with us," John Blackley says of the happy times in Erbismule. Martin, incidentally, had composed the squads' 'Easy! Easy' single.

"Even though I was a wee bit of a bit-part player, going to that squad was like going to meet your mates," says Blackley. "It was great, honestly. I knew I might be sitting up in the stand or on the bench but the standard of training was good, the banter was good and honestly it was a great squad to be about.

"They were all great characters and they all had something for that particular group. We used to split up. You'd get Bremner, Morgan, Law and Donald Ford, there would be about seven or eight of them and then there would be what we used to call the young group. There'd be Dalglish, McGrain, myself and Hutchison. Honestly, I used to love getting picked for the squad just to go down and enjoy the training and enjoy the banter."

Willie Morgan is in agreement. "The nice thing about the squad was that everyone got on together with no cliques. All you did was go training and come back, a couple of bottles of wine and then played cards as we did most of the time. The fact that all the players got on so well together made it easy. It was a nice time. The facilities were great, nothing but good. There was no sense of boredom at all and we played cards and skittles."

The manager was able to list the same 11 who had performed so well against Brazil to face Yugoslavia. This was in fact the first occasion Ormond had fielded the same team in consecutive matches although a settled side was not always his priority, as he tended to select the best players for a particular game.

Intensifying the pressure Ormond was under were the dozens of reporters who surrounded him, of various nationalities and with microphones and recording devices thrust close to his face during press briefings. "We know the job that faces us," he told the cosmopolitan audience on the eve of Scotland's date with destiny. "We go into the job as underdogs just as we did against England and Brazil. The first goal will be vital and I would think that whoever scores first will win this match."

Scotland could take heart from their recent victories under Ormond against Czechoslovakia and England plus the draws against Brazil and West Germany which had been moral victories. Amid the inconsistencies against lesser sides these performances had proved that Scotland were capable of rising to the occasion and it was hoped for the same application in Frankfurt. History also favoured the Scots who had not lost to the Yugoslavs in four meetings.

Although the Scottish support had increased with each match, Scots fans were, as expected, heavily outnumbered by Yugoslavs working in the Frankfurt area. Some of the Scots fans who had been in Germany for a week were sleeping rough and down to their last few Deutschmarks.

The German polizei were on standby for possible trouble between the rival fans and there were a number of isolated incidents. Dumbarton fan Andy McArthur, aged 16, was staying in the tourist town of Rüdesheim am Rhein some 30 miles from Frankfurt. "Myself, 'Be My' (on account of his surname being Valentine) – a Hearts fan from Edinburgh – and a Hibs fan by the name of Steve, were strolling in liquid form along the river front. Some banter was shared with a couple of passing Yugoslavs who responded to the banter with battery – they were soberer, bigger and demonstrably more violent than us, which resulted in a doing being meted out that left me with the pointer finger of my left hand pointing at 90 per cent in the direction it shouldn't have."

When the story was retold one of their party had retribution in mind. "Davie from Clydebank wore a pair of black Dr Martens, rolled-up denims and braces over his Scotland top. He looked just like a tough youth who had learned the hard way in a detention centre – which was exactly the case. I became the lead scout, sent into bars to look for our prey."

The culprits were located in a downstairs bar and invited outside to continue the matter. As Andy started to ascend the stairs he heard the sound of breaking glass and a commotion as Davie took matters into his own hands and shouted for Andy to get out before climbing the stairs himself.

"In the early hours I was encouraged by Be My to visit the A&E at the St Joseph's Krankenhaus where they fitted a stookie from elbow to fingertips. The stookie certainly impaired my applause at the game in Frankfurt, but I know I would have got a much better view of the proceedings than the Slavs if indeed they made it. If so, I'm sure at least one would have been wearing an eye patch and possibly a parrot."

Today Andy has a constant reminder of his trip to West Germany. "The finger remains, thick in the middle and still slightly bent to the right – a memory of a great experience at the World Cup that I didn't really need a bust finger to remember it by! I should probably have got an operation on my return, but I headed directly off to BB camp in Torquay."

Stuart Borrowman recollects the mood in Frankfurt. "Scottish football fans in those days sometimes regarded foreigners as being inferior and that was certainly the impression with the Slavs. There was this feeling of 'who the hell are these people to be challenging us?' They were different to us and there was that kind of animosity but I don't remember any physical confrontations."

"There was definitely tension between both lots of supporters," says Robbie Jenkins. "There was a lot of Scots guys that wanted it as there was a few Yugoslavians but I don't think there was any major stuff. I had a couple of beers with some of them and they were alright."

Playing in the all-white strip worn in Norway, Jordan kicked the first ball of the most vital match Scotland had ever taken part in amid a cacophony of noise in the searing afternoon heat of 22 June.

Again the contest was physical with both Bremner and Lorimer sent crashing to the ground in the opening stages. The Slavs appeared largely content to defend but looked dangerous when they ventured forward.

Jordan forced a save from Marić before a fine move involving Jardine (pronounced as "Jardeen" by English commentators) and Morgan found Hay, whose cross was completely missed by the keeper who watched the ball bounce behind.

The news at half-time was that, as expected, Brazil were leading Zaire – but only by one goal.

Jardine was playing the game of his life and tried his luck with a low drive which Marić held as the sun beat down and the Scots, Slavs and Germans present roared and sang their appreciation.

Hutchison was introduced for Dalglish whilst Karasi replaced Bajević for the Yugoslavs as the players began to tire with time running out for Scotland to find that vital goal. There were under ten minutes left when Džajić beat McGrain just inside the box and crossed for Karasi who scored with a spectacular diving header.

Ormond sought desperately for a way to retrieve the situation and decided to introduce Johnstone for Buchan with five minutes left. On what had already proved to be a frustrating afternoon his attempts to attract the referee's attention were unsuccessful. The linesman also sought acknowledgement from the Mexican official who was too caught up in the play to notice Jinky striding restlessly on the touchline. As the minutes ticked by Ormond gave up and the player returned to the bench.

The outnumbered Scottish supporters still waved their flags. "We will never be beaten until the last whistle," Bremner had said and those words found justification when his side found extra legs and launched another attack. Hutchison skipped past a defender and reached the byline before sending a low cross into the six-yard box. Lorimer looked to be in a good position but sliced at the ball which then broke to Jordan. The striker, with perhaps a split second more to think, kept his head and with determination etched on his face, controlled the ball before thumping it low and hard just inside the post. "Brave, brave Scotland!" uttered a clearly emotional Arthur Montford during his STV commentary.

Jordan punched the air then celebrated briefly with Jardine and Bremner before rushing to retrieve the ball and, along with his team-mates, somehow summoned up the extra energy to rush to the halfway line.

Scotland poured forward again with seconds left and Jardine found Morgan on the right wing who was about to cross when the final whistle sounded.

"The heat wasn't an excuse, we all loved playing in the sunshine, believe me!" says Willie Morgan. "We did our best but ..." His voice tails off as he reflects on that fateful afternoon.

After an agonising few minutes the players were shattered to learn that Brazil had beaten Zaire by the minimum requirement of three goals, meaning Scotland had exited the tournament on goal difference.

Tears were shed amongst fans and players alike and even hardened journalists could not suppress their disappointment. But it was a disappointment etched with pride and a sense of injustice that Scotland, having played so well, were unbeaten in the tournament but would be home in a couple of days whilst the World Cup continued.

When the players eventually made their way on to their coach for the last almost silent trip back to Erbismule hundreds of supporters who had been waiting burst into song with "We're on our way to Argentina, We Shall Not Be Moved."

Back in their complex Jardine told Ian Archer: "It was like running through a furnace out there. I couldn't catch my breath. When that goal of theirs went in I was done. I've never felt so bad in my life." Davie Hay told Jim Blair, "One break in the three matches would have made all the difference. I'm convinced had we beaten Yugoslavia we would have been capable of winning the World Cup."

No one dared to speak about what many were thinking – that just one more goal in the opening match against the Africans would have been massive.

"The saddest thing of all for the team and the World Cup is that we are a better side than Brazil and Yugoslavia," wrote Doug Baillie for the *Sunday Post*.

Supporters on the Cross Travel package had the option to extend their stay with match tickets available through to the final itself. Tommy Collin had kept his options open but only had home on his mind after the disappointment of Scotland's exit. "Me and my pal Ronnie flew with Cross Travel," he recalls. "I took a blank cheque in case Scotland got through. But after the Yugoslavia match, the disappointment was so intense that we decided to go home. Later on we realised that it was the wrong decision. Eight years later in Spain I stayed all the way through to the final and it was an amazing experience!"

Stuart Borrowman shared Tommy's grief. "I was absolutely, massively disappointed and thought we had been a complete failure. It was only when I got home I realised that people watching the World Cup thought Scotland had done wonderfully well and were a great source of pride to the nation. In Frankfurt after the Yugoslavia game that was not the impression, you felt Scotland had lost when we should have won.

"We were gutted and thought we had blown it through missed chances. We had bought tickets for the next round on the assumption that Scotland might have finished second and there was disappointment we were going to watch Brazil when it should have been Scotland that was there."

Archie Macpherson can still recall "the sense of anti-climax and disappointment". He adds: "At that stage we didn't appreciate the achievement of actually getting to the World Cup. It was obviously a disappointment not going on as other nations did to the final stages. The fact that we were unbeaten ... I suppose that took away a certain amount of the disappointment."

The players, although shattered, were determined to enjoy their last night in Erbismule as Willie Morgan relates: "In the hotel complex after the match Rod Stewart, Billy Connolly and Lonnie Donegan came back with us and we celebrated as you do. It was a great campaign and we were unlucky. We had the hotel to ourselves and had a good night. I think we all went to bed between two and five o'clock. Billy and Rod slept on my floor because they couldn't get a room with the tight security. I gave them a blanket and a pillow and they slept on the floor together between the twin beds. As sad as it was it was still a great campaign."

"It was a nice night in many ways," says John Blackley, his voice mixed with both nostalgia and disappointment. "It must have been a real sad time for a lot of them, too, because they could have been playing in the next round. That was one thing about that squad: they always knew how to celebrate. We were allowed a drink or two and Willie Ormond did enjoy a drink."

"We called Willie the Pink Gin Kid," laughs Willie Morgan. "It was a different era then. The players played hard and partied hard. It went with the territory."

A campsite had been set up for Scottish supporters close to the University Clinic in Frankfurt. Stuart Borrowman was one of the campers and he remembers being woken early on the Sunday by some uninvited visitors.

"The morning after the Yugoslavia game a carload of Slavs came in early, tooting their horns and showing off that they had put us out. What they didn't realise was that they couldn't get out the other end so by the time they had turned round some people were out and had stopped them. To my memory there was nothing physical – nobody fired a blow or anything like that but it became a stand-off. The Scottish guys were demanding to speak to the British Consul before they would let them go.

"An official from the Consul came – we got the third secretary or someone who was deemed not to be senior enough. We wanted somebody more senior, anxious to make as much of the situation as we could before they were allowed to leave but to the best of my memory nobody got hurt."

The *Sunday Mail* encouraged fans to greet the team when they landed in Glasgow, giving the precise arrival time as 12.55 on the Monday afternoon. This was picked up on by some of the dailies and, depending on which newspaper you read, between 6,000 and 10,000 supporters cheered as the players crossed the tarmac 24 days after they had left for Belgium. The scenes at the airport were more in keeping with the arrival of pop stars than footballers.

The players themselves had anticipated nothing more than perhaps a few family members to greet them as John Blackley recalls. "We were just expecting to pick up our cases and jump on a bus and go into the centre of town. I could not believe the crowd that came out on that day; I don't think any of us could."

As the fans sang and cheered, Willie Ormond was seen to wipe a tear from his eye. Once again he was surrounded by reporters armed with notepads and a microphone was thrust in his face. In an interview broadcast on STV the manager was visibly emotional as he struggled to speak.

"We did something in Germany that other teams didn't do: we went forward and we played football," he said, regaining his composure. "I think we showed we are one of the best teams in the world. We are a world-class team now. I'll tell you something now and I can say this from the heart – these people back in Germany, they are very happy that we are out."

As the sound of "Bonnie Scotland We'll Support You Ever More" rang out the players boarded a single-decker coach. A few of them stood on seats to wave from the open skylights whilst others had climbed out on to the roof of the bus as they left the airport terminal.

Hundreds more fans lined the route to the North British Hotel, next to George Square where a large crowd had gathered.

"I don't think any of us believed the amount of people at the airport and on the journey home into Glasgow," says John Blackley who will always cherish those memories. "It was phenomenal. We had a wee reception at the hotel then my wife took me home."

There has always been a question mark over Jimmy Johnstone's non-appearance at the tournament and speculation that the manager had been pressured by the SFA to keep him on the sidelines following his misbehaviour in Largs and Oslo. The fact that Ormond attempted to introduce him in the final game suggests otherwise.

In a 2017 interview with the *Scotsman* Tommy Hutchison revealed that Ormond also planned to send Jinky into the latter stages of the match with Brazil. "But the game was going at 100 miles an hour and there only being a couple of minutes left so he said to Willie: 'Nah, you're okay.'"

"I still think Jimmy Johnstone should have played against Brazil," John Blackley reflects. "It was such a bad Brazil team and they tried to kick us off the park. Jimmy would have got us free kicks in areas and possibly a penalty because he had such ability."

Johnstone was not alone in missing all three matches, with Cormack, Donachie and Ford amongst eight of the 22-man squad who did not take part.

Debate continues over the margin of victory against Zaire and the fact that Scotland's rivals had the advantage of playing the Africans knowing Ormond's men had only scored twice against them. Given the nervousness prevalent amongst the players ahead of their first appearance at the World Cup it is worth considering how they would have coped if facing tougher opposition in the opener. It is conceivable that the experienced Yugoslavs or Brazilians may have profited from Scottish nerves so it could very well be argued that the unrated Zaire were ideal as first opponents.

Whilst most observers point to the lack of goals in the first match and failure to win the final game, John Blackley pinpoints the middle fixture as decisive. "Everybody says we should have beaten Zaire by more and I agree with that, but I'll tell you what – I always say that Zaire were never a 9-0 team and I still think there's been a conspiracy with the Yugoslav coach of Zaire. I honestly thought Zaire were not a bad side.

"I think most of the lads in that squad would think with huge disappointment they just failed especially when you look at the Brazil game because I think they came off that park knowing they should have beaten them. It was the second game and on that particular day we should have beaten Brazil. Wee Billy missed that chance and it was just one of those days how the whole thing turned out. Yugoslavia were a right good side but Brazil were there to be beaten and that's the one where we should've got the two points."

After the host nation triumphed in the tournament's final on 7 July analysis of the results confirmed that only one team had remained unbeaten throughout the tournament – Scotland. It is worth pointing out that a number of other nations – East Germany, Yugoslavia, Brazil, Holland, Sweden and Poland – also survived the first round unbeaten, and all reached the second phase. So it is possible to read too much into the unbeaten factor as those other sides only lost after competing in a further three games. Scotland won one match from three but the standard of the opposition they faced should not be dismissed in any assessment of their performance at the 1974 World Cup.

Would Scotland have fared any better had Tommy Docherty still been in charge? Although nothing is certain, qualification against the Czechs would have been likely under Docherty given the team spirit he had built up and his impressive record. That said it was Ormond who discovered Hutchison and brought Jordan into the side and his decision to introduce the latter against the Czechs at a crucial stage in the match resulted in the winning goal.

It would be wrong to ignore Manchester United's relegation from Division One in 1973/74 under Docherty and there is the possibility that the good form with Scotland may not have continued. Had the Doc remained in charge of Scotland on a part-time basis his split duties would have probably been blamed for United's decline.

"He took over an ailing club anyway; we were struggling before he came," says Willie Morgan. "I don't put relegation down to him. Some of the buys he made at the time weren't the best and we went down but came straight back up. And he made some great buys and got the team playing again."

It is certain that Docherty would have imposed stricter discipline on the players during the World Cup trip and might well have stressed the importance of a greater winning margin against Zaire.

He may also have succeeded in countering the players' nerves ahead of the opening game but ultimately it all came down to the last match and it is difficult to see what any other manager could have achieved from the players that fateful afternoon against Yugoslavia.

In 1978 Docherty launched a libel action against Willie Morgan over comments the player had made on Granada television about their time at Old Trafford. It ended up in the Old Bailey with the Doc's defence dropping the case during the third day of the trial. Willie was awarded costs and the two have never crossed paths in the intervening 40 years.

To his credit Willie does not let the incident cloud his judgement of the Doc's time in charge of Scotland. "I truly believe that, despite my differences afterwards with Tommy Docherty, if he had stayed on as the manager of Scotland we could have won the World Cup that year. I honestly believe if he had stayed on he would have gone on to become the greatest Scottish manager ever. As the manager of a club you were with him every day and he was just completely different."

Once the disappointment had passed there were valid grounds for optimism and a belief that the team could go on to achieve something special if the players and manager were kept together. The manager, both trainers and each player later received a bonus of £500 from the SFA for competing at the World Cup.

The qualifying draw for the 1976 European Championships had been made in mid-January of 1974 and was given little prominence, coming just 11 days after the World Cup draw. Spain, Romania and Denmark were the nations Scotland would compete against in Group 4 with only the highest-placed side qualifying.

On Monday 21 October Willie Ormond announced his first post-World Cup selection for a friendly against East Germany at Hampden ahead of the opening European qualifier with Spain the following month. Bremner and Hay were both unavailable due to injury and Denis Law had retired from the game at the end of August.

Those three aside, Ormond listed each of the men who had played during the World Cup and, had they been available, at least two of those omitted would certainly have been included. Schaedler, Ford, Donachie and Allan, who had not played in Germany, were absent. In their places came Kenny Burns, Derek Johnstone, Alex Forsyth and 21-year-old Middlesbrough midfielder Graeme Souness.

One break from tradition was the relocation of the squad's base eight miles south from Largs to Seamill, which was said to be more spacious. The change was never acknowledged as a consequence of the rowing-boat incident during the Home Internationals. "It may well have been a factor," considers Rodger Baillie. "The Queens was perfectly adequate although I'm not sure if there was any en suite. They did more or less have to queue up to take a bath and some of them didn't like that. It seems to have been too much of a coincidence, really."

After Lorimer withdrew, Celtic striker Dixie Deans was called in following his hat-trick in the League Cup Final against Hibs on the Saturday. Watched by Ormond, Deans had also hit three against the same side seven days earlier in a league fixture.

"I was hoping for that call but I wasn't expecting it," Deans told Ian Archer for *The Herald*. "I've been playing well and hoped that it would be enough ... I'm delighted." The journalist also spoke with the newly appointed captain Jardine who revealed: "I admit it took me about three weeks to get over the disappointment of that World Cup. It was all so hopelessly emotional."

As many of the players had not seen each other in the four months since Germany the gathering was in some respects a reunion and the same team spirit was soon rekindled.

The SFA was more than a little concerned at the East Germans' plan to fly into Glasgow on the day of the match, as any delays would put the game in jeopardy. Communications were twice sent urging the German party to arrive a day earlier and an entry for the minutes of the committee meeting of 11 October reads: "Despite repeated appeals the German Democratic Republic refused to alter their travel arrangements." A sum of £250 had been advanced to the Germans to cover "out of pocket expenses". This sum was recoverable when a return match was played at a date suitable to both associations.

Given the huge interest generated in the summer the attendance of 39,445 can be considered disappointing but can be partly explained by the SFA's insistence that the match be made all-ticket with no sales permitted on the evening. The crowd figure was consistent with a midweek Home International, suggesting that the hard core of the Scottish support was around 40,000 at that time.

When several hundred ticketless fans turned up the police allowed some turnstiles to accept cash, contrary to the pre-match agreement. A loudspeaker announcement ten minutes after the start advised that a cash gate would be open behind the North Stand for those who had not already left the area.

There was almost a sensational start. Although the East Germans had kicked off they lost possession when Forsyth intercepted and headed a long ball forward which Deans ran on to only to be floored inside the box by Kische with a mere ten seconds on the clock. "It looks like a penalty!" claimed Archie Macpherson commentating for BBC Scotland's *Sportsreel*. Jack Taylor, alas, did not agree although he had shown no hesitation in pointing to the spot in the opening minute of the biggest game of all, the World Cup Final.

The Germans made their intentions known after 15 minutes when, after a late tackle, the previously thought invincible Holton had to be stretchered from the field.

Debutant Souness looked at home from the start and played a fine ball through to Dalglish who was felled by Kreische, and this time Taylor gave the penalty. Following his success against the Welsh Jardine took the kick. He hit it straight in the centre of the goal and Croy, who had started to go to his left, stopped the ball with his legs.

Dalglish then fed Jordan, who was pushed in the box for Scotland's second penalty of the evening. As captain, Jardine could have taken the kick but allowed Hutchison, who had been second in the penalty trial, the opportunity. It was a decision which would have dire consequences the following month but Hutchison scored easily by placing the ball to the keeper's right as Croy again went left.

A couple of minutes later Jardine tapped a free kick to Johnstone who sent it into the six-yard box where Jordan was sent flying as he rose to connect. Just as it looked like a third penalty would be given the ball broke to Burns who scored on his debut.

Eleven minutes into the second half Jordan unleashed a spectacular left-foot shot on the turn from 25 yards which cracked off a post before rebounding into play. The striker was static for a few seconds trying to comprehend just how the ball had stayed out.

The icing on the cake came when Deans squared for Dalglish to score with a low shot from almost the same piece of turf on which Jordan had cursed his luck.

The football writers could not heap enough praise on the team after the 3-0 win and considered there were no failures as the summer form continued. "This was as solid a Scotland performance as any, a million light years away from those stuttering and nervous occasions which have been the curse of our game for most of our history," wrote Ian Archer. "The Scots humiliated the East Germans," gushed Hugh Taylor, adding, "The score could have been doubled. It was roses all the way with Scotland hammering into attack from start to finish."

And things would get even better ... briefly.

The SFA admitted they had made an error with the all-ticket decision and reconsidered the policy for the Spain game. Ultimately there was no change, with tickets again required as demand increased following the East German result. Hay and Holton were still injured when the pool was named but Bremner was back as captain. The Spaniards, too, had problems with six of their regular side unavailable.

A suggestion by the Scottish Women's FA to host a ladies' game as pre-match entertainment was "declined with thanks" by the SFA. Four years earlier a letter from UEFA had been considered by a meeting of the Executive and General Purposes Committee. They had enquired as to the SFA's attitude towards women's football and the Women's Football Association, which sought recognition in Scotland. "The Committee were unanimous in their refusal," reads the entry in the minutes of that meeting.

The SFA was vindicated when it was announced that only a few of the 100,000 tickets remained unsold compared to the 60,000 they had to dispose of after the East Germany match.

Ormond acknowledged that the Spaniards would prove harder to break down than the Germans, but there was a confidence amongst both the players and supporters which at times surpassed that witnessed during Docherty's days, and a belief that this Scotland side were capable of achieving success.

Freezing fog threatened a postponement with many Glaswegians struggling through a thick blanket to reach work. Fog was still forecast for late afternoon so there remained a question mark over the game as the players waited anxiously at Seamill. "It would be a tragedy if the game had to go off now because we are ready for action," an eager Bremner told the *Evening Times*.

The conditions cleared enough to allow fans to view the frosty pitch and the match went ahead with over 92,000 inside Hampden Park in freezing temperatures.

Those fans were warmed after 11 minutes as Bremner celebrated his return with only his third international goal. It began with a Johnstone corner which Deans headed goalwards. Iribar in the Spanish goal let it spin from his arms and Bremner reacted in an instant to prod the ball into the net. He had scored from a similar position to the missed opportunity in the Brazil game.

"Oh why are we so good?" was the song from the huge crowd and they soon roared again as Migueli handled a Deans cross and the Austrian referee signalled a penalty kick.

If you were to pinpoint a moment in time of supreme optimism amongst the Scottish support it would be at that particular point. Following a good showing in the World Cup and the performance against the East Germans the prospect of establishing a two-goal lead over Spain was enough to warm any Scotland fan on that cold November evening. Little over an hour later it had all gone horribly wrong and a cloud of doom and gloom replaced the fog over Glasgow's south side.

After the failures of Morgan (twice), Bremner and Jardine from the spot the responsibility rested with Hutchison who had netted so confidently from 12 yards against the East Germans.

As in the previous match he hit it to the goalkeeper's right but looked on as Iribar blocked the shot and instantly silenced the cheers of the expectant crowd. The ball lay unattended for a split second as the participants, Hutchison in particular, remained static before the goalkeeper smothered it as Jardine closed in.

Nervousness then crept into the Scots' play and the Spaniards equalised nine minutes before the interval when Martinez headed on for the unmarked Quini whose shot was helped over the line by Harvey. Worse was to follow after an hour's play when a promising Scottish attack was intercepted and, with McQueen and Burns caught napping, Quini again found himself all on his own and beat Harvey.

Lorimer and Dalglish were introduced for Hutchison and Deans but a Burns header that rolled along the top of the crossbar was as close as Scotland came to salvaging a point. Before full time gaps were visible on the terraces with some older spectators recalling a defeat to Poland nine years earlier when a winning position had been surrendered in a 2-1 defeat that had all but ended qualification hopes for the 1966 World Cup.

"The penalty would have finished the Spaniards. Perhaps we committed ourselves too much to attack and now we have to beat them in the return game. Indeed we will have to win all our matches now to qualify," a disappointed manager told *The Herald*'s Jim Reynolds, who also extracted Hutchison's thoughts. "I scored from the spot against East Germany and I decided to take the kick the same way. My big regret, however, was not following up the rebound. If I had gone for it I could have scored."

The SFA Annual Report later lamented the miss from 12 yards with the following entry: "It appeared in the early stages that we had the ability and the spirit to win. A missed penalty kick wrecked the team's composure and the will to win."

Scotland had now missed five times from their last seven penalties, with Hutchison's the most crucial of all. Having already beaten the Danes, Spain were in a strong position to qualify, with their next fixture the return game against Scotland.

The final international of the year was the Under-23 match with England in Aberdeen. The fixture, which had so often been cursed by bad weather and cup replays in its February-to-March slot, took place earlier in the season on 18 December. Both managers faced selection problems with the England squad altered so much that a loose page detailing a revised pool was inserted into copies of the match programme. Sir Alf's successor Don Revie took advantage of the UEFA rule which allowed the inclusion of two players above the age of 23, Denis Tueart who was 25 and 27-year-old Phil Boyer. Ormond, however, refused to exploit the loophole insisting that an Under-23 team should be just that.

The year was to end in further Scottish disappointment as Revie's makeshift squad recorded a deserved 3-0 win with the overage players responsible for much of the damage. Unmarked, Tueart thumped a Boyer cross into the roof of the net after 33 minutes, a goal from which the Scots failed to recover.

Minutes after the break Tueart scored again after Jim Stewart had fumbled a lob from Mike Lyons on to his crossbar from where it landed kindly for the striker. Jim Brown immediately replaced Stewart although as James Sanderson reported for the *Daily Mirror*, "This made no difference at all as the Scots had collapsed completely. The final indignity came with three minutes to go when full-back Steve Whitworth came down on the overlap and walloped a very good shot past Brown." Sanderson also noted that "the 14,141 frozen fans were sporting enough to give England an ovation despite showing anger and disappointment at the flop of the Scottish team."

Reflecting on a year that had promised so much, Ian Archer shared his assessment with readers of the *Glasgow Herald*: "This year had been a bad and a good year, but 1974 will be remembered more in sorrow as the calendar closes. The defeat by Spain has rubbed all the gloss from the week of World Cup delirium. We have moved neither forward nor backwards, only two steps sideways."

1975

*"It now seems that only a miracle result
in Bucharest will save Ormond."*
Alex Cameron, Daily Record

A result in the return match with Spain in February was vital to Scotland's European Championship prospects. Defeat would see the Spaniards stretch their lead in the group to six points and all but end Scotland's qualification hopes after two games.

There were some surprises in the 18-name Scotland squad with Charlie Cooke recalled after four years in the wilderness and Bobby Clark, who had last played in the St Valentine's Day Massacre two years earlier, also returning. Cooke had impressed the manager whilst he had been checking Davie Hay's fitness during the Chelsea vs Leeds game on 18 January.

It was feared Scotland could be without their Leeds contingent when a postponed FA Cup replay with Wimbledon looked likely to be played in that same first week of February. A telephone call from Willie Allan to his newly appointed counterpart in the south, Ted Croker, resulted in a hastily arranged meeting of the FA Cup Committee.

A decision was taken to postpone the replay until the following week with Croker quoted in the *Glasgow Herald* saying: "We decided to do everything possible to help Scotland. We had to bend our own rules which say that rescheduled ties should be played as soon as possible." A grateful Willie Allan told the newspaper: "We are delighted and indebted not only to the FA but also to Leeds United and Wimbledon."

Davie Hay's comeback was short-lived as he suffered from a thigh knock against Leicester but was the only withdrawal from the squad who flew from Glasgow to Valencia on Monday 3 February.

Jordan, who the Spanish were said to fear, started up front alongside Burns, with Cooke also in the line-up. "Had anyone suggested this to me a month ago I would have laughed in their faces," the delighted 32-year-old told the *Evening Times*'s Jim Blair.

The match took place in a hostile atmosphere with 40,000 Spaniards enraged when the Scottish players broke away to practise before the Spanish anthem had ended. Seeking to retrieve the points squandered at Hampden, Scotland took a sensational lead within two minutes. A Burns shot came down from the underside of the crossbar where Jordan reacted quickly to force the ball over the line. Television viewers were treated to the surreal image of the players celebrating wildly in front of a silent crowd.

Remembering Hutchison's penalty miss, the Scots continued to press for a second goal with the home side clearly shaken. McQueen headed over then Dalglish miskicked in front of goal – all within the first ten minutes. Spain only threatened occasionally but equalised in controversial circumstances midway through the second period.

A cross from the left was headed goalwards by Megido whose effort was saved but not held by Harvey. As a cluster of bodies fought for the loose ball the Belgian referee signalled for a penalty, judging correctly that Buchan had punched the ball. The linesman then motioned towards the centre circle, indicating that the ball had already crossed the line before connecting with Buchan's hand. The Spanish players surrounded the referee and harassed him all the way to the touchline where, after consulting the linesman, a goal was awarded. It was difficult to understand how the linesman, who was some 30 yards from the incident, could be so certain although there was no doubt that Buchan had handled.

Scotland continued to press but failed to find a winner. The point gained in Valencia would normally be considered an excellent result but the loss of three points to the Spaniards meant that they already looked likely to win the section.

There were shades of Frankfurt when a couple of hundred travelling fans cheered the players as they boarded their coach outside the Luis Casanova Stadium and the Scottish press were unanimous in their praise for the players' efforts.

"A mystery goal in a moment of chaos robbed Scotland of a victory. Scotland had played with all their World Cup poise and authority until that unlucky break," wrote Hugh Taylor for readers of Thursday's *Daily Record*. "You can't fault Scotland for lack of courage," he continued. "Let's be proud of a team who fought against all the odds, dreadful refereeing and vicious fouling which went unpunished."

The *Record* also recorded Ormond's thoughts: "The referee must have crawled out of the home dressing room. I don't often criticise referees but Delcourt was a real homer. The ball was at least two feet off the line and even when we scored the referee was looking around to see if he could give another decision."

Jim Blair's *Evening Times* piece adopted a similar tone: "This was as good a performance as I've seen from Scotland since Willie Ormond took over as Scotland manager 21 games ago."

Blair had managed to catch a few words with the officials who defended their decision to allow the goal. Alfred Delcourt told him: "I saw a Scotland player clearly arm the ball. Naturally my first reaction was to blow for a penalty. There were many players in the penalty area and I honestly could not see whether the ball was on the line or over it." His linesman Francis Rion was of the view that Delcourt had blown his whistle to indicate a goal. "I was in line with play and when I heard the whistle I immediately pointed to the middle of the park because the ball was definitely over the line by at least half a metre."

At the 17 February meeting of the International and Selection Committee the team manager was asked to explain his criticism of the referee. Willie Ormond then found himself censured for the comments from which the committee wished to disassociate itself. At the same meeting the manager's request for an assistant was sanctioned on the understanding that it would not be a full-time appointment.

There was a change in policy for the following week's Under-23 international in Wales. Ormond had been unhappy with Don Revie's inclusion of overage players at Pittodrie but this time he chose to take advantage of the ruling and included Tommy Craig and Rangers goalkeeper Stewart Kennedy in the pool. Partick Thistle manager Bertie Auld criticised Ormond for failing to watch his players, suggesting that he did not know the location of Firhill. It was rumoured that Thistle had made an official complaint to the SFA over what they considered a snub of their club by the national manager.

The game at Swansea did not go well with the Welsh recording only their second victory in the series. Kennedy was considered Scotland's best player and was credited with limiting the final result to 2-0. "He will assuredly play for Scotland one day, probably soon," Ian Archer confidently predicted.

The goalkeeper had already saved well from Cartwright before Roberts headed a free kick down for Smallman to net just ahead of the half hour. Kennedy saved again when Flynn had looked certain to score as the inexperienced Scots struggled to muster any threat. The other Stuart Kennedy, the Falkirk full-back, intercepted a cross with his elbow on 73 minutes and Leighton James completed the scoring from the penalty spot. There were few positives to be taken from the match and Archer described the performance rather eloquently with: "as flat as last week's beer".

Jock Stein accepted the SFA's invitation to assist the manager for the trip to Sweden in mid-April. With the Under-23s and the senior team both playing friendlies on the same day in Gothenburg, Stein took charge of the youngsters which significantly reduced Ormond's workload. The appointment sparked speculation regarding Ormond's future and whether Stein sought a move from Celtic Park. Stein quickly quashed the rumours and pledged his future to Celtic whilst stressing that he had only agreed to take charge of the Under-23s for one match.

The selection of both squads was still Ormond's prerogative although he was hindered by Leeds' European Cup involvement which ruled out seven players. Bertie Auld was said to be delighted at the inclusion of Hansen and Rough whilst Motherwell striker Willie Pettigrew was a newcomer to the 34 names spread over both pools. Falkirk's Kennedy did a Jim Cruickshank by turning up at the airport without his passport but there was sufficient time for an emergency document to be issued.

With the two venues in close proximity the Under-23 match commenced at 5pm and the full international two and a half hours later. As Ormond looked on, the youngsters got the day off to a good start with a much-improved performance from the game in Wales.

Scotland dominated the opening half but it took 41 minutes before they took the lead courtesy of a free kick from captain Tommy Craig. This from Ken Gallacher's *Daily Record* report: "The Swedes expected a short ball. Instead Craig lobbed it over the wall and it went past the startled keeper and into the net."

A half-time change of goalkeeper saw Rough replaced by Jim Brown, who was beaten within ten minutes when Sjostrom levelled. Seconds later a Jim Pearson header was cleared from the goal line by Werner who still had a further part to play in the match when, ten minutes later, the Danish referee considered he had handled although no one else in the ground seemed to have noticed. Craig regained the lead from the penalty spot and won the match for Scotland.

For the later match in the Ullevi just three players, McGrain, Jardine – the captain – and Dalglish, remained from the game in Valencia in what was a makeshift line-up. Four new caps started including goalkeeper Kennedy and Ted MacDougall, scorer of 22 goals for Norwich that season. A Parlane header looked to have put Scotland ahead but the striker was flagged offside. The opposite linesman aided the home side just as the interval beckoned. Connecting with a pass from Edstrom, Thomas Sjoberg lobbed the ball over Kennedy and into the net but looked a couple of yards offside. Led by Jardine the Scots protested but the goal stood.

A long-range strike from Bobby Robinson hit the crossbar and Scotland were heading for defeat when Dalglish sent over a perfect cross from the right which MacDougall controlled before scoring with a spectacular shot to earn a deserved draw with four minutes left.

Willie Ormond left Sweden early the next morning bound for Madrid and the qualifier between Spain and Romania, hoping for an unlikely result in the visitors' favour.

He left Madrid a happy man after the hosts played out their second consecutive 1-1 draw, meaning they now had six points from four matches when they might have expected to have eight.

Leeds' progression to the European Cup Final in May meant that their players would not be available for the Home Internationals.

This affected three of the competing nations but Ormond's selection suffered most with the loss of several players. Gordon McQueen was available, however, as a sending off during the second leg of the semi-final with Barcelona excluded his participation in the final.

On the first day of May Willie Ormond named a total of 21 players for five matches to be played over 19 days. In addition to the Home Internationals a friendly had been arranged with Portugal at Hampden and the season concluded with the European qualifier in Romania. He stuck by the players who had accompanied him to Gothenburg with the only newcomer being Tottenham midfielder Alfie Conn, once of Rangers. Bruce Rioch, first selected under Docherty three years earlier but who had later withdrawn, was called in after starring in Derby County's championship-winning side.

The Portugal match was promoted as part of a celebration marking the 800th anniversary of the granting of Glasgow's Burgh Charter and was a useful warm-up just four days before the opening Home International. Rioch started, with Jardine retaining the captaincy in Bremner's absence. The early stages of the game were low-key before Scotland took the lead courtesy of an own goal with two minutes of the first half left. McQueen sent a powerful header goalwards which Damas managed to push on to a post. The ball spun out of goal where it struck the heel of the unfortunate full-back Artur and rebounded into the net.

The half-time entertainment saw the Wombles take part in a penalty kick competition. The furry inhabitants of Wimbledon Common were well ahead of their time, promoting the benefits of recycling rubbish to help the environment, and were in town as part of the Glasgow 800 celebrations. That very week the children's favourites featured in the charts with their latest single, "Wombling White Tie and Tails". The recently launched *Scottish Daily News* reported on its front page: "The lovable characters from Wimbledon danced and cavorted with children in the Buchanan Street pedestrian precinct whilst the Radio Clyde lunchtime show was belting out their greatest hits." Following lunch at the City Chambers Princess Anne apparently refused to be rushed to her next engagement until she had heard her favourite song, "Remember You're A Womble".

Unfortunately the Hampden crowd were less appreciative as David Stephen, a spectator at the match recalls. "They were having a kick around," he laughs, "and the crowd treated them with foul-mouthed obscenities including, 'If you hate the fucking Wombles clap your hands!'"

It was hoped that the Wombles were not too emotionally scarred from the experience and that they remembered more the warm welcome the children in Buchanan Street had given them during their visit to Glasgow.

Three minutes after the restart Fraiguito almost equalised but his shot came back from a post before Toni thumped the rebound goalwards for Kennedy to make what was his second and final save that night. Artur almost completed an unenviable double but Damas succeeded in touching Artur's wayward back-pass over the line, although the defender was still credited with the winning goal.

The squad then headed to their Porthcawl base ahead of the opening Championship game in Cardiff. The Scotland manager criticised the Ninian Park surface in conversation with Ian Paul of the *Scottish Daily News,* saying: "The pitch is in such a shocking state that it made me change my plans – particularly as far as one player is concerned. In this condition there are bound to be errors and I think the game will be like a cup tie – fast and furious."

Whatever the conditions the crowd were treated to an enthralling contest with *The Herald*'s Ian Archer going so far as to describe the game as "the most splendid international of recent times – a landslide of a match. This was football of the United Kingdom at its enduring best."

High praise indeed though one suspects a report on the first 45 minutes without the benefit of watching the whole game would have been typed with rather less enthusiasm.

Parlane headed a Macari cross narrowly over inside the opening minute before goals by Toshack and Bryan Flynn put the Welsh in a seemingly invincible position by half-time. The opener came after Kennedy had saved from Flynn. Then Jackson booted the ball off the line before Toshack shot home through a crowd of players. Flynn's goal oozed quality. In a lovely passing movement he played a one-two with Toshack before lashing the ball into Kennedy's bottom right-hand corner. "A masterpiece of a goal!" raved ITV commentator Brian Moore.

Scotland were back in the hunt nine minutes after the restart. Following a free kick which looked to be heading out of play Parlane caught the ball on the byline and his looping cross was met by Jackson who headed the ball beyond Davies. Within eight minutes the score was levelled in spectacular style. Arthur Duncan cut in from the left and passed to MacDougall, who laid the ball off for Rioch to thunder a shot high into goal from just inside the area.

The action was far from over and within a minute Kennedy performed heroics as he dived to fist a Toshack header out then recovered to block as Mahoney pounced on the rebound.

Scotland twice struck the frame of the goal. This from Jack Harkness's *Sunday Post* report: "A magnificent Parlane shot almost broke the crossbar and a full-blooded shot from McQueen had the crossbar twanging like the strings of a banjo. A matter of inches might have had us celebrating a magnificent victory." McQueen's strike had actually hit a post but the margin was still inches, nonetheless.

Reflecting on the draw Ormond told the press: "Those last minutes … I didn't know what to think. One moment the ball was in the Welsh goalmouth, the next in ours, and you didn't know whether you wanted the match to stop or go on forever."

The night before the Northern Ireland match Hampden hosted a game between Scotland's Under-23 side and Leeds United. This was ideal for both teams with the Under-23s playing in Bucharest at the end of the month whilst Leeds were preparing for the European Cup Final nine days later. As the club season had concluded Jock Stein had again agreed to take charge of the Under-23s for their two matches.

There were six Scots in the Leeds team who took an early lead when Lorimer sent one of his trademark volleys beyond Alan Rough. Scotland responded with three goals in a 15-minute spell, firstly through a Craig volley before Conn got the better of three defenders and scored from an angle. Alex Forsyth then curled a 20-yard free kick around Leeds' defensive wall and past Harvey in the 27th minute. Before half-time Lorimer then made it 3-2 with another powerful drive as described by Bob Patience in the *Daily Record*: "Bremner split the Scots defence and Lorimer hit a magnificent shot on the drop past Rough."

The second half was punctuated by numerous substitutions for both sides and there was no further scoring in what was considered a useful exercise. Following another fine performance Tommy Craig was tipped to progress to the full international side before long.

With the attendance announced at just under 10,000 the SFA was criticised for the choice of venue, with a number of readers voicing their disapproval in the *Aberdeen Green Final*'s Sportsbag. Under the pseudonym "Sick of Travelling" – with name and address apparently supplied allowing the writer to receive their £1 postal order prize for publication – one fan ranted: "To play this match at Hampden only 24 hours before the Northern Ireland game was absolutely ludicrous. Time and again the Glasgow football public have not turned up for matches with nothing at stake. In future let's see the under-23s play their home games at Tynecastle, Dens or Pittodrie. Come on SFA – give it a try. You know it makes sense."

Stein's management skills made an impression on Alfie Conn. When the ex-Ranger made a high-profile transfer to Celtic a couple of years later, Conn cited the opportunity to work under Stein as the main factor in his decision to cross the great divide.

A much larger crowd of almost 65,000 left happy after the Northern Ireland match. A Ted MacDougall header from a Duncan corner put Scotland on the road to victory inside the first quarter of an hour, sparking a predictable chorus of "Bring on the English!"

After 20 minutes Dalglish accepted a throw-in from Rioch before beating Jennings from a tight angle for the second goal. Scotland eased off after half-time and Kennedy looked comfortable coping with efforts from O'Neill and Spence as thoughts turned to the road south. With ten minutes left Parlane played a one-two with Dalglish before sealing the 3-0 victory with a low shot for his first and last international goal.

Hugh Taylor told readers of the *Daily Record*: "This was football played with ability and with confidence … Scotland set themselves up for a wonderful Wembley with a devastating display."

Rival reporter Ian Archer was in complete agreement: "This was a Scottish performance as solid as any. The goals are coming and the Home International Championship is there to be won." *The Herald* journalist also observed that: "Scotland's supporters were wearing so much tartan that strangers could have thought they were at a convention for the Bay City Rollers."

Scotland had now lost just one of their last 11 matches and, following England's 2-2 draw with Wales at Wembley, hopes were high for a positive result on the Saturday. So well had the team performed in the two Championship games that no mention had been made of the missing Leeds' contingent. Jardine had proved himself a great captain and he and McGrain had now established themselves as an attacking full-back partnership. Kennedy had deputised well in goal following a good season with Rangers and Rioch and MacDougall looked completely at home in international football. So there was much to be confident about.

Supporters were angered when the National Union of Railwaymen voted in favour of strike action with no underground trains running to Wembley Stadium on matchday. The decision had been taken as many members feared for their personal safety. During Scotland's last visit Joe Wireko, a guard on the underground, had been beaten up so badly after the game that he lost the sight of an eye and had not worked since.

NUR spokesman Bob Kettle defended the action of his members, denying they were discriminating against Scots. "We are protesting against hooliganism in British football in general – and we are not singling the Scots out for special treatment," he read from a statement.

The match did take place in an escalating climate of football violence and a few months later London Underground workers, again concerned for their safety, staged a 24-hour strike around the QPR vs Manchester United fixture which closed half of the Central Line. This went some way to vindicating Kettle's claim that their action at the time of the international was not specifically anti-Scottish.

British Rail then cancelled all trains to Wembley Central on the Saturday, concerned at the increased demand for that service. "Because of the tube strike everyone would want to travel by train and we just couldn't cope," read an official statement. Buses to the stadium were also suspended as London Transport workers expressed solidarity with the underground staff.

A climate of fear was reported with many Londoners apparently going away for the weekend and even taxi drivers said to be considering taking a rare Saturday off, with trouble anticipated. Many of the pubs in London's West End remained closed and shop windows in the Wembley area were boarded up. Some feared that the lack of transport to Wembley would inflame the situation and local MP Doctor Rhodes Boyson, concerned for the safety of his constituents, called for the match to be postponed.

The *Sunday Mail* tracked down Joe Wireko to his home in Harlesden, just a few miles from Wembley Stadium. "Of course I feel bitter," he told the newspaper. "Those hooligans ruined my life." The article revealed that Mr Wireku, a Guyanese, now wore dark glasses and never left his home without the aid of a walking stick. He told how he had been knocked on to the track and confirmed he had been unable to return to work in the intervening two years.

Daily Record journalist John Jackson walked the eight miles from Euston station to Wembley on the Friday and his report listed directions for the trek he had apparently completed in two hours and five minutes.

It has to be said that the Scottish fans, whilst often credited for their fanaticism at this time, were a rougher crowd than the self-policing Tartan Army of later years, who prided themselves on making friends with the locals and a lack of arrests on foreign travels.

Much of the repertoire at all Scotland matches had anti-English overtones and there had been a steady decline in the attendance of England fans at both Hampden and Wembley since the end of the 1960s. One favourite amongst the fans was: "If you hate the fucking English clap your hands", and another, "If you hate the English bastards clap your hands". In context these songs were part of football culture at the time and were adaptations of club songs against rival teams heard on the terraces every week.

There was, to a degree, a lack of respect for the residents of London during the biannual invasions. It is also fair to say there was never a full-scale riot and given the numbers who travelled the potential for mass hooliganism existed. Nevertheless, what might be described as a "we are the people" mentality was prevalent within the Scottish support which converged on the capital during the seventies.

"That's exactly what it was," says Hearts supporter Stuart Borrowman who had been a Wembley regular since 1969. "It's a small country going to the big man's capital hoping to be noticed. There was an immature thing about going to London in the sense that you wanted them to notice you. You would think you were in an inferior place against an inferior team and something of that applied – that we were better than these people."

The mood seemed more sinister in 1975 with the number of obstacles placed in the way of fans heading for Wembley. Perhaps the returning Wombles had shared their experience of the nasty Hampden crowd with the capital's residents.

The first supporter to appear in court, John Jarvie from Edinburgh, stood in the dock of Bow Street Magistrates' Court on the Friday clutching a tartan scarf and hat. He pleaded guilty to being found drunk in the Strand, explaining to the judge: "We always get drunk before and after the game. It's a tradition." Jarvie was fined the sum of £1.50 for his behaviour.

The Aberdeen *Evening Express* quoted 20-year-old John Downie from Ayr, who had arrived by train on the Friday. "There's bound to be vandalism tomorrow. You're obviously going to have trouble after fans have been drinking and are then faced with hours of marching."

There was an increasing shortage of match tickets amongst Scottish fans with many travelling without, and the situation seemed to be even worse in 1975. The *Evening Times* quoted one fan from Airdrie who had travelled in a party of two coachloads. "This year only ten out of 90 of us have tickets. There will be 20,000 Scots in Wembley without tickets."

All of the off-field publicity did nothing to dent the confidence emanating from the Scottish base at Harpenden. In the *Scottish Daily News*, Willie Ormond had a message for the supporters: "I know our fans will reach Wembley one way or another and to reward them we will be putting something extra into our game. I can assure them it will be worth the effort getting there. We have been playing well and I am confident we can win the Championship."

"It is hard to remember," wrote Ian Archer, "when the English journey was undertaken in such good heart." This captures perfectly the mood of optimism with which Scots travelled to Wembley in 1975, confident of their first win there since 1967.

To avoid the walk a number of supporters made their way to Wembley on the Friday and Nich Seade, manager of the London Esso Hotel close to the stadium, told the *Evening Express*: "We have 600 paying Scottish guests and several hundred non-paying guests." He had allowed hundreds of fans to stretch out on the deep-pile carpet in the hotel's banqueting room once the bar had closed. Whilst admitting he had feared trouble, Mr Seade told the newspaper that the unofficial guests had been well behaved.

Stewards inside the stadium had checked all the toilets and bins late on the eve of the game in case anyone had tried to conceal themselves after the Friday evening dog racing.

A total of 27 supporters appeared at Marlborough Street Magistrates' Court on the morning of the match where fines ranging from 50 pence to £10 were handed out for a range of offences including stealing milk, drunkenness and using insulting or threatening language or behaviour.

Most fans did walk to Wembley with hundreds of extra police officers on the route, indicating the way to the stadium. Others paid inflated taxi fares or turned up in various vehicles with enterprising Londoners offering spaces in vans and trucks with cash required in advance.

Fans with local knowledge, such as 15-year-old Stirling Albion supporter David Stephen, who was staying with an aunt in the capital, mapped out alternative paths. David was making his first trip to Wembley and found a route which saved his legs from the long trek. "We caught a tube to Golders Green and then a bus to Wembley. If everyone had known it would have been pandemonium. Although the bus was full there wasn't, like, thousands of people. My first view of Wembley was from the top deck of a red London bus – and it was quite spectacular."

Stevie Newlands from Dumbarton was the guest of an aunt in Bayswater Road, along with two friends. "Our briefs had come from my Aunt Ellen's pal 'Johnny the Fruit' who plied his trade – in fruit and veg – from a barrow outside Lancaster Gate tube station," Stevie fondly remembers. "Johnny was a fine guy, a true Londoner and great England fan. At a time when very few Englishmen ventured north of the border for the Hampden fixture, frightened of the reception they guessed awaited them, Johnny enthused about how he had been received in Glasgow over the years. With Johnny the Fruit's cooperation, getting to Wembley in the face of the tube strike posed no difficulty. He arranged a coach to pick us up outside the Swan pub on the Bayswater Road, and by the time we reached Wembley, the few spare seats, as well as the whole passageway, had been filled with Scotland fans who had probably resigned themselves to walking all the way to Wembley."

There were 7,500 police officers on duty in the vicinity of the stadium, a figure almost twice the number normally required for a Wembley international. One ambitious attempt by an unknown number of ticketless fans to enter the ground was successful until some of those officers stumbled across their plans. Probably inspired by the BBC prisoner-of-war drama *Colditz*, a tunnel had been dug which led under the perimeter fence and inside the ground. A spokesman for the Metropolitan Police told the Edinburgh *Evening News*: "I don't think many got in and even if they did, they would still need to show a ticket before getting into seats or on to the terracing, so it would not have done them much good."

Knowledgeable fans were aware that once the perforated portion had been removed from tickets at the turnstile only a glimpse of the stub was required to pass through the second gate. It was simple enough to enter with a stub, then, on the pretence of a visit to the toilet, return with tickets collected from others already inside to distribute to waiting friends.

Some ticketless fans scaled the 60-foot fences and a BBC News team captured one supporter jumping from a fence before being hauled through a high window by others who just managed to grab his outstretched hands before he fell. Robbie Jenkins was one of those watching from the ground and is visible in the first few seconds of the footage.

He still recalls the incident with some trepidation. "This guy had obviously had a bit of a drink and he jumped and he missed the window and by luck there's this big bruiser of a guy who grabbed his arms about halfway down his arse and managed to pull him up. I remember at the time just being horrified because, just for two seconds, you thought, 'he's dead', because he'd jumped and missed before they grabbed him."

There are countless tales of ticketless fans' efforts to enter Wembley from the period, including swallow dives beneath turnstiles and middle-aged men crashing through stadium roofs exclaiming, "I'm in!" to those gathered round concerned for their safety.

Those fortunate to get their hands on a ticket often kept it concealed on their body, perhaps down a sock with pockets not considered safe enough.

If anything, there were more Scottish fans than ever before inside Wembley, with "Bonnie Scotland We'll Support You Ever More" echoing from the crowd as the teams appeared from the tunnel. "There must be 60,000 or 70,000 Scotsmen in the ground," said BBC commentator David Coleman, who still referred to "Sandy

Jardeen". Other estimates put the number as high as 80,000 with other ticketless fans milling around outside.

The 11 players who had ended the match against Northern Ireland started against England, including Conn who had replaced Robinson late in the Northern Ireland game. Backed by the noisy crowd, a confident Scotland started well and from a MacDougall cross Parlane controlled inside the area before miskicking. The ball broke to Dalglish whose powerful shot was well saved by Clemence although offside had been given.

Channon then won the ball in the middle of the park and found Francis whose shot from 30 yards flew past the static Kennedy and into the net after five minutes. "Kennedy was left looking at space … he never even moved!" Coleman observed.

Stunned, Scotland piled forward and won a free kick in an effort to retrieve the situation. Conn's forward pass was blocked and England broke quickly. Ball fed Keegan, whose cross was headed in by Beattie for 2-0 with just seven minutes on the clock. The image of the beaten Kennedy staring skywards from the Wembley turf is one of the most enduring from the day.

Just eight minutes into the game Stevie Newlands realised that his day was fast unravelling. "Things had been going remarkably smoothly with half a dozen pints in the Swan and timely transport to the game. But they went pear-shaped shortly after. Scotland found themselves two down after seven minutes, and I sank to the terracing, head in hands, trying to shut out everything that had just happened in the last few minutes. Moments later my mourning was disturbed by a warm sensation spreading down my back. Looking over my shoulder, there was my mate Graeme Dick – his namesake in hand and slightly unsteady on his feet – spraying some of the lager he'd taken on in the Swan pub down my back. It was 2-0 down to England with the whistle hardly blown … and I had thought things couldn't get worse!"

There were good claims for a penalty when an Arthur Duncan cross clearly struck the arm of Bell but it was ruled unintentional. In a promising move Dalglish fed Parlane, whose angled shot from eight yards beat the goalkeeper but struck the outside of the post. "So unlucky!" uttered Coleman. Conn and Rioch then both fired wide before England struck again after 40 minutes when Bell collected a Keegan pass some 25 yards out and his speculative shot rippled the net.

Ormond's men were staring at a humiliating defeat when MacDougall played the ball against the arm of Todd and the referee pointed to the spot. Arguably the handball had been less deliberate than the earlier incident involving Bell.

Skipper Rioch kept his cool, stepped forward as if to put the ball to Clemence's right, then hesitated before calmly placing it to his left. The captain did not react and walked away expressionless as the fans sensed a glimmer of hope at the end of the half.

Soon after the restart Francis shot narrowly over. Then it was almost 3-2 as an alert Duncan intercepted a back-pass from Todd. He dragged the ball away from Clemence before shooting towards the empty goal only to see the ball roll into the side of the net. Scotland were refusing to give in but were clearly having no luck when a second goal would have given them a major boost.

Any thoughts of a comeback were extinguished when Francis scored for the second time. A free kick was touched to him but the ref ordered a retake. Exactly the same move saw Francis's strike deflected beyond Kennedy, who for once could not be blamed.

Minutes later Lou Macari was sent into the cauldron in place of Ted MacDougall. "I remember wondering what I was going on for," Lou laughs. "You always wanted to play but by then you realised it was a lost cause. You just want to get as many caps because it wasn't that easy to get them, but I try to forget those games when we got beat by five by England!"

The final nail in Scotland's coffin came from another free kick which saw a Ball header rebound from the crossbar. Dave Watson then slammed the ball against the post when it looked easier to score before David Johnson shot into the net.

It might have been six but a Channon shot was cleared by McGrain, almost from the goal line, before Clemence produced the save of the afternoon. Hutchison, who had replaced Duncan, curled a shot from 25 yards which looked destined for the top corner before the goalkeeper dived to fingertip the ball over.

At the end of the match hundreds of Scottish fans invaded the pitch, scoring imaginary goals and dancing a jig, before squatting around the centre circle. For a time they refused to leave, perhaps re-energising themselves for the long walk back. One was said to have taken the penalty spot Rioch had netted from as a souvenir.

A group of supporters from Eyemouth had hired a coach to take them to and from the stadium and one of them, Tommy Collin, recalls the journey back. He had been travelling to Wembley since the match in 1963 and was aware of a decline in the fans' behaviour. "I do remember fans walking back as our bus moved slowly away from the ground but it was not our finest hour. Fans were peeing in residents' gardens, others sleeping on lawns, urinating and falling into bushes."

Stuart Borrowman had arranged a lift from a pub in Acton which was still a six-mile hike from the ground. Thirsty by the time he arrived, the barmaid innocently enquired of the result. After being informed her next question was received with less tolerance. "But was it a good game, though?" she asked.

Willie Ormond looked completely devastated when interviewed on BBC1's *Grandstand*. "Six times they went up the park and five times England scored," he reflected.

The game had been effectively lost after seven minutes yet Scotland had enjoyed little luck. Although Ormond's claim of five goals from six attacks was not 100 per cent accurate, it was not too wide of the mark. The game might have ended 5-3 or 5-4 and had Duncan's effort found the other side of the net to make it 3-1, who knows? Even Jimmy Hill in the BBC studio considered Scotland had nothing to be ashamed of. The polar argument is that England only required half a dozen or so efforts to secure the result and may have pushed forward more had the score been closer.

The experience and leadership of the absent Bremner may have had an influence on the game but in fairness little excuse was made of the missing Leeds contingent which constituted half a team. This is perhaps an indication of the Scottish talent available at the time.

Although the performance had been nowhere near as bad as in the centenary St Valentine's Day massacre, Willie Ormond had now twice conceded five goals to England, or three times if the Inter League match at Maine Road was taken into account.

The predicted vandalism, fears of which were intensified by the result, did not materialise and MP Doctor Rhodes Boyson, who had feared for the safety of his constituents, was quoted in the *Daily Record* saying: "The international match turned out to be one of the most peaceful ever. If the Scots continue to behave that way there's no reason I should resent them coming back next time."

Mrs Malka Lewin, wife of the chairman of the Wembley Residents' Association, was also impressed, telling the *Record*: "We were given to understand that they would tear the place apart but the Scots were, if anything, quieter than other fans."

A total of 59 fans had been arrested on the Friday night and a further 74 on the day of the match. Commissioner Robert Bryon, in charge of policing at the stadium, told the *Scottish Daily News*: "Considering the size of the crowd everything went very well. Most of the incidents only involved over-enthusiasm."

The pre-match optimism was eclipsed by a mood of depression. Murray Stevenson wrote in the *Scottish Daily News*: "The saddest Wembley sight was the Scotland team bus, curtained like a hearse, winding its way through the masses of shattered fans at the start of the long trek home. Not a cheer was raised nor a word of condemnation spoken. The silent sickness afflicted us all. The sea of tartan had become a slow, sweeping ocean of tears."

Willie Ormond had to motivate his players for the vital match in Bucharest eight days later and morale was not improved when Martin Buchan walked out, upset at not playing at Wembley. In a letter to the SFA, reprinted in the *Scottish Daily News*, he gave his reasons as: "I was told I was wanted for Wembley then I was asked to sit on the bench. I did not refuse to be a substitute but I did not feel it right I could go to Romania without a game under my belt."

In the same journal Ian Paul summed up the mood: "The defeat by England and the rebellion of Martin Buchan have drained a side whose confidence was at a peak when they headed for London."

Much of the focus of the Wembley inquest was on Stewart Kennedy, who told Ian Paul: "I am desperate to play in Romania and If I'm picked and have a good game then I would die happy. It was a day when everything went wrong for me although I've got to defend myself by saying I honestly felt solely at fault for the second goal only." The goalkeeper's reluctance to move as Francis's shot flew past him to open the scoring had been highlighted, but even if he had dived it is unlikely he would have prevented the goal. ·

The Scottish *Daily Express* invited readers' views on Kennedy for their Sports Forum. The response was close with 52 per cent of the respondents backing the goalkeeper. J. Anderson of Leith voted in his favour, writing: "Of course Kennedy should retain his place.

He saved Scotland from defeat in Wales, played exceptionally well against Northern Ireland and has played well for Rangers all season. So why drop him because he has an off day?" O. Robertson from Ayr disagreed: "Kennedy was the complete failure and should not be given another chance. He shattered the confidence of the whole team and England were by no means a great side." Perhaps the most reasoned contribution came from Stirling resident David McCallum: "It was not only Kennedy who was caught cold on Saturday. It was the entire Scottish team, and the media, with the odd exception, who thought that our team had only to turn up to win."

Stuart Kennedy never did represent Scotland again. Ormond fully intended to play him in Bucharest but a twisted ankle, the price of stopping a penalty from Alex Forsyth during a training session, ruled him out. Jim Brown of Sheffield United deputised to earn his one and only full international cap.

Rumours that Under-23 manager Stein would soon be replacing Ormond resurfaced after the Wembley defeat as the SFA party flew from Glasgow on the Wednesday. In a *Daily Record* piece titled "Ormond's Last Chance" Alex Cameron wrote: "It now seems that only a miracle result in Bucharest will save Ormond."

The pressure was mounting on the manager whose players were up against a side who had not lost a match in Bucharest since 1967. But he still found time to send a good-luck telegram: "From Willie Ormond and the Scottish squad" to "Billy Bremner and the Leeds team" for that evening's match in Paris.

Ormond must have felt the whole world was against him when Bremner and Jordan, who had been expected to join the squad following the European Cup Final, both withdrew.

The Under-23s were up against Denmark and Romania in Group 4 of their own European Championship, a new competition. The Spaniards had opted out of participation in a section where the winners progressed to the quarter-finals.

Stein's men played in Pitesti the day before the big match, achieving a creditable 2-1 victory in an 80-degree heatwave.

Willie Young opened the scoring in the 34th minute with the captain at the heart of the move. Tommy Craig curled a free kick over the wall where Young trapped the ball and dummied the goalkeeper before netting from a tight angle.

The Romanians fought back and Rough produced a series of saves either side of the interval before conceding in the 65th minute to a long-range Bolania shot.

Then Pettigrew "with astonishing coolness drove the ball low into the net" (Alan Herron, *Sunday Mail*) following a long run from Conn with 15 minutes to play. Six minutes from time Beldeanu watched as his 20-yard rocket shot struck a post.

Rough's goal survived further close calls before the end with one effort seemingly handled wide by a Scottish defender only for the referee to award a corner as the Scots clung on for the points.

The watching Ormond clearly sensed the hovering shadow of Stein as BBC Scotland radio commentator David Francey recalled in his 1988 autobiography *And It's All Over …*

Francey told of a visit to Ormond's room in Bucharest after he had returned from Pitesti. He found the manager lying on his bed and the first thing he apparently said was: "You saw the game this afternoon, David. One thing you've got to say about Jock: he's a lucky bastard." Ormond was presumably thinking back seven days to the match at Wembley where Scotland had enjoyed no luck.

Alan Herron's *Sunday Mail* match preview summed up Ormond's position. "Willie Ormond can expect little sympathy if he loses this match. Those in authority out here are only interested in victory. If Scotland lose then Ormond is a loser. The word is out that the axe is ready to fall." Referring to the post-World Cup optimism of the previous year, Herron concluded: "It is a sorry state Scotland finds itself in after so much pride and what looked like a bright future." And all of this because of one defeat to England.

Scotland's first ever meeting with Romania kicked off in front of 52,000 fanatical locals in conditions recorded by Jim Blair of the *Evening Times* as "best known to dry cleaners back home". Gordon McQueen was made captain and Aberdeen's Willie Miller, who had expected to feature in the match at Pitesti, made his debut. This illustrated another benefit of the Under-23 double header, particularly away from home: the option to "promote" a player to the senior squad if required.

The home side dominated the early period although Scotland held out until the 19th minute when Georgescu leapt to head a Lucescu cross into the net. Parlane looked to have levelled in the 35th minute when he knocked the ball in after a Macari effort had been saved, but the Turkish referee mysteriously ruled it out and McQueen was booked for protesting. It was later explained that the referee had penalised Macari for handball as Parlane's shot had struck him before entering the net.

Jim Brown kept Scotland in the match with two fine saves from Dobrin in the second half and as the large clock inside the stadium indicated the 90 minutes were over Scotland gained a free kick. Dalglish floated the ball into the box where McQueen, with his back to the goal, turned and fired into the corner of the net with his right foot. Willie Ormond jumped up and down as the goal was otherwise greeted with the same eerie silence as Jordan's strike in Valencia had been four months earlier. It was timed at 89 minutes and gained Scotland their second point from three group matches.

Archie Macpherson commentated on the match: "I remember the incredible ending to the game in particular when everybody ripped up their intros. Thinking back, as I can recollect, I think it was the obituaries they were writing for Willie. There is no question about it – it was an execution if that last-gasp goal hadn't gone in."

Around 100 Scottish supporters travelled to the match, one of whom was Robbie Jenkins. "It wasn't the friendliest place going; you just felt you weren't too welcome, but that could have been propaganda about what Scottish or British people were like. We were invited along to the British Embassy after the game to get some drinks. I thought 'don't fancy that much' but a few of us went along to the embassy and they had McEwan's Export and everything there and it was a pretty good time. Some of the players were there because it was the end of the season and everybody got well tanked up, including the players."

On departure supporters on a charter flight found their remaining currency to be worthless as Robbie explains: "The flight was two o'clock in the morning and you weren't allowed to take any of their money out of the country and you couldn't change it back because it was the middle of the night. That was deliberately done so the police would get a bit of money. 'You can't take our money out,' that's what it was; it was their money and you had to hand it over to the police. They thought this was a great thing and they would just take the money, but a lot of the guys started ripping up Romanian banknotes and the police were going absolutely mental." The supporters were of course committing a serious offence which could have resulted in severe punishment during the days of Ceauşescu's reign.

In spite of the draw speculation persisted over Willie Ormond's position. Before departing from Bucharest SFA president Rankin Grimshaw criticised Ormond's record in the lobby of the Park Hotel in the company of pressmen, indicating that he had lost confidence in him after the Wembley defeat.

The manager did receive some backing in the media with Ian Paul writing in the *Scottish Daily News*: "If the continued rumours about this being Willie Ormond's last chance are correct then I would say he took it. How many international sides decimated by injuries could have come here and nearly won?"

Paul's view was not shared by all, as Rodger Baillie remembers during a tedious four-hour delay in the airport. "Rankin Grimshaw more or less indicated to Willie in Bucharest Airport where we had an interminable wait on the way back that his time was up."

When the flight finally got underway, Ormond sat next to Stein, an image remembered by David Francey in his autobiography: "Ormond had to suffer the acute embarrassment of sitting beside Stein on the plane knowing that the knives were out for him in high places."

"I don't know if it was actual friction between the two of them," ponders Rodger Baillie, "but certainly the suggestion was that Stein was in line to take over but I don't recall there being actual friction. If there was a coolness, it wasn't evident to anyone."

This view is shared by Archie Macpherson, who rejects the suggestion. "Overshadowed? No, there was nothing, Stein kept himself well apart. There was no sense of thinking that Stein was overwhelming him in any way that I can recollect. I think there would be a sense that some journalists might have sensed that. I was quite close to Stein at that stage and I never at any time felt that he was looking down his nose or being rather superior to Ormond, I never got that impression from him about that."

An announcement of one form or another was anticipated when the International and Selection Committee met the following week but Ormond's position appears not to have been on the agenda. The situation was finally clarified at the 7 July meeting. In Ormond's presence, Rankin Grimshaw delivered a statement to the committee that his remarks in Bucharest were personal and not the view of the association. Intriguingly, SFA chairman Bill Lindsay announced that neither the manager's position nor his contract had at any time been discussed, indicating that business would continue as usual under Ormond. This does rather suggest that the widespread speculation over Ormond's future had accelerated after Grimshaw's comments had been misinterpreted as representing the SFA Committee, but another incident cannot be overlooked.

In the early hours of 5 July, just two days ahead of the SFA's endorsement of Ormond's position, Jock Stein had been involved in a serious car crash on the A74 whilst driving home from Manchester Airport following a family holiday in Minorca. At the time of the committee meeting he was in intensive care at the Dumfries and Galloway Royal Infirmary so it would clearly not be a suitable time to make an announcement regarding his future. His club had recently made their displeasure known over reports continuing to link Stein with the national job.

Rodger Baillie believes there may have been rather more to the timing of the manager's endorsement. "Jock was more or less on his death bed and that probably saved Willie. I think you could assume with some proficiency it may well have saved him."

Ormond was able to call upon the Leeds contingent when he named the pool to travel to Copenhagen early in September. Martin Buchan, who was said to have apologised for his walkout during a face-to-face meeting with the manager, also returned. With Jordan injured, Aberdeen striker Joe Harper came in. As Stein continued his recovery Aberdeen boss Jimmy Bonthrone took charge of the Under-23 team.

Reflecting on the trip to Copenhagen in his biography, *Leeds and Scotland Hero*, Peter Lorimer paints a picture of a drinking culture within the Scottish camp which was by no means confined to the playing staff: "Willie Ormond seemed to be drinking more and more and trainer Ronnie McKenzie was never more than a glass behind him."

The Under-23s kept up their 100 per cent record in the group with a narrow win played on what reports of the time describe as a village green setting before a decent crowd of 5,685 in Frederikshavn.

Scotland were troubled by the Danes early on with Dave Narey heading one effort off the line before Des Bremner netted the only goal just before half an hour, scoring with a dipping shot from 15 yards. After the break the Scots were rarely troubled by the hosts and Bonthrone told the reporters he considered it to have been "a very professional performance".

For the senior game in Copenhagen there were six changes from Bucharest with Harvey, Bremner, Lorimer, Buchan, Harper and Hutchison in at the expense of Brown, Munro, Parlane, Miller, Macari and Duncan. Coincidentally, Harper's two previous appearances had also been against Denmark in Tommy Docherty's era and it was Scotland's third appearance in the Idraetsparken in little over four years.

Rioch forced a save from Jensen after two minutes before Dalglish fired over. But the Danes fought their way back into the contest with Simonsen narrowly missing the target.

The home side grew in confidence in the second half which made Harper's goal, against the run of play after 51 minutes, all the more welcome. A Lorimer corner eluded its target of McQueen and the ball fell perfectly for the Hibs man to score. Simonsen threatened again with a shot which thudded off a post before the ball was scrambled away. The Scots clung nervously to their narrow lead and held on for the points with the Danes considered unfortunate to have lost.

SFA assistant secretary Ernie Walker told the *Evening Times*'s Jim Blair that Harper's goal might be worth as much as £100,000 to the association. "It could mean we will now get around 50,000 at Hampden for the next game against Denmark. Had things not gone our way, we might have been lucky to get 15,000." With the final fixture being another home game – against Romania – there was still a slim chance of topping the section but only if Romania could defeat Spain in November. Thoughts of Hutchison's missed penalty in the opening game were never far away when assessing the group table.

But headlines of a more serious nature overshadowed the result when rumours of player misbehaviour in a Copenhagen nightclub slowly began to surface.

It was the following weekend when, in response to an item in a Danish newspaper, the first reference to "the Copenhagen incident" featured in the Scottish press.

It was alleged that a number of players had visited Bonaparte's nightclub in the early hours after the match. Mention was made of a lamp being broken by drunken players who were asked to leave at around 4am when the police were summoned. There were also rumours of a fight between Billy Bremner and John MacDonald, the North of Scotland SFA council member, back at the team hotel.

Even sports journalists who had been in Copenhagen had been completely in the dark as Rodger Baillie recalls. "We did fly back on the same chartered plane but we knew absolutely nothing about it. In fact if my memory serves me right the actual story didn't come out until two or three days after we had flown home. The *Daily Record* picked up on it and sent a reporter out and that's how it all came about."

With the SFA unable to ignore the developing story, an emergency meeting of the International and Selection Committee was called for Monday 8 September to discuss the alleged misconduct of certain players.

The outcome of the meeting was that five players received lifetime bans from playing for Scotland. Article 15 of the minutes of the meeting simply states: "The Committee considered reported alleged gross breaches of discipline on the part of five players, following this match, and decided that the players, William Bremner, Arthur Graham, Joseph Harper, Patrick McCluskey and William Young would not again be selected to represent Scotland." The players were not summoned to offer any defence and neither was John MacDonald present although he had submitted a report detailing his encounter with Bremner.

Erik Hyldstrup, secretary of the Danish FA, thought the punishments unwarranted considering no arrests had taken place. He was quoted in the newspaper *Politiken* saying: "There was very little basis for the charges against the five. There was no police complaint against the incident in the nightclub when the Scottish players were thrown out and no names were given in the police patrol's report."

Bremner, approaching his 33rd birthday, was the only one of the five to break the wall of silence in the press. "The players' side of the case has not been heard," he told *The Herald,* intimating that the meeting had not been balanced. "I was not involved in any fight and was not punched by anyone. I still consider the whole affair to be little more than a storm in a teacup." Bremner subsequently refused to comment on the evening's events which brought a sad end to his international career of ten years, during which he had represented his country a total of 54 times.

Over 20 years later, whilst working on his biography *Keep Fighting* with journalist Paul Harrison, Bremner finally spoke about the events of Copenhagen. He recalled that a drink had been spilled over a member of the hotel staff before the players' visit to Bonaparte's. He described the events at the nightclub before the police were called as "innocent fun".

Bremner then admitted to his involvement in the trashing of MacDonald's room, and when confronted called the official "a boring fart". MacDonald responded by saying he would make sure Bremner never played for Scotland again before punching him to the floor.

In his biography Peter Lorimer recalls events before his team-mates left the hotel for the nightclub. The hotel prices were so extortionate that the group collected duty free bottles from their rooms and made no attempt to conceal them, pouring their own drinks on the hotel bar which the manager objected to before calling the police.

Willie Young, in an interview for the *Scotsman* in 2015, confirmed that the police had been called to the team hotel before the quintet headed to Bonaparte's by taxi, although no names were taken and no arrests were made. Young's recollection was that the manager of Bonaparte's had demanded the equivalent of £800 for a broken light bulb and that they had suffered some rough treatment from the police with Bremner apparently thrown down a flight of stairs. Back at the hotel they had no idea as to the identity of the room's occupant with the SFA men still socialising. Young confirms that the returning MacDonald disturbed them before punching Bremner after the player had attempted to apologise.

MacDonald's written report was hugely influential on the bans handed out and his promise that Bremner would never again play for Scotland proved accurate; the individuals were subsequently and infamously dubbed "The Copenhagen Five". It is quite possible that had Bremner gone to his own hotel room on returning from the nightclub, rather than to MacDonald's, the punishment would have been less severe.

"He was an extremely stocky little man, a very nice man that was not somebody to be messed about with," Rodger Baillie recollects of MacDonald. "He was very well rated in the halls of the SFA and was a very close friend of Ernie Walker's, who did have influence above perhaps what was a normal SFA councillor. But by all accounts Bremner was totally out of order. Even by Scottish standards it was one of the more bizarre episodes."

Although Jimmy Bonthrone accepted the SFA's invitation to oversee the Under-23 side for the return game with the Danes at the end of October, the situation changed when, under pressure, he quit the Aberdeen manager's job on the 16th of the month. He then advised the SFA he was unable to assist them for the Under-23 game. The Dons were joint second bottom in the Premier League table having won just one of their opening seven games.

"It's something we could have done without," Willie Ormond told Shearer Borthwick of the *Evening Times*. "We must have someone available to run the Under-23 team as I can't be in two places at once." A subsequent plea from the SFA persuaded Bonthrone to take charge for the game at Tynecastle where a win would secure top place in the section.

When Ormond dictated to reporters the names of the players selected for the two matches against Denmark, he paused during the Under-23 list. "Bremner," he said, before adding, "Des of Hibs that is – not Billy."

Asa Hartford, who had last played under Docherty in Brazil, came in as a straight replacement for Bremner with the manager explaining that the two were so similar he could never have played them in the same side.

This is not something that the player was aware of. "No, not at all. I wouldn't have said that but at that time in my career wee Billy and Alan Ball were the two players, I was trying to get bits out of both of their games if you know what I mean. Alan Ball to me was the best around at that time so maybe I took too much of Billy Bremner on board and then couldn't get in the team! But they were the two midfield players I most admired that played at that time."

One manager who certainly thought Billy and Asa were a good fit was Leeds manager Don Revie, who had signed Asa from West Brom in 1971 only for the deal to be unexpectedly cancelled following a medical.

A large crowd of 16,441 watched Bonthrone's Under-23s maintain their 100 per cent record in Edinburgh with a side dominated by future internationalists. Andy Gray, recently transferred to Aston Villa for £100,000, found the net twice with headers from Gordon Smith crosses. The Danes pulled one back right on half-time when Jan Hansen flicked the ball home from six yards.

Scotland piled on the pressure after the restart and Conn was denied by what Jim Reynolds described in *The Herald* as "an unbelievable save" from Poulsen. Two goals in quick succession on 74 and 75 minutes sealed a 4-1 victory and sent the crowd home happy. First Gray completed his hat-trick as he knocked in a Pettigrew effort which might have found the net anyway, before substitute Bobby Prentice, playing on his home ground, beat two defenders then the goalkeeper for the goal of the game to set Scotland up for a quarter-final appearance.

It had not been clear who would take over the Scotland captaincy with Buchan a contender, a suggestion which led to some criticism after his walkout earlier in the year. When Buchan and McQueen both withdrew Ormond made the surprise decision to call on the services of 33-year-old John Greig and immediately named him as skipper for the night.

John Greig had last played for Scotland at Wembley four years earlier and his recall boosted the attendance to 48,021. Scotland pressed from the kick-off with Lorimer, Dalglish and MacDougall all going close, but the visitors stunned the crowd in their first venture over the halfway line when Bastrup beat Harvey with a header midway through the half. Ormond later told the press: "At half-time I just told them to keep playing and it would come right in the end." His no-panic policy proved correct three minutes into the second half when Houston's free kick was headed down by Jackson for Dalglish to at last beat Larsen.

Another free kick six minutes later saw Scotland take the lead with a well-rehearsed but comical move. Both Rioch and Lorimer ran over the ball before Rioch, exploiting the Danes' confusion, hammered it through the wall and against the stanchion behind Larsen. MacDougall scored the third and the margin of victory might have been greater than the final 3-1 result.

Scotland were two points adrift of the Spaniards, both of whom had one game to play. If Romania could defeat Spain in Bucharest a couple of weeks later a home win over the Romanians would see the

Scots top the section on goal difference. As the Spain–Romania game was scheduled for a Sunday afternoon, STV were permitted to screen it live, with Willie Ormond a guest in the studio.

The Spaniards established a two-goal lead after 56 minutes before a Georgescu penalty prompted a fightback which brought the scores level with ten minutes to play. The Romanians might have even won the match but it ended all square and left the Spaniards in an uncatchable position, three points clear of Scotland and Romania. Again, mention was made of Hutchison's missed penalty when Scotland had led Spain in the opening match, and in truth all of the other results had been impressive, particularly the draws in Valencia and Bucharest. It would, of course, be unfair to blame Tommy Hutchison for Scotland's failure to qualify as he was by no means the only player to miss a penalty kick for Scotland during that period.

There was little time to reflect on what might have been for the manager as the qualification draw for the 1978 World Cup was being made in Guatemala four days later. "It's just Scotland's luck to be handed such a hard group," Ormond grumbled to the *Evening Times*'s Shearer Borthwick, adding: "We never seem to get a break." Retrospectively these comments now seem like an overreaction as Scotland were drawn in a group of three with the winners qualifying. Old foes Czechoslovakia plus Wales were the other teams in the group.

The remaining matches against Romania the week before Christmas were now both meaningless. Bonthrone again agreed to take charge for the Under-23 game at Falkirk which still drew a crowd of 8,419 to Brockville Park.

Pettigrew pounced on a pass-back ten minutes from half-time and made no mistake from 15 yards for the opener. His second came shortly after the break when he latched on to a headed flick from Joe Craig to finish. But the goal of the match belonged to Des Bremner – a 25-yard shot which looked all the more spectacular as it struck the crossbar before landing in the net.

Skipper Craig then completed the 4-0 scoreline from the penalty spot after his namesake Joe had been fouled by Ciocan with eight minutes left.

Representatives from Arsenal, Tottenham, Aston Villa, Sunderland and Newcastle had watched £250,000-rated Willie Pettigrew whom Bayern Munich were also said to have an interest in.

A paltry 11,375, only about 3,000 more than watched the Under-23s, bothered to turn out at Hampden where Jim Cruickshank returned in goal after four years. Ayr United's John Doyle gained his one and only cap that December evening with Andy Gray also debuting. Buchan, as had been predicted for the Denmark match, was given the captain's armband with John Greig named as one of the substitutes.

Doyle almost enjoyed a dream debut inside two minutes but could only hit the side netting with the goal gaping, after connecting with an off-target Gemmill shot.

When Dalglish was felled a foot outside the area close to half-time Rioch prepared to take the free kick. "Do you remember that wonderful left-footed free kick he took against Denmark?" Archie Macpherson asked *Sportscene* viewers, pondering, "I wonder if the Romanians saw any hint of that?" One suspects not as the three-man wall was quite inadequate to deal with Rioch's blockbuster from almost the corner of the area, which rocketed spectacularly into goal.

The match deteriorated into a physical encounter after the break with Doyle and Dinu both booked after one incident before the visitors drew level after 74 minutes with a goal completely missed by the BBC cameras.

"I did the commentary and it was absolutely incredible," says Archie Macpherson of an occasion he has never forgotten. "What happened was we had a director, I can't remember his name now, who wasn't a regular director.

"When you are sitting in a broadcasting van you have three or four different cameras to pick from and he picked the wrong one at the wrong time. It was only the principal camera which records so he was on the wrong shot at the time."

The surviving footage shows an image of the centre circle before cutting to a shot of Zoltan Crisan celebrating, having apparently tucked the ball beneath Cruickshank's body whilst Archie informs viewers: "It's a beautiful equaliser!"

So was Archie looking at the monitor or did he actually witness the goal? "There's a point. Do you know something, I can't remember ... I can't remember if it confused me or not. I'd have to think back very hard on that."

Neither side was able to find a winner although the Romanians seemed happier with the draw as their players celebrated as if they had won.

The SFA Finance Committee later recorded a loss of £343.70 on the Hampden game as opposed to a profit of £20,768.48 for the Danish fixture.

Scotland finished the group in third place, level on seven points with Romania but three goals worse off, which probably explained the Romanians' Hampden celebrations. Although the last match had been an anti-climax Scotland had lost only once in the section, crucially in the first match with Spain, whose points total was two greater than the Scots.

Television companies in Romania, Libya, Tunisia and Yugoslavia threatened to withhold the £2,450 fee due to Eurovision for BBC Scotland's coverage of the final game, in protest at the omission of Zoltan Crisan's equaliser. The Romanians, in particular, sensed a conspiracy. "The only comment I can make is that there was a regrettable human error," BBC press officer Douglas Low told the *Sunday Mail*.

1976

"For all his great goalkeeping, that seems to be all people remember him for – that game at Hampden."
Eddie Gray on Ray Clemence

Willie Ormond's focus in the first few months of 1976 was very much on the Under-23 side as they prepared for their quarter-final ties. He had the annual match with Wales as preparation in early February and took control of the team whilst retaining Bonthrone as his assistant.

Tommy Craig collected a pass from Bremner before scoring with his trademark left foot to give his side a 20th-minute lead in Wrexham and, close to the break, in-form Pettigrew, again being watched by scouts of English clubs, netted a second from close range.

Gordon Smith was felled by Dwyer in the second half, giving the captain the opportunity to score from the spot. Craig's kick was saved but, as others hesitated, Pettigrew reacted quickly to give his side a three-goal lead.

Two late goals made the scoreline more respectable for the home side. Mickey Thomas scored first, then, with two minutes remaining, Deacy converted from the second penalty of the evening following a foul on Johnson by Chic McLelland. Scotland held on for the 3-2 win, an impressive seventh victory in succession. When asked his opinion of Pettigrew's performance Ormond told Ian Archer, "He has just confirmed that he is the best striker in Britain right now."

The Under-23s faced Holland in the two-legged quarter-final tie in March and travelled to Breda for the first match. Ormond rued the loss of the in-form strike force of Gray and Pettigrew who withdrew after the weekend's league matches. The influential captain was also absent with Craig required for Newcastle's FA Cup replay against Bolton although his overage replacement was the more than capable Kenny Dalglish.

Ormond listed six full internationalists in the starting line-up and Scotland looked comfortable after a goalless first half. The restart was delayed after a bottle was thrown into the Scottish goalmouth and within three minutes Rough was beaten by a curling Van Diensten shot.

Kist then headed in the second goal in the 71st minute as the tie looked to be slipping away from Scotland.

During the last few minutes more missiles were thrown at Scottish players from behind the goal and play was interrupted. An announcement advised that the match would be abandoned if the disorder continued and the game was allowed to run its course. The Danish referee later told the press that had just one of the plastic bottles thrown been glass, he would have had no hesitation in calling a halt. Following the 2-0 defeat Ormond insisted that the tie was far from over.

The Inter League meeting with the English took place at Hampden on 17 March, seven days ahead of the Under-23s' second leg. "Hampden Goes On Trial Tonight" was the lead article in the match programme by Scottish Football League president Bill Lindsay. He described the attendance of 18,548 for the last Inter League fixture at the stadium as inadequate. "Hampden is a stadium which needs a big crowd to bring life to any game," he wrote, concluding, "If we do not get the support at the Queen's Park ground then I think places like Pittodrie, Tynecastle, Easter Road and Dundee must be considered." The old stadium certainly failed the "trial" with fewer than 9,000 turning up on the night.

The only goal of the match came as early as the third minute when a Tueart corner was headed on by Doyle for Trevor Cherry to beat Jim Stewart. Shilton, so often the scourge of the Scots, was almost caught out just before the hour mark but he managed to touch a 40-yard Joe Wark lob over at the last second.

Jimmy Greenhoff twice went close for the visitors in the closing stages, but Cherry's early goal was enough to win the game. "It was difficult to understand how the Scots were able to achieve so much possession, and it was fortunate for the Football League that their opponents were able to make so little use of it," noted *Daily Telegraph* reporter Robert Oxley. The Scottish League had now failed to defeat their southern counterparts since the win at Newcastle ten years earlier. The last home triumph was way back in 1961.

The poor turnout provided further ammunition for critics of the fixture and the 1976 meeting was the last played between the two sides. Throughout the history of the 72-match series the Scots had triumphed 18 times, well behind the English total of 40 victories.

A Scotland Select side played a Rest of Britain XI at Fulham in a benefit match for Alan Mullery on the night of Monday 22 March. Unlike John White's testimonial at Tottenham 11 years earlier there was no SFA involvement in the match. Along with two Italians, Terry Cooper and Norman Hunter guested for the Scots in what Jack Steglees described in his *Daily Mirror* report as a "light hearted game". Hunter headed the Scots into the lead, after which goals from Steve Perryman and Jimmy Greaves gave the British side the advantage. Lorimer then made the half-time score 2-2 before Alan Ball netted the second-half winner. Steglees had typed: "The goodwill even extended to allow Spurs defender Willie Young to wear the dark blue shirt again." Billy Bremner had initially been included but was one of a number of withdrawals which led to the addition of the non-Scots.

Both Hampden and Pittodrie had been considered as venues for the Under-23 quarter-final two days later but Easter Road was chosen. The decision had been taken ahead of the Inter League match although the poor Hampden turnout vindicated playing the game away from Glasgow.

Joe Jordan, who had last featured in a Scotland jersey in Valencia the previous year, came into the team with Craig and Pettigrew returning.

With the possibility of penalty kicks deciding which side reached the semi-finals, Ormond told the *Evening Times*'s Shearer Borthwick: "All 16 players, including the goalkeepers, have practised taking penalties – but I hope it won't come to that."

As 32,583 spectators looked on, Scotland got the early goal they sought when Derek Johnstone headed in a Craig free kick after 15 minutes. A Frank Gray volley was miraculously turned around by Shellekens as the Scots, urged on by the noisy crowd, produced wave after wave of attacks. From Smith's corner Johnstone's effort rebounded from the goalkeeper but Colin Jackson was on hand to knock the ball in to send Easter Road into a frenzy.

Scotland looked capable of scoring a third at any moment but the interval came too soon. In the second period Jordan smashed the ball off the face of Shellekens' crossbar and watched as Pettigrew headed the rebound over. There was a moment of déjà vu five minutes later when Craig crossed for Jordan to head against the bar and again the ball fell for Pettigrew, who this time shot wide of the target.

Thirty minutes of extra time continued in the same vein with the Scots creating the greater chances. But no further goals meant that the semi-finalists would be decided by the drama of a penalty shoot-out.

The kicks were taken at the traditional away end of the ground which was full of home supporters that evening. After Willie Miller had scored, loud whistles greeted Nanninga but he remained calm and beat Rough. Jordan then saw his effort saved before Van Rijnsoever gave the Dutch a 2-1 lead. Brownlie scored Scotland's third then the crowd went wild as Meustege shot against the crossbar. Three kicks each and all square at 2-2. Frank Gray and Van Diensen were both successful, leaving the captain to take his side's fifth. Craig had scored from the spot against Romania but missed in Wrexham and there was silence as he struck the ball, which the diving goalkeeper stopped. All the pressure was now on Kila who successfully converted to send the Dutch through and thousands of Scots heading for the exits much later than they had expected. Some of the Scottish players slumped to the turf in tears as a memorable campaign, which had included just that one defeat in Breda, ended in disappointment.

"That miss will live with me a long time, I didn't get enough behind it," Craig told Shearer Borthwick. Ironically Tommy Craig was the last ever player to kick a ball for Scotland at Under-23 level. Following the tournament's final, won by Russia who had disposed of the Dutch in the semis, the criteria was changed to Under-21 with the option of including two overage players continuing.

Switzerland visited Hampden on 7 April for the year's first full international. This was the payback for the game played in Berne three years earlier when George Connelly had gone AWOL. As with the Portugal match the previous season the scheduling of a warm-up game ahead of the Home Internationals illustrates how seriously the tournament was viewed at that time.

Ted MacDougall was withdrawn by his club, Norwich, for a league game at Everton on the same evening, after which a letter arrived at the SFA from his manager John Bond. The correspondence advised that MacDougall felt jaded even before extending his season and did not wish to be selected for the Home Internationals. Willie Ormond's response was that the striker would no longer be considered for Scotland so long as he was the manager.

A total of six players were promoted from the Under-23 squad in what was viewed as an experimental line-up. Tommy Craig, Rough, Pettigrew and Alex MacDonald all made their debuts with Tom Forsyth awarded the captaincy.

Following a near five-year hiatus Eddie Gray was back in the team: "I had a bad thigh injury which kept me out of the game for a long time and I hardly played any games in 1972, 1973 or 1974, and was initially told I would have to pack the game in. I got on well with Willie Ormond who I remember as a player and he had a good knowledge of the game."

Another who returned to the starting line-up was John Blackley who had last featured against Zaire but had continued as a regular member of Ormond's pool.

The crowd numbered less than 16,000 and the television companies ignored the match, with some critics suggesting that the exercise was worthless.

Although brief muted renditions of the song can be heard on the BBC Sport recording of the match at Ninian Park the previous year, it was really during the Swiss game that "Flower of Scotland" was sung to any great degree. It was first heard as the band played "God Save the Queen" before the Swiss anthem was jeered. This began a pre-match ritual of trying to drown out Her Majesty's tribute at every international. "Flower of Scotland" had first been issued on the Corries' second album in 1972 and had been gaining popularity since being released as a single two years later.

Everton manager Billy Bingham watched as Pettigrew opened the scoring inside two minutes, accepting a Dalglish cross before turning and shooting into the net. The rest of the evening's entertainment did not live up to the lively start, with a McGrain cross-cum-shot which glanced off the crossbar the only other incident remotely close to a goal in the first half.

Hibs' John Blackley was well acquainted with Pettigrew's abilities. "Willie Pettigrew was a typical goalscorer and he went through a season where he scored so many goals it was unreal. Willie was quick and direct and a good finisher, so it was no wonder he was hitting the headlines. He wasn't terribly big, about my height, and wasn't great in the air – but put him through and he was on to it to stick the chance away."

Pettigrew was taken off injured during the second 45, during which Burgner in the Swiss goal made just two saves worthy of Note: – one from a Gray header, the other a shot from MacDonald – whilst his colleagues posed almost no threat at all.

Aside from goalscorer Pettigrew, the other debutants, Rough, MacDonald and Craig, were said to have done little wrong in the 1-0 victory. The latter two never played for Scotland again whilst Rough went on to represent his country a total of 53 times and played in two World Cups.

The SFA later recorded a loss of £721.76 on the evening although the deficit would have been covered had highlights been broadcast on television.

The following day the SFA unveiled the new-look Umbro strip Scotland would begin wearing during the Home Internationals, complete with a diamond pattern on the sleeves of the jersey which was the first major change in the association's 103-year history. Replica tops were made available for supporters to purchase with royalties from sales benefitting the association.

Secretary Willie Allan told the media: "The Committee who decides this feels that it must move with the times and must explore every avenue to raise money." The wording of Allan's statement hinted that he himself, often accused of a reluctance to change, may not have been in favour of the decision. President Rankin Grimshaw enthused that: "For the first time in our history Scotland supporters will be able to buy identical jerseys – and this includes a quality Scotland badge reproduction." The SFA was believed to have received a payment of £10,000 from Umbro for the rights over the strip plus a percentage of all sales.

"Commercialism," wrote Ian Archer in *The Herald*, "which dominates much club football – has entered into Scotland's affairs."

Willie Ormond took a Scottish League side north to Elgin for a show game with a Highland League Select XI on 19 April, a Monday evening. The selection was almost entirely from First Division clubs plus winger David Cooper of second-tier Clydebank, who was emerging as a promising talent. There were three Kilmarnock players in the starting line-up along with two each from Partick and Falkirk. The final scoreline of 3-0 in favour of the Scottish League does not tell the full story with the opening goal only coming in the 69th minute through Joe Craig, following what Arthur Montford would have described as "a stramash".

Watched by just over 2,000 spectators, the Highlanders had almost scored straight from the kick-off when Louis Duncan just failed to connect with a low cross. In the second half Inverness Caledonian's MacKintosh headed against the crossbar before Montrose's Les Barr scored directly from a free kick for 2-0. Craig grabbed his second with a glancing header to complete the scoring four minutes from time.

The manager considered the trip had been a useful exercise and was quoted in the Aberdeen *Evening Express* saying: "I am strongly in favour of coming back next year ... however, I don't know if I'll be in the job this time next year." Ormond's last comment may have been partially said in jest but ongoing speculation continued as to whether his contract, due to expire at the end of 1976, would be extended.

On that same evening the Scottish Professional Youths Under-18 side overcame hosts France to win the Cannes International Youth Trophy with a goal from Gordon Boyd. The success of Andy Roxburgh's youngsters implied that Scotland's international future was in safe hands.

Willie Ormond now looked ahead to the British Championship. "Its high time we won this tournament," he told the press on the eve of the opener against Wales, "and there's no reason, with all three matches at Hampden, why we should not do it."

With Hampden Park required for the European Cup on 12 May, the original date for Scotland vs Wales, the international was brought forward to the preceding Thursday. Archie Gemmill was given the captaincy with Queens Park Rangers midfielder Don Masson selected for the first time as the players, along with many spectators, showed off their new strips.

Scotland controlled the first half but it took 38 minutes before Pettigrew ran on to a pass from Gemmill to break the deadlock – a typical Pettigrew goal. The margin became two when Rioch headed home an indirect free kick from Gemmill from three yards before the interval.

"Easy! Easy!" and "Flower of Scotland", which always died out after the opening verse, was the fans' response to the goals.

Wales responded on the hour mark when Forsyth felled Leighton James in the box allowing Arfon Griffiths to score from the penalty, the first player to beat Rough in a full international.

Eddie Gray headed in a long cross from Jordan to complete the scoring at 3-1 as the fans struck up the annual offering of "Bring on the English".

The non-appearance of substitute Dalglish brought a run of 33 consecutive Scotland appearances to an end, one short of George Young's record. Little mention had been made of this statistic before the game and even the match programme ignored the prospect of Dalglish equalling the milestone.

The inevitable rumours speculated that Ormond had been instructed to omit Dalglish and most neutral observers would agree that his absence from the starting line-up was odd at the very least. Dalglish did later surpass Young's record with an unbroken run of 43 international appearances which commenced with the very next match and continued into 1981.

Little over 40 hours passed before the players took to the field against Northern Ireland on the afternoon of Saturday 8 May.

Pat Jennings' goal looked to be leading a charmed life with Jordan twice denied by the woodwork in the early stages as Scotland attacked relentlessly.

The opener arrived midway through the half with Jordan this time the provider, cutting the ball back for Gemmill who had time to control it before calmly beating Jennings.

Scotland had a golden opportunity to double their lead seconds after the restart when Jennings fouled Jordan as he was about to shoot.

Rioch took the penalty but the ball came back into play from the keeper's right-hand post. Aware that he could not kick it twice in succession, Rioch cleverly stepped over the ball allowing Dalglish to strike a shot against the underside of the crossbar and seemingly over the line only for the referee to mysteriously award the Irish a free kick. It was later explained that although Rioch had not played the ball he had been in an offside position as Dalglish struck his shot.

The goal was delayed by little more than a minute when Masson scored with a low shot from 20 yards, and the margin was soon three in what was a hectic start to the second half.

This from Stewart Brown in the *Edinburgh Football Pink*: "Ireland were being taken apart and Masson dribbled round two men, coolly looked up and lobbed the ball through and Jordan dummied it so that Dalglish could move in from the left to stroke the ball into the net."

"Don Masson and Archie Gemmill are here to stay and Don Revie had better look out!" enthused Bill McFarlane in the *Sunday Post* as he reflected on the 3-0 victory.

There was now a real belief that Scotland could defeat England and claim the home title. That optimism had of course been evident ahead of the 5-1 reverse 12 months earlier following an identical result against Northern Ireland.

The Strathclyde Regional Authority had imposed a crowd limit of 85,000 on the Scotland vs England match, making it the first to be played in front of fewer than 100,000 people – other than the midweek 1973 centenary game.

Of the 85,000 printed, a mere 7,390 standing tickets were available to the public via the postal ballot. Each SFA councillor had been allocated 30 seats, 50 enclosure and 30 standing tickets.

The *Sunday Mail* published the names, addresses and telephone numbers of all the council members encouraging supporters to contact them for tickets. This later led to the SFA's legal agents raising the matter with the Press Council which rejected the complaint.

There was one public sale for the England game, which took place on the morning of the Northern Ireland match. Hibernian made the remaining 760 of their 1,200-ticket allocation available after supporters' clubs and season ticket holders had been catered for. Fans queued outside Easter Road overnight and the briefs were all sold within an hour, leaving hundreds disappointed.

The Scotland squad were back at Hampden on the Wednesday evening to witness Bayern win the European Cup against St Etienne. The England players viewed the match on television in their Troon hotel after manager Revie, who attended the game, considered it was too cold for them.

Tommy Docherty controversially claimed that his player Buchan ought to play ahead of Forsyth against England. "When you talk about Buchan and Forsyth it's like comparing a thoroughbred with a Clydesdale, a Rolls-Royce with a van. It's got to be Buchan," the Doc imparted with Bill Brown of the *Evening Times*.

Andy Roxburgh's Scottish Youth team did a lap of honour with the Cannes trophy before the kick-off as a passionate crowd waved hundreds of Lion Rampant flags. Roxburgh sat next to Ormond in the Hampden dugout during the match in which the English support was clearly down again and barely noticeable.

Forsyth started despite, or perhaps in spite of, Docherty's advice and Pettigrew was listed as a substitute with Eddie Gray included. With both nations on four points the British Championship trophy awaited the winners.

A shot from Masson and a Dalglish header were both saved by Clemence before Mick Channon gave England an early lead from a McFarland cross.

Scotland fought back and from a Masson corner Jordan powered a header against the bar and over.

A near identical move brought the scores level after 18 minutes. This time Eddie Gray sent a high corner into the box where Masson bulleted a Jordanesque header beyond Clemence and high into the net.

Eddie remembers the move had been rehearsed: "I practised them and used to swing them under the bar; you try to hit an area with your corners."

Roared on by the crowd, Scotland poured forward with Masson directing the midfield like a veteran. On the stroke of half-time a Dalglish run was halted by Clemence as he was about to shoot. There was astonishment when the Hungarian referee failed to award what most considered a blatant penalty and the teams headed for the tunnel with a chorus of "You're a bastard referee" ringing in their ears. Mr Palotai later explained that he had blown for the interval before Clemence's intervention.

Within four minutes of the restart Scotland were ahead through one of the most famous goalkeeping blunders of the time. Jordan made the goal, collecting a through ball from Donachie just inside the England half. Showing tremendous determination and stamina he beat McFarland before driving on until he was almost level with the penalty spot. He shrugged off a challenge from Todd before passing to the incoming Dalglish who appeared to control the ball before striking a low shot which squirmed from Clemence's hands, through his legs and into the net. Dalglish later admitted he had mis-hit the ball when shooting. "Clemence seemed to have it covered low at the left-hand post," noted Stewart Brown for the *Edinburgh Football Pink*, "but somehow the ball slithered behind him into the net to the immense joy of the Scots who seemed oblivious to the latest shower of rain."

Joe Jordan may not have been the most prolific of Scottish strikers, with 11 goals in 52 appearances – many of which came in important matches – but his efforts that afternoon demonstrated that there was much more to his game.

England responded, although Rough, whom some had feared might freeze like Kennedy had the previous year, was not called upon to make any significant saves. In a breakaway McGrain found himself racing in on Clemence but shot straight at the keeper from the 18-yard line.

The crowd cheered again as Rough beat Keegan to a through ball before dancing around him and passing to McGrain, who lost possession before Keegan's curling shot drifted just wide as the goalkeeper scurried back to his line.

With two minutes left Keegan headed on to Pearson who laid the ball off for Channon. The striker looked certain to score before Forsyth slid in to rob him with a match-saving tackle which ensured the 2-1 victory. The "Clydesdale's" intervention had been executed with precise timing and skill and was the last significant kick of the afternoon.

"For some of them who were at Wembley last year and who suffered the indignity of a heavy defeat this is sweet, sweet revenge indeed," was how Archie Macpherson described the scene as the players showed off the Home International Trophy to the adoring crowd.

"I'm a very happy man indeed, Archie," Ormond told Macpherson in a post-match interview for *Sportscene*. He felt that his side could have been 3-1 up at the interval and singled out Forsyth's performance without referring to Docherty's comments: "Tom got his tackle in and saved the day." The manager went on to state his belief that the team could only get better the more time that they played together.

Docherty was later big enough to withdraw his remarks over Forsyth although it would not be the last time he would have advice for his successor. There was a perception that the Doc had never been able to fully let go of the Scotland team following his departure.

Since losing in Belgium on the way to the 1974 World Cup Scotland had lost only twice – to Spain at home, when a missed penalty would have given them a two-goal advantage, and the heavy loss at Wembley when the squad had been depleted by Leeds' involvement in the European Cup Final. In Rioch, Masson and Gemmill, Scotland seemed to have found the perfect midfield combination and once again it felt good to be a Scotland supporter.

Mick Channon had been the first player to disappear into the tunnel, telling pressmen: "I couldn't stomach to see the bastards doing a lap of honour." With Alan Ball's international career over the Scots now had a new target of hate. Before Ball, Bobby Moore had been singled out for similar treatment.

"For all his great goalkeeping that seems to be all people remember him for, that game at Hampden," says Eddie Gray of Ray Clemence. The game ranks highly in Gray's memory. "I don't think you can ever forget your first cap, which was against England at Wembley in 1969. But to play for a Scottish team that beat England, that's right up there, that takes a bit of beating."

A few weeks later World Cup qualifying opponents Czechoslovakia defeated West Germany in a penalty shoot-out to win the European Championship Final, highlighting the improvement to their side since their last visit to Scotland.

In August Rangers hosted a pre-season sponsored tournament, the Tennent Caledonian Cup, involving themselves, Partick Thistle, Manchester City and Mick Channon's Southampton.

Channon was jeered from the start of his side's opening game against City and targeted with chants of "Ee Aye Addio, Channon is a poof!" and "If you hate Mick Channon clap your hands." In what would be unthinkable today the Ibrox choir loudly sang "Scotland two England one, Hallelujah" between their traditional offerings.

Readers of the following day's *Evening Times* were incensed at comments the player made during an interview conducted at Southampton's Stirling University base.

"The only good thing about Scotland is the road leading out of it to England," he told journalist Tina Kerrigan before describing Glasgow as "an ugly, horrible place".

When the Saints met Rangers in the final of the competition that evening the abuse only lasted for several minutes before Channon was withdrawn through injury. During his brief appearance he had opened the scoring in a match Southampton went on to win.

The player was more diplomatic the following day when featured in the *Daily Record*, saying he understood why the Rangers fans had given him a hard time. "I'm a country boy at heart," he told the newspaper, "and since all I've seen of Scotland is Glasgow, I am not much impressed but I'm no more impressed by London, Liverpool or Manchester." He justified his post-match comments in May with: "I'm a professional and don't like being on the losing side so perhaps people will understand the Hampden remark." Within that context fans could be more sympathetic as players and managers often have to live with comments made in the aftermath of a defeat when it is perhaps not the best moment for them to air their views.

Willie Ormond was grateful for the visit of Finland in September ahead of the World Cup qualifier in Czechoslovakia the following month. He intended to play the same personnel and formation he had in mind for the game in Prague. Although the quality of the Finnish players could not compare with the European champions, Ormond's intention was to use the exercise to familiarise the players with the strategy.

Again the turnout of 16,338 was poor considering that Scotland had won six and drawn one of their last seven matches. The public's response was consistent with club football where gates were showing an alarming decrease compared to the same stage of the previous season.

Czech boss Vaclav Jezek and Wales manager Mike Smith watched from the Hampden stand as a goal-hungry Scotland strolled to a three-goal lead inside 25 minutes. Rioch struck first, letting fly from all of 30 yards although goalkeeper Alaja really ought to have kept the shot out. Rough then had to look smart to get down to a close-range Paatelainen header before Scotland were gifted a penalty kick. There was no appeal from Andy Gray as he rose to head for goal, but the referee indicated a push to the bewilderment of the Finns.

Following Rioch's miss against Northern Ireland Masson netted easily from the spot, sending the goalkeeper in the opposite direction from the ball. Dalglish then cheekily flicked the ball in from close range for 3-0 and goal number four arrived in first-half stoppage time when Andy Gray connected with a cross from his namesake Eddie to power the ball past the Finnish keeper.

Harvey replaced Rough for the second period although there were times when it appeared Scotland could have played without a goalkeeper. Eddie Gray took off on a run from midfield and shrugged off two defenders to net from a tight angle, before Andy Gray scored the goal of the night ten minutes from time. The Aston Villa striker controlled a pass from Dalglish on his chest and, as it dropped, turned and smashed the ball into the top corner. This goal was later voted Goal of the Season by *Sportscene* viewers and the 6-0 scoreline was Scotland's largest victory since an 8-0 win against Cyprus in 1969.

To aid Scotland's World Cup preparations four of the five Premier Division games scheduled for Saturday 9 October were cancelled with only Hearts vs Ayr United going ahead.

Another fixture which took place that afternoon was between Scotland's Under-21 side and Premier League bottom team Kilmarnock at Rugby Park. There were 2,859 spectators watching Roxburgh's Under-21s prepare for their game in Czechoslovakia with a 3-0 win. Both the listed overage players, Bobby Clark and Pat Stanton, featured although David Cooper was in action for his club at Hamilton and joined the squad later that evening.

Scotland led early when John Wark thrashed the ball into the net but it was not until the 56th minute that they struck again when substitute Dave McNiven shot past McCulloch. The final goal arrived shortly afterwards when Craig Burley gave the goalkeeper no chance with a powerful shot. Roxburgh was said to be satisfied with the exercise but fully expected a tougher challenge in Czechoslovakia.

"The game at Rugby Park saw everything going our way," Bobby Clark remembers, "and was a good build-up for the game in Pilsen."

Charter flight BR8011 carried both squads from Glasgow to Prague the following day. On arrival the Under-21 squad made the

60-mile journey to Pilsen, the venue of their match which Ormond chose not to attend.

The Under-21 tournament mirrored that of the Under-23s with the youngsters playing the day before the big game. The Welsh FA had declined to take part so Switzerland made up the three-team group.

Bobby Clark's influence was important both off and on the park. "It was a fun trip and there were quite a lot of budding internationalists in the selection. Pat Stanton was really the captain but both of us had the role, as overage players, to look after the younger ones. Andy Roxburgh was in charge and did an excellent job with the team. He was meticulous in his preparation and even brought board games to play in the hotel. No iPhones or computers in those days and the TVs were of course not in English."

Roxburgh's men were the better side and probably deserved more than the point gained from the match in which they created five goalscoring opportunities against the home side's two.

Clark did well to turn a free kick from Farkas around a post then, just ahead of the break, Burley headed a corner goalwards only to see it cleared off the line.

After changing ends the Czechs pressed forward with more urgency but it was Cooper who almost won the game two minutes from time with a left-foot shot which came back into play from the crossbar. Roxburgh was said to be reasonably content with the goalless draw in what was Scotland's first official Under-21 international.

The more important business of World Cup qualification began late the following afternoon. Several hundred Scottish supporters had made the journey including a party who had travelled all the way from Moffat by coach. One of them had been forced to shave off his beard at the border to match his passport photograph.

There were two changes in Ormond's line-up from the Finland game, against a side that were not only European champions but were undefeated in their last 23 matches.

Scotland settled into a controlled and disciplined performance, occasionally venturing out of defence where McQueen and Jordan both went close with headers. Just two minutes from the interval, centre-half Anton Ondrus elbowed Andy Gray off the ball, sending him to the turf. The Scot rose before landing a right hook to Ondrus who fell clutching his face. The linesman had witnessed the whole event and both players were ordered off by the Italian referee.

The sending off aside, the players had successfully carried out the manager's instructions and there was little warning that the game would be lost beyond retrieval just a few minutes into the second half. Following a quickly taken corner Rough did well to save a powerful close-range Nehoda drive which rebounded 20 yards to Panenka, who lashed the ball high into the net. Just two minutes later McQueen misjudged a free kick from the left which allowed Petras to score with a fine diving header. As bedlam erupted in the noisy crowd all around them the Scotland players wondered how it had all gone so wrong so quickly.

A series of saves from Rough prevented a heavier defeat and the goalkeeper was the player who earned the most credit from the 2-0 defeat.

Hugh Taylor introduced his *Daily Record* match report with the following: "Two minutes of sheer horror destroyed what looked like a World Cup dream come true for Scotland. For 45 minutes they had played superbly in the continental manner ... the Czechs were worried sick. What went wrong?"

Gray was handed a three-match ban for his ordering off, which ruled him out of the remaining qualifiers for Argentina. Victory against Wales at Hampden in November was now essential to keep Scotland's World Cup chances alive.

With the continued cooperation of the clubs the squad again assembled six days before the match. With England due to play a qualifier in Rome their First Division programme was also postponed which obviously benefitted both Scotland and Wales. The Scotland party watched Rangers win at Kilmarnock on the Saturday in the day's only Premier League fixture.

The SFA's Executive and General Purposes Committee later rejected claims from a number of clubs for loss of income due to rescheduled matches ahead of the World Cup qualifiers. This was a change in policy from 1973 when two clubs had been compensated under similar circumstances. The Committee expressed the view that the purpose of the postponements was to enhance the chances of World Cup qualification, with the minutes of the meeting stating: "Any success would rebound to the benefit of the clubs."

The manager was refreshingly confident of victory, simply telling reporters at Seamill: "I know we will win ... we have better players."

Ormond got just the start he wanted after 15 minutes when McGrain sent a dangerous ball across goal. Dalglish cleverly flicked it on before Ian Evans, attempting to clear, stuck out a leg and stabbed the ball behind Dai Davies for the opener.

Rioch then sent a pass into the area which caused panic in the Welsh defence, before Jordan was felled by Evans. "That must be a penalty!" insisted STV's Arthur Montford but the West German referee begged to differ.

In the second half a Rioch volley rebounded from a post before Gemmill had similar bad luck, his angled drive from a Hartford free kick smacking against Davies' crossbar and over.

The Welsh almost snatched a point late in the game when Toshack, completely unmarked, connected with Thomas's cross only to misdirect his header, allowing Rough to save.

John Blackley vividly recalls the incident: "I was playing against John Toshack and we were one-nothing up. There was a chance and I couldn't believe Toshack was standing about 12 yards out and the ball was coming to his head and I thought, 'here we go' – and he missed it! That's a wee memory I have of that particular game. What a chance – I could not believe that guy missed a chance with his head."

It was the type of opportunity the striker specialised in converting for Liverpool and he held his head in his hands once it had gone.

Although the own goal was perhaps not the most satisfactory way to win the match, Scotland's ruthless attacking play had deserved the two points. "There was tremendous pressure on us all to win the game," Ormond told Jim Blair for the *Evening Times,* adding: "I was pleased with the attitude of the players. They got the result that mattered and that's the most important thing."

"They had some good players like Leighton James, Mickey Thomas and big John Toshack but we dominated that game," Eddie Gray recalls of what turned out to be the last of his 12 internationals. "I was privileged to play with a lot of terrific Scottish players," he reflects. "It's something you look back on with pride but the overriding factor for me was just not playing enough games for my country through injury. That's how I looked at it."

Scotland's next match in their quest to reach Argentina was not for another ten months when Czechoslovakia were to visit Glasgow. Before then the Czechs were due in Wales.

With the manager's contract due to expire on 31 December the uncertainty which had clouded Ormond's time in charge of Scotland continued until a week after the Welsh match. He was then offered a new deal which would retain his services until the end of June 1980 although he did not immediately agree to the terms. After consideration Willie Ormond signed the contract on offer although no one at that time could have foreseen that he would take charge of the side just once more.

In the last few days of 1976 the SFA released details of a trip to South America at the end of the season, where they would play three matches including one in Argentina in preparation for possible World Cup participation. It was also announced that assistant secretary Ernie Walker would be taking over from Willie Allan in the New Year with Allan approaching the 20th anniversary of his appointment. The SFA Annual Report described Walker as "a young man, enthusiastic and of proven ability and efficiency".

1977

"It is doubtful if any single event since the last war had the impact on the Scottish people that our qualifying to play in Argentina had."
Ernie Walker, SFA Annual Report

There was a touch of irony about Wales's visit to Edinburgh for an Under-21 friendly in February 1977 given that their FA had declined to take part in the European tournament where they would have faced Scotland. This followed the series of Under-23 fixtures which dated back to 1958.

Torrential rain limited the crowd to 4,538, but those who braved the elements were rewarded with a thrilling match. Scotland took a fourth-minute lead through Paul Sturrock before the visitors levelled 15 minutes later when Nick Deacy slotted home.

In a game which swung from end to end, Wark put Scotland back in front in the 52nd minute with a fine angled drive. Sayer's equaliser four minutes from the end looked to have denied Roxburgh the win, until Roy Aitken sent a long ball to the edge of the area which Parlane headed on for McNiven to volley high into the net for the winner. It was a fitting climax to an excellent match.

The pool for the Under-21 qualifier in Switzerland at the end of March was a strong one.

Only five of the original 18 named did not represent the full squad at some point in their careers.

"The two overage players were myself and Bobby Clark who was nearly as old as the coach Andy Roxburgh," laughs Asa Hartford.

The goalkeeper also recalls the evening: "It was played in a big stadium and it seemed empty. A little bit like when I played for Queen's Park in Hampden before a couple of thousand."

Scotland dominated possession with Cooper and Sturrock performing well on either wing, but their crosses found no takers. The Swiss then took a second-half lead.

Michel Decastel sent a cross over from the byline which swerved at the last second before striking a post and landing behind Clark. A miserable evening was completed six minutes from time as Jan Piero Zappa connected with a free kick to guide a powerful header into the net. Before the end Cooper shot against the crossbar, just as he had late in the game in Pilsen, and Roxburgh was left to rue the lack of an accomplished finisher.

The unexpected loss meant that Scotland had collected just one point from the opening two matches but with two home games to come there was still a belief that they could top their section.

The big news that same evening was Wales's unexpected 3-0 victory over Czechoslovakia in Wrexham, which was witnessed by Ormond. This was as much a boost to Scotland's qualification prospects as Denmark's draw with the Czechs in the 1974 qualifiers had been. All three teams in the group were now level, with two points each and the same number of games played.

Both the Under-21s and the full side were in action in friendlies on the evening of 27 April. Whilst the seniors entertained Sweden in a return game for the Gothenburg match, the youngsters played England at Sheffield United's Bramall Lane.

With Leeds, Aston Villa, QPR and Manchester United taking part in league matches that midweek many of the first-choice Anglos including the established midfield trio were unavailable for Hampden. This meant only four England-based players were selected – Burns, Hartford, Donachie and, unexpectedly, Willie Johnston. Johnston had last played for his country against Denmark in November 1970 when he was a Rangers player back in the days of Bobby Brown. His performances in the First Division for West Bromwich Albion had alerted Ormond, who viewed him as a replacement for the injured Eddie Gray.

The unexpected recall delighted the player: "I was out a long time. Tommy Docherty wouldn't pick me as I just didn't get on with him. I wanted to get back in the Scotland team when I went to West Brom but we got relegated the first year I was there. It was one of my ambitions to play again for Scotland and I was over the moon getting back in the team. Willie Ormond phoned me the week before to say that he had picked me and that I would be playing. So instead of him reading the team out on the Tuesday night I knew I was playing. He told me to behave myself because the SFA didn't want me there – that's what he said anyway. I had been a bad boy a couple of times but I was playing well at West Brom." At this point in the conversation Willie laughs in the way that only Bud can.

Ormond made Dalglish captain of his country for the first time with Ronnie Glavin, scorer of 26 goals for Celtic that season, the only debutant in the starting line-up.

The standard midweek friendly crowd of 22,659 included Welsh manager Mike Smith. Although Scotland had the better of the early chances the Swedes soon settled and were quick to break when the situation allowed. A golden opportunity squandered by Johansson, who fired wide with only Rough to beat, proved crucial. Within three minutes Scotland were ahead – through an own goal. A long Donachie free kick caused problems for the Swedish defence and the ball fell perfectly for Hartford at the edge of the area. His chipped shot bounced from the inside of Hellstroem's right-hand post before striking the goalkeeper and rebounding into his net after half an hour.

The Swedes were not finished and equalised in quite spectacular style after 51 minutes. A long goal kick was controlled by Sjoberg who released the ball for Benny Wendt, who shot high into the net from all of 30 yards.

It took Scotland just a few minutes to regain the lead in a move begun and completed by the captain. Dalglish beat a couple of Swedes before releasing the ball to McGrain. The defender took off goalwards then passed to Dalglish, whose shot took a deflection before entering the net via Hellstroem's left goalpost. There then followed an amusing moment as the goalscorer hopped for ten yards before retrieving his boot which had come loose as he struck the ball.

The 3-1 scoreline was completed when Jardine sent a cross into the six-yard box. The ball bounced once on the turf at the perfect height for Joe Craig, who stooped and scored with a diving header just three minutes after he had replaced Burns. This meant that Craig had scored for Scotland before he had kicked the ball.

"Johnston, back after seven years, brought an exciting brand of wing play to the side and it was a night when McGrain stamped his world class all over the game." So wrote Jim Reynolds in *The Herald*. He had taken over as the journal's lead football writer following Ian Archer's move to the Scottish *Daily Express*.

Although the evening sparked the revival of Willie Johnston's international fortunes it proved to be John Blackley's last Scotland appearance. "I got taken off and Davie Narey came on for his first cap," he looks back. "In many ways that was the sign that there was a young Narey, and there was a Willie Miller coming through and they were starting to make their name so that was more or less my final swansong." Blackley did remain part of the squad for another 12 months and was in the provisional pool for the 1978 World Cup. "I was a defensive reserve for Argentina but I can't have any complaints really," he modestly reflects on his days with the Scotland squad.

Roxburgh's Under-21s went down to a single Laurie Cunningham goal in Sheffield with the 20-year-old's performance dominating even the Scottish football headlines. Hamilton goalkeeper Rikki Ferguson fumbled a free kick after 18 minutes and was fortunate to see Bertschin somehow drive the ball into the side netting when it looked easier to score.

The Aberdeen *Press and Journal's* correspondent Jim Dolan thought Ferguson had a "nightmare debut", noting that: "He had dropped four balls inside the first half hour." Ferguson was replaced by Partick's Billy Thomson at the break and within a few minutes Cunningham had knocked a Peter Barnes corner past Thompson for the winner.

"Cunningham made history by being the first black player to wear an England jersey and score a goal on his debut," wrote Sandy Beveridge for the *Daily Record*. His efforts brightened the match in which Scotland hardly made a chance." The very next day Scottish football was thrown into turmoil when Hearts were given permission by the SFA to approach Ormond with a view to filling their vacant manager's position.

The Tynecastle club had just been relegated from the top flight for the first time in their 103-year history and manager John Hagart's resignation had been accepted.

Hearts targeted the former Hibs player as the man they believed could return them to the Premier Division, dangling a carrot of £10,000 which was £2,000 greater than his SFA salary. Tynecastle chairman Bobby Parker sounded confident that he would get his man, whilst Ormond initially made no comment.

The following Wednesday Ormond released a pool of players for an exhibition match between a Glasgow Select and a Football League side at Hampden on 17 May, part of that year's Silver Jubilee celebrations. He tendered his resignation with the SFA the next day, 5 May, and also listed two squads, one for the Home Internationals and South American tour and another for an Under-21 tournament in mid-June.

An SFA statement came from secretary-in-waiting Ernie Walker containing the following: "The Committee has reluctantly agreed to Mr Ormond's request and in doing so express their appreciation of his services to the SFA. He has had considerable success and we wish him all the best. The Committee will take immediate steps to fill the vacancy."

The speed of Ormond's departure, which had been initiated less than 24 hours after the Sweden match, was as staggering as the timing of it. As with Docherty's resignation Scotland were halfway through a World Cup qualifying campaign – and were now without a manager three weeks before the Home Internationals which would be closely followed by the South American tour.

Ormond, who had recently opened a pub in his home town, gave the usual stock answers that others quote when leaving international jobs for club positions – too much travelling, too much spare time and a desire to work with players on a daily basis.

In the four years and two months he had been in charge of the national side Willie Ormond had overseen 38 matches. Of those, 18 had been won, eight drawn and 12 lost.

In November 1981, four and a half years after his resignation, Ormond finally broke his silence in conversation with *Sunday Mail* journalist Don Morrison. "I've always resisted talking about my quitting. Basically it was about the money and subsequent events have proved me right. I always believed there was no way the post of Scotland manager should be second best," he told the reporter. Elaborating on this he admitted to being "astonished" by the salary Hearts had offered him which was "a considerable increase on what I was getting from the SFA". He had hesitated over the Hearts deal before signing at the end of 1976. It was also believed that an uneasy relationship with his employers and the uncertainty over his future at the time of the match in Bucharest had contributed to his departure.

"I got the feeling that Willie Ormond wasn't comfortable dealing with the so-called big names like Bremner and all these people, although I don't remember anyone speaking up or undermining him in any way," Asa Hartford reflects. "I just felt that he wasn't as comfortable around them as the Doc who was a larger-than-life character. When the Doc was there he would be here, there and everywhere cracking jokes and jumping about but Willie was more reserved and you wouldn't see him as much. I think Willie was just a different type of fella. There's nothing wrong with that; it's just different personalities."

Jock Stein, Derby County boss Dave Mackay and Bill Shankly were the first to be linked by the press with the vacancy with, at that point, no mention of the SFA's eventual choice.

On 10 May Stein issued a statement which ruled him out of the Scotland job. He said: "My future is with Celtic and that is where I'll be next season." This was a massive blow for the SFA, who were believed to have been optimistic of luring him from Celtic Park. It was believed that the venue for the following year's World Cup was a factor in Stein's decision as he had unpleasant memories of his club's treatment in the World Club Championship in Argentina in 1967.

Rodger Baillie, who knew Stein for many years, believes he seriously considered the offer. "They had offered him it before he went back in 1978. I think there were at least three separate occasions to my knowledge when they had tried to get him. Yes, I think he toyed with the idea. I am sure he was tempted but for whatever reason he rejected it."

Ally MacLeod, who had succeeded Jimmy Bonthrone at Aberdeen, then emerged as the clear favourite and permission was requested by the SFA to speak with him.

MacLeod, aged 46, had enjoyed relative success as manager of Ayr United, establishing them as a Premier League side. A shock and, crucially, televised 3-0 win over Rangers three days before Bonthrone left Pittodrie in October 1976 alerted the Aberdeen board to his potential. Ally saved the Dons from relegation that season – but only just, with a victory in the very last game. In the 1976/77 season the Dons won the League Cup – defeating both Old Firm sides in the process – and finished third in the table.

MacLeod saw his long-term future at Pittodrie where he was confident of building a team which could challenge the Old Firm, and he had never considered himself a candidate for the national job. He did, however, agree to a meeting with the SFA on return from his club's end-of-season friendly in Yugoslavia.

This few days spent away from the limelight gave Ally time to think about his future. There was a niggling doubt that the call may have come too early in his career, countered by the fear he may only get one opportunity to manage his country. "I argued with myself for hours," he later recalled in his autobiography *The Ally MacLeod Story*. He eventually decided that should he be offered the Scotland job on his return he would not be able to turn it down.

On Tuesday 17 May MacLeod drove from Aberdeen to Glasgow for a meeting with Ernie Walker and three members of the SFA Executive Committee. At this point the press were in the dark over the liaison and Ally entered 6 Park Gardens after knocking on a side window.

Following amicable discussions the committee members agreed to his conditions and he was offered a contract of £14,000 per annum. MacLeod accepted but, just as he had done at Ayr United and Aberdeen, rejected the offer of a contract, preferring to keep his future options open.

With the agreement still secret Walker then attended the Jubilee match at Hampden that afternoon. This was Ormond's last duty as an SFA employee where the Glasgow Select defeated Don Revie's English League side 2-1 in the presence of the Queen and the Duke of Edinburgh. Whilst at Hampden Walker notified journalists of a press conference he had arranged for 11 o'clock the following morning at Park Gardens.

Although the Jubilee game was played in a good spirit there was some crowd trouble and sectarian songs were sung on the terraces.

The Queen had left the stadium at half-time with Revie's side a Dennis Tueart goal to the good. A Jardine penalty and a winner from Dalglish gave Ormond the win although he confessed to having mixed feelings throughout the afternoon. There was a trophy for the winning side and, in a nice touch, Glasgow Select captain Dalglish insisted Ormond collect it.

By the following morning, before Walker had briefed reporters, the secret was out and Ally's entrance was greeted with sarcastic cries of "Surprise! Surprise!" from some of the pressmen. Walker then left the room, leaving the reporters and photographers in the company of the new manager.

MacLeod credited his predecessor, acknowledging that the squad Ormond had selected for the Home Internationals more or less contained the names he would have chosen. "I never played for Scotland," he imparted, "so this is obviously my best chance to prove myself at the highest level. I enjoy a challenge and of course I was born to be successful. I am my own man."

Ally's first selections were to bring Lou Macari and Davie Cooper into the pool as replacements for Pettigrew and Eddie Gray, who had already pulled out of Ormond's original 22. Macari had been out since the game in Bucharest two years earlier and was said to be out of favour with Ormond, whilst Cooper had been due to travel with the Under-21s.

Reacting to Macari's international recall, his club manager Tommy Docherty had a final pop at Ormond and was quoted in the *Evening Times* saying: "Thank goodness Scotland now have a manager with common sense." Ormond hit back with: "I ignore Tommy Docherty completely."

Willie Pettigrew was due to enter hospital for a nose operation in June and the Sweden game was his last match in a Scotland jersey although he did later feature for the Scottish League side on a couple of occasions. Curiously, despite all the interest from English and continental clubs, he played all his football in Scotland having submitted then subsequently withdrawn a request for a transfer from Motherwell. Pettigrew remained at Fir Park until 1979 when he signed for Dundee United.

Seven days later Ally MacLeod was back in Glasgow to meet up with the home-based players ahead of the Welsh match in Wrexham on 27 May. The party headed south to their base in Chester where they joined the Anglos, many of whom knew very little about Ally MacLeod.

MacLeod had a habit of appointing his own captain when taking over. At Pittodrie he had replaced Bobby Clark with Willie Miller and he chose Rioch, now an Everton player, to skipper the side for the home series. "I had never even met Bruce until he joined up with the squad on Wednesday," the manager told Jim Reynolds. "But having watched him and having talked with him I am convinced he is the right man for the job."

MacLeod, who was more Docherty than Ormond personality-wise, was popular with both the media and the football public and his optimistic nature had increased the profile of the clubs he had managed. He believed in entertaining the fans and always made himself available to attend supporters' functions. During his playing days at Blackburn Rovers, Ally had discovered that the media could be a useful ally. At a meeting of the Players' Union a vote was about to be taken over possible strike action should the football authorities not agree to abolish the maximum wage. It was Ally MacLeod who suggested allowing the press to witness the vote, which resulted in front-page headlines and nationwide publicity for the players' grievances.

There were said to be more Scots than Welsh amongst the 14,469 in the Racecourse Ground where one prominent banner contained the message "GOOD LUCK ALLY, ABERDEEN STILL LOVES YOU".

Scotland's game plan appeared to be one of containing the Welsh then attempting to snatch a goal on the break. This was contrary to the new manager's philosophy which had always been about attacking, entertaining football.

The home side dominated and Rough touched a 25-yard dipping shot from Sayer over for a corner from which Deacy's header was cleared from the line by McGrain.

Scotland were fortunate to go in level at the break and the second period continued in the same manner with a Joey Jones strike from 20 yards smacking the face of Rough's bar. The Scots clung on and almost stole victory in stoppage time when Burns headed McGrain's cross into the path of Hartford.

"Knocked down from Burns and a goal from Hartford!" exclaimed ITV Sport's Hugh Johns before he corrected himself with: "No! It had to be ... there was the winning of the game." The midfielder had sent his shot across the face of the goal and just wide as the crowd expected to see the net bulge. "I had a chance right near the end. I missed it, blew it – I was never a finisher anyway!" Asa says with a laugh.

The manager's press briefing was at odds with the reporting of the match. "It was a reasonable performance ... We just did not look like losing ... We were never really under any real pressure and we might have won it in the end," were some of his thoughts on the game.

Doug Baillie's *Sunday Post* piece opened with: "Ally MacLeod got what he was looking for in his first game as boss – a side which doesn't lose. When I tell you that Wales could have played without a goalie, you will understand what I am on about!" To put the result in perspective, there had been a spate of call-offs, and a draw on the ground where the home side had recently taken the European champions apart might be considered an achievement. But Scotland had no right to expect anything like the same amount of luck when the two countries met later in the year on World Cup business.

Obviously irritated by some of the criticisms, MacLeod promised a change of tactics for the Northern Ireland game. Jordan was passed fit for the match on the Wednesday and MacLeod told Jim Reynolds: "My job as manager is to win games but if we can win games and entertain the fans then that is all the better. At club level I was always conscious of that and I don't intend to change now."

Scotland fans had a new song that summer which was sung repeatedly during the Ireland game, although they could not themselves claim to have rewritten Doris Day's classic for the football terraces. Versions of "Que Sera Sera" had been heard from Manchester United and Liverpool supporters during their sides' progression to the FA Cup Final that same year with the line "The future's not ours to see" replaced with "We're going to Wembilee". There was some confusion amongst Scottish supporters with some singing "wherever we'll be" and others "whatever will be" for the second line.

Apart from a first-minute scare when a McIlroy goal was disallowed for an infringement, Scotland produced a performance that sent their fans heading to London full of hope. A larger than normal turnout of almost 45,000 watched Dalglish pounce on a long kick from Rough before sending the ball rolling beyond Jennings and into the empty net.

The blond head of Gordon McQueen rose to meet a long Masson free kick after an hour of play and the ball looped past Jennings and over the line for 2-0. Dalglish, having a fine match, then almost broke the Hampden crossbar with one shot.

With around ten minutes left a Masson corner caused panic in the box and after a scramble the ball fell at the perfect height for Dalglish to head home from close range to record a result of Scotland 3 Northern Ireland 0 for the third successive year.

Throughout the week Scottish newspapers relived previous Wembley trips though the memories of retired players, with fans invited to share their recollections in the build-up to the game of the year.

There was always something special about the biannual pilgrimage, with younger supporters reared on tales from fathers and granddads of two overnight journeys on the great adventure. The fact that the trip was every other year and not an annual event added to the anticipation, with supporters saving up for the next journey south immediately on their return.

In the match programme Billy Bremner tried to explain what the fixture meant to the supporters. "Some of them exist for a year just looking forward to the day when Scotland and England play each other," he told journalist Frank Clough. "As soon as the Hampden match is over they start saving their cash for the Wembley match. They are the greatest fans I've ever known, they make you feel that you would rather die than let them down."

"Wembley is where a lot of Scots become more Scottish than they ever knew they were," William McIlvanney wrote for the *Daily Express*. "Some approach it as a kind of profane equivalent of Lourdes. Every two years they stagger hopefully back, their inferiority complexes swathed in alcohol, their insecurities bandaged with tartan."

In the same newspaper John McKenzie considered: "On every pilgrimage, no matter how well or how badly Scotland have been playing, miracles can suddenly become possible. And not one of the thousands of Scots who travel south for this game can possibly envisage defeat."

MacLeod named the same starting line-up as the Northern Ireland game, telling MacKenzie: "I think we have better players and a more settled formation than Don Revie can offer, but it is important that my players don't get carried away with themselves. They must tighten up sensibly at the start and give themselves a chance to settle down before going out to win the game."

Scottish confidence was boosted by England's recent form – they had lost their last two home matches to Holland and Wales. More Scots than ever seemed to be in London with hundreds cooling off from the sunshine in the fountains at the traditional gathering point of Trafalgar Square.

"The biggest tourist attraction in London today was the thousands of Wembley-bound Scots," wrote the *Evening Times*'s Bill Brown, who continued: "Americans gawped at them, French, Japanese and Germans took hurried snapshots, Arabs stood amazed as – with war chants, banners and bottles – the invading force took over the Piccadilly region bloodlessly."

As well as "Que Sera Sera" the fans had another new song that weekend which had again originated during that season's FA Cup. There were in fact two versions – "Wembilee, Wembilee, We're the best team in Europe and we're going to Wembilee" or alternatively "We're the famous Tartan Army and we're going to Wembilee."

The term Tartan Army first came to be associated with the Scottish support around this period but already had roots away from the world of football.

A terrorist group of that name had attempted to further the case for Scottish independence through a bombing campaign, the targets of which included pipelines pumping oil from the North Sea to the mainland. One *Evening Times* headline from September 1975 read: "Tartan Army – Scotland's IRA".

Less sinister were the tartan-bedecked girl-fans of the Bay City Rollers who had also been referred to by the term in the earlier part of the decade. Large remnants of woven tartan had been sliced into dozens of scarves and sold to eager fans ahead of Rollers' concerts. It did not take vendors long to realise that Scotland football fans were another potential market for the offcuts, as Ian Archer had noted in his report on the Northern Ireland game two years earlier.

During MacLeod's time at Pittodrie, Aberdeen's followers were referred to as Ally's Red Army, which paid homage to Manchester United's followers. It was therefore a natural progression for the press to rename the Scottish support as Ally's Tartan Army.

Fans disembarking from overnight trains on the morning of Saturday 4 June were greeted by the sight of hundreds of their compatriots sleeping rough in stations whilst others stretched out on park benches using flags as blankets. The accommodation shortage was caused by a clash between the match and the Silver Jubilee weekend although at least the trains were running to the stadium.

The Scottish fans inside Wembley virtually turned the fixture into a home game and there could have been no more than 15,000 English supporters in the crowd. Of the SFA's 29,173-ticket allocation only 3,565 had been available for public ballot. Forgeries had been in circulation and some of the gates had been forced open by supporters in no mood to be denied entry.

Wales's drawn match with Northern Ireland on the Friday left them with four points in the table which meant that a Scottish victory would see retention of the Championship with five points accrued.

Willie Johnston was making his debut at the ground: "I was in the squad for the 1969 and 1971 games but it was my first game at Wembley and it was brilliant. Most of us were playing down there at the time and we fancied our chances."

The two sides entered to a deafening roar before being introduced to the Duke of Edinburgh. Inside the first minute McGrain passed the ball back to allow Rough an early touch, a pre-planned move after the nightmare start Stewart Kennedy had suffered during the last visit.

Stuart Pearson and Jordan both tried their luck with headers before Johnston beat Phil Neal to set up Hartford. The net rippled, but Asa's shot had slammed into the outside of the goal.

The singing of the Scots fans had never let up but intensified just ahead of the break after Neal handled a Johnston cross. Hartford chipped the free kick into the area where McQueen leapt to an incredible height to power a header down and beyond Clemence as bedlam erupted all around the stadium.

Asa Hartford does not recall the goal as a rehearsed move. "If it was there I would have taken it. In those days it was more or less if the free kick was on the left it was going to be a left-footer and if it was on the right it would be a right-footer. We probably wouldn't have rehearsed it ... I might have seen Gordon moving."

Hardly anyone noticed as Jordan limped off to be replaced by Macari during the uproar.

"I was desperate to get on because the signs were there that we were going to beat England," says Lou.

The teams headed for the tunnel with a chant of "We Shall Not Be Moved" echoing all round. This was followed by a chorus of "Sailing" which would have pleased Rod Stewart who was watching from the stand.

Scotland scored again just beyond the hour mark. The move began when Hartford found Johnston with a pass. The winger's cross from the goal line was headed down by Rioch for Macari who either miskicked or dummied the ball which allowed Dalglish to pounce. His first shot was blocked but he forced the rebound over the line which looked to have sealed victory and the Championship.

"Phil Neal the full-back just seemed to get too close to Willie and left that wee bit of space inside," is Asa Hartford's memory of the goal. "When I was playing at West Brom with Willie he would always say stick it in behind the right-back and Willie would chase him down and buy himself a bit of space. I've probably overhit it slightly but he had fantastic pace to get there and put it in. He went crashing into the photographers," Asa laughs, "but he did amazingly well to get there."

"Asa ... what a ball he gave me," Willie Johnston recalls. "I was going at about a hundred mile an hour to catch it. I just caught it and crossed hoping someone was on the end of it and Lou and Kenny were there."

"I do remember, yeah. I didn't dummy it!" laughs Lou Macari. "You don't dummy anything inside the box! No, I attempted to get on the end of it but I couldn't. My intention was to make a connection with the ball but I didn't. But everything went right for us."

"You'll Never Walk Alone" echoed around Wembley Stadium accompanied by a mass of yellow, red, blue and white flags. The choice of song was significant in the changing demographic of the Scottish support. It had been turned into a football anthem on the famous Spion Kop at Liverpool accompanied by a display of red and white scarves. Other clubs followed – with one notable exception. The song was never heard at Ibrox; Rangers' supporters considered it to be associated with Celtic and it was often said that Rangers were the only fans in Britain not to sing "You'll Never Walk Alone". Similarly Celtic followers almost exclusively refused to sing "We'll Support You Ever More", the adaptation of "Bread of Heaven" believed to have originated at Ibrox. One reader's letter to the *Celtic View* in October 1970 referred to attempts by some of the Parkhead faithful to start the chant as "sickening, sheep-like imitations of the support of another team. The Welsh supporters in our ranks will forgive me if I ask them to refrain from singing their national anthem."

Adaptations of Celtic's "Hail Hail!" anthem were also sung by fans of other Scottish clubs, as were versions of Rangers' chants throughout the 1960s and 1970s. But as the years passed non-Old Firm fans deleted these offerings from their song sheets to the point where today "You'll Never Walk Alone" is largely considered the property of Liverpool and Celtic. "Sailing" was also not on the Ibrox choir's playlist but if anyone doubts these songs were heard at Wembley in 1977 the evidence exists in the ITV Sport library.

The only lull in the atmosphere came as the match entered its final stages when McQueen was ruled to have fouled Trevor Francis before Channon beat Rough from the penalty spot. It had been a soft award but ensured a nail-biting last three minutes, as England poured forward to try and save the game. A cacophony of whistles and jeers rang out as Channon headed a cross for goal which Rough pushed over for a corner. The keeper was then cheered as he clutched the kick confidently but despite Scotland's performance it had been very close to a draw. Although it may not have seemed like it the referee played no additional time and as the players in blue celebrated a trickle of fans cleared the three-foot barriers around the track and entered the playing area.

Before long thousands had streamed on and Rioch was carried shoulder high, punching his fist in the air, as was Rod Stewart who had made his way down to join in the celebrations. Eventually the entire playing surface was covered by jubilant supporters singing their new "Que Sera Sera" song with the police and stewards looking on helplessly. Some fans scaled the crossbars which gave way due to the numbers, sending the culprits crashing to the turf. As supporters carved out chunks of the grass to take home as souvenirs the plea on the scoreboard, "In the Interest of Safety Will You Please Clear the Pitch Slowly", went largely unnoticed.

"I tried to get the net but I cut my hand trying to break it," remembers Robbie Jenkins. "I was with a mate and we got a couple of bags full of turf. We even tried to get through to the players' tunnel as the police were heavily outnumbered."

Andy McArthur was not amongst the first batch of invaders. "I stood on the touchline for a while just to absorb the moment," he reminisces. "There I noticed, to the side of me, a policewoman standing open-mouthed. I followed her gaze over my shoulder to where a huge police horse was standing within touching distance. The rider's head was slumped forward, in an 'I give up' kind of expression. The reason being was an older guy in a tartan bunnet and rosette slowly feeding the horse a tin of McEwan's Export. The bloke was clearly a little the worse for wear, but he was making a fine and successful effort to pour the bevy carefully to avoid any spillage ... the horse didn't spill a drop. When the horse had finished I commenced my quest for a piece of the park."

The damage to Andy's hand from the Yugoslavs near Frankfurt did not hinder his task. "The early invaders had made it easy for me. I found a rough edge where a chunk of turf had already been removed. All that was required was to get a grip and peel off a new piece ... nae problem; no need for shoe heels or proxy garden tools!

"My clump of turf was from where Gordon McQueen rose like a Scottish salmon to head home. It fitted neatly inside my bunnet, and there it stayed safe for the rest of the night. Most of this slice of turf ended up in our garden in Dumbarton, where it quickly became a favourite spot for our dog Frisky to relieve himself. A small piece went into a matchbox and on to a lecturer at my university who had asked: 'Were you there?' On replying, 'Yes', his next questions were: 'Did you get any?' followed by 'Can I get a bit?' He did, and I recall I did remarkably well in the exams that summer."

Most of the players had reached the sanctuary of their dressing room before the events had got out of control and Willie Johnston remembers surveying the scene with his manager.

"We were in the dressing room and Ally MacLeod said to me: 'Bud, come on and see this.' We went and stood at the top of the tunnel and looked out on to the park and he said: 'It's like Culloden!' That was a great day!"

Bobby Clark also watched from the mouth of the tunnel. "I remember coming back up to watch the Scotland fans celebrate. It was all very good natured and although there was damage done to the field there was no hostility and the police seemed to have a friendly attitude to the whole affair."

Bobby's Aberdeen clubmate Gordon Strachan was a spectator that day and later told how officers of the Metropolitan Police actively encouraged him to enter the playing area.

Asa Hartford: "I certainly didn't see what went on and I wasn't aware of that at all until we came up the tunnel say half an hour later and saw the devastation. There was damage, no doubt about that, but it was celebratory. I must have met 100,000 people myself that had been to Wembley on that day!"

Lou Macari took rather longer to vacate the pitch: "When the final whistle went you were well aware that it was going to be an achievement to get to the dressing room. Most people thought there was no point in even trying it because the tunnel at Wembley is quite a distance from the playing surface and it depends on where you are at the time on if you can get to that tunnel or not. They just swarmed the whole pitch, didn't they? It was tougher getting to the dressing room than it was beating England!"

There are accounts of some supporters exiting the stadium as late as 10pm, leaving behind a playing surface looking more like a patchwork quilt than a football pitch, with large bare patches and an absence of goalposts and netting.

"Wembley went mad that day," says Lou Macari. "It's hard to tell the supporters of nowadays that Wembley, England's home ground, was full of Scots supporters but that's the way it was back then."

That evening Ally MacLeod enjoyed the limelight in the team's hotel, the St Ermin's, close to St James's Park. Retrospectively, his comments to Jim Reynolds, as documented in *The Herald*, were frighteningly accurate. "I have had only good times in my short spell as Scotland manager ... but, as in everything else, the bad times have still to come."

Fans in London celebrated well into the night, leaving a mountain of empty cans and bottles to be cleared from Trafalgar Square. London had been draped in Union Jacks ahead of Jubilee Day on the Monday but the Lion Rampant and cross of St Andrew were more prominent in the capital that evening now that the ten-year wait for a Wembley victory was over.

There is a recording of a punk concert in south London that evening during which the band are occasionally drowned out by the victory songs of Scots in the crowd. Similarly, viewers of BBC2's cricket coverage on the Sunday at Lord's heard Scottish chants throughout the match between Middlesex and Hampshire and tartan-clad supporters could be seen on the steps of the Taverners Bar drinking beer. This was a well-researched move by fans still in the capital, with cricket matches one of the few sites in London where it was possible to purchase alcohol on a Sunday afternoon.

Hitch-hiking and sleeping rough were normal for a lot of Scotland supporters in those days and one London-based fan, Adrian Haren, used to vacate his home from the Thursday until the Monday to feel part of the Wembley weekend. Another, Robbie Jenkins, hitched from Elgin with a companion and planned to sleep in King's Cross Station before seeking a lift home in the morning. A real football man, Robbie was used to hitching, regularly making the return trip to Glasgow for midweek internationals and Rangers games despite no north-bound public transport being available afterwards.

"I remember the police pushed us on a train to Aberdeen. They just wanted us out and we were just going to crash out in the station. With no tickets we got all the way up for nothing. When we got off the train in Aberdeen it was like you had come back from a war," he reminisces. "The police and all the people waiting applauded you off the train. When we got back to Elgin we planted the turf in my back garden. Almost every day there were people knocking at the door before and after going to school asking, 'Can we stand on the Wembley turf?'"

The press reaction to the pitch invasion was mixed as illustrated by the *Daily Record* editorial on the Monday which was titled "We Wish They Hadn't Done It" and included: "The invasion of the Wembley pitch, the damage caused by exuberant but irresponsible souvenir hunters cannot be condoned. Yet shouldn't we try to put it all in perspective this morning? Although the chaotic scenes on the pitch DID spoil things, let's not allow them to completely cloud a wonderful victory. And let's make sure such an invasion can never happen again – anywhere."

Ian Paul penned an article for *The Herald* headed "Tartan Schizophrenia" which contained the following: "Scotland's football fans, the best and the worst in the world, demonstrated at Wembley the schizophrenia which characterises our soccer army.

"During the game they were humorous, at times hilarious, providing the kind of atmosphere which had to be experienced to be believed. But the scenes at the end, when goalposts, fences and large chunks of turf were ripped up, revealed the less than admirable side of the Scottish fans' make-up."

Archie Macpherson had continued to commentate for BBC Scotland viewers as the supporters dug up the pitch. "Obviously I was overjoyed with the victory and I suppose spiritually speaking I could understand what was going on out there although in a sense it was hard to take ... I suppose you might say it was over the top. But I never expressed any of that feeling at the time as the English around me were rather tut-tutting about the whole affair. No, I don't have any unpleasant memories about that at all."

Few of the Scots in the crowd – and many remained on the terraces – would consider that the post-match celebrations in any way spoiled their day in the sun. A Metropolitan Police spokesman was quoted in the *Daily Record* with guarded praise for the supporters: "The fans compared favourably, to say the least, with our Cup Final visitors."

Ally MacLeod had a knack of getting off to a good start when taking charge of a new team. At Pittodrie he had achieved victories over both Old Firm clubs within weeks of his appointment and he had now repeated this success at international level. But there was little time to reflect, with the squad due to reassemble on the Thursday for departure that evening to South America. MacLeod had told his players that anyone who did not wish to take part in the tour would not be considered for the remaining World Cup qualifiers. Still suffering from the injury picked up at Wembley, Jordan elected to travel although he was unable to take part in any of the matches. Another who would not play, Davie Cooper, completed a £100,000 transfer to Rangers from Clydebank the day before the party set off.

Bobby Clark, who had played under Ally during his spell at Pittodrie, was pleased to be back in the squad. "Willie picked the squads for the Home Internationals and the South American tour and I was delighted to be part of it. Ally breezed in and enjoyed his early time with the team. I think he looked on me, as the older goalkeeper, to look after the goalie workouts with Alan Rough and Jim Stewart at practice."

Conditions were cramped on the British Caledonian 707 aircraft from London to Santiago with most of the passengers on the long flight exercising stiff limbs in the aisle of the plane and grateful for a short stop in Brazil where they were briefly allowed to disembark. The tired Scots arrived 26 hours after leaving Glasgow and three days ahead of their opening game and were met by local television and newspaper reporters keen to interview the British champions. A handful of supporters even travelled with them, still cheered by the glory of Wembley.

When asked to name Scotland's best player Ally responded to the Chileans that Jordan was "the best centre-forward since De Stefano", adding that half a million pounds could not buy the striker. This was classic Ally MacLeod who, aware that Jordan would not be fit, was attempting to divert attention from those who would play in Santiago.

The fixture in Chile had been criticised because of the fascist government in power and the choice of venue. The National Stadium had been used as a gaol for political prisoners during a military coup four years earlier and a number of them were said to have been tortured and executed there. A campaign to have the game called off involved the Scottish Trade Union Congress, the Scottish Chile Defence Committee and other left-wing groups. Supporters in Wrexham for the Home International had been handed leaflets urging fans to ask the SFA to think again. But the association were adamant that the tour arrangements could not be altered and there was never any question of changing the schedule.

As well as training, the squad played golf and some players went to a horse racing event as they acclimatised ahead of the opening game. The match started at half-past midnight British time on the morning of Thursday 15 June, with Radio Scotland providing a commentary for those still awake. There was no television coverage.

Willie Johnston is still troubled by the conditions the players encountered. "The bullet holes were round the dressing room where they shot all those people. It was a terrible thing, shocking. They didn't tell us but we found out later that's where they were shot. We just wanted to get the game played and get away."

Dalglish opened the scoring from just inside the area at around the 20-minute mark and the lead was soon doubled as confidence oozed throughout the side. Chilean goalkeeper Nef dropped a free kick taken by Johnston and Macari reacted first to hit the ball into the net. In what seemed a dream performance Hartford added a superb third, accepting a pass from Macari before shooting high into the goal from the edge of the area.

Jim Stewart replaced Rough for the second half and was soon beaten when Crisosto stabbed in from close range following a defensive mix-up. Macari then missed an easy chance before turning a McGrain cross over the line for 4-1.

Crisosto grabbed his second to make the final score 4-2 and although MacLeod's men looked jaded towards the end the result had never really been in doubt.

"Chile are not the best team on this side of the world, but we scored four goals in South America," the manager shared with Jim Reynolds for *The Herald*'s back page.

Ally MacLeod was not the only one impressed with the Scottish performance, which encouraged offers of additional matches against Peru and Bolivia. These were reluctantly turned down by the SFA which was unable to extend the length of the tour.

The party flew directly to Buenos Aires the following day and were astonished by the levels of security which greeted them. A convoy consisting of six police cars with sirens blaring plus two outriders in front cleared a path through the city's traffic on the 30-mile journey from the airport to the Plaza Hotel.

The match took place in La Bombon1era, the home of Boca Juniors, which was full to its 57,000 capacity. England had played in the same stadium the previous week and Don Revie, as well as sending a good-luck message to MacLeod, warned him not to expect impartial refereeing. Trevor Cherry had been ordered off following an incident involving Bertoni, who most observers had considered to be the guilty party.

The game was shown live on BBC Scotland on the Saturday evening and was the last Scotland international to be screened in black and white, with the Argentinians promising colour transmissions for the World Cup 12 months later.

A shower of ticker tape welcomed the teams, a feature that would become a familiar sight at the World Cup and the paper littered the pitch throughout the match.

"That was a special experience," says Bobby Clark. "The terraces seemed to rise almost vertically on all sides and it was fairly obvious why it was called the 'Chocolate Box'.

"I can remember the stadium; it was packed," recollects Lou Macari. "They were going mad the whole time. They never stopped singing, never stopped shouting. One of the most intimidating atmospheres probably I've played in front of. I can see the fencing now around the stadium. Thank goodness the fencing was up!"

Asa Hartford agrees: "It was a terrific atmosphere, they had a stand there where the crowd seemed to be nearly on top of you."

Willie Johnston was visibly singled out for rough treatment and Pernia was booked by the Brazilian referee for his second assault on the winger early in the match.

Two further fouls, which ought to have resulted in Pernia's dismissal, were ignored and when Johnston reacted verbally the Argentinian was clearly seen to spit in his face.

Scotland controlled the midfield during the first half with Rough rarely called into action but events after the interval made headlines for the wrong reasons.

With 56 minutes on the clock Pernia punched Johnston in the kidneys out of sight of the referee, with play at the other end of the pitch. As Johnston lay on the turf the referee, on instruction from his linesman, sent the Argentinian from the field. What happened next was recorded by Hugh Taylor for the *Daily Record*. "We applauded as referee Filho sent off Pernia. We stared in amazement as he turned to Johnston and ordered him off. It was incredible, and no wonder Johnston was in tears. If he had done anything it was to stand up to an opponent." Willie remembers the incident as if it were yesterday. "I never touched the boy. They dragged me off because he was getting sent off. Honestly, they were animals; on the park they were up to every trick in the world."

Asa Hartford sensed that the writing was on the wall before a ball had been kicked: "In those days you would stand either side of the halfway line for the kick-off, like the outside-left against the right-back, and the fella was spitting at Willie then. You knew it was just a matter of time. It was quite a physical battle. After he got sent off Willie was fairly distraught because he thought he wasn't going to play against Brazil in the Maracana where everybody wants to play."

Scotland gained a penalty kick with 13 minutes remaining after a foul on Dalglish by a defender with the surname Killer. Masson, scorer of Scotland's previous penalty, against Finland, kept his composure in the hostile environment and scored with ease.

The joy turned to anger when Forsyth was said to have pushed Rossero in the box just three minutes later, enabling the balance to be redressed. Anticipating that Passarella would place the kick to his right, Rough dived in that direction only for the ball to enter in the centre of the goal. Forsyth later claimed that Rossero had dived whilst Jim Reynolds' view was that he had tripped over the ball.

The resulting draw would normally have been considered an excellent result, and retrospectively is one of the best achieved on foreign soil by the national side, but it did not seem like that at the time. Martin Buchan told Reynolds that the players were so disgusted with the referee that they had considered leaving the pitch after the equaliser. "At that point we felt like walking off," he told the journalist. "After all that had gone before, that penalty decision was the last straw."

Don Masson was in a similar frame of mind, as Jim Blair reported in the *Evening Times*: "We didn't draw the game, we were cheated out of winning it. We got a penalty, so they had to get one. Just like they had a man sent off, so we had to have one sent off too."

One walkout did take place, when the Argentinian manager Carlos Menotti continually deflected questions about the violent conduct of his players. When he accused the Scots of the same misbehaviour the Scottish reporters walked out en masse from the press conference.

There was unanimous sympathy for Willie Johnston with the manager absolving him of any blame and telling the press that he would definitely start in the final tour game in Brazil.

Over 40 years later Willie has never forgotten the manager's support. "Ally always said to me if it had been my fault he would never have picked me again. They were unbelievable. You didn't want to go back to Argentina, put it that way. And what did I do? I went back! But we should have beaten them that day. We played them off the park, honestly."

Flanked by their police escort, the SFA party were happy to head for the airport on the Monday where their 2pm flight to Rio de Janeiro was delayed by four hours. The manager profited from the impasse as a sweep was held amongst the party to guess the eventual departure time; it earned MacLeod £30.

The game had originally been scheduled for Sao Paulo but was rearranged for Rio a few weeks earlier, where the party enjoyed the luxury of the Sheraton Hotel.

The squad's new base was far removed from the metropolis of Buenos Aires with the beach within touching distance, two outdoor swimming pools and a brace of tennis courts within the complex. They had three days in which to acclimatise before their appointment in the Maracana.

"We had a hotel overlooking Copacabana beach – it was just something that as a footballer then it would never have happened to you," says Lou Macari. "It was a real eye-opener for you with all the sights in Rio that we went to. Trips abroad were something that all the players looked forward to as you would never have seen these countries."

"The players obviously love this setting, but they are here to do a job and they will not have much time for enjoyment," MacLeod told Jim Reynolds. Although he came across as easy-going, Ally was a strict disciplinarian and had seen a lack of it affect results during his time as a player at Blackburn Rovers.

Ally was already looking 12 months ahead and shared some of his thoughts with Reynolds. "This is perhaps the most difficult task Scotland has had to face. Winning the British Championship gave me a thrill, but really the World Cup is what it is all about. People may laugh when I say that is our aim, but I am deadly serious." He also told the journalist that the Brazilian media had intimated to him that they considered Scotland to be the third best team in the world. During the tour MacLeod stressed to the elder members of his pool that 1978 would quite probably be the last opportunity they would get to play at a World Cup.

Davie Cooper described the mood of the squad for the *Rangers News*: "It's hard to explain but all the guys over there would have died for their country. I was sure big Gordon McQueen was going to burst into tears when he realised his injury was going to keep him out of the three games. I realise manager MacLeod did me a terrific favour when he included me ... and it was a wonderful experience to mix with Scotland's best players."

Of the four survivors from Scotland's previous visit to the Maracana five years earlier – Donachie, Buchan, Hartford and

Macari – only Macari failed to make the starting 11 due to an injury sustained in training. Brazil, who had not lost a match in the famous stadium for 13 years, were at full strength.

Torrential rain was blamed for the "poor" crowd of 60,763, which left the ground approximately two-thirds empty. The Scots displayed signs of nervousness in the opening period with the fluency of previous performances missing. Rough almost single-handedly kept the game at 0-0, saving Rivelino and Cerezo shots inside the first 20 minutes.

As the half drew to a close Cesar looked certain to score from two yards before Rough saved the day again.

A tired Johnston had to be replaced by Jardine after an hour and it was beginning to look as though MacLeod's men may hold out for a draw. But then two goals in quick succession settled the match. "We had done well against Argentina and Chile but when we played Brazil we were all knackered and some of us didn't want to play," are Willie Johnston's recollections. "Brazil at least tried to play football. They could be physical, but they weren't as bad as what Argentina were. Argentina were just dirty thugs." The opener came with 20 minutes remaining when substitute Zico's free kick curled into the net from the edge of the box. It would not be the last time Rough faced a Zico free kick in his international career. The goal was greeted with firecrackers and the banging of drums which had barely diminished when Zico passed to Cerezo whose shot went over Rough and into the net to finish the scoring.

The manager offered no excuses for his first defeat in six matches – with five of those games away from home. Scotland had failed to win a corner kick against Brazil and MacLeod's own hand-written notes were a realistic assessment. They included the following: "Well beaten by a better team ... Humidity seemed to drain our midfield ... Never in the game in the second half."

Willie Johnston recalls: "It was a long season for us and then to go and play three games like that after you've had a hard season ... Honestly, it is hard with all the travelling but it was a good experience."

Davie Cooper's observations of the Brazilians were printed in the *Rangers News*. "I didn't think they were all that good. They never seemed to take on an opponent and beat him. All they did was take the ball up to him, give a shimmy and then roll it sideways to someone lending support. Good running off the ball but not as skilful as they were made out to be." Cooper himself was one of the last of a dying breed of Scottish wingers who thrived on the challenge of taking on and beating opposition players.

There was a feeling of anti-climax after the loss to Brazil but the tour was considered a success, as Ernie Walker told Jim Blair. "I feel we've achieved our purpose for this trip. The results were important, but it was also about experience for the players, manager and officials." The association's Finance Committee later calculated a loss of £13,723.40 on the trip although if it benefitted World Cup qualification the deficit would be more than covered.

Whilst the senior side had been in South America, Andy Roxburgh had taken an Under-21 squad to France to participate in the European Youth Tournament in Toulon. They played four matches between 12 and 19 June on the Cote D'Azur. The tournament format comprised two groups of four with the winners of each section contesting the final.

A practice match at Largs on 9 June against Northern Ireland's full team, who were preparing for a World Cup qualifier in Iceland, ended in a 1-1 draw. That result was a massive boost for the Scots, ahead of the trip, with Sammy McIlroy equalising Paul Sturrock's first-half goal.

Roxburgh's men lost their opening Group A match with Hungary 1-0 with Fuko's 33rd-minute winner coming against the run of play.

Their next match two days later was a real thriller with the young Scots beating Portugal 4-3. Wallace headed the opener but the lead was short-lived as poor defending contributed to the loss of two goals in a four-minute period. Second-half goals from Joe Craig, Wallace and McGarvey gave Scotland a 4-2 lead before Gomes reduced the deficit late in the game. This set up a decider against the hosts with a place in the final at stake.

Again, there was only 48 hours between matches but Scotland gave a good account of themselves in that last group game in front of 20,000 spectators. Both sides enjoyed good spells but a winner four minutes from time scored by Gerard Soler took France into the final against Bulgaria.

Roxburgh's men were not quite finished and played Italy before the final to decide fifth place, watched by 13,000 spectators. Scotland gained a 12th-minute lead through John Wark but needed a late equaliser from the same player to secure a 2-2 draw. The Scots had a marginal advantage for a five-minute spell during the first period when Prandelli was sent to the experimental "sin bin" before being allowed to re-join his team-mates. A penalty kick lottery then took place to separate the sides. After Thomson had saved from Bodini, the shoot-out turned to disaster for Scotland. Wark, Hansen and Aitken all missed whilst three Italians were successful, clinching fifth place for their team.

Almost unnoticed, on 1 July, Willie Allan left his position as SFA secretary with, as had been announced at the end of 1976, Ernie Walker succeeding him. It was the end of Allan's controversial reign which had begun exactly 20 years earlier.

Journalist Rodger Baillie looks back on a time of change within Park Gardens. "The major difference was that Ernie was aware of all the financial advantages that could be gained and Willie Allan was very old school," Rodger says. Ernie brought in Bill Wilson who was a commercial manager and he really made a massive difference in getting deals that I don't think they had ever dreamt of before. A lot said Willie Allan was impossible to deal with and he wasn't, but he was very much old-school SFA and he could be quite terse with you. Personally I would say I got on reasonably well with him but Ernie had a much more astute idea of how to deal with the media."

"I had known Ernie before he became secretary," says Archie Macpherson, "and I got to know him. He was a football man unlike the previous ones and he was snappy and intelligent to write some of his official statements for the SFA. To my mind he was the best."

One of Walker's first acts was to abbreviate the outdated title of International and Selection Committee to the more appropriate International Committee. Ever since Bobby Brown's appointment ten years previously the manager had been allowed complete control of team selection. In future the selectors would be referred to as committee members or by some in the media as "The Blazers".

Article 11 was recorded in the minutes of the International Committee meeting of 19 July thus: "The cases of the players who were disciplined following the match Denmark v Scotland, played on 3 September 1975, were considered and having agreed that the sentences imposed had now served their purpose, it was agreed that the ban on their being selected to represent Scotland be raised forthwith." Whether the suspensions would have ended under the previous secretary is unknown and, significantly, John MacDonald, who had been involved in the incident with Bremner, was no longer a committee member. Of the five, only Harper and Graham went on to play for Scotland again.

Ally MacLeod had one final opportunity to assess his players before Czechoslovakia's visit, when Scotland flew to Berlin to take on East Germany in September, the agreed return fixture for the Hampden friendly of 1974. They were greeted at Berlin Airport by a party of Scots Dragoon Guards, one of whom played the bagpipes as the party boarded a coach which took them through Checkpoint Charlie.

The manager told the press that although he wanted to win he also planned to experiment with the more important Czech game in mind. Leeds' Dave Stewart, who MacLeod had signed for Ayr United ten years earlier, started in goal with the manager stressing that Rough would have been first choice had the match been a competitive fixture.

Welsh manager Mike Smith's presence in Berlin concerned MacLeod enough for him to confide in Jim Blair: "I don't want to show our full hand. It would be foolish to give too much away."

The match began at 5pm local time with Jordan and McQueen both starting for the first time since Wembley. Scotland controlled the game in the opening half hour and Jordan went close when his header from a Dalglish cross was saved by Jurgen Croy. Just weeks earlier Dalglish had been transferred from Celtic to Liverpool for a fee of £440,000.

The Germans showed a more physical side to their game as the match wore on with Jim Reynolds' *Herald* report noting: "Konrad Weisse, a man who plays his football with all the finesse of a hammer thrower, chopped down Joe Jordan with sickening regularity." Stewart, keen to grasp the opportunity, impressed in goal and prevented Scotland going in a goal down with a fine stop from Weisse just ahead of the interval.

Stewart was, however, beaten in the 59th minute when Schade scored after running on to a through ball. The defence was exposed again 15 minutes later and Buchan floored Hoffman when he looked sure to score, but Stewart capped a fine performance by diving to block Dörner's penalty.

The policy of delivering high balls in Jordan's direction had been effectively neutralised by the East Germans and it was to be expected that the Czechs would also have taken Note: of this tactic which had cost them in the 1973 match. The single-goal defeat to the East Germans provoked an out-of-character outburst from the manager in the press room. "They are the dirtiest international side I have ever seen – even worse than the Argentinians. They committed an amazing number of off-the-ball fouls that went unpunished."

Alex Cameron sympathised with MacLeod, informing *Daily Record* readers: "The Czech referee was really the villain of the game. He allowed far too much pulling. Scotland were unlucky not to draw but the East Germans gave a sharp reminder that Czechoslovakia will not be easy to beat in two weeks' time."

Later that evening Scotland faced Switzerland in an Under-21 qualifier at Ibrox. MacLeod had chosen the side ahead of the German trip, leaving ex-Hearts boss John Hagart in charge on the night.

An action-packed four-minute period just ahead of the half-hour mark saw the Swiss take the lead with their first attack through Brigger. Scotland responded seconds later as Ian Wallace swivelled to shoot low into the net from 18 yards. After a further three minutes Burns won a soft penalty following a challenge by Weheli, only for Narey to blast the ball well wide of the target.

Shortly after half-time a shot from Schonenberger beat Stewart but rebounded off the bar. Scotland then went ahead after Wallace back-headed a cross from Graeme Payne into Cooper's path. Cooper made no mistake. Wallace notched his second before the end to seal a fine 3-1 result and give Scotland three points.

Ally MacLeod spent considerable time at both BBC Scotland's Queen Margaret Drive and STV's Cowcaddens studios where he was given full access to recordings of the Wales v Czechoslovakia match and West Germany v the Czechs in the European Championship Final. As well as noting any potential weaknesses in the opposition he also planned to learn from any mistakes made by his own players during the game in Prague.

Surprisingly there was no request for clubs to postpone league fixtures ahead of the Czechoslovakia match, which may have been related to the SFA's refusal to compensate clubs who had cooperated for the opening two qualifiers.

After a three-hour delay leaving Prague the Czech party missed their connecting flight from London to Glasgow and had to endure an overnight train journey which arrived in Central Station around 7am on the Tuesday morning.

After checking into the Eurocrest Hotel in Erskine the secretary of the Czech FA contacted FIFA with an unsuccessful plea for a 24-hour postponement of the match. This could only be considered with the SFA's cooperation and, not surprisingly, this was not forthcoming. The entire hotel staff then walked out on the Tuesday evening as part of a dispute over working conditions before relief workers were brought in to cater for the guests.

The travelling Under-21 players had almost no recovery time before heading to Edinburgh for Tuesday evening's match. Hagart was again in charge at Tynecastle and appealed for a large crowd. He got his wish with the turnstiles clicking over 14,000 times – almost four times the number that had watched the Swiss match at Ibrox. There was a terrific atmosphere in the ground and Scotland struck the woodwork twice early on through McGarvey and Burley.

The crowd were briefly silenced when Kroupa's angled shot went into the net after striking an upright, to give the visitors the lead. Scotland equalised when Burley forced the ball in at the second attempt. The crowd were still singing when Sturrock headed in minutes later to "put Tynecastle into a state of near delirium", according to Ian Paul's *Herald* report.

Showing no signs of travel fatigue, the Czechs created the better second-half opportunities but Hagart's men held on to finish 2-1 winners and complete their fixtures with five points, two ahead of the Czechs who still had to play Switzerland where a win would see them qualify on goal difference.

"The same will do tomorrow night," uttered at least one fan exiting Tynecastle. Although the backing had been excellent both numerically and vocally, club rivalry had reared its head during the match with "Flower of Scotland" and "Bonnie Scotland We'll Support You Ever More" alternating between chants of "If you are a Hearts supporter clap your hands" and anti-Hibs songs. Not all of the participants were necessarily of a maroon persuasion, as a small group, on meeting friends at Haymarket station, were heard to comment: "We were Hearts fans for the night." There had likely been an element of self-preservation in their behaviour, as in those days failure to clap at the appropriate moment could result in questions being asked or even a punch.

The Czechs ultimately won their outstanding fixture 2-0, causing Scotland to regret the earlier loss in Switzerland.

Czechoslovakian woes continued the following day when Under-21 goalkeeper Pavel Macek was arrested after stealing goods worth £16 from two stores in Glasgow's Argyle Street. He was fined £20 at Glasgow Central Court after admitting the offences, after originally pleading not guilty.

Like Hagart, MacLeod appealed directly to the fans through the press. "We've got to pull together on this one ... What I'd like is for the fans to give us a Wembley-like reception throughout the game." He dismissed the disruption to the opposition's preparations with: "I'm more concerned with what Scotland do than to worry about the Czechs' excuses."

The manager admitted to Jim Reynolds that some of the expected enthusiasm had been missing during the last international. "In East Germany I could sense before the match that something was wrong. Even in training I felt as though everything was forced. I could tell the difference immediately on Monday. They are all looking forward to this one and they have the real World Cup spirit."

With all the 85,000 tickets long sold out and a new SFA secretary, STV were given permission for a live transmission of the game. This was only the second occasion a home World Cup qualifier had been shown live with the Czechs providing the opposition both times.

"The noise is deafening!" said ITV's Brian Moore as the teams lined up. The manager's instructions to attack from the start were carried out as first Dalglish shot wide and then Masson had a long-ranger saved.

Scotland won a corner on the right after 18 minutes. If, as the manager suspected, the Czechs had been watching the game in Berlin they certainly had not done their homework. As Johnston's corner came over Jordan outjumped a defender and powered a header into the same net he had struck against the Czechs four years earlier.

It was 2-0 ten minutes before half-time when Jordan and Michalik both jumped for a Johnston cross. The goalkeeper caught the ball then lost it allowing Hartford to slot into an empty net from almost the penalty spot. There was a brief hesitation in case Jordan had impeded the keeper but the goal stood.

In what really was a dream performance a third goal arrived from a Masson corner just nine minutes after the turnaround. The ball was cleared out to the edge of the area where Jardine cleverly returned it with a strong header which Dalglish, with his back to goal, diverted into the net.

"Why are we so good?" sang the crowd, who were now quite accustomed to watching a winning team.

The only blot on the evening came ten minutes from time when Rough was beaten by a 30-yard Gajdusek shot which he later admitted he ought to have halted.

Although the 3-1 victory had contained none of the drama of the 1973 encounter it had been the perfect team performance, with the European champions looking second best all evening. The lion's share of the crowd refused to leave for around 15 minutes as a chant of "We want Ally!" rang out. Eventually they dispersed into the night when it became clear that the team would not be reappearing. "This was not a night for a lap of honour," MacLeod told the *Record*'s Ken Gallacher. "We will only do that when we have qualified for the World Cup finals."

During a brief pitch-side interview with STV's Alex Cameron, Ally singled out Masson as "the finest player in the world tonight", before rushing down the tunnel to join his players.

"I honestly think that was Scotland's best ever performance in an international," the manager told Jim Blair the following day. There was no shortage of journalists who shared that view. Alex Cameron said: "I have been watching Scotland for many years but for me this was our finest hour and a half." For Ian Archer: "This was the ultimate evening. Scotland played poetic football, worthy of a place in history. It was all the stuff of dreams. They were all heroes, the punters and professionals on a night that no one will ever forget." Jim Blair said: "No praise is high enough for this Scottish performance. They won a match they had to win (and won it well) ... and this has been our downfall in the past."

The result meant the Scots topped their section on four points with one match to play against the Welsh. Another victory would secure a place at the World Cup whilst a draw would still leave the door open for Wales to qualify on goal difference depending on the outcome of their final game in Czechoslovakia.

There had been much speculation about the venue for the Welsh match on 12 October, with both Cardiff and Wrexham's grounds considered inadequate for the occasion. After a failed attempt to increase the Ninian Park capacity from 14,000 to 25,000, the Welsh FA looked further afield. At one stage it seemed likely that Wembley might stage the match with Villa Park also under consideration.

Liverpool's Anfield was announced as the chosen venue on the penultimate day of August with Welsh FA secretary Trevor Morris explaining: "Anfield is just as accessible to many people from north Wales as Wrexham is. They can easily get there in less than an hour."

The SFA was allocated 25 per cent of the 49,500 capacity, a total of 12,000 tickets. Surprisingly the association decided against a ballot and made half of the tickets available for public sale through the established network of outlets used for the sale of Hampden tickets. These businesses were a mix of sports shops, travel agents and newsagents, stretching from Nairn in the north of the country to Dumfries in the south. The remaining 6,000 tickets were allocated to clubs and associations affiliated to the SFA. Ernie Walker revealed that each of the SFA's councillors were allocated six stand and four terrace briefs which amounted to almost 500 in total.

The public sale had taken place two days before the Czech match and all the outlets reported a complete sell-out within 30 minutes. As that particular Monday was a local holiday in Edinburgh, Ronnie Simpson's sports shop did not make their allocation available until the following day. This resulted in some unsuccessful fans from the west travelling to the capital and queuing outside the Rose Street store overnight. This caused some resentment amongst locals turning up closer to opening time who found the tickets were already accounted for.

Initially the Welsh FA dealt with postal applications from Scotland, but this policy was soon halted due to the numbers received and postal orders returned to Scottish addresses. The Welsh made the mistake of holding a public sale with no checks made on those handing over cash. A request from the SFA for an increased allocation following the Czech result was rejected by the Welsh. Judging by the thousands singing "We're all going to Anfield!" after the third goal against the Czechs, there was clearly going to be a number far in excess of 12,000 Scottish supporters in Liverpool.

Doigs Tours offered a return coach journey to Liverpool departing from Glasgow at 11am and returning directly after the match for £7.50. Cross Travel offered a more upmarket package flying to Liverpool with two nights in the city at the cost of £69.

British Rail laid on four Football Specials for the game with two leaving Glasgow, one from Edinburgh and the Aberdeen departure stopping in Dundee. The extra trains could accommodate a total of 3,600 passengers. Return fares were fixed between £8 and £12 with all purchasers required to fill out a questionnaire detailing names and addresses.

Even the total number of tickets printed would have been inadequate to fulfil Scottish demand with Anfield only accommodating half of Wembley's capacity, which Scottish fans had more or less filled just a few months earlier. The hunt was on to secure those precious tickets with contacts in England applying to the Welsh FA just as they were expected to do for the England v Scotland matches. A further 1,000 tickets were sent to the SFA when the Anfield crowd limit was increased by 2,500 about a week before the fixture. This increased figure of 13,000 was consistent with the 25 per cent allocation of the new 52,000 capacity. Season ticket holders at Liverpool had had the opportunity of purchasing one ticket each.

Again, clubs were not requested to cancel league games on the Saturday and MacLeod attended Partick Thistle v Celtic where Danny McGrain's name was absent from the team list. The full-back had been taken off against Hibs seven days earlier, suffering from an ankle injury. He had also missed a midweek League Cup tie and had withdrawn from the match at Firhill in a bid to improve his chances of playing at Anfield.

McGrain travelled with the Scotland party on the Monday but, along with Rioch, was ruled out of the match. Their places were taken by Willie Donachie and Lou Macari. McGrain's injury was much more serious than first realised and he did not play again all season. "For me it's like missing a Cup Final, only worse because this is my country

Tommy Docherty, right, revitalised the Scotland team when appointed manager in 1971. Billy Bremner, pictured left, said, "He puts arrogance into you and tells you the opposition aren't entitled to be on the same field" (Eric McCowatt)

The feel-good factor continued into the World Cup qualifying campaign. Peter Lorimer nets against Denmark, 15 November 1972. Within weeks Scottish football was shocked when the Doc left to take over at Manchester United, a decision he later regretted (Eric McCowatt)

Hampden's greatest night – Jim Holton rises to equalise against Czechoslovakia as the Scots qualify for the 1974 World Cup finals. 26 September 1973 (Eric McCowatt)

Joe Jordan scores in the 88th minute against Yugoslavia to briefly keep Scotland's [playing in white] World Cup hopes alive. 22 June 1974. "We will never be beaten until the last whistle," Billy Bremner had vowed (Getty)

With no public transport to Wembley in 1975, fans either had to endure a long walk or find alternative means, such as these supporters who travelled to the stadium in a furniture lorry. 24 May 1975 (Getty)

With the scores level on aggregate, Willie Ormond prepares a strong Under-23 side for extra-time against Holland. 24 March 1976. Players from left to right: Peter Dickson, Joe Jordan, Tommy Craig (no. 6), John Brownlie and Willie Miller. The Scots lost on penalties in what was their last ever Under-23 fixture (Eric McCowatt)

A lack of funds did not prevent supporters travelling to matches. Unlike the Tartan Army of later years hitch-hiking and sleeping rough were a way of life for some fans during the 1970s. Supporters catch some sleep in Euston Station ahead of their victory at Wembley, 4 June 1977 (PA)

Ally's Army turned Wembley into a home match. The watching police and temporary barriers were powerless to prevent the pitch invasion at full time (PA)

"Que sera sera" – although good at the time, the post-match celebrations were a major factor in the demise of the traditional Wembley weekend (Eric McCowatt)

On top of the world. After an outstanding start, Ally MacLeod was the King of Scotland in June 1977. He assesses the conditions at La Bombonera in Buenos Aires ahead of a match Scotland ought to have won. Twelve months later Ally's whole world collapsed when he returned to Argentina (PA)

Kenny Dalglish's late header seals qualification for the 1978 World Cup on a dramatic night in Liverpool, 12 October 1977. The local newspaper described the evening as "The night the city will never forget" (PA)

13th October 1977. Clearing out the Kop the morning after. Despite a ban on bottles, empty containers of Pomagne, Gordons, Carlsberg, Smirnoff, Cointreau, Newcastle Brown and others litter the terraces, whilst a couple of tartan scarves remain tied to a barrier. One local resident described the area around the ground as "a great bin" (Getty)

Whilst many others had turned back, Robbie Sterry reached the promised land of Argentina after a long journey fraught with danger. Robbie is pictured here in Cordoba

"No Mendoza!" was the chant from these irate fans who targeted the players at the end of the draw with Iran. Robbie Jenkins is in the centre of the second row, wearing a cap. Others pictured in the front row include John Duffy, Jim Grieve, John Cullen and John McKenzie. 7 June 1978 (Alamy)

Joy at last in Argentina as Archie Gemmill's penalty gives Scotland an early second half lead against the Dutch. 11 June 1978 (Getty)

Jock Stein was the popular choice to pick Scotland up from the debacle of Argentina. Here he watches his side collapse after taking an early lead at Wembley. 26 May 1979. Note the newly erected fencing around the spectators since Scotland's previous visit (Getty)

Scottish fans in good spirits ahead of the European Championship qualifier in Norway one year to the day after the Iran nightmare, 7 June 1979

involved and the prize is the greatest in the game," a shattered Rioch told Horace Yates for the back page of the *Liverpool Daily Post*.

The advance guard of Ally's Army began arriving in the city on the Monday with the majority of them seeking match tickets. Some fans knocked on former Liverpool manager Bill Shankly's door hoping he may be able to help. Police patrolled the Anfield perimeter on the Tuesday evening in case anyone attempted to scale the high walls around the ground.

The *Liverpool Echo*'s matchday edition said: "Around 400 Scots who had made no arrangements for accommodation wandered around Liverpool all night. Scores slept huddled under blankets and flags in Stanley Park where some found shelter under the bandstand." Locals going to their work that Wednesday morning were shocked to see many Scots already drinking from tins of beer. On the day of the game the Scots took over Liverpool city centre with the Welsh fans expected to arrive closer to kick-off time.

Scottish fans were critical of the ticket allocation and took offence at advice to watch the game on television. "I can tell you this: there will be as many in Liverpool tomorrow as there were at Wembley for the English game and it doesn't matter whether or not they have tickets," Jim Thomson from Dumbarton told *The Herald*. "Why should we stay in Scotland and watch the game on TV? It doesn't matter what happens – we will be at the game."

Following the pitch invasion at Wembley, there were fears of trouble in the Anfield area with schools closing early and pubs around the ground not opening. The majority of cafes, shops and off-licences also remained closed with some boarded up. The Anfield Residents' Association wanted the match to be called off with one anonymous member quoted in the *Liverpool Daily Post* saying: "We are piggy in the middle. There are Welsh and Scottish supporters and this is going to be a battlefield."

Bill Shankly appealed for calm, comparing the Scots with Liverpool supporters who had travelled to Rome for the European Cup Final that summer. "Don't confuse excitement with troublemaking. The Scots fans will be no trouble to you," he told the *Echo*.

Liverpool FC secretary Peter Robinson told the *Daily Record*: "The ground is impenetrable. Fans without tickets have no hope of getting in. We extended the outside walls to 17 feet after Celtic were here 11 years ago and some of their supporters had climbed over – this won't happen again." This cut no ice with the travelling fans as Fifer Ian Souter told the *Liverpool Daily Post*: "The gates will go down at Anfield just as they do at Wembley every two years. I come from Lochgelly and 680 people are coming down and 20 have tickets."

That was the mentality of the time, whereas in later years ticketless Scottish football supporters would travel to away matches resigned to watching the action on big screens in designated fan zones away from the stadium; that was out of the question in the 1970s. Ally's Army were determined to turn up at the ground and would not be denied entry.

The famous Spion Kop was allocated to the Welsh supporters whilst the smaller Anfield Road end plus some stand seats were the official Scottish sections. Ally MacLeod predicted that the majority of the crowd would be backing his players. "I expect we will have between 25,000 and 30,000 fans," he told the *Liverpool Daily Post*, adding, "Wales think they have the Kop but they'll find it full of Scots."

Thousands walked to the ground, forcing traffic to grind to a halt as nervous locals watched from behind curtains. One group marched all the way in single file until police realised they had a ladder between their legs.

Close to kick-off a crowd estimated at 5,000 forced open a double gate at the Anfield Road end which led directly on to the terracing. Some fans were injured in the crush and the *Scotsman* reported: "Hundreds of people poured through the opening and it was several minutes before police could regroup and charge the supporters with batons. With ten minutes to go until the start of the game police regrouped and pushed back the crowd, forming a human wall against the open gates. As the game kicked off and the roar rose from inside the ground, those with and without tickets who could not get in pushed again, and again the police barrier broke. More supporters streamed in. Half an hour after the start many supporters were still trying to get in."

A number of fans climbed through a hole in the roof of a gents' toilet whilst some turnstile operators accepted bribes. This led to overpopulated terraces with the consequence that some latecomers with tickets were refused entry. Various estimates put numbers outside the ground at between 8,000 and 10,000. The *Liverpool Echo* related: "After half-time as hundreds of supporters realised entry was impossible, they ran through the streets of the area chanting and throwing cans and on several occasions mounted police were forced to disperse them."

Earlier, the Welsh had spread themselves around the Kop but as kick-off approached more and more Scots entered, forcing them into a corner. A number of bottles were thrown before order was restored. It was obvious to those standing at both ends that the terraces were over-capacity and there was little room to manoeuvre with fans crushed against barriers during frequent crowd surges.

The expectation levels were far greater than they had been for the Czech match in 1973, when a win had earned World Cup qualification. Doubts had been cast over the team's chances on that occasion but for the game in Liverpool there was almost an assumption that Scotland would win. "It's Argentina or bust," wrote Hugh Taylor in the *Record*. Jim Blair's *Evening Times* column contained the following: "It's almost zero hour ... the tension is mounting ... all eyes will be on Anfield tonight."

Stuart Borrowman was a spectator at the game and had also attended the Czechoslovakia match four years earlier. "In 1973 the mood was a sort of 'Can't quite believe it but we've succeeded'," he said. "But at Anfield there was a bit of 'Who the hell are Wales? Who are they to be getting in our way? We are bound to beat them'. You felt it had to happen – like it was fate. It was the completely opposite feeling before that game."

"It was a different atmosphere at Anfield," Robbie Jenkins recalls. "Both brilliant atmospheres but in different ways as in we were there to conquer Wales. The Czech game was different – it was a phenomenal atmosphere urging Scotland to victory."

Robbie vividly recollects the tension around the ground. "There were absolutely loads of people without tickets and I just felt it was overpowering. Like at an Old Firm game when it could be friendly but you feel the slightest thing and it could kick off to something unfriendly, and that's what I felt about the Scotland v Wales game. I felt if Scotland had lost that game there would have been trouble because everybody was up to such hype. People had been drinking a lot and it was one of these games where there was a potential for trouble.

"I remember there was people talking about storming the gates. There were thousands there without a ticket, people hanging about outside desperate for a ticket, so it just seemed like it could kick off. Everyone was so tensed up you just think it won't take much.

"It was a sense of desperation as much as anything else. There was an element amongst the Scottish support you were expecting something from the team. We were going there expecting to beat the Welsh."

Archie Macpherson surveyed the scene from the television platform ahead of the kick-off and still remembers the words of his co-commentator Jock Stein. "'I hope to God we win,' he said to me. 'If we don't I think they'll take Liverpool apart.'"

Despite the run of recent good form there was an air of nervousness inside the Scotland dressing room, as remembered by Willie Johnston: "There was a lot of pressure that night. I think that's the only time I've really felt nervous ... I was always a bit nervous but I had a few extra fags before I went out. In the dressing room before the start of the game we couldn't wait to get out because the nerves were jangling."

"Willie was quite nervous before many games in those days and he used to have a puff before big games like that," laughs Asa Hartford at the memory of his team-mate drawing on a cigarette.

The players walked out to a wall of noise and, just like Wembley, the game was like a home match for Scotland. "When we came out and saw that it was just amazing. That was a brilliant atmosphere," Asa reminisces.

The support the team received that evening is fresh in the mind of Lou Macari. "The prize was going to the World Cup so we were ready for it but when we walked out the tunnel that was the clincher. The ground was nearly full of Scottish supporters. There was that many there it was no longer an away match, it was a home game and the fact you felt it was a home game gave you that little bit more belief that you were going to do it.

"You think: 'Bloody hell we can't lose here, no way can we lose. We've got all these people supporting us, it's going to happen for us.'"

The volume barely let up throughout the 90 minutes on a dramatic night which would, like the Czech game of 1973 and the England match a few months earlier, go down in Scottish football folklore. Never to be forgotten by those who were fortunate enough to be there and if you weren't present you really could not have an accurate perception of the occasion.

From a Macari cross Dalglish, making his 50th appearance, flashed a header narrowly wide after four minutes. Shortly afterwards the Liverpool player looked sure to score after pouncing on an error by David Jones but lost his footing as he tried to round Dai Davies. Having survived a 15-minute onslaught Sayer shot past as the Welsh began to settle and half-time arrived with the contest still scoreless. In that first half Scotland had earned five corners with the Welsh yet to win their first.

The St John Ambulance crews treated over 200 casualties inside the ground. Included in that figure was one man who was successfully revived with oxygen at the side of the pitch. He had collapsed after being crushed and had been close to death. Another fan was passed above the heads of those packed on the Spion Kop and then over the perimeter fence. He was rushed to Walton Hospital but died of a heart attack.

Wales's best opportunity of the night came around the 60th minute when Toshack controlled a header from Yorath before lobbing a fine effort from around 15 yards which Rough, diving athletically, managed to touch on to the top of the crossbar and into the Kop.

Scotland then rallied in search of the goal they knew would take them to Argentina. The Welsh hacked the ball to safety after surviving one incredible scramble, which was described by Arthur Montford as "an unbelievable 60 seconds of pure drama".

The second half had flashed by so quickly that it seemed that only ten minutes had been played rather than there being 11 remaining, when Johnston launched a long throw high into the box from the left touchline.

"I was throwing it long at that time," says Willie. "I would throw it into the box for big Joe or big Gordon when he came up, and once it was in there it was up to them." Jordan and Jones went up together and the ball was clearly punched away after which referee Wurtz signalled a penalty kick. For once the Scots fans were silent with only the jeers of the Welsh audible as Masson prepared to take what Arthur Montford, the tension evident in his commentary, described as "the most important football moment in Don Masson's long and distinguished football career", adding, "and I can hardly look".

Masson kept his cool whilst Montford lost his, exclaiming: "It's there! It's there!" as the ball hit the net, like a demented fan on the packed terracing. Archie Macpherson's reaction for BBC Scotland viewers was: "The Scottish supporters are going mad! You have never heard noise like this in all your life!"

Scottish flags fluttered around the ground as "Que Sera Sera" was adapted to "We're going to Argentine" which rhymed better than "Argentina" and contained the required number of syllables.

"Flower of Scotland" was rising to a crescendo when Dalglish leapt to head substitute Buchan's cross into the net with three minutes remaining, sealing a 2-0 win and a place at the World Cup.

One solitary fan breached the police cordon at full time and was promptly and heavy-handedly dealt with by the oficers, resulting in a number of bottles being thrown in their direction.

The Welsh fans and players were shattered and there was a suggestion that the handball had been perpetrated by Jordan although this was largely lost in the euphoria of the evening. Expecting the team to return, the crowd waited for the best part of 30 minutes before it dawned on them that there would be no lap of honour. The players had been waiting in the mouth of the tunnel but had been refused permission to take a bow by the Merseyside Constabulary.

The manager paid tribute to his goalkeeper and the supporters in the press room: "Alan Rough had the save of the match and that set things up for us," said MacLeod. "It's a marvellous result and I'm so pleased for all those fantastic fans."

It was not until the next edition of the *Sunday Mail* was published that the penalty controversy gathered momentum, with a picture appearing to show long-sleeved Jordan handling the ball. After launching the ball into the box Willie Johnston had had his suspicions. "After the game I said to big Joe, 'Did you?' and he came back with 'What do you think?' I said that I saw a hand going up that was all. Joe just sat there in the dressing room."

"I actually thought it was a penalty. I think I claimed for it," says Asa Hartford.

Joe's clubmate at Leeds, Eddie Gray, has this to say: "Big Joe's so-called handball? He still says he never handballed it, adamantly!"

Wales had been unfortunate in terms of the opening goal, since a draw would have kept them in with a chance of qualification. And it should not be forgotten that they only lost at Hampden due to an own goal. Yet Scotland had undoubtedly been the better side in both matches, unlike the Home International in Wrexham when the Welsh had dominated. Taking Toshack's late miss at Hampden into account, these incidents illustrate the thin margins between winning and World Cup participation.

"THE NIGHT THE CITY WILL NEVER FORGET" was the *Liverpool Daily Post*'s front-page headline above an article which generally praised the behaviour of the Scots. "It was impossible to avoid admiring the passion of the thousands wearing the tartan," said reporter Charles Lambert. The locals offered opposing views with a greater number speaking in favour of the supporters than criticising them although inevitably some were of the belief there would have been more trouble had Scotland lost. There were 300 injuries, many caused by crushing or by head wounds inflicted by police batons during the rush on the gates. More than 50 arrests inside the ground were reported.

The *Liverpool Echo* claimed that Bridewell Prison had experienced the "busiest night in its history with 120 arrests". A spokesman for British Rail told the *Daily Post* that the special trains had all left Edge Hill without incident. "We have had no trouble with any of [the passengers]. They have been well behaved, formed queues as we asked and did as they were told."

One resident of Anfield Road, Mrs Ivy Gordon, told the *Echo*: "They were wonderful. At other big matches we have had bricks thrown through the windows, fights and damage to gardens, but tonight there was nothing but good nature." Mr Bob Connelly of Crosgrove Road agreed, but criticised the closure of pubs and cafes in the vicinity of the ground. "Their behaviour has been impeccable, but the police have shown a great deal of aggression and I'm surprised more of the fans have not lost their temper." Commenting on the debris left behind, another local described the area as "a great bin".

The *Echo* also contained a report of vandalism to a vicarage opposite the Kemlyn Road stand. "Forty supporters climbed over a barbed wire barricade put up by the Reverend Michael Smart at his home. In an orgy of destruction they jumped on the church's minibus, and hurled slates from the garage roof from where they threw cans and bottles down on passers-by." The Reverend Smart, who was said to have been cowering inside with his wife and two young children, told the newspaper: "I have never known anything like it – they terrorised the family."

Other accounts included an elderly woman who invited four ticketless but grateful fans into her home to watch the match when she realised her television could receive BBC Wales. Many locals stood on doorsteps after the game offering water in a variety of containers to grateful and thirsty supporters of both teams. As with the predicted riot at Wembley in 1975, many supporters had made a conscious effort to try and improve the image of the Scottish fans.

Thomas Cook's Glasgow branch received their first enquiry about Argentina shortly after opening at 9am the following morning. Travel agencies around the country were soon dealing with similar queries but before long it was obvious that nothing like the thousands who had followed the team to West Germany would be able to afford the trip to South America.

At the end of November Ally MacLeod and Ernie Walker flew to Argentina to check out potential accommodation and training facilities even though the fixtures would not be allocated until January. Provisional bookings were made at all of the World Cup venues, to be confirmed or cancelled once the draw had been made. The SFA was later criticised over its organisation for the tournament but this move was one step ahead of Scotland's as then unknown opponents.

The duo returned with a much-improved opinion of Argentina than their summer experience in Buenos Aires. "The trip was invaluable and we both feel that the finals will be a great occasion," Ernie Walker told the *Evening Times*. "We were both struck by the enthusiasm and efficiency of the Argentinians." The year 1977 had been the best ever in which to be a Scotland supporter, with 1978 promising to be even better. The SFA secretary composed the following text for the association's Annual Report: "It is doubtful if any single event since the last war had the impact on the Scottish people that our qualifying to play in Argentina had. Whatever happens, win or lose, to have qualified again is an accomplishment for which, justifiably, the Association and all who are interested in Scottish football may be proud."

9

1978

"So don't cry for us Argentina, just cry for Iran and Peru. And when we have finished with Holland they'll sign Johan Cruyff on the Brew."
Andy Cameron, Klub Records

The draw for the 11th World Cup finals took place in Buenos Aires on Saturday, 14 January and was relayed live on STV. As in 1974 Scotland were one of 16 participants and the only British side taking part. Two nations would progress from each group of four and there was optimism when Scotland were given what was considered by many to be a favourable route to the second phase.

Ian Archer, in Argentina for the draw, was certainly optimistic, telling STV viewers: "Holland, Iran, Peru and Scotland – surely a passport to the last eight. Iran and Peru are the two minnows, so it could be that when we get to Holland we've both qualified already." The order of fixtures for Scotland was Peru first followed by Iran then the Dutch.

Ally MacLeod, along with Ernie Walker, was also present in Buenos Aires and told the *Sunday Post* by telephone: "It couldn't have worked out any better if I'd planned it myself and we must have a fair chance of moving into the latter stages."

The following day Walker and MacLeod flew to Córdoba, the venue of Scotland's opening two matches, to confirm the provisional accommodation booking they had made in November. When they arrived in Alta Gracia, 23 miles from Córdoba and with a population of 3,000, they discovered that the Iranians had already visited the Sierras Hotel and had attempted to bribe the manager into cancelling the SFA booking.

A number of sports writers found themselves redundant the following Saturday when bad weather all but wiped out the Scottish football calendar. Some editors quickly arranged for journalists to meet the returning manager in London ahead of his return to Scotland.

"I was on the *Sunday Mirror* when Ally and Ernie Walker came back from the draw," remembers Rodger Baillie. "Five or six of us flew down to Gatwick to meet them and he was ebullient and full of life and that's where he came out with the line – he actually didn't say we would win it – but come out with we will win a medal which was a hostage to fortune. I don't know if he actually did say we'll win the World Cup but he certainly came very close to it."

That same month the first Argentina-bound supporters left Scotland prepared to sacrifice their attendance at the Scotland v England match in favour of the World Cup. Unable to afford flights to South America, John Grigor and three colleagues handed in their notices at Butlin's holiday camp in Ayr. Their gateway to the Americas was Freddie Laker's DC10 Skytrain. Laker Airways was one of the first budget airlines and had offered a one-way London to New York fare of £59 the previous year. The trio had a vague plan to find work en route.

"I didn't know how far New York was from Argentina. We were going to get Greyhound buses but we hadn't really a lot of plans," Ayr United fan John reminisces. "The important thing was getting to the right continent and giving ourselves plenty of time to do it. I was only 18 at the time when I left with £100 in my pocket – that was four weeks' wages!

"We got jobs in bars in the Bronx where we got fed and got beer off them and a bed. We had absolutely no idea how we were going to get back home or anything. You didn't think about these things. We met other people in New York who were trying to get to Argentina too."

During this period Ally MacLeod became one of the most prominent personalities on television and in the newspapers. He had guested on four different programmes in as many days over the New Year period. *Hogmanay Sportscene* and *Scotsport* were familiar territory for the national manager who also popped up in Grampian's *Welcome to the Ceilidh* and an edition of STV's *Sounds and Sweet Airs,* in which both he and host Kenneth McKellar sported tartan bonnets.

A weekly slot each Sunday afternoon on *Scotsport*, 'The Ally MacLeod File' later allowed him to look ahead to the tournament alongside Ian Archer. Ally also appeared on *Blue Peter*, presented a television commercial for Argentina '78 carpets and enjoyed a brief stint as a disc jockey on Radio Clyde.

This over-exposure would later be used as ammunition by critics when results went against Scotland, with the accusation that MacLeod was too busy selling carpets to watch the opposition. The promotional work had been arranged through an agency recommended to him by Jock Stein. Tony Meehans also represented a number of players who appeared in their own advert for Chrysler Avenger cars. It is practically impossible to imagine Stein promoting the sale of anything let alone carpets and MacLeod himself later admitted he had perhaps been guilty of spending too much time in the spotlight. The carpet commercial enjoyed regular screentime but in reality would have taken less than a day to produce.

The first fixture of 1978 saw Ally MacLeod take full control of the Under-21s against Wales on 8 February. The match had been switched to Chester at short notice with the original Wrexham venue required for an FA Cup replay involving Newcastle. MacLeod returned to Thornton Haugh which had served his players well before the qualifier against Wales. He also went back to Anfield where Liverpool defeated Arsenal 2-1 in the first leg of the League Cup semi-final 24 hours before the Chester game.

MacLeod paid particular attention to the form of the once-banned Arsenal centre-half Willie Young and told Jim Reynolds before the game: "It is the one position where we could have problems for the World Cup and I could not pass up the chance to see one of the candidates in such an important match." Young was said to have a poor game and MacLeod told Alan Davidson of the *Evening Times*: "Kenny Dalglish apart, I didn't see too much to impress me."

Wales dominated the first half and took the lead when Robbie James beat Billy Thomson with a swerving shot from 25 yards. Thomson almost single-handedly kept Scotland in the game with a fine second-half performance as his team-mates struggled against a physically stronger side.

In only their second opportunity of Note: Scotland almost stole a draw two minutes from time when Gordon Smith's header from a Neil McNab corner was booted off the goal line by Wayne Hughes to preserve the 1-0 result.

What the manager really wanted was full international matches and a friendly was arranged with Bulgaria at Hampden on 22 February. Ally's selection contained two surprises: Coventry goalkeeper Jim Blyth and Nottingham Forest midfielder John Robertson.

"I have no intention of playing somebody who has no chance of going to Argentina," MacLeod told the press at Park Gardens. Blyth had produced an outstanding display for his side in a victory against Liverpool earlier that month, highlights of which had been featured on BBC Scotland's *Sportscene*.

The Saturday before the match threw up all kinds of problems. Firstly, bad weather allowed just four Scottish fixtures to go ahead, with frozen pitches wiping out the rest of the calendar. Just one game, Queen's Park v Clyde, had taken place on the Hampden pitch since 10 December and with the Bulgarians due to fly in on the Monday the conditions were of grave concern. The FA Cup was also affected and the Derby v West Bromwich tie was rescheduled for the same evening. In addition, Notts Forest rearranged their League Cup semi-final with Leeds for the Wednesday, all of which deprived Scotland of Masson, Rioch, Johnston and Robertson with Buchan, McGrain and Andy Gray all out through injury.

That Saturday morning the manager, the SFA secretary and two members of the International Committee inspected the Hampden pitch and decided that the conditions were suitable for the game to proceed. There was a gamble involved because any deterioration in the pitch meant compensation, said to be between £25,000 and £30,000, to be paid to the Bulgarians in the event of a wasted journey.

Graeme Souness and Under-21 star Ian Wallace were amongst the replacements called in to the squad. By the Tuesday the weather was no longer considered a threat and there were no further pitch inspections planned. Celtic's rearranged Scottish Cup tie with Kilmarnock was postponed on the Tuesday then rescheduled in direct opposition to the international.

Flooding after an overnight thaw led to the cup tie being called off again and an inspection at Hampden by match referee Pat Partridge. With rain forecast in the afternoon Partridge delayed his decision and it was just before 5pm when the green light was given for the game to go ahead, with many supporters already heading for Glasgow.

Just six of the Anfield line-up started with Blyth and Stuart Kennedy earning their first caps and Willie Miller his second. Continued rain had little effect on the turnout which was massively underestimated. Organisation was poor with only a limited number of turnstiles operating, which led to chaotic scenes outside Hampden. With no organised queues a mass of bodies converged on those gates, causing some supporters to give up and return home. Although the scenes could not be compared to those in Liverpool it took some attendees half an hour to enter by which time Scotland were behind.

Not that the late arrivals would have been able to tell as they entered a party atmosphere which seemed to have continued from the Anfield Kop. "Que Sera Sera" was now an established favourite with Andy Cameron's World Cup novelty release "Ally's Tartan Army" also sung repeatedly.

Alex Cameron's *Daily Record* report adequately summed up the mood: "The days of coming to cheer Old Firm players are over. There wasn't one Rangers or Celtic player in the line-up at the kick-off yet there was an incredible reception from the crowd – despite the lashing rain."

The truce was briefly broken when the Celtic anthem "You'll Never Walk Alone" was countered by a response of whistles even though it had been sung loudly during the previous few matches.

Blyth could have done without the loss of the early goal on his international debut, when Zdravkov punted a long ball forward for Mladenov to strike a spectacular right-foot shot high into the net from 12 yards. As already noted, this did nothing to silence the mood of the crowd and, typical of a MacLeod team, they then threw six and sometimes seven men into attack.

The pressure paid off shortly before half-time when a Donachie cross was headed out as far as Hartford who beat three men before being tripped. The ball broke to Dalglish who swept it over the line but his and the crowd's celebrations were halted as referee Partridge had already signalled for a penalty kick following the foul on Hartford.

In Masson's absence Gemmill, also deputising as captain, took the responsibility and made no mistake by placing his kick high to the right of Staikov.

Scotland continued to pour forward in the second half and introduced Wallace and Johnstone for Dalglish and Jordan, but it was McQueen who went closest when his header from Johnstone's cross came back from the crossbar seven minutes from time.

That looked to be the final opportunity but there was a dramatic ending just two minutes later: Souness ran from his own half past three Bulgarians before feeding Wallace just outside the area. The striker strode forward and shot beyond the diving Staikov to send the fans home happy still singing the Andy Cameron song.

"That was a terrific atmosphere out there," Wallace told *The Herald*. "I'm used to playing before big crowds at Coventry, but they are nothing like that."

The attendance of 59,524 was described by Ernie Walker as "astonishing". Responding to accusations of poor organisation the secretary told the *Evening Times*'s Alan Davidson: "I think it took everybody by storm and I think it's a reflection of the huge interest there is in the international side in World Cup year. It was a marvellous turnout when you consider the weather, the withdrawals from the squad and the uncertainty about the match." Certainly the prospect of a full house under more favourable circumstances was quite conceivable.

The gamble in going ahead with the match had paid off with the SFA later calculating a profit of £35,364.41, once outgoings had been deducted from receipts, programmes sales and television revenues.

By the end of March the four fans who had set off from Ayr were still in New York – ten weeks after their arrival. "We had no money left for a long time," says John Grigor. They did, however, have return tickets for the Skytrain and the party split with two of them continuing to Argentina whilst John and one other reluctantly decided to return home on 1 April. They consoled themselves with hopes of attending the Scotland v England match – if they could find tickets.

At New York airport they found the next available seats were not for a further three days, a period John recalls with no great pleasure. "We had nowhere else to go to except sleep at the airport so I had to go and beg with my tartan bonnet. We had cigarette papers and we pinched fags out of the ashtrays and made roll-ups. We had run out of money and there was no way you could reach any money then so you had to beg and quite often it was just a cup of tea or coffee you had." They were not short of company, however, as they encountered another 40 to 50 returning Scotland fans at the airport whose World Cup dreams were also over.

"We should never have gone into New York in the first place," John reflects today. "The two that went on I've never heard from since and I can't even remember their names. I got slagged rotten when I came back to Ayr. I didn't have a job or nothing and my mother wasn't pleased." John, who has attended every World Cup Scotland have taken part in since 1978, speaks in a voice which is a mixture of both nostalgia and regret. "Although some people call it a disaster I still have regrets about not making Argentina to this day because it was such a high that we just felt we were going to win the World Cup."

Unable to arrange another international for April, MacLeod took charge of a Scotland XI to play Rangers in John Greig's testimonial match at Ibrox on Sunday 16 April. It is difficult to gauge how seriously this fixture was taken as there was no scope for preparation, with the players turning out for their clubs 24 hours earlier and only assembling on the Sunday. Nevertheless, Ally fielded a strong side with a starting line-up of Blyth, Brownlie, Whitaker, Masson, McQueen, Rioch, Robertson, Wallace, Jordan, Hartford and Gemmill.

The two Old Trafford players drove north on the Sunday morning but were held up in traffic which delayed the kick-off by 20 minutes. Tom Forsyth and Derek Johnstone were hastily transferred from light blue to the white of the Scotland XI to make up the numbers, only to revert to their club colours when Jordan and McQueen arrived courtesy of a police escort which had enabled them to bypass the congestion.

Johnstone scored with a header after 50 seconds and as Jim Reynolds observed in his *Herald* report: "The Scottish side were prepared to amble their way through and they paid the full price for it."

Greig found the net after an hour when Jardine's ball across the face of the goal allowed him to finish from four yards. To say that Greig looked to be in an offside position would be an understatement but what referee could deprive a man of a goal in his own benefit game? Bobby Russell, often tipped for a full cap, scored three minutes later and again shortly afterwards. Ten minutes from time Greig scored a goal more worthy of the occasion when he beat Blyth from 15 yards to complete the scoring at 5-0.

Jim Reynolds summarised with: "As a testimonial match it was ideal. As a trial for Scotland's World Cup squad it was a disaster bordering on humiliation. Rangers looked as if they wanted to win from the start while too many of the Scots were apparently not willing to expend too much energy on their traditional day of rest."

As far as the 65,000 crowd were concerned there was no great Rangers–Scotland love-in. Most of the attendees wore club favours with some also sporting a concession to the national side such as a tartan scarf tied to a wrist. Save for one chant of "Scotland! Scotland!" at the start the terrace anthems were those normally heard on the Copland Road slopes with each goal cheered enthusiastically and the result rounded off by a chorus of "Rangers five, Scotland nil, Hallelujah!" It is highly likely that the fans of every other club would have behaved in the same manner, for, even in those heady days of 1978, supporters' loyalties lay primarily with the side they watched most weeks of the year.

Just three days later a Scotland Select played against a Highland League side at Kingsmill Park in Inverness. Unlike the 1976 match in Elgin, which had featured a Scottish League XI, this fixture had SFA recognition. With MacLeod watching the England v Brazil friendly at Wembley, his chosen assistant took charge of the Scottish side.

"Scotland World Cup assistant manager John Hagart danced a jig of joy on the pitch when substitute Gordon Cramond flicked home the last-gasp equaliser which saved his side from a humiliating defeat," began Bill McAllister's *Press and Journal* match summary. Watched by a crowd of 4,301, Inverness Caledonian striking partnership Billy Urquhart and Ray MacKintosh had given the Highlanders a two-goal lead by the 65th minute before late strikes from Alan Sneddon and Cramond salvaged the draw which sparked Hagart's impromptu dance routine.

The following Wednesday MacLeod took a Scottish League side to Verona for a match against a strong Italian B team. Seven of those who had played at Kingsmill Park started, with Willie Pettigrew supplementing the attack. The expected 30,000 crowd was reduced to around 10,000 by "a thunderstorm of immense proportions", reported Ian Paul in the *Glasgow Herald*. The home side were expected to win but the Scots, watched by Peru manager Marcos Caleron, took most of the plaudits as they earned a fighting 1-1 draw. The Scots were fortunate to hold out until the 60th minute when Roberto Pruzo scored, but Ally's men responded within four minutes when Graeme Sinclair's cross was headed in by Dougie Somner.

A matter of inches prevented victory when a Pettigrew effort struck the crossbar before the end with Italian manager Enzo Bearzot praising the "approach and technique" of the Scots. None of the players on display that afternoon even made the World Cup squad so Caleron had something of a wasted journey.

On 14 April, about a week after John Grigor's return, 19-year-old Robbie Sterry left Perth for Argentina with £500 in traveller's cheques in his pocket. After his travelling companion had backed out Robbie followed in John's footsteps on the Skytrain from Gatwick, at the start of a trip which would be fraught with danger.

Whilst on the road Robbie became something of a celebrity in the Scottish newspapers as the fan who had broken off his engagement with a local beauty queen who had been crowned Miss Perth to head to the World Cup.

As Ally MacLeod was sometimes heard to say, never let the truth get in the way of a good story which was certainly the case here, as Robbie had actually left the relationship around eight months earlier which did not stop reporters tracking down his ex-fiancée as the tale grew arms and legs.

"I looked at a huge map of the world in the Sandeman library in Perth and saw only one road going from Mexico to Chile, the Pan American Highway, and assumed they only had one road so how hard could that be?" Robbie remembers, admitting, "I think that I was very naive and probably none too bright. It was an adventure for me more than anything but one way or another I believed that I would get there. I planned to swim across the Darién Gap which didn't look very big on the library map."

His survival kit included camouflage face paint to sneak across borders and the minimum of clothing, but no map.

Unlike John, Robbie did not hang about in the Big Apple and, after a night in the YMCA, headed for the Mexican border on a Greyhound bus for $69. He then undertook a 680-mile, 36-hour train trip to Tapachula in the Gulf of Mexico, an uncomfortable journey he shared with pigs and donkeys that peasants were taking to market. Robbie then made the relatively short journey to Guatemala City where he spent a few days with a local girl during which a surfing escapade saw him encounter the first of his brushes with death on the epic trek.

A freak wave saw him washed up on the beach in a semi-conscious state before he was resuscitated by his anxious companions. When it was time to move on Robbie, by chance, found himself in the bus station queuing behind two other Scots who were also bound for Argentina. They were David Ednie and Brian Fleming from Edinburgh.

"I spoke no Spanish and had no maps and they seemed to know what they were doing," Robbie recalls. "They took me under their wing and introduced me to a guy from Crieff that they had met earlier that day, Ralph Dargie. Ralph had previously made it to Panama but had gotten sick and was on the way back to Scotland when he met Dave and Brian who convinced him to carry on. I think for sure that if I had not encountered Dave and Brian in Guatemala I would not have made it to Argentina. Maybe I would have but probably not.

"We bought a ticket all the way to Panama for around $35 but could only travel during the day. At a stopover in Nicaragua we were having a beer in a dirt-floor bar when another guy walked up to us and introduced himself as Jimmy Burns from Rothesay. From then on we all travelled together. When we hitch-hiked we would split into two groups but for the most part we travelled as five, commandeering the back-five seats of the cheap buses that we used for transportation."

The quintet made up approximately one-quarter of the Scots who reached Argentina after travelling overland – and one of them almost turned back. Their exploits took supporting Scotland to a whole new level and by comparison the eight-mile walk to Wembley in 1975 was a mere stroll in the park. Once in Panama they had to wait for a few days for a flight to take them across the Darién Gap to Colombia, a part of the journey Robbie had initially intended to swim.

Robbie has never forgotten that flight. "The propeller plane took three attempts to get off the ground which left us wondering what was happening but we finally got up in the air for the hour or so flight. Halfway through, the plane literally went sideways and we were heading down. People were screaming, shouting and praying and it was pandemonium. I was sitting next to Ralph who by now was crushed up against me in the window seat. There was lots of shit running through my mind and Ralph ever so calmly commented, 'It looks like we're going to miss the games.' Looking down at a muddy brown river and the tops of trees the plane finally levelled off and we limped into Medellin happy to be alive."

The next leg of the journey required a trek of some 1,200 miles to Peru, negotiated by hitch-hiking and a number of buses, one of which lost a wheel which, Robbie recalls, "fell off and bounced through the scrub alongside the bus".

They arrived in Lima early one morning ready for the 500-mile trip south to Peru's second city of Arequipa. During the journey Robbie went through "probably the most profound experience of my young life".

Three tickets were purchased for one bus with the other two men following some 30 minutes later on the next departure.

After a few beers near the coach terminal they decided to try and travel together on the later bus. "Dave and Jimmy, who spoke the best Spanish, went back to the station to see what they could do," says Robbie. "Dave talked a man travelling with his wife and kid into taking our three tickets and giving us theirs so that they would be on the earlier bus. They were more than happy with this as it saved them sitting around for another hour or so. We left the little bar with a wooden case of beer and commandeered our five back-of-the-bus seats and off we went.

"About an hour or two into the journey we were stopped by police or military and had to leave the bus while it was searched. About 100 yards ahead was a bus that was smouldering, with the smell of burnt rubber still in the air. All the luggage doors had been blown off and the windows smashed and there was a tarpaulin some ways off to the side with lumps under it which we took to be bodies. We were told that a bomb had gone off on the bus (the one that left before ours) and that was why we were being searched. Ralph, Brian and I had had tickets on that bus until Dave and Jimmy swapped them.

"All of us were stunned, three of us for realising that we were supposed to be on that bus and the other two for what they had inadvertently done to a family of three. Sobering up was pretty well instant and we continued on in silence. I remember Dave grabbing a newspaper in Arequipa and looking for a report of the incident but finding nothing." Had the authorities been aware of the travellers' late change of plans, they would, of course, have been considered suspects for the bombing.

Back home Andy Cameron was by no means the only entertainer to realise the potential of a novelty disc, as World Cup fever swept the country. Others who got in on the act included Bill Barclay, Johnnie Beattie, Calum Kennedy and the Alexander Brothers, and at one point there was even a World Cup chart in one of the newspapers. Other merchandise available included T-shirts, mugs, tankards, shoulder bags, sweaters, posters and a variety of glossy publications as manufacturers capitalised on the opportunities presented by Scotland's success.

On 3 May the manager announced his selection of 22 players for Argentina from an initial list of 40 he had named in March. These players would also represent Scotland in the Home Internationals. Souness, a late addition for the Bulgaria match, had impressed enough to earn a seat on the flight with McGrain's injury ruling him out. Six reserves were placed on standby to allow for late withdrawals, including Andy Gray whom many believed merited a place in the 22.

The Aston Villa striker had been unavailable for the 1977 Home Internationals and South American tour and had also withdrawn from the Bulgaria match due to injury. Whilst suspended from the home game against the Czechs due to his ordering off in Prague, Gray had pulled out of the Under-21 pool for the game at Tynecastle and when Ormond had been in charge the player had also withdrawn from two Under-21 matches early in 1977. This cast doubts in Ally MacLeod's mind over the player's fitness and he later claimed that Gray had also called off from Villa games he had been planning to attend to monitor his form. Much of the player's unavailability was due to the committed style of Gray's play which displayed no fear when diving for low crosses in crowded goalmouths and which ran the risk of a defender's boot connecting with his head.

With Jordan, Johnstone and Harper in the 22, Scotland were not short of goalscorers but many felt Gray was more worthy of a place than Harper whom the manager was accused of favouring due to their time together at Aberdeen.

"I should be going for I feel I have done enough to earn the trip," Gray told the *Record*'s Jack Adams, adding, "I am bitterly disappointed. This is the biggest setback of my career."

As Lou Macari remembers, no one dared take their place for granted. "I'd been in the Scotland team at Anfield but I wasn't sure of a place. I was sweating 'Oh God I hope he picks me. I hope he realises I played in the last game,' because I looked at all the players that were possibly in contention for the midfield area where I played. When you looked at the larger squad you thought, 'I might not make this' and the relief when the squad was announced and you were still there and you think 'Wow I wonder what this is going to be like?' as very few of us had been at a World Cup."

On 6 May MacLeod summarised with Alex Cameron during the STV commentary for the Scottish Cup Final. Derek Johnstone scored for the 38th time that season as Rangers defeated Aberdeen to clinch the domestic treble.

The cup final sports edition of the *Evening Times* contained an article penned by Hugh Taylor titled "Now It's For Real Ally". Taylor's piece was the first to hint that the manager may have been neglecting team matters with the following text: "Ally MacLeod will today I trust come to the end of extra-curricular activities when once again he dominates our television screens for STV on the Scottish Cup Final. Scotland's team manager will be rolling up his carpets, being piped ashore from *Blue Peter*, storing his disc jockey's badge in a drawer and throwing away his bumper book of jokes ..."

Ally MacLeod's reluctance to study his World Cup opponents would later be one of his most heavily criticised decisions. He had always planned to watch Iran in a friendly in Paris on 8 May but this was ruled out when the fixture was rearranged for the night before Scotland's Home International against Northern Ireland.

In *More Than Argentina – the Biography of Ally MacLeod*, his son claims: "On many occasions he said to the SFA he wanted to go and watch opposition but they wouldn't fund trips so he had to rely on video." There is no mention of any such requests within the minutes of SFA meetings for the period although such matters may have been discussed privately with the secretary. The suggestion that overseas trips were vetoed for reasons of cost do, nevertheless, contradict the sanctions for previous visits to South America by Docherty, Ormond and MacLeod himself, as recently as January 1978, all of which were to check on accommodation and facilities.

Archie Macpherson had been met with a positive response from the BBC in London to a suggestion that a film crew might cover a match between Peru and Argentina on 23 March. This would form part of a World Cup preview and BBC Sport was keen to get the manager on board, with the Corporation covering all expenses.

"I contacted Ally and he said he would get back to me but he never did," recollects Archie. "I tried again several times but he didn't want to go. It was as simple as that and London could scarcely believe this."

In the manager's defence his own notes document that during this period he was driving hundreds of miles to watch players as he sought to finalise his World Cup squad.

Two days after the Peru v Argentina match he travelled to the Newcastle v Everton fixture on Good Friday specifically to monitor the form of John Blackley, who pulled out of the home side just ahead of kick-off. The following day he watched St Mirren v Motherwell before driving south on Easter Monday to take in the game between Leeds and Wolves, then stayed overnight to watch Leeds again against Leicester the next day.

Ally MacLeod undoubtedly did spend many hours analysing video footage supplied by Brian Moore at ITV Sport on the Philips format. Moore's cooperation was just one example of the goodwill extended to Scotland's World Cup bid from south of the border with Brian Clough another ally.

Mike Smith submitted a dossier he had compiled on Iran after Wales had played them in mid-April. As with the lack of goals against Zaire four years earlier, Ally's decision not to spy on Scotland's opponents first hand was raised at the time but became much more of an issue after the team's elimination.

Arthur Montford asked Ally directly about this in an STV interview shortly before the tournament and found the accusation skilfully deflected. Montford said: "You haven't bothered in your preparation to go to see Iran, Peru or Holland." MacLeod's response was: "Basically what I have decided to do is to try and win the World Cup by preparing my own team to perfection."

Concentrating on the strengths of his own players had served Ally well in international football, particularly so in the match against

Czechoslovakia, and the confidence he had in their ability apparently gave him no reason to change this policy.

The initial post-Anfield interest in travelling to Argentina had petered out, with the cost of packages to the World Cup way beyond the means of most supporters. At an early stage Thomas Cook had affiliated themselves with the World Cup organising committee and were able to supply quotes the day after Scotland's qualification. Their packages started at £930 for the first two weeks with an initial price of £1,106 quoted for 24 nights, which included tickets for ten matches including the World Cup Final. This later rose to £1,395. At the end of April the travel agency estimated they had a mere 20 bookings from the whole of the UK.

Cross Travel, which specialised in catering for fans of Scottish clubs as well as the national side, had to abandon plans for a trip despite a lot of interest. Another tour operator, Border Travels, felt that the enquiries had actually cost them money. "I'm sick of it," the company's Mr McGill told the *Evening Times*, explaining, "At one time I was spending five or six hours a day dealing with World Cup queries with very little to show for it."

The only other organised trip from Scotland was assembled by AT Mays who catered for a similar number to Cook's – around 20. These included a young couple from the Borders, some oil-rig workers, two competition winners and a few regular supporters who had saved hard for the trip. Many fans would have been only too happy to go into debt for a chance to go to the World Cup but credit cards were for the wealthy in the 1970s and bank loans were only available if you met strict criteria following a meeting with your bank manager – and that's if he would agree to meet you in the first place.

On the Monday after the cup final Tommy Docherty placed both Don Masson and Bruce Rioch on the transfer list at Derby County. They had been amongst the Doc's first signings after taking charge the previous September but they and the club's form had suffered as Derby fought against the threat of relegation. "I expected more from them … They have turned out to be poor investments," are two of the Doc's comments to the press but he wished them well, adding that they would be in the shop window in Argentina.

By 1978 both Wales and England had returned to play in Belfast but despite what was described in the SFA Annual Report as "an impassioned plea by the president of the Irish FA" the SFA was still reluctant to travel to Northern Ireland, which ensured all three of Scotland's Home International matches again took place in Glasgow.

Lessons had been learned from the Bulgaria friendly and all three matches were made ticket-only and, for the first time, colour coded. Section N tickets for the East Terrace, for example, were printed on red card for the England game with white tickets required for access to O, whereas white tickets had been printed for section N for the Northern Ireland match. Following a timely inspection of Hampden Park on 22 March the Safety of Sports Ground certificate was increased to 88,000 allowing an additional 3,000 tickets to be printed for each match.

The squad met at the North British Hotel in Glasgow city centre on 10 May, three days before the game against Northern Ireland and two days after Rioch and Masson had been transfer-listed. A large crowd had gathered as the players boarded the coach to take them to their training base at the Dunblane Hydro, scenes which Alan Davidson described in the *Evening Times* as "yet another indication of the fever which is gripping the country".

Dalglish and Souness were not present but had a watertight alibi as they were playing for Liverpool in the European Cup Final later that evening. Following his sensational first season on Merseyside, Dalglish was widely expected to be one of the superstars of the World Cup.

The Hydro was not so isolated as to deter excited fans, and crowds of autograph hunters turned up in search of their heroes on a daily basis. Ally MacLeod was grateful for three competitive games before the World Cup, with the Home Internationals now considered of lesser importance.

On the Saturday afternoon Scotland and Northern Ireland lined up at Hampden for the eighth successive year in front of 64,433 spectators. The Liverpool two, fresh from collecting European Cup medals, were listed as substitutes with Robertson making his debut on the left wing in place of the unfit Johnston. Asa Hartford was forced to withdraw as a substitute due to a freak accident.

"I was going to be a sub and was warming up in the bath area," Asa recalls, "where a bottle of oil had been spilled on the floor. As I fell, my hand jammed against the glass bottle that had fallen and it cut my wrist so I had to get it stitched." The team sheet was hurriedly amended to list Joe Harper in Hartford's place on the bench.

David Stephen lived in Bridge of Allan, three miles from the squad's base, and remembers a story which circulated amongst the locals. "There was a rumour that one of the players was in a pub in Dunblane and had cut himself on a pint glass or a beer bottle and that was why he missed the game."

This misinformation was a foretaste of things to come once the squad had relocated to South America.

Scotland launched into attack from the off and in doing so left themselves exposed in defence. After 26 minutes Armstrong moved in from the left then passed accurately for the on-rushing Martin O'Neill to shoot first time into the net from 14 yards. The goal stunned the crowd and, unlike the Bulgaria game when the Scots had also gone behind, the fans became restless before breaking into slow handclaps. The mood changed ten minutes later when the unmarked Johnstone rose to head Rioch's cross into goal from six yards. Jordan limped off at the interval and was replaced by Dalglish.

The second half continued in the same lacklustre pace as the first, with Rough saving from O'Neill before a number of Scottish attacks were thwarted by some tough tackling. The match finished 1-1. After the drama of the Bulgaria game the afternoon had been something of a let-down.

Jardine had struggled to complete the 90 minutes after taking a knock, was subsequently ruled out of the remaining Home Internationals and did not train for over a week.

"Winning is not anyone's divine right, but it is amazing – even a bit frightening – when a draw is treated as a national disaster," the manager shared with *The Herald*'s Ian Paul. Hugh Taylor was philosophical and considered the draw may prove to be a good thing: "Now there's no chance of big-headedness taking over," he typed.

Souness and Dalglish started against the Welsh the following Wednesday with a fit Johnston replacing Robertson and Blyth taking over in goal. The midweek fixture attracted an even larger crowd of 70,241. Hartford, too, returned; the Northern Ireland game was the only one Asa failed to feature in during Ally's time as manager.

"From my point of view there were six midfield players – Bruce, Lou, Don, Graeme, myself and Archie – vying for three positions," Asa reflects. "He always picked me – but I didn't know that at the time. I wouldn't have thought, 'Aye, I'm playing'. You don't think like that. Looking back on it you get the feeling that he fancied me more as a player than Willie Ormond did. With Ally everything was fine."

Scotland took the lead in spectacular style after 12 minutes. Dalglish split the defence with a pass for Gemmill who, with just one touch, crossed the ball perfectly for Johnstone to head into the roof of the net from 15 yards. It was the striker's 40th goal of the season – and none of his goals had been from the penalty spot. Dalglish then pounced quickly on a defensive mix-up before shooting narrowly over, as the Scots played with a confidence which had been lacking in the previous game.

There were 31 minutes on the clock when Phillips sent a long ball to the edge of the box which Curtis headed on for Dwyer. Dwyer's shot beat Rough but was blocked on the line by McQueen, who collided with a goalpost. Following a delay the defender was taken off and replaced by Forsyth.

Johnstone's goal still separated the sides as the game entered its closing minutes, when Forsyth handled a cross, gifting the Welsh a golden opportunity to snatch a draw from the penalty spot. MacLeod replaced Johnston with Robertson, causing a delay before Flynn could take the kick. The tactic appeared to have worked because Flynn's effort struck the outside of Blyth's right-hand post and was cleared to the relief of more than 70,000 people.

"Que Sera Sera" was in full swing when a moment of madness brought an abrupt halt to the singing. Stuart Kennedy passed the ball back to Blyth who rolled it out for Donachie with the match in its dying seconds. Instead of playing the ball upfield the defender chipped it back towards his goal and watched as it sailed past the helpless Blyth to earn the Welsh a point.

MacLeod expressed sympathy for Donachie in the press, adding: "It was a big improvement on Saturday and a splendid goal but I consider we missed too many chances and that is something we must work on." In truth Wales were due a bit of luck in the fixture but the draw meant Scotland could not retain the Championship trophy they had won for the last two seasons regardless of the result against England.

Asa Hartford remembers Mick Channon sending his Manchester City clubmate Donachie a telegram which read: "Same again on Saturday please."

The players enjoyed a break at Perth races where all but two of the party observed the 7pm curfew for dinner at Dunblane. Those in question had found themselves drinking in the company of American film and television star James Garner, whose hugely successful BBC1 series *The Rockford Files* was popular at the time. Garner was taking a golfing holiday in Scotland and invited the duo to join him back at the famous Gleneagles Hotel where the socialising continued.

It was the following day when the players returned to the Hydro with their absence somehow kept from the media. A number of reporters sensed a story but their enquiries were met by a wall of silence as another pre-World Cup scandal like the Largs incident was the last thing the SFA wanted. The involvement of a Hollywood star could well have boosted the story to a higher profile than Jimmy Johnstone in a rowing boat. Whether or not the episode affected team selection is unclear but the players in question were certainly reprimanded for their Gleneagles sleepover.

The massive demand for Scotland v England tickets resulted in thousands of forgeries changing hands in pubs in Glasgow and Edinburgh and commanded front-page news. Serious Crime Squad officers conducted a raid on Glasgow Printing in the city's Buchanan Street early on the Thursday morning where printing plates and forged tickets were seized. The inquiry had begun some days earlier following a tip-off that fakes were being sold in Glasgow pubs and discos on what was described as "a very large scale". A statement from Strathclyde Police said that "several thousand" fake tickets were in circulation for section N of the uncovered terracing.

The SFA announced that all 15,000 genuine £1.50 tickets for that section had been sold. The counterfeits were quite convincing but had a couple of flaws, most noticeably a line where the genuine briefs had a dot next to the serial number. Extra security was planned for section N with fans required to present tickets to police for inspection before being allowed near the turnstiles.

One newspaper report detailed how a stranger had walked into a garage workshop in Glasgow's Cumbernauld Road and sold 25 tickets to mechanics at £5 each.

Two men appeared in private at Glasgow Sheriff Court on the Friday charged with conspiring to commit the crime of fraud and were detained in custody pending further inquiries.

Gordon McQueen's injury was more serious than had been initially believed and he was also ruled out of the England game. Thousands of fans from all parts of the country converged on Glasgow for Scotland's final match ahead of the World Cup. The weather was perfect and everyone was in good spirits as Scotland sought their third win on the trot over the Auld Enemy.

Despite Johnstone's two goals he was surprisingly replaced by Jordan. The explanation given by the manager was that as Jordan had only played 45 minutes in the first match, he was in need of game-time ahead of the World Cup.

"Hampden was a sea of yellow flags and stupendous noise as England kicked off," read Hugh Taylor's match report for the *Evening Times*'s sports edition. Every touch by an England player was booed in the early stages and there seemed to be no visiting supporters present at all. A Hartford lob bounced from the crossbar after six minutes and was rushed behind by Mills as the visitors' defence appeared to panic. It was as close as Scotland would come to scoring all afternoon.

"It was all Scotland with the blue midfield in command ... making England look no more than an average side," Taylor recorded of the first half.

After the break England were more adventurous and Francis shot narrowly past. A Johnston cross eluded Jordan but landed at the right foot of Hartford who hurried his shot straight at Clemence; it began to look as though it would not be Scotland's day. The crowd continually called for Derek Johnstone but with the limited number of opportunities created it was doubtful if his introduction would have affected the score.

There was almost an inevitability about the match's only goal seven minutes from time. Peter Barnes sent over a cross from the left which Rough, rising with Francis, appeared to catch. But the ball fell perfectly for Steve Coppell, who fired into the empty net.

Rather than demoralise the crowd the goal had the opposite effect as the fans burst into a repeated chorus of "We're gaun tae Argentine" and refused to leave the terraces at the end until the players came back out. This reaction to a defeat was quite unprecedented as far as Scottish football was concerned and, for once, losing to England, whom Ally considered had been "outclassed", did not seem to matter. The manager's assessment was shared by most of the

Scottish sportswriters and his Northern Ireland counterpart Danny Blanchflower, who was quoted in *The Herald,* saying: "It was daylight robbery ... there was no comparison between the teams."

The official attendance of 88,319 indicated that some supporters had been able to enter with forgeries despite the additional checks. Discussions later took place with the SFA's printers and it was agreed that additional security features would be incorporated into future match tickets.

The squad departed Dunblane on the Sunday to spend a few days with their families before reassembling for the trip to South America. Gordon McQueen continued to receive round-the-clock treatment in the hope he would be ready for the Peru match.

In South America Robbie Sterry and his four companions, still stunned by their near-death experience, had travelled 1,500 miles south from Peru into Chile. They arrived in Santiago on a Sunday when there was no transport to help them cross the Andes, but they were content that their final destination of Argentina was at last within their grasp. As Robbie recalls, the locals made them welcome. "The SFA had been criticised for playing there but the decision went down well with the Chileans, and a few times during our trip to Santiago we had people go out of their way to buy us a beer," he said.

"We started walking and eventually got picked up in an open truck carrying open-topped freezers and we each got to sit in one. Reaching the border we found that there was a three-kilometre tunnel to go through to get to Argentina so we started hoofing it only to be shouted back by the police. We didn't understand why until a train came rumbling through it, one train one way, another train the other, then cars in both directions. It was freezing up there and by now everybody waiting around knew what we were doing and why, so we had rides pretty quickly that took us through the tunnel and into Mendoza."

The following day they split into two groups and hitched the 300 miles to Córdoba, agreeing to reunite in the main square, Plaza San Martin. Córdoba was the venue for Scotland's opening two group games with the third scheduled for Mendoza. On arrival, Robbie, Ralph and Brian were surprised to bump into two other Scots there, Adrian Haren and Gerry Keenan.

The two Celtic fans had first met during the 1974 World Cup and, in Prague in 1976 along with four other supporters, had pledged that should Scotland qualify they would, by hook or by crook, all meet up in Argentina – which all six of them did.

They had been the first fans to arrive in Córdoba the previous Sunday, two months after setting off on 23 March. Adrian and Gerry had also travelled via New York and, armed with their Bible and a publication titled *How to Hitch South America*, had arrived ahead of their target date of 1 June. Both experienced hitch-hikers, they had never doubted they would reach their destination. Lifts had come fairly easily apart from one occasion when they spent a full day at the Mexican border during which only two vehicles passed – neither of which had stopped. After the hikers gestured with a "V" sign one of those cars had reversed and a pistol was pointed at them.

The pair had another bad experience in Costa Rica when police searching their belongings stole some of their cash. They were also dumped in the middle of a desert by one driver when he discovered they had no marijuana. These issues aside, they had encountered great hospitality on the road with food and shelter offered by strangers resulting in only a few occasions when they were forced to sleep rough. Adrian and Gerry had attracted a lot of interest when in Los Angeles where again they were invited to stay with several families.

Robbie Sterry's first taste of Argentinian hospitality has never left him. "Locals started asking us why we were there and when we explained they wondered why we were so early," he recalls. "Lots of questions and we drew quite a crowd." With Robbie now down to his last £100, their first few nights in Córdoba were spent sleeping rough in the bus station with their backpacks tied to their feet, until a local helped to find them a place to stay.

The next morning the travellers sought out tickets for Scotland's opening matches which were on sale through a bank. Robbie Sterry says: "We went into a gracious old building and were standing in line for a few minutes. Apparently word had gotten out that we had hitched to Argentina and we were approached by a bank official who, after a few questions, took us to the front of the line and saw to it that we had our tickets. A few shouts went out and before we knew what was happening everybody on all three open terraces of the interior of the bank were clapping and cheering us. We were gobsmacked."

"We went back out to sit in the Plaza San Martin and within a couple of hours there were so many people around us that police on horseback showed up to control the crowds which were spilling out on to the streets. Strangers brought us beer and sandwiches and those who spoke English questioned us and translated back to the masses. It was literally surreal, we were nobody special but were treated like royalty.

"From many later conversations I came to realise that the bulk of Argentinians thought that the effort we had made to get there, when they were wondering if anybody would show up in their troubled country, was a thing of beauty. We were not rich people [but] humble and straightforward and I believe that resonated with them more than anything. We five could walk through the streets and be pulled into pizza joints and given free food and beer. Everywhere we went people wanted to be with us, wanted to feed us, to look after us."

On Thursday 25 May the squad changed into their light blue SFA suits in their Glasgow hotel rooms ready for the journey to Prestwick. On the way to the airport they had one other engagement which necessitated a diversion to Hampden Park.

What was billed as a World Cup Gala Night would retrospectively be criticised as a premature celebration of World Cup success. The reality was that consultations had taken place between the SFA and Strathclyde Police over concerns at the number of well-wishers who might turn up at the airport. During the discussions the secretary suggested the Hampden event to allow supporters to see off the players in a manageable environment. Ally MacLeod was said to be against the idea which would be consistent with his refusal to partake in a lap of honour after the Czechoslovakia game, but he would later be accused of arranging the event to fuel his ego.

One myth regarding the send-off is that Hampden Park was filled to capacity – there were exactly 22,732 present, most of whom had paid 30 pence for a ticket. Half the ground remained closed. The initial plan had been to allow free entry but again there were concerns over numbers and Queen's Park FC were given permission to charge a nominal admission fee. For a further 30p a programme similar to those printed for Hampden internationals was available and British Rail ran special trains from Glasgow Central to Hampden for a return fare of 45 pence.

The gates were open from just before 6pm with STV broadcasting live from the stadium an hour later.

Andy Cameron introduced each player to the crowd and each one waved as he walked to the centre circle from the tunnel. In a nice touch Danny McGrain took part although he would be heading for home and not Prestwick later that evening. Accompanied by pipes and drums, the squad then paraded a giant Argentinian flag around the open sections before boarding an open top double decker bus which made two circuits of the pitch before heading to the airport.

"That should never have happened," Willie Johnston reflects. "The players didn't want it, honestly. We didn't want to go on the bus around Hampden Park. We would have preferred to turn up at the airport and just go."

Asa Hartford agrees: "It was the sort of thing that happened in America where you get introduced individually on to the pitch. I don't think any one of us felt comfortable. It's only from the tunnel out to the middle of the pitch but it seemed like an awful long way. In the bus going down it was amazing. There were people turning out all the way to Prestwick."

Thousands of people of all ages lined the route, with entire families waving and cheering. Huge flags were draped from bridges on that fine summer's evening.

The estimated 4,000 fans who did turn up at Prestwick perhaps vindicated the decision to stage the Gala Night. The viewing gantry was packed with fans wearing tammies and Scotland tops as the party were piped on to their British Caledonian aircraft with "Flower of Scotland". The charter flight took them directly to Buenos Aires where they transferred to an air force plane which flew to Córdoba Airport. There they were greeted by two bands and a group of kilted schoolchildren carrying a giant saltire, and around a dozen of the growing band of supporters who had hitch-hiked across. Two of those fans, Richard Grassick and Robbie Sterry, had beaten the players to their accommodation after unsuccessfully seeking employment in the Sierras. Their tour of the hotel was to prove useful at a later date. Coaches transported the party on the 40-minute journey to Alta Gracia but the vehicle with the team on board broke down just before reaching the hotel and the weary players had to walk through crowds of locals lining the streets.

Tired and to a degree irritable, the squad had arrived a full eight days ahead of their opening match.

The nearby training facilities were found to be inadequate and the team used them just once, as Lou Macari remembers: "Ally warned us before we got there on the first day. He stood up and said, 'By the way, lads, when you get to the training pitch it might look okay from the bus but when you get on it you'll find out it's not grass!'"

The manager later noted in his internal SFA report on the trip: "During my January visit I was assured that the Argentinian FA would bring the pitch up to standard. Attempts had been made to do this, but the end result was poor and conditions were completely unsuitable to carry out training. The alternative offered was in Córdoba next to the stadium. At no time could we carry out any practice in private ... Iranian and Peruvian delegates attended all our sessions." On the Saturday evening Johnston, Jardine and Rough visited a nearby casino, returning just ahead of their curfew. Finding a side gate locked they took a short cut over a fence which alerted security men. Ernie Walker was informed and confirmed that the trio were residents but the matter did not end there and local newspapers reported that the players had been drunk.

More than 40 years later Willie Johnston recalls that evening. "Myself and Sandy Jardine came in the back door one night and we nearly got arrested at gunpoint," he says. "It was all blown up by the press, the least wee thing. They were getting stories back home about boys turning up late and everything but we were all good professionals. We would maybe have a drink just like a normal game when if you were out you'd maybe have a couple of drinks on a Wednesday or a Thursday night. It was your routine."

Further inaccurate stories of excessive drinking contributed to bad feeling within the camp amongst players who would soon get bored.

This misreporting by the Argentinian press was fuelled by the legacy of Largs in 1974 and the Copenhagen Five, along with an assumption that most Scots were avid whisky drinkers. This explained the lengths taken by the SFA to keep the James Garner Gleneagles episode under wraps.

Some accounts of drunken players could be attributed to supporters in replica tops sinking the local brew. Rodger Baillie recollects seeing images of fans in the Argentinian press: "They inferred that it was players that were drinking away."

In its 31 May edition the Argentine newspaper *Clarin* carried the following: "There are all sorts of rumours about the Scots. Some are true, some are invented. Cigarettes at any time and visits to the casino are not." The following day's edition was rather less balanced and included: "It is very well known that the freedom this delegation has. These likes are divided between golf, sightseeing and drinks. Of the 38 boxes of whisky they brought in their luggage, hardly one is left in a full, unpreserved state."

"I was leaving Alta Gracia on one occasion," recalls Rodger Baillie, "and it was Stuart Kennedy's birthday. An Argentinian photographer asked him to pose taking a swig from a Coca-Cola bottle to celebrate and this appeared in an Argentinian publication the next day as Kennedy drinking alcohol."

Robbie Jenkins was on the AT Mays' package and was based in Córdoba: "We were in the same hotel as Ron Greenwood, Dave Sexton and Clive Thomas, the Welsh referee. The thing I remember was going out of our hotel and nobody went near them. When we came out we were surrounded by hundreds of people wanting our autographs. I don't think it was a mistake and they thought we were players. That was rubbish, they knew we weren't players. The people in Córdoba made us feel like superstars. Córdoba wasn't like Buenos Aires and we were strangers; we were exciting strangers to them."

"We started hanging out in the Sorocabana, a cafe on the corner with glass walls which became the Scottish contingent's base of drinking and socialising," says Robbie Sterry. "After the flying fans arrived that place became impossible for Argentinians to enter unless they knew a Scotsman. When the singing started and the pipes came out there was always a crowd spilling on to the streets to watch us. During the day mothers would bring their children with their white school smocks on to speak to us in their school-learned English and have us sign their smocks, even though we explained that we were fans and not players. It didn't matter. What a crazy and beautiful time that was. It almost brings a tear to my eye remembering all the generosity we were surrounded by."

The hospitality of the locals even extended to what may have been perceived as undesirables back home, as Robbie Jenkins remembers.

"Me and two other guys and one woman, typical of Scots, were sitting on a wall drinking a bottle of wine in Córdoba and this guy came up and asked us to come in the evening to this celebratory thing. We were not so sure about that but he insisted. 'You must come,' he said. This guy was the equivalent of the Lord Mayor and we were there as his guests. It was a wee place called Jesus Maria just outside of Córdoba and we had an absolutely amazing time."

The swimming pool in the Sierras complex held no water during the Scots' stay and there were complaints about the standard of rooms, some of which were said to be without a window. The players soon renamed the hotel the Chateau Despair, and with swimming removed from the curriculum the only options to pass the time between training sessions were golf, cards or head tennis as there were no rackets or even a net available.

"It wasn't the best place, put it that way," Willie Johnston looks back. "They never did their homework for that one as there wasn't a lot to do. There was a swimming pool but there wasn't any water in it, but it wouldn't have mattered anyway because it was freezing."

Lou Macari says: "It wasn't even a hotel. It was something that had been built into rooms and a reception area. There was no front door entrance where you went into the reception.

"What was clear was that nobody from Scotland had been to look at it because if they had been out there and said it was okay then they should have been locked up." As we know both the SFA secretary and manager had visited the Sierras not once but on two occasions.

"You're not looking for luxury," says Asa Hartford, "but it was a bit of a let-down. The rooms were not great, the toilet leaked from upstairs and water would drip through into the bathroom in our room."

The daily training sessions in Córdoba required a 90-minute round trip by bus which added to the dissatisfaction. "I think it was 30 kilometres and then afterwards if you'd been sweating you were sitting on the bus coming back getting cold," is Asa's memory of those uncomfortable journeys.

Following the fabricated press reports the squad were forbidden from leaving the hotel as Ally's SFA report documents. "At first I allowed players to play golf or visit Alta Gracia for one hour. These privileges were withdrawn and the players confined to camp for the last ten days, except for the training sessions in Córdoba. This can lead to boredom, but good results on the field soon lift this state of mind." The restriction of movement did nothing to improve the mood within the squad as the days after their arrival dragged by.

"Our hotel meals were good initially but they began to be the same," says Bobby Clark. "Looking back it would have been good if we could have had a warm-up game against someone about three days before the Peru match. The squad perhaps lost their edge due to the timing and location."

"You were aware of security around the hotel," says Asa Hartford. "It does sound farcical but you would see people sweeping up leaves and so on and just looking around and you knew they weren't gardeners. They were security people around the hotel."

At Dunblane the mood had been positive with access to snooker and golf and visits to the Hydro from the likes of Rod Stewart and Billy Connolly reducing the tedium. Things had not been so well planned for the players' stay in the Sierras.

Bobby Clark says: "The excitement continued into the early days in Alta Gracia but, in retrospect, eight days was a little too long to be in a place where phone calls were difficult, the TV was in Spanish and although there was a golf course and tennis courts the days were long. In Dunblane players could call home, could watch TV and read the newspapers. Personally I was not over-bothered as I wrote a daily piece of around 600 words for the Aberdeen *Evening Express* so that kept me busy and I also, as a back-up, did not have the immediate pressure of knowing I would play. I knew from the outset that Roughie was the number one and possibly Jim Blyth was two but I had come off a good season with Aberdeen where we just missed out on winning the double, so I was ready if needed."

"There was nothing to do and there were armed guards all around and therefore boredom became a serious thing," is Lou Macari's recollection of those days in the Sierras.

The squad did have access to a video tape player but the only English language recordings available were of series such as the period drama *Upstairs Downstairs,* which was not particularly to their taste. STV partly remedied the situation by supplying football tapes and the players watched a recording of the recent Peru v Argentina game that the manager had declined the BBC's invitation to attend.

At a meeting with the players the manager was asked about the bonuses available. Ally's account of this meeting is summarised in his SFA report, thus: "The players suggested they would want £20,000 per man to win the cup and various other large sums for qualifying, etc. Needless to say I did not agree with their attitude and refused to take the position any further. In fact several harsh words were said to me at this meeting."

On the third day in the Sierras some of the players requested a meeting with both the secretary and president of the SFA to discuss the bonus issue. This was declined by Walker as such a meeting might have been perceived as undermining the manager's position, given that Ally had already refused a similar request. The lack of clarity over money issues had first been aired in Dunblane but had not been resolved to at least some of the squad's satisfaction.

A few days later Rioch, as captain, approached Ernie Walker with the same request and, apparently, the manager's consent. In his report to the International Committee the following month, Walker's opinion was that only a few of the players had a grievance over money but that their dissatisfaction was having a disruptive effect on the whole squad. Rioch had intimated he personally had no desire for such a meeting and again the request was refused.

The supporters in Córdoba were unaware of the unrest amongst the players and were in great spirits ahead of the Peru match. Some reports listed the ratio of women to men in the city of Córdoba as around seven to one, which naturally went down well with the visiting fans.

There were an estimated 600 to 700 Scottish supporters in Argentina. The official figure of supporters who had booked flights or packages from Scotland was 540 although this did not take into account fans living outside of Scotland and those who travelled overland. Whilst this may seem a relatively low figure considering the interest at the time, to put it into perspective the total number of Dutch fans who travelled to the first round of the World Cup was exactly 46 and Scotland were almost certainly the best-supported European side in the opening stages.

A strange episode occurred in the lead-up to the opening match when a couple sought out Robbie Sterry in the Sorocabana. "I'm still not sure why," says Robbie, "but he was a journalist and she was supposedly a physiotherapist attached to the team and they were telling me that they could get me into the team hotel."

After a drive to Alta Gracia they found the Sierras surrounded by armed guards. "I was wearing the team jersey which was probably one of only two shirts that I owned. A soldier approached and handed a clipboard to me with a list of names and checkmarks. I realised it was a list of which players had gone into town and who had returned. Willie Donachie was out so I checked him in and the soldier escorted me into the gate with a 'Buenas noches senor' whilst the journalists remained outside."

Remembering the layout from the job interview, Robbie made straight for the bar area. "Nine or ten of the team were sitting around with a couple of bottles of beer. Silence, then 'Who are you?' Just a fan. 'How did you get in here?' I explained about Willie and then the patter began; they thought it was pretty funny. I was asked how I got to Argentina, how old I was." "Does your mother know you're out?" quipped one player. "He told his mum he went out for a shovel of coal!" joked another. "I was ordered a beer and sat down and answered questions about my trip," Robbie adds.

Robbie's account confirms that there was no blanket ban on alcohol within the Sierras.

"I was asked if I needed any money," says Robbie, "and even though I was skint I replied no, with too much misplaced pride. I told them all I wanted was for them to win games but they were going to have a whip round for me. I did get autographs of everyone there and still have that yellowed piece of hotel stationery to this day.

"Suddenly half a dozen soldiers burst in and one of them pointed me out – I'm guessing Donachie had tried to get back into the hotel. I think it was McQueen and Jordan who stood up and protected me and refused to let the soldiers take me away. Four or five of the players escorted me to the gate where the two Argentinians who had brought me were happy to see me.

"Back in the Sorocabana I was the centre of attention with a pile of beers supplied, as I repeated the story many times. That led to an interview with ITN's Trevor McDonald the next day with a phony hitch-hiking scene outside of Córdoba. I later read that Ally MacLeod denied it had happened and at that time I realised that something was off. It had happened and why would it throw a bad light on anyone?"

Ally did indeed dismiss the story in response to a question from the *Record*'s Gordon Airs at a media conference. The reporter told how Ally "exploded, shouting in front of journalists: 'It's just rubbish. It never happened! People are saying these things to put us in a bad light!'" After defending his players over fabricated tales of drinking it does seem odd that the manager would similarly dismiss a factual event in the same manner. Before a ball had been kicked Ally MacLeod was clearly feeling the strain of the World Cup, just as his predecessor Ormond had done four years earlier. For Ally the pressure was about to intensify.

The manager's popularity even extended to Argentina as Robbie Jenkins recalls. "There was Ally's Bar in Córdoba and I'm sure the guy said his wife came from Peterhead but nobody ever met her. I think he just stuck a pin in the map and said 'my wife comes from ... Peterhead!' It was just a ramshackle bar, basically. You would think even if she wasn't interested in football she would still come down and talk to people about back home or whatever."

The opening match had a Saturday evening kick-off in Scotland, guaranteeing a bonanza for off-licences and pubs as the long-awaited day of 3 June finally arrived. Sports shops were sold out of Scotland strips whilst television rental companies reported a late demand to take advantage of special deals for the latest colour sets. The *Daily Record*'s front page described the mood as "Saturday Night Fever", in homage to the musical released the previous year, and stated: "For every Scots fan who has travelled to Argentina to cheer the team, thousands will be giving front room support around their TV sets when the 8.45 kick-off rolls around."

There was still no improvement to McQueen or Jardine ahead of the game. Along with the absence of McGrain, Donachie's suspension, following a booking in the game at Anfield, further depleted the defence.

This allowed Kennedy to come into the side with Forsyth, Buchan and Burns forming the rest of the back four. Jordan was chosen ahead of Johnstone to partner Dalglish up front and the manager expressed his belief that Willie Johnston was the key to unlocking the defence from the left wing.

During the flight from Prestwick MacLeod had discussed the first opponents with Hugh Taylor, intimating that he felt Peru were a good side going forward but suspect when retreating back to defend. "I've studied Peru and I've had thorough reports on them, they are really slow," he told the journalist.

In a press conference held by the Peruvians in Córdoba on 1 June captain Hector Chumpitaz had told reporters: "No one must underrate us. We are a much better team as Scotland will find out on Saturday." Assistant manager Alexandre Hereria was equally confident, predicting: "Juan Munante is a jet ... and he will fly past a Scotland defence as Donachie is suspended." Like Cubillas, Munante had played against Scotland at Hampden six years earlier.

As was normal for an Ally MacLeod team the Scottish players were instructed to seek an early goal which almost came in the opening minute when a fierce Hartford drive went narrowly behind. The goal did arrive after 15 minutes when Masson sent Rioch through. Quiroga pushed the captain's shot back into play but straight to Jordan who made no mistake.

Scotland then seemed to switch off with the midfield lacking coordination and passes regularly going astray. Rough saved well from Oblitas and Munante but was unable to prevent Cueto's fierce drive from the edge of the area hitting the back of the net just as the sanctuary of half-time was in sight.

Peru had ended the half in the ascendancy and the Scottish players were in need of one of their leader's motivational team talks.

Asa Hartford can remember those crucial few minutes. "I do have recollections of that ... we probably still weren't able to sort it out at half-time. That is when the managers earn their corn if things are going wrong. The dressing room was split into two parts. It wasn't like it was a square or horizontal room and he would be talking but only half the dressing room would hear him, so it wasn't ideal.

"I think it was Bruce Rioch that ended up getting us all together, getting the lads from one part into the other which would probably be a tight squeeze. It probably should have been Ally who said 'just come in here for a few minutes'."

"I've worked with some managers that talk for the duration of half-time and the players go out more confused than when they came in due to their attention span. Maybe even if he had done it just before we went out on to the pitch, gathered everybody together, but that didn't happen and I don't think that helped us either."

Ally's SFA report indicates he held a different view and includes this passage: "As the first half finished several players, particularly Burns, became too casual, allowing Peru to gradually take over. The interval put things right ..."

After the resumption Quiroga turned over a Jordan shot from two yards when a goal looked certain, but the Scots lost their way again as Peru gained in confidence. Against the run of play Scotland were awarded a penalty when Rioch was fouled by Diaz. Just as he had at Anfield, Masson hit the ball to the goalkeeper's right but Quiroga dived to turn it around the post.

The miss visibly affected the team's performance further and from that point Peru were in complete control. On 72 minutes Cubillas blasted a ferocious right-foot shot inside Rough's near post from 25 yards and the humiliation was completed three minutes later when the same player smashed a free kick through a six-man wall for 3-1.

Asa Hartford pinpoints a major factor in the defeat. "We didn't know anything about the opposition teams. Peru had two wingers who were lightning quick, Oblitas and Munante. The two of them were flying machines. You were finding things out about them actually on the pitch. You'd think someone would have picked out a few of the players. We thought we would have got to know a bit more about the opposition."

Robbie Jenkins knew someone who worked for the British Consulate in Lima. "He watched Peruvian football every week and sent a letter to the SFA saying he could provide updates and all the rest of it. He got a letter from someone – not MacLeod – who basically said, 'We don't need your information.'"

Lou Macari had been introduced for Rioch with the scores level. "Because Ally was an optimistic fella who always wanted to send out good vibrations it was just a game where the opposition were as good as us but no one really thought that before the game because of the hype surrounding the Scotland team. But if you played the same game now against Peru in South America, people wouldn't be looking upon it as a Scottish win."

Archie Macpherson once wrote, "Ally MacLeod could only fail to sparkle when he was asleep", but there was no sign of any such sparkle when interviewed by Arthur Montford soon after the defeat. Viewers of ITV witnessed an edgy, nervous man far removed from the bubbly, optimistic character who had regularly dominated their screens. When Montford suggested he may have underestimated the opposition MacLeod went on the defensive responding: "We did our homework on them. I've said all along that Peru were no easy meat." On his team's prospects in the tournament Ally would not be drawn, commenting that they "would have to soldier on".

Morale amongst the squad reached rock bottom the following evening when news broke that the results of a urine sample Willie Johnston had given indicated he had taken a banned substance. The player admitted to swallowing two Reactivan tablets shortly before the match, pills which were regularly supplied by his club doctor at West Bromwich and considered no more than a mild stimulant.

There then existed the real possibility that Scotland could be expelled from the tournament and, attempting to limit the damage, a hastily arranged meeting of the International Committee told the player he would be sent home and banned from representing his country again.

SFA assistant secretary Peter Donald drove Johnston all the way to Buenos Aires where he was deposited in a hotel and booked on a flight via Rio and Paris to London the next day. Ironically Johnston had not initially been summoned for the urine test as there had been a mix-up and Gemmill had incorrectly been called.

There was sympathy for Willie amongst his team-mates, who had largely been kept in the dark over his expulsion. Asa Hartford said: "There were no goodbyes. He was cast out and we felt sorry for him. He had been bundled out and nobody got to see him and didn't know that he was going. In those days you thought of drugs as heroin and cocaine. The doctor came round the room with a scroll of about 400 banned tablets but you wouldn't know right from wrong. The overall feeling was not anger. We just felt sorry for him."

Although Scotland were not expelled from the tournament there was still the possibility of a points deduction later should they acquire any, which could yet deprive them of a place in the second phase.

Willie Johnston's international career had been interesting. Having appeared nine times for Scotland between 1965 and 1970, he then spent a period of over six years in the wilderness. Unexpectedly recalled in Willie Ormond's last game in 1977, he was then included for MacLeod's first squad as Ormond had already registered the players. Clearly rated by MacLeod, he won a further dozen caps bringing his overall total to 22.

The manager's SFA report records his views on the Reactivan incident. "I feel that Johnston did not really appreciate that he had taken drugs, it seemed it was normal practice at WBA," it says. "I would record that it was rather out of stupidity than an act of wilfully taking drugs."

Johnston's room-mate Masson then confessed to having taken the same tablets but later retracted this, claiming it was an attempt to support his colleague. The decision was taken to exclude Masson from any further international duties but not to send him home as this would have attracted further scandal. The manager disagreed with this as he felt the presence of a banned player would be detrimental to the already low morale.

"The secretary informed me later that Masson denied taking the tablets and made the excuse that he thought he was helping Johnston if he said he took Reactivan. I personally believe he took the tablets," Ally noted in his report. "I informed Masson that I would no longer consider him ever again for team selections as I felt I could no longer trust him."

The SFA's stance was that the player had either, A, taken the banned tablets or B, lied about taking them but if so there is a case for saying he at least answered the question honestly. Had he denied the offence he may very well have taken part in the other two matches.

Ally MacLeod reneged on an agreement to appear live on BBC1 on the Monday evening during a special link-up with Frank Bough in the London studio. A telephone number had been issued inviting viewers to speak directly with the Scotland manager but he was replaced by Denis Law, who was with the BBC in Córdoba.

The recently appointed SFA president, Willie Harkness, chose to break with tradition and appealed directly to the squad to tackle the remaining games in the "spirit expected of Scottish players".

A meeting did later take place between the players and the SFA to clarify the bonus structure. Walker, Harkness, vice-president Tommy Younger and chairman Tom Lauchlan addressed the squad in the lounge of the Sierras. In addition to the normal match fee of £100 a similar amount would be paid to each player for a win. At that point a total of £145,000 had been accumulated from the various World Cup promotions from which the players' royalties would be calculated. A sum of £40,000 would be paid directly from the SFA into the players' fund if they reached the second phase, £95,000 was the incentive for a third-place finish and £210,000 would be paid should they triumph in the final itself.

Walker's report includes the following: "Four or five players spoke out in terms of disagreement and a few made it quite evident by their expressions and muttered comments that they wanted no part of the complaints and that they had little time for their self-appointed spokesmen."

"There was a meeting regarding bonuses," says Bobby Clark. "Personally, I never got involved in any of the discussions as I was very happy to be at a World Cup. This should have been handled immediately the squad was announced and before we left Scotland. But again, hindsight is 20/20!"

The outcome of the meeting was that the SFA was not prepared to offer any more than the bonuses proposed before departure, with Walker of the opinion that the manager had not adequately communicated the details to the squad. The manager's own report contains the following observation: "The meeting with the secretary, chairman and vice-chairman did nothing to ease the problems, but, in fact, divided the squad."

Rodger Baillie says: "The question of the bonus was never settled even to the extent of Willie Harkness calling a press conference on the Sunday to put the SFA's side of it. I think the SFA had every reason to assume that it had been settled before they left Scotland. In the general atmosphere of dissatisfaction within Alta Gracia the grumbling about the bonus did become more of a factor than it should have been."

The previously cordial relations between manager and journalists had deteriorated following the Peru result and an uneasy atmosphere hung over the daily briefings at the Sierras. During one, MacLeod had those journalists fixed in his sights as he hinted at a siege mentality within the squad. "I think I have made myself too available and been too accommodating with certain sections of the press," he said. "I know people back home are hearing stories ... we'll get together like the dirty dozen and defy them."

Unfortunately, Ally did not get the same response from his players as his predecessor had in the England game following the Largs episode four years earlier.

In Córdoba the fans were of the belief that the performance against Peru had been a blip and that the unrated Iran would suffer the backlash. There was an undercurrent of resentment amongst some of those who had travelled overland towards the competition winners and the SFA, which had dismissed requests for match tickets out of hand.

On the day of the Iran game a bedsheet was spread out in the Plaza San Martin. A pot of paint and a brush were acquired and the words "FUCK THE SFA" were painted in large letters on the white sheet. After the handiwork was attached to two poles the message was left for all to see on the cobbles of the square. The plan was to raise the banner at half-time with the TV companies tipped off to expect something behind the goal during the interval.

A local woman complained over the banner which she mistook for a political message and got into an argument with "Mad" Rab Rodger from Kirkintilloch. The resulting exchanges resulted in 15 Scottish supporters being detained in the local jail where they listened to the first half of the match on the radio trying to make sense of the Spanish commentary. Earlier during their stay in Córdoba another member of the group had set fire to a Union Jack being carried by a well-intentioned but badly advised Englishman, who had expected a friendly welcome from the Scots.

Donachie returned from suspension for the must-win game with the recovered Jardine replacing Kennedy. Macari and Robertson also came in with Gemmill starting after Rioch failed a fitness test.

By all accounts the team were confident in the changing room ahead of the match but that optimism seemed to evaporate once they took to the field. The change in atmosphere was a factor with just short of 8,000 in the Chateau Carreras Stadium, some 30,000 down on the opening game. It seemed that the locals, too, had become disheartened with the Scottish team.

Asa Hartford found the occasion surreal. He says: "It was devoid of any sort of atmosphere – you just couldn't take in the enormity of what was at stake. I do remember thinking: 'There is nobody here and you can't take in how much this means.' It was like a practice match when you play on the training ground and there's no pace to the game."

"You could actually hear people shouting because of the lack of atmosphere at the game," says Lou Macari. "The stadium wasn't all that great, there wasn't stands on all sides and it was a bit spooky. Us Scottish players, whether it be at Hampden Park or Wembley or Anfield were used to atmosphere and noise and people going crazy." When reminded of the attendance, Lou's reaction is: "A World Cup game with 7,900!"

Hartford had a shot blocked early in the game before the Iranian keeper Hedjazi produced two fine saves, turning a Robertson free kick behind and a back-header from Dalglish over. This could not disguise the habit of midfield players misplacing passes and a strange lack of motivation which had been less evident in the Peru game.

Two minutes from the break Scotland had the type of luck that had deserted them. Jordan challenged Hedjazi for a cross and the ball broke to Eskandarian 12 yards out who inexplicably, and under no pressure, hooked the ball into his own net. The Scottish players captured by the television cameras did not even react to the gift, which added fuel to later theories that some of them wished to return home at the first opportunity.

Following an intervention by the British Consul in Córdoba jail a decision was made to release the 15 Scottish inmates. They were given transportation to the stadium and, after initially being refused entry, took their places in the crowd where they retold their story.

Before too long they probably wished they had remained in the cell. The goal did nothing to improve the second-half performance and disaster struck when Iran equalised. A cross from the right was headed out by Jardine as far as Danaifar who strode forward and appeared to beat Gemmill with ease. There was no denying the quality of the finish as he smashed the ball beyond the helpless Rough from a tight angle.

Regular close-ups of the Scottish bench focussed on Ally MacLeod who appeared to be in a progressively worse state as the minutes ticked away. With 15 minutes remaining Dalglish was replaced by Harper, much to the frustration of Derek Johnstone. Again this was seen as favouritism by MacLeod for his old Aberdeen player but behind the scenes there had been a rift between the Rangers player and the manager, who was of the impression Johnstone only wanted to play in his preferred centre-half position.

At this stage Denis Law shared his thoughts with BBC Radio 2 listeners back home: "We all said before the World Cup started the exclusion of Andy Gray was so important. We brought players who can't score goals. Jordan is good in the air but he is not a great goalscorer. We relied on Kenny Dalglish so much but he hasn't shown his form at all. And there we've got an Aberdeen player and I don't think Joe Harper has played for a month to five weeks so when you've got to rely on players to get you goals it's a sad reflection that Andy Gray is not in the pool."

"It was infuriating to observe given that we expected a rebrand from the first match, which just didn't happen," was Archie Macpherson's view. "It was just dreadful, an awful game."

As the nightmare continued a winning goal for Scotland never looked likely, with only a Jordan header from a Hartford free kick troubling Hedjazi.

The last close-up of Ally MacLeod captured a broken man with his head in his hands. He looked ill, as though life itself was being drained from his body. "Anybody watching television saw the man almost disintegrating at the touchline," recalls Rodger Baillie.

Ally's greatest asset as a manager was his ability to motivate players but the scarcest commodity on the pitch against Iran had been motivation and he had been unable to either understand or change the situation. "I was so sure in the dressing room they would play well," he later told STV. "Everyone looked as though they were dying to get out there."

Those 90 minutes were a low point in Asa Hartford's international career. "That was the worst game any of us had played in," he says. "We had to win and we could only draw with Iran. Near the end one of their fellas was put through and Kenny Burns was chasing him. Although he was a top player, Burnsy wasn't a quick player and I thought 'this could get worse'."

The final whistle sent a group of fans heading to the edge of the stand as close as they could get to the players' tunnel. One, Jim Grieve, threw his Scotland jersey towards the team and a host of expletives was aimed in their direction accompanied by a couple of flags. The chants included "We want our money back" and "No Mendoza!"

"You could understand the fans shouting and some were spitting, shouting 'No Mendoza!'," Asa Hartford recalls of that dark night. "You could clearly hear them all shouting abuse and you think well, it's fair enough isn't it? They've travelled all that way and we've been really poor."

Commentator David Francey's assessment for radio listeners was: "We didn't play well and too many mistakes were made during the game here and the one before. The exclusion of Andy Gray was very important and there were poor performances by too many of the Scottish players like Dalglish who we relied on so much. Iran could possibly have won the game."

When the team coach was held up outside the stadium supporters were able to vent their anger at even closer range. There is a suggestion that some irate fans were directed to a vantage point by a television crew.

Robbie Sterry says: "I don't remember how I got there but I was with a crowd and we ended up on an elevated road about 30 feet above where a luxury coach was parked. The Scottish team left a building and made their way to the bus and that's when the abuse started. It was positively hateful, most of us broken-hearted and embarrassed vented at the top of our lungs for a good ten minutes as the bus was loaded. No need to go into what was said but I assure you it was the worst insults that anyone could spew on another group of humans. All of the players had their heads down and only a few glanced up, scarves, tammies and the occasional team jersey were thrown to the ground landing nowhere near the bus. Had there been rocks around I guarantee the bus would have been stoned."

His namesake Robbie Jenkins was at ground level. "There were people that were shaking the bus and all the rest of it. There were enough supporters there shouting abuse but there was a minority that were trying to push the bus over and it looked like at one time it could get out of hand because people felt so let down."

Even those who hadn't played in the match felt the fans' fury as Masson and McQueen discovered on their way to the coach. Robbie Jenkins says: "Masson's going, 'You wouldn't believe what happened to us!' He was going on about how hard it was, how boring it was and all the rest of it. Lots of people had given up their jobs, hitch-hiked down or got Greyhound buses or spent their life savings or whatever and I completely lost the plot with him. I mean if you can't play for your country and have a couple of weeks of hardship then sorry mate but we've gone through more hardship than you. He might well be right, it might be a bad training complex and all the rest of it but don't try and make Scottish guys that have given up everything feel sorry for you because most people would have loved to have been in his situation. If big McQueen hadn't been there that could've turned nasty because a lot of guys were pillorying Masson quite a bit and the more he spoke the more he was digging a hole for himself. McQueen was the one who was saying 'Come on guys, cool it down. I know we're all disappointed.' If he hadn't been there I think that somebody would have slapped Masson. Maybe I'm wrong but I thought that at the time and I still think that today.

"I know that today you get well-off people going to Scotland away games, staying in top class hotels and the likes, but in these days it was mainly working class people that went to games and for most it was a major financial outlay, and Masson came out with all the wrong things to say to people that had made tremendous sacrifices to get there."

Many of the fans involved in the scenes around the team coach had travelled overland and, as we have seen, in some cases put their lives on the line to reach Argentina. They had no idea how they would get home and were very much aware that the players would be travelling back in comfort by the quickest route. Their anger had been further fuelled by rumours that the players had been squabbling over money.

Robbie Sterry adds: "Just as the bus pulled away an armoured vehicle drove up the road mounted with what we assumed was a water cannon. Now that the team had gone the crowd turned en masse and shouted at the cannon but more with protestations that it could fuck off. We were done and did not have anger for them. We were more trying to convey that there was not going to be a riot and we just wanted to be left alone, which we were."

Back in the Sorrocabana the stunned and angry supporters attempted to drown their sorrows, occasionally singing "Why are we so bad?"

The one shred of comfort was the result from the other Group 4 match in which Peru had drawn with the Dutch. This meant that

Scotland were not yet eliminated from the tournament but required a three-goal victory in their last group game to progress.

"It's difficult to beat the Dutch at any time ... it looks an impossible task," Ally told Arthur Montford, refusing to pass the blame on to his players. MacLeod was loyal if nothing else and took the flak when he might have spilled the beans regarding the bonus rows.

The manager faced calls for his resignation from journalists he had considered friends. "I won't quit here!" he responded. "You will have to wait until we get home." From an English perspective, Colin Malam, football correspondent for the *Sunday Telegraph*, reflected on the manager's behaviour later in the year for his *World Cup Argentina* review, saying: "There were those of us who suspected MacLeod of being quite mad."

Rodger Baillie says: "I remember one press conference after the Iran draw and he sat there as a dog wandered by and he said 'this is my only friend in the world'. I don't recall this, but some people say that the dog then bit him! I honestly can't remember if that was fake news or true."

Someone dispatched a brick through one of the windows of 6 Park Gardens after the game and the front page of the Scottish *Daily Express* carried the headline: "End of the World".

The manager's fall from grace was both spectacular and immediate. The *Evening Times* devoted its centre pages to images of Ally's promotional ventures including his carpet advertisement and one of him wearing a crown. A number of pre-World Cup quotes were recycled, particularly in relation to his own abilities and those of Willie Johnston. He would later be ridiculed as a Pied Piper cartoon-type character who had misled a gullible nation into unrealistic territory.

"We all liked Ally," says Lou Macari. "He was a good character, he was a football man so enthusiastic that you were desperate to win for him. Everyone got carried away but I think we got carried away by the quality of the Scottish team. It had unbelievable quality in it. I don't think it helped either that we were the only British country there because the spotlight fell on Scotland and there were pages to be filled every day by the English reporters."

Bobby Clark knew the manager well and recalls the impact the results had on him. "Having been coached by Ally at Aberdeen I never thought anything would be too much for him, but after both the Peru and Iran games he lost his sparkle. I remember walking past his room one morning, the door was open and he was sitting alone looking very forlorn. I walked past, stopped and then went back and sat with him for a few minutes. I felt he was all alone. I told him we had one game left to salvage some pride. I think I cheered him up but he was down and was feeling the pressure fanned by disappointment. Football can be a very cruel game sometimes and it takes a strong character to handle the ups and downs of a World Cup."

Lou Macari criticised the SFA's organisation of the trip during an ITV interview. His comments were considered inappropriate and he became the third player on the trip to be suspended although none of the officials in Argentina could have possibly seen the interview. Unlike Johnston and Masson, Lou was never officially banned by the SFA. The minutes of an International Committee meeting the following month recommended the team manager "should give serious consideration to subjecting the player again to these arrangements which he professes to find so unsatisfactory".

A number of the fans who had hitch-hiked to Argentina stuck to their "No Mendoza" pledge and, with funds running low, stayed in Córdoba rather than make the 300-mile journey. This meant that some of those arrested ahead of the Iran match only watched one-and-a-half games at the tournament.

Robbie Sterry chose to remain in Córdoba with his Argentinian girlfriend. "I didn't go to Mendoza but stayed with Carol and her father during the game. I didn't see it on television either as at that time you had to go to the cinema to watch a game. I felt way too cheated and disgusted with the SFA to want to make the effort to go to Mendoza."

"When we shifted our headquarters to the San Francisco Hotel in Mendoza there was a general feeling of having started afresh and the atmosphere improved," reads the SFA secretary's report. In excess of 2,000 telegrams arrived at the hotel, some addressed to the manager and others to the players, urging them to put the previous disappointments behind them and do their best against the Dutch. Ally made a point of passing selected messages to the players as their spirits rose.

In the hotel, at the foot of the Andes, the fit-again Rioch had a private meeting with the manager in his room. As team captain, he suggested that the way to defeat the Dutch might be to play a 4-4-2 formation in which Souness could play a key role. Rioch left the manager with his suggestion, which he decided to take on board. This was reflected in his starting 11. Jardine and Burns made way for Kennedy and Forsyth whilst the midfield comprised Rioch, Souness, Gemmill and Hartford with Dalglish and Jordan up front.

When taking the importance of the fixture and standard of opposition into account the Iran match is considered Scotland's worst ever performance. What followed four days later was the polar opposite and for a few wonderful moments the impossible dream really did look possible.

"The Scots put all their disasters behind them with a display of fast, crisp, aggressive football which had the local fans and the few Scots supporters left cheering with emotion," read Alex Cameron's *Daily Record* account.

As they had in the previous two matches Scotland started on the attack but they enjoyed no luck when, after six minutes, a fine cross by Souness was met by the head of Rioch who watched as the ball bounced back from the bar. Jordan then sent Dalglish through who found the net after chipping Jongbloed but a foul had been given against Jordan.

Cameron's *Record* report included the following: "Scotland in these vital early minutes certainly looked better than they had done in the games against Peru and Iran. They hustled and harried the Dutch and pressed them into making chancy pass-backs."

Just as the players rediscovered the form they had shown during qualification the roof fell in when Johnny Rep intercepted a Kennedy back-pass. Attempting to retrieve the situation, the full-back won the ball but Rep went down and a penalty was awarded. It looked a harsh decision and even the gods seemed to be against Scotland. "That's the story of Scotland's World Cup so far," said a dejected Arthur Montford as Robbie Rensenbrink found the corner of Rough's net meaning Scotland needed four goals to progress.

Salvation came on the brink of half-time when a Souness cross was headed down by Jordan for Dalglish to hook in the equaliser. The two players who had looked reluctant to celebrate the own goal against Iran displayed broad smiles as they hugged each other before Hartford and Souness joined the celebrations.

Just one minute after the resumption Souness and Krol went for a cross inside the area and the Liverpool player somersaulted to the ground. Again the Austrian referee pointed to the spot and again the award seemed soft. Gemmill took the responsibility and Scotland led 2-1.

The dream was on as the second period passed its midway point when Gemmill took a pass from Dalglish and danced around three defenders before slotting the ball past the advancing keeper. Bedlam erupted in bars and living rooms around Scotland as grown men hugged each other, unconcerned at the spilling of drinks. David Coleman famously told BBC viewers: "Scotland are in dreamland!" In the *SFA Football Annual No. 1* Ian Peebles captured that glorious moment amongst the SFA party: "Everybody went slightly mad. SFA men jumped up and down hugging each other with players in the row in front of us doing likewise. Bobby Clark was shouting 'I told you we could do it ... I told you!' Sandy Jardine just stood with his hands in the air and a huge smile on his face."

After all the previous disappointments it really looked as though it could be Scotland's day with the impossible looking increasingly likely.

But the celebrations were silenced only three minutes later when Rep sent the ball into the roof of Rough's net from 25 yards, meaning Scotland now needed a further two goals.

Forsyth ought to have scored in the dying seconds, heading over from two yards, but there was barely time for Jongbloed to take the goal kick before the referee's whistle ended Scotland's 1978 World Cup adventure.

The fans had mixed emotions as the players left the pitch. Robbie Jenkins says: "Most people who went to Mendoza thought we were out, we didn't go there expecting to win. Everybody was pleased that we had done well against arguably the best side in the world. There was disappointment but the real anger and disappointment was against Iran. The obvious thing was why couldn't we play like that in the first two games? That was the disappointment, just knowing we had that performance in us."

Along with Peru, the Dutch qualified from the section on goal difference from the Scots, with an identical record of one win, one loss and a draw. They then progressed all the way to the final in Buenos

Aires. Had Scotland won the match in Mendoza by the required margin the spectre of a points deduction may have come back to haunt them.

The Willie Johnston incident merited the loss of two points although as Scotland had lost to Peru this had not been invoked by FIFA. It is quite conceivable that had their side been facing elimination from the tournament the Dutch FA may have addressed this issue, seeking to progress further.

In the *SFA Annual* Ian Peebles noted that one person remained in his seat during the pandemonium which accompanied Scotland's third goal – Don Masson. Clearly Masson had no wish to extend his unhappy stay in Argentina, the likelihood of which increased with each Scottish goal.

During Ally MacLeod's last press conference in the San Francisco Hotel, he defended his players and accused certain reporters of fabricating stories of misbehaviour. The squad, he insisted, had been "the best behaved and best disciplined I have ever worked with". This public backing was not reflected in the internal report Ally submitted to his employers, which contained the following: "Generally speaking the 22 players made up a good squad, were well disciplined and easy to handle with the normal one or two exceptions. The squad had its usual quota of petty grievances and these became magnified when the results went against the team."

On the flight home Derek Johnstone informed the manager he no longer wished to be considered for international duty should he be in charge. Along with the still injured McQueen and the two back-up goalkeepers, the Rangers striker was one of four squad members who had failed to feature in any of the three matches.

Asa Hartford remembers the contrast in the two journeys. "The thing that sticks in my mind was that when we went out we went with British Caledonian. When you were having food it was the silver condiment holder and silver knife and fork. But we came back with your knees underneath your chin at the back of the plane." The Scottish party arrived back in Glasgow on 15 June exactly three weeks and a lifetime since the send-off from Hampden.

Although they were never going to receive the type of welcome the 1974 squad had enjoyed there were a number of supporters waiting and no sign of a lynch mob. There would have been some apprehension amongst the players given the anger they had encountered after the draw with Iran. Jack Webster reported in the Scottish *Daily Express* that "several hundred supporters chanted words of encouragement". There is no doubt that the performance in the last match had brought a smile to the faces of Scotland fans again and for a short time this eclipsed the events of Córdoba.

In his lengthy SFA report the SFA secretary recorded: "The Committee is of the opinion that the morale of the players was seriously affected by the numerous distortions, exaggerations and, in some cases, quite hysterical comments by the media." Walker still defended the much-criticised choice of accommodation in Alta Gracia which had been earmarked during the trip at the end of 1977. "As I was jointly responsible with the team manager for the choice of that particular hotel, I wish to put on record that I do not accept the criticisms and that, in my opinion, the Sierras Hotel was perfectly adequate for our purposes."

In the manager's report Ally took a similar view to the secretary: "In my opinion the hotel at Alta Gracia was satisfactory. The squad, with the normal one or two exceptions, accepted that the hotel, although not a luxurious abode, was well above the average Argentinian hotel. Several players indicated that they were not happy with the hotel. This is normal, and if they had been based in the Hilton, something would have been found to be wrong even there."

Whilst the Sierras may not have been up to the standard of hotels in other parts of Argentina it may very well have been the most suitable to accommodate a large group in the Córdoba area in 1978. It was certainly good enough for the Iranians, who had attempted to outbid the SFA, and the Dutch who moved in during the second round, although it is significant that the hotel's two defenders were also responsible for its selection.

Rodger Baillie's views have not changed over the years. "All that you have read about it was perfectly true. I was always a bit surprised because Ernie Walker was an extremely shrewd administrator. I can only think that promises were made by the authorities in Argentina that the hotel and also the training area, which was appalling, would perhaps be improved. It wasn't a tumbling ruin but it was not up to what you would expect." Rodger's assumptions, as we have seen, are quite correct in regard to the training pitch which proved to be unusable despite promises by the organisers.

"I never covered a tournament when there was such a frenzy for stories," the journalist reflects. "There was a lot of misinformation. The BBC national news on the Monday after the game in Mendoza led their one o'clock bulletin with the news that Ally had resigned and he hadn't. Even somebody as respected as the BBC came out with that and anything went."

On the manager, Rodger says: "Ally was a lovely man but he was not suited to be an international manager. He had never been in charge of a club team in a European tournament so he had no experience as regards outwith the domestic scene. He didn't go to watch Peru, Iran or even Holland.

"He'd done well with Aberdeen so it wasn't a total shot in the dark but his experience outwith the domestic scene was limited. He was partially responsible for the whole circus which surrounded the build-up but, to be fair to him, not totally.

"There were team selection problems. He only brought Souness in in the last game which made a tremendous difference. He didn't pick Johnstone but selected Masson and Rioch whose form had dipped quite alarmingly at Derby County. So there were myriad factors that came into it. I wouldn't put the whole blame on him by any means but he was a factor – but you couldn't dislike him."

Asa Hartford looks back on the 1978 World Cup with these thoughts: "The lack of information about the opposition cost us dearly but it was the players' fault. The players have got to hold their hands up. When you look at the squad – the six midfield players – we should have at least qualified. There were a few things that Ally maybe brought on himself like saying we're going to come back with some sort of medal but that was the way he handled things. He was this showman I suppose, a bit like Tommy Doc."

Even allowing for the failure to win a match in the Home International series, when Scotland ought to have beaten the Welsh and had played well during the England game, Ally's time as Scotland manager had been successful right up until the squad left for Argentina.

In Alta Gracia he was unable to cope with the combination of disastrous results and low morale. There are reports of Ally going

AWOL, confined to his room in the days following the draw with Iran, but some players cannot recall this so the story may well be exaggerated. Perhaps his initial feeling that the opportunity to boss Scotland had come too early in his career had been correct. Yet the managerial inquest would have been avoided had the team scrambled a win against Iran which would have alleviated much of the gloom. But when assessing his overall record it would surely be wrong to ignore the success MacLeod brought to the Scotland job so soon after his appointment, particularly in the performances against England, Chile, Argentina, Czechoslovakia and Wales.

Willie Johnston had arrived back in London on the day of the Iran match where his club manager Ron Atkinson succeeded in shielding him from the media frenzy waiting at the airport. The payback for this was an exclusive interview Atkinson had arranged at a BBC studio. So did Willie watch Scotland's other matches or did he try to ignore the tournament in what was clearly a tough time for him? "I got home and they were playing Iran – I watched a bit of it in London. I watched the Holland game; that was unlucky."

Despite a return to Rangers in 1980, whilst Ally MacLeod was managing Motherwell, albeit in a lower division, Willie and Ally's paths never crossed again. "I went to Vancouver Whitecaps after West Brom and when I came back to Rangers I never met him again."

A number of Scotland fans were in Argentina until the final itself. "We had people on our trip who had won the raffle but like everything else the people who won it were not diehard Scotland supporters and the first time they had been at a Scotland game was in Argentina," remembers Robbie Jenkins. "We made great friends in Córdoba and when it came to the final a lot of these guys were fed up once Scotland went out and they were going to chuck away their World Cup final tickets. We said don't be silly, we'll give them away to people we know in Córdoba. We gave them to them for nothing and I remember a guy about twice the size of me crying his eyes out, hugging me."

A handful of supporters still remained in Córdoba after the tournament's conclusion – the remnants of Ally's Army. Their long journey to Argentina had been an adventure with the expectation of good football its reward. The return trip, with funds almost exhausted, was a less exciting prospect. A couple of the fans considered using a canoe to cross the Gulf of Darién which would at least save the cost of an airfare. Others, unable to face the long trek back, were repatriated by the British Embassy after agreeing to repay their airfares once home, with travel restrictions imposed until the debt had been cleared.

Robbie Sterry and Richard Grassick set off on the long road back together around 5 July. After reading about his planned trip to Argentina in the *Daily Record*, Robbie had written to Richard in Kirkliston suggesting that the two of them journeyed together. As the pair had never previously met they failed to rendezvous as arranged in London before eventually meeting up much later in Córdoba.

Leaving Córdoba, where Richard had sold his camera to supplement their dwindling funds, they chose to bypass Mendoza and made for Salta in the north-west of Argentina, where they hoped to jump a freight train and cross the Andes into Chile.

After sneaking on board they were discovered a few hours into the journey and escorted to the caboose at the rear of the train where they sat with two soldiers who were on their way to the military checkpoint at the border. "By this time I was wearing a number 10 Argentinian jersey – Kempes – which I had traded for my Scotland shirt after the final, and they befriended us and fed us for the rest of the trip," Robbie recollects. "Or I should say until the engine shit itself and we were dropped off at a siding with a loaf of bread and a chunk of salami!"

The following two nights were spent stranded halfway up the Andes. "There was not a soul in sight, just a rocky barren landscape with peaks in the distance. There was a stone railway building with a well beside it where we would drop a bucket down and winch it up to get water and we spent two nights in there." Perhaps the Mendoza route would after all have been a better option.

Finally, a new engine arrived and they continued on the train to the army base at the border where the stowaways were introduced to the base commander who made them welcome. Robbie recalls: "We were told that a train would come and haul the wagons back down into Chile and that they would let us know when it was leaving. We slept in the barracks and helped out during the day baking bread in an outdoor wood-fired oven. We were treated like minor celebrities and everyone wanted to talk to us and hear about our trip. Our soldier buddy woke us up one night and said the train was leaving. He guided us to the right one and we climbed on to the ladder between the carriage's ... it was fucking Baltic at that altitude."

The train moved off slowly but stopped after an hour as guards with flashlights and German shepherd dogs searched the trucks in scenes reminiscent of a spy movie or prisoner of war escape film. "The dogs smelled us. We were told to get off the ladders we were clinging to," Robbie relates. "I tried but was frozen in place and could barely move so two soldiers helped us down and we were escorted to a small warm hut where we were given coffee and some cake."

After their passport numbers had been recorded, Robbie observed a change in the mood of their captors. "We explained our situation and informed them that we had very little money and were trying to get home from the World Cup. The Chileans had heard about the Scots and broke into smiles. We were allowed to get in the caboose at the end of the train where they had a pot-bellied wood stove which they cooked on and we were fed. I believe today, now knowing what a Canadian winter is, that we could have died on that ladder.

"It took around 30 hours to get off the mountain and down to the flatlands. About four hours before our arrival the train stopped and one of the drivers climbed up a telephone pole which had stirrups up one side just for that reason. He hooked up a couple of wires to the lines and started tapping away. Richard and I looked at each other and thought that this must be a telegraph, never having actually seen one except in old movies. Little did we know that it was for us they were telegraphing.

"We pulled into a deserted station in Antofagasta late afternoon on a Sunday and were met by two guys wearing trench coats and English-style trilby hats. They showed us their credentials which identified them as Interpol and off we went to another office to repeat our story. Our passports were taken and after about an hour the guy who left with them returned and his mate put a stamp in our passports as we had obviously crossed a border without going through the normal channels. Then they drove us to the outside of town to the Pan American Highway so we could again begin hitching back north. They dropped us off on the coastal road where we stripped and had a bath in the Pacific Ocean, bloody cold and hard to make soap work in salt water. It had been eight or nine days since my last shower.

"What excellent people we encountered on that part of our journey. Everyone was in synch with the Scots who were too poor to fly to the World Cup but were desperate enough to hitch-hike for their love of their team and country. Diehard football fans to be sure."

Ally MacLeod attended a meeting of the International Committee at Park Gardens on 10 July where he faced some tough questions from the six committee members and chairman Tom Lauchlan. He was then asked to vacate the room before later being recalled and informed that a vote was narrowly in favour of him continuing as Scotland manager. The decision had been split with three in favour of retaining his services and three against, with the chairman's casting vote going in Ally's favour.

Although relieved to still be in a job and, therefore, exonerated for at least some of the blame for the summer's events, Ally MacLeod was aware that it would be difficult to continue in the long term without the support of all the committee members.

He refused to speak to reporters as he left the building having vowed to be less accessible to the media. Ally's SFA report on the World Cup had adequately expressed his view: "I, personally, feel that the press did not play ball with the squad, and in fact, abused the privileges given to them. I feel a long and hard look at future press privileges should be taken."

Almost certainly responding to criticism of his failure to spy on Peru, MacLeod flew to Oslo at the end of August to take in the match between Norway and Austria, Scotland's first two opponents in the European Championship qualifiers. Portugal and Belgium made up the numbers in the tough group of five from which only the winners would go to the finals in Italy, a tournament in which Scotland had yet to take part.

Pressmen inside Park Gardens were surprised to find the list of players for the Austria game in September dictated by assistant secretary Peter Donald and were advised that the manager had left the building. Tom Lauchlan, whose casting vote had resulted in Ally's retention, told Alex Cameron: "I assumed he would be present … I shall certainly ask the reason for his absence." Ally later claimed that he had had to attend to a family matter that afternoon.

The manager's pool omitted 11 of the Argentina squad. Aside from the banned players, Burns, Jardine and Robertson were dropped with Rioch unavailable through injury. Harper was out but Andy Gray was included – again a likely reaction to criticism.

Derek Johnstone's absence was explained by his defensive role for Rangers that season, with the players' post-World Cup comments to the manager kept private. MacLeod later intimated he had been unhappy with Kenny Burns's form during the matches in Córdoba and his SFA report had singled out the player for criticism during the Peru match. This was completely out of character for Ally, who had not withdrawn the player and indeed stuck with him for the duration of the Iran game.

Before the trip to Austria MacLeod took charge of the Under-21 team who hosted the USA's full side in a challenge match at Pittodrie on the afternoon of Sunday 17 September. The venue was not ideal for the manager as he was flying from Glasgow to Vienna the following day. The Americans were approaching the end of a seven-match European tour with a pool of players whose average age was 22.

With the second half broadcast live on *Scotsport*, the crowd numbered just below 6,000. The young Scots took an early lead through Jim Melrose but paid the price for complacency when Dale Russell equalised a minute after the break.

Scotland responded with two goals in quick succession midway through the half. First Neil Orr's strike from 40 yards struck a post then entered the net via the back of unlucky goalkeeper Dave Brcic before Murdo MacLeod scored with another powerful shot to record a result of 3-1.

The legacy of Copenhagen and Alta Gracia continued in the run-up to the game as some Austrian newspapers featured cartoons depicting drunken Scottish footballers. "All the players will be completely behind the manager," Archie Gemmill told the *Record*'s Alex Cameron, adding, "You can take it we are pleased he has been given, if you like, a second chance."

On the afternoon of the game Ally declined an invitation to attend an SFA/press function, choosing instead to go for a walk as the players slept. Rodger Baillie remembers the occasion.

"The SFA did make some kind of attempt to build bridges again with the press and there was a reception for the hacks in Willie Harkness's suite which was very affable. I can remember when entering looking along the corridor and Ally was kind of hidden behind a pillar trying to see who was going in."

Hugh Taylor noted in the *Evening Times*: "Compared with the bubbling, eager, voluble publicist of the World Cup MacLeod was almost a hermit in Austria."

The manager selected an attacking line-up with the aerial threat of Jordan and Gray up front whilst the fit-again McQueen returned to the centre of defence. Gray said he was delighted to be back and was unconcerned that the referee for the evening, Italian Alberto Michelotti, was the same official who had sent him off in Prague two years earlier.

There were over 62,000 in the Prater Stadium, around 2,000 of whom had travelled from Scotland. For many of those fans the trip was the next best thing to attending the World Cup with more than a few of them venturing overseas for the first time. Some Rangers fans had arrived in Vienna after travelling from their side's European Cup tie in Turin the previous week. Tickets delivered from Park Gardens were accompanied by a letter from Ernie Walker which concluded: "Have a good trip and thanks for your continued interest in the Scottish team despite recent events."

The Austrians, with star striker Hans Krankl, had performed well in Argentina, exiting the tournament after the second round.

Scotland fell behind in the 27th minute when the ball broke to the unmarked Pezzey who had all the time in the world to shoot past Rough. The two Scottish strikers did not appear to be gelling and the Austrians extended their lead in the 48th minute when Schachner somehow scored from a seemingly impossible angle with Rough looking suspect.

Arthur Graham replaced Jordan after an hour, four minutes before a freak goal seemed to finish the contest. Kreuz mis-hit a cross which flew skywards before dipping behind Rough and into the net as the sound of thousands of air horns was heard for the third time that evening. Now facing the prospect of a heavy defeat, Scotland instantly pulled a goal back when McQueen connected with a Donachie free kick to power in a flying header.

The goal lifted the side and they scored again to silence the home fans. A Gemmill corner found McQueen but this time his header was blocked on the line before Gray reacted to head into the net. The Scots in the crowd were buoyant and with their side continuing to attack were beginning to sense a draw was possible.

The ball boys positioned around the pitch were then withdrawn and valuable time was lost due to there being a running track around the pitch. Ally MacLeod can be seen in television footage retrieving the ball and returning it to his players on a number of occasions.

There was almost a fairy-tale ending when Hartford snatched at a chance from six yards with a couple of minutes remaining, but he missed the target – it had been that close to 3-3.

"The only thing that comes to mind in that game was a fella kicked me in the balls, one of their midfield players!" is Asa Hartford's abiding memory of the Prater Stadium.

The manager was more like his old self speaking to the press after the 3-2 defeat. "I thought we played tremendously well. With a bit of luck in the closing stages we could even have saved the game. This must have been one of Scotland's greatest displays in Europe."

Not even Ally MacLeod himself could have realised at that point how little time he had left as the national manager. Just two days later he bumped into Ayr United vice-chairman John Ferguson in a corridor at Park Gardens. Ferguson was exiting a committee meeting and mentioned to Ally that his club would soon be seeking a replacement for manager Alex Stuart, whose resignation was believed to be imminent. Stuart resigned later that same day and an approach was made for Ally to return to Somerset Park the following Tuesday.

Ally asked for 24 hours to consider the offer which was believed to mean a reduction of £3,000 per year in wages. But after meeting with the Ayr board he accepted the position later that same day. The MacLeod family still lived in the town and the decision was made after weighing up the result of the International Board's vote plus his uncomfortable relationship with the Scottish press, which was damaged beyond repair.

The change of manager would have been of no importance to Robbie Sterry and Richard Grassick, who were still trying to find their way home. In Córdoba they had befriended a Scot whose father was the British ambassador to Ecuador and he had suggested they look him up in the capital city of Quito on their way back. As well as an open return for Laker's Skytrain from New York to London, Richard had a ticket with Lufthansa from Ecuador to Guatemala so the pair hitched from Chile through Peru before eventually reaching Quito.

"We were invited into the residence in a very nice part of town where we showered, were fed and did laundry," Robbie recalls. Richard, very nobly, attempted to exchange his ticket for two shorter journeys which would at least see them bridge the Darién Gap, but the agent in the local Lufthansa office refused to entertain the idea.

Back at the embassy Richard was permitted to telephone a *Daily Record* reporter he had met in Argentina and the pair's dilemma was explained. He was told to call back the following day with the journalist pledging to try and help.

The follow-up call brought welcome news as Robbie remembers. "He explained that we could go back to the Lufthansa office and all would be well. Why? He had called the airline and explained that the back page of the *Record* would be a full-page story about how Lufthansa were not helping out two World Cup stragglers and how did he think that would play out with ticket sales in Scotland?" They were taken downtown in a chauffeur-driven car where the agent was only too delighted to hand over two tickets from Barranquilla on the north coast of Colombia to Guatemala.

This really raised their spirits and they spent a further three days as guests of the ambassador before hitch-hiking to the coast for their flight.

"From Guatemala we jumped a train and got into the States with six dollars left between us which we spent on Big Macs at McDonald's," says Robbie. "We got a ride all the way to Chicago where a young guy picked us up and took us back to his house where his father, realising we were broke, gave us two days' work cleaning out the inside of two tanker trailers. They had been used to make an emergency run to Detroit and needed to be cleaned before being put back into use. The guy's surname was Montgomery and he owned Montgomery Tank Lines and had Scottish heritage. He paid us $100 each and got us a ride to Detroit on one of his trucks where we crossed into Windsor in Canada."

Robbie intended to look up some relatives in Canada and they made it to his mother's sister's house in Seaforth, Ontario, where "we were force-fed every two hours until we put back on a few of the pounds that we had lost during the trip".

There was yet another twist in the tale of Robbie's 1978 adventure: "I ended up seeing my mother for the first time in 12 years. I didn't even know she was there."

The two travellers parted company a week or so later with Richard seeking out an old friend before heading to New York and the Skytrain.

The SFA pledged to appoint a replacement manager before the Norway match in October with the names of Stein, Jock Wallace, Turnbull and Roxburgh linked to the vacancy. Stein had only recently taken on the manager's role at Leeds United and it was clear that the timing was not ideal but there was an indication that his wife was not keen to move away from Glasgow.

Jock Stein was very astute at dealing with the media and a call to sports writer Jim Rodgers set his plan into operation. At Stein's request Rodgers asked Archie Macpherson to telephone him in Leeds. "It was really just a couple of phone calls that were made to me and me to him that provided his interest in me helping him publicise the fact that he would be interested in the job," the broadcaster remembers today.

Stein suggested that Archie might care to mention his name in connection with the Scotland job should he be appearing on that evening's *Sportsnight*. "But you can't say you've been speaking with me," he insisted.

"The SFA only need to pick up the phone to Jock Stein and they will have their new manager," is how Archie raised the matter on air that same evening.

Just as Stein had planned, the comments were quickly seized upon and he was heard downplaying the suggestion on the radio the following morning to the effect that Archie Macpherson's words ought to be taken with a pinch of salt.

But the International Committee took the bait and a secret meeting was arranged at Hampden on 4 October, away from the prying press at Park Gardens. Ernie Walker, Willie Harkness, Tommy Younger and Tom Lauchlan met with Stein for just over half an hour.

Although he had turned down the position on two previous occasions Stein agreed to a four-year contract after just 44 days at Elland Road. The Leeds board tried to keep him but they parted on good terms with Stein admitting: "I feel I have let a lot of people down."

Ernie Walker described the Hampden meeting as harmonious but would not discuss the salary, which was speculated to be around £25,000.

The SFA Annual Report later recorded: "There was nobody else in the field whose qualifications for the job could even remotely approach Mr Stein's and the International Committee had little hesitation in asking him to join us at Park Gardens."

A letter submitted for the *Daily Record* Sportsbag by Willie Stewart of Glasgow Tollcross Road represented the views of most supporters: "The rest of the world can stop laughing at us now that Jock Stein is the boss. For the first time we have got the right man for the job."

Stein took office on 5 October and told the press the same day: "I am still hopeful that we can qualify from the group. I wouldn't have taken this job if I didn't think we could get some success and obviously the European Championship is part of that aim. I feel that we have a good pool of players, but everyone has different ideas about players and there are some I would like to see in the squad."

The 18 selected by Stein for the Norway match contained no fewer than 13 "Anglos" and just one Old Firm player – Tom Forsyth. Stein also chose a similar number for the Under-21 fixture with the Norwegians and asked Hibernian manager Eddie Turnbull to oversee the youngsters. Stein was quick to point out that Turnbull was only in charge for that one match as he did not wish to rush into making a decision about a full-time assistant. The choice was an interesting one as the managers had previously had their differences whilst Stein was in charge of Celtic, but he clearly rated Turnbull as a coach and saw him as someone he could work with.

Rodger Baillie had many dealings with both men. "Looking back on it and knowing Jock as I did, I don't think there were many managers that he actively disliked. I do think, in fact, this rivalry with Eddie is somewhat exaggerated. A professional rivalry, yes, but on another level it really wasn't a factor."

At this stage Robbie Sterry was still in Canada. After leaving his aunt in Seaforth, he hitch-hiked to Thunder Bay in Ontario where his father lived and secured enough employment to purchase a seat on the Skytrain.

In Thunder Bay Robbie was invited to turn out for a local soccer side, Finlandia United, where: "It surprised the shit out of me to find Richard Grassick, whose buddy had moved up there and had invited him to play for the same team. Small world!"

Robbie hitch-hiked the best part of 1,000 miles to New York before flying to London, finally arriving home in Perth on his 20th birthday, 16 October, just over six months after setting off.

Newspaper reports naming Robbie as the last man back from Argentina were inaccurate as it was another few weeks before Adrian Haren walked over the doorstep of his Surrey home for the first time in eight months. Adrian had worked his passage back to Europe on a cargo ship from Buenos Aires to one of the German ports from where the rest of the journey home was little more than a short hop by comparison.

The managerial arrangement continued for the Under-21 match with Stein notifying Turnbull of the starting XI before both men sat together in the Easter Road dugout. Unfamiliar with each other, the players started nervously until Ray Stewart strode forward in the 37th minute to unleash a 20-yarder to open the scoring.

Stein was seen to hurry down the tunnel at half-time suggesting he had some wisdom to impart to the players although Turnbull was very much his own man who would have had an input into any discussions.

Whatever was said by whom worked, as the Scots completely overwhelmed the Norwegians in the second half. George McCluskey capitalised on a half chance before skipper Ally McLeod (no relation to the former manager) scored the goal of the match. The Hibs striker struck the ball from just outside the box and watched it hit the underside of the crossbar before landing behind the line. McCluskey then stabbed through the goalkeeper's legs for his second. Wark made it five with another long-range effort before Jacobsen replied for the visitors six minutes from time to make the final score 5-1.

Stein's Hampden selection was a line-up that would have been completely unacceptable a decade before. For the first time in the history of the SFA an international side was completely populated by Anglos with Jim Stewart chosen ahead of Rough in goal. The manager's choice of goalkeeper may have been influenced by a recording of the match in Vienna supplied by BBC Scotland and there was a touch of irony considering Stewart had only joined Middlesbrough after an attempt to lure Rough from Firhill had failed.

Aberdeen full-back Kennedy would probably have featured had he not failed a late fitness test, which opened the door for Frank Gray to earn his second cap. Jordan was also dropped with Dalglish and Andy Gray preferred as the strikers.

"When I named the players I did not consider which club they played for," was Stein's response to the press regarding the Anglo issue on the eve of the game.

The SFA had decided against making the match all-ticket with payment accepted for all sections on the night apart from the South Stand. The situation outside the ground mirrored that of the Bulgaria match with too few gates manned. This led to chaos with some latecomers leaving rather than literally trying to fight their way inside. The attendance topped the first home match following the 1974 World Cup – an astonishing 65,372 inside despite heavy rain and a strike by Glasgow busmen. Robbie Sterry, who had returned from Argentina a week or so earlier, was not amongst the crowd, however, spending the evening at home in Perth.

The mood of the fans was positive with "We'll Support You Ever More" greeting the teams. Norway forced two corners inside the opening few minutes and scored from the second as Aas headed past Stewart. The crowd stayed behind the team and a Gray header from a Gemmill cross was saved well by Jacobsen and a Dalglish volley booted from the goal line as Scotland camped themselves in their opponents' half. The equaliser came after half an hour when Hartford hooked the ball towards Dalglish, who scored with a header. Norway still threatened occasionally although Scotland created so many chances that it seemed only a matter of time before they took the lead.

The same pattern as the first half continued after the break with Scotland piling forward before the visitors broke away to regain the lead. Mathisen directed a cross for Okland at the far post, who netted with a fine diving header. Both the crowd and players were again stunned and when the singing did restart it was to the tune of "What a load of rubbish".

With Scotland committed to all-out attack, another breakaway saw Johansen strike Stewart's crossbar, an incident which proved to be a turning point.

Just eight minutes remained when Gray headed a Hartford cross down for Dalglish to bundle in from two yards. Scotland were not finished and there was a dramatic end when Souness sent Graham through for Birkelund to upend him in the box for a clear penalty.

With two minutes left, Gemmill kept his head and scored easily to give Scotland the lead for the first time on the night and two vital points.

Just in case Jacobsen had done his homework, Gemmill had been astute enough to place the penalty to the opposite side of the goal than he had in Mendoza.

"Scotland have done the impossible!" was Arthur Montford's assessment. His view was replicated by the *Evening Times* sport's headline of "The Great Escape".

It had been a quite incredible match during which Scotland had been in danger of another embarrassing result. It had also been one of the most exciting Hampden internationals for many a year with so many chances created that on another day might have produced six or seven Scottish goals.

Stein was philosophical in the press room afterwards, imparting: "Some things came off, others didn't, but it was a good result especially after that first goal by Norway gave us a mountain to climb."

Seven days separated Stein's next appointment when he took charge of the Scottish League side for their first match against their Irish counterparts in nine years. With Rangers, Hibs and Aberdeen all in European action the same evening Stein's selection came from Dundee United, Morton, Celtic, Hearts, Partick and Motherwell with Rough given the opportunity to impress the new manager. The series of fixtures between the two had begun in 1893 and the Irish had never won in Scotland, but they came within less than 20 minutes of doing just that at Fir Park.

The visitors led after 20 minutes through a goal by Tom Armstrong of Ards. The Irish then set up camp in their own half for most of the remainder of the match with goalkeeper Barclay the equal of the Scots' many efforts. Even when Barclay was beaten by a Hegarty header the ball rebounded from a post and into his arms.

The equaliser came in the 73rd minute when Pettigrew drew Barclay from his line before slipping the ball low into goal to complete the scoring at 1-1. In a fixture historically dominated by the Scots the result was the first time that the sides had drawn with just one more meeting, the 56th, taking place in Belfast two years later.

In their quest to reach the European Championships Scotland faced another tough away match in Portugal before the end of the year.

Stein watched the Portuguese win in Austria in mid-November, two weeks ahead of Scotland's trip to Lisbon. Alberto's last-minute winner halted the Austrians' strong start but also lifted the Portuguese into second place in the group, a point ahead of Scotland.

Stein took the party to the Palacio hotel in Estoril which had been the base for his greatest triumph, the European Cup Final of 1967.

The Under-21 side showed the watching senior squad the way with an excellent 3-0 win in Lisbon's Restelo Stadium where the noisy Scottish contingent outnumbered the locals in the 1,000-strong crowd.

An even first half was scoreless before Scotland took control after the turnaround. McCluskey first drew the keeper then sent the ball into the corner of the net after 54 minutes. With the midfield combination of Aitken, Bannon and Wark gelling well, the contest was effectively ended eight minutes later when McLeod was brought down by Alhino. The home players complained at length over the penalty award but McLeod was unfazed and scored easily. McLeod provided the icing on the cake four minutes from the end by slotting home from close range.

There was a completely different atmosphere inside the Stadium of Light the following evening where 70,000 patriots roared their side on. The 1-0 scoreline did not reflect Portugal's superiority on a night when Alan Rough returned in goal.

The only goal came just ahead of the half-hour mark when Alberto netted after a 40-yard run.

The Portuguese ought to have doubled their lead in the second half when Sheu unleashed a spectacular shot from all of 30 yards which Rough could only watch cannon from the face of his crossbar to safety. Scotland came closest to scoring when McQueen's header was cleared from the line by the head of Alhinho.

"We could have taken a point, but that does not disguise the fact that it was a poor performance," Stein told the press, adding, "We didn't play well until it was too late."

Scotland had now failed to win in a competitive match overseas since Copenhagen three years earlier, apart from the Holland game in neutral Mendoza.

The Herald's sports headline spared readers the need to read the accompanying article by stating "Portugal Shred Stein's New Lions to

Shreds", whilst Alex Cameron's *Record* report began with: "Scotland's soccer story continued last night as one of dismal failure."

The defeat in Lisbon brought the disastrous year of 1978, which had promised so much, to an end, with Scotland's European Championship prospects already looking slim.

1979

"Is there an Englishman in the house?"
Wembley Stadium announcer

One positive factor for Scotland's European Championship hopes was that each of their three main group rivals had yet to visit Hampden Park with the Belgians due in Glasgow on 7 February for the first international of 1979.

After the congestion preceding the Norway match one of the suggestions to ease the flow through the turnstiles had been to either round up the terrace admission of £1.70 and £1.80 to £2 or down to £1.50. The SFA chose the £2 option – then made the game all-ticket! The tickets themselves were of the previous standard with the recommended security features only incorporated for the England game at the end of the season.

Another severe winter threw the game into doubt with only three domestic matches played on the Saturday prior to the international. On that day SFA secretary Ernie Walker advised that the Hampden pitch was playable but delayed a final decision until the squad were due to assemble on the Monday. The Belgians were said to be happy with this arrangement as they were not due to travel until the Tuesday. The Under-21 match was, however, postponed as the Tynecastle surface had no prospect of staging the game and there were no guarantees that an alternative venue would be playable.

The situation was uncannily similar to the Bulgaria game 12 months earlier. Then the SFA had gambled on the state of the pitch rather than calling the match off although the circumstances were different this time. Whereas the alternative to the friendly going ahead had been cancellation, the Belgium match would have had to be rescheduled in the event of a postponement.

Following consultations with local referee Ian Foote the match was called off on the Monday morning with most of the England-based players already in Glasgow. The announcement came just as Graeme Souness had arrived and he was reported to have done an immediate U-turn and driven back south. Consideration had been given to keeping the players together at Largs for a couple of days but with some of the Anglos now available for midweek club matches that idea was abandoned.

The cancellation disappointed Stein, who believed that the timing would have favoured his side as the Belgians' domestic season had only recently restarted. The SFA advised that all tickets sold – said to number around 40,000 – would be valid for the rearranged date which had still to be agreed. Initially it was said there would be no refunds issued but there was a change of policy at a meeting of the International Committee the following week. Whilst tickets would still be valid for the new date, refunds could be claimed by ticket holders within a four-week period. It was further announced that the income from ticket sales would be invested in a special fund until the match was played with the accrued interest donated to a charity selected by the association. Much later in the year a cheque for £6,200 was presented to the Scottish branch of the Variety Club of Great Britain to aid in the purchase of two coaches for handicapped and deprived children.

Ironically the Hampden pitch was said to be playable on the Wednesday. An offer to reschedule the game for 28 February was rejected as the Belgians had an Army Cup match that evening.

Scotland were then out of action until the Home International series in May, which would be five months after their last match in Lisbon. They would then play a total of five games in just under three weeks beginning in mid-May. Eddie Turnbull was again invited to assist Stein during the busy end to the season.

There were some new faces in Stein's pool for the British Championship and George Burley, John Wark, Paul Hegarty and Alan Hansen all made their debuts during the opener iat Ninian

Park where Dalglish was given the captaincy. With Arthur Graham and Hansen surging forward there was no hint during the opening period of the heavy deficit the Welsh would inflict on Scotland. Hugh Taylor's summary for the *Evening Times*'s sports edition noted: "Scotland were stringing passes together in fine fashion. Wales could not match Scotland for skill or artistry."

Scotland self-destructed before the half hour when a stray pass from Hegarty allowed Alan Curtis to create an opening for Toshack who strode past Hansen to beat Rough from an angle.

Stein's men hardly deserved to be behind but Toshack scored again in the 35th minute after Rough had blocked his first effort.

After half-time Scotland continued to press but panicked into hurried finishing whilst the Welsh looked comfortable and Toshack completed his hat-trick by heading in a cross from Curtis.

With Hartford and Wark both given offside after finding the net, Scotland had enjoyed no luck in the match, but there was no disguising yet another disappointing result. The 3-0 defeat was Scotland's heaviest ever loss to the Welsh – with the ruthless Toshack exacting some revenge for the perceived injustice of Anfield. The large travelling support did not sound too dejected as their "Wem-bi-lee-bound" chants drowned out the home fans at the end.

With some justification Stein claimed Scotland had not played badly but was not blind to the faults, telling Hugh Taylor: "The team played better than you would think from the score but it's true the central defence didn't work out as I hoped that it would."

Hansen and Wallace made way for the more experienced McQueen and Jordan for Northern Ireland's visit to Hampden on the Tuesday, with Everton keeper George Wood taking over from Rough.

An Old Firm championship decider on the Monday must have had some effect on the Hampden attendance of 28,524 but had minimal influence over Stein's selection. Jardine and Bobby Russell, who may not have played anyway, were the only Old Firm players named in the squad, both of whom had been released to play at Celtic Park.

It was one-way traffic in the first half with Graham being continually denied by Pat Jennings whilst Wood touched the ball just once – to catch an off-target effort by Nelson. The match developed into a duel between Jennings and Graham after the interval as the lack of a goal tested the patience of the crowd. In the 76th minute Jennings again thwarted Graham then saved as Dalglish struck the rebound. The ball then broke for Graham, whose shot through a ruck of players finally beat the seemingly invincible goalkeeper to break the deadlock. In total Graham alone had had eight attempts saved by Jennings but the goal was enough to earn his side two points.

It seemed impossible but even more Scotland fans travelled to London in 1979 than had two years earlier. One supporter, Jim Mallon from Cumbernauld, was so desperate to attend his first Wembley international that he offered to trade his G-registered Volvo for three match tickets.

Again, forgeries made front-page news with a large number of standing tickets for J and K sections – the SFA's allocation – circulating in the Aberdeen area. The Wembley tickets were more complex than those for Hampden and the fakes were considered to be of a high standard but could be detected by holding the watermark to the light. In excess of 1,000 forgeries were believed to have changed hands, generally for £5 – twice the face value of genuine tickets. Once the existence of counterfeits had been publicised there were reports of fakes changing hands for a couple of pounds.

Traditionally the supporters who travelled to Wembley had always been a cross section of football fans leaning towards an older age group who saved hard for each trip. This changed in the 1970s when an increasing numbers of younger fans with disposable income and more energy started to travel and did not overly concern themselves with trivialities such as match tickets and accommodation. This new generation of fans could amass the necessary funds for a weekend in London in a couple of months whereas their elders would have saved for two years to finance the trip.

"If you see the pictures of the guys on the park in 1977 they all look like they're about my age then," says supporter Stuart Borrowman who was 24 at that time. "My impression of the previous generation was it was guys that had saved up in a club for two years and it was their only break and that was the big thing. It was older guys who would go heavy on the drink but maybe didn't go wrecking things or whatever."

A glance at images of the more restrained pitch invasion in 1967 certainly confirms those supporters as part of an older age group.

As the support increased so did the levels of misbehaviour with one particular incident resulting in the death of a fan on the Thursday overnight Glasgow Central to Euston service. John Murray, 21, from New Cumnock had only been offered a match ticket that very evening after which he rushed home to pack a bag and join the train.

There were over 500 supporters on the overcrowded service with some sleeping in the corridor of the train whose coaches were split into seating compartments. Amongst the travellers were 12 heavily intoxicated members of a gang known as the Govan Young Team who boasted about boarding without rail tickets. Trouble flared soon after departure and an unscheduled stop was made at Dumfries where several fans were escorted from the train. Shortly before 1am more troublemakers were taken off at Carlisle.

Trouble continued as the gang rampaged through the corridors with reports of smashed glass and assaults on passengers. It was alleged that one of the gang members was about to molest a sleeping girl in the same compartment when John Murray and another man intervened. This resulted in the two good Samaritans being stabbed with a flick knife then chased along the corridor over sleeping bodies. A witness later recalled how the two were so terrified they tried to open the doors of the moving train to escape their pursuers. After further stab wounds both men collapsed and the train guard radioed ahead for assistance when the train halted at Warrington Bank Quay station shortly after 3am. Police and ambulances stood by as everyone was taken from the train and interviewed. One female supporter from Dumfries discovered £120 had been stolen after a knife had been used to slash her pocket. The money was later recovered by police.

John Murray was pronounced dead from five knife wounds to his chest but the other stabbing victim survived after treatment at Warrington Infirmary. Twelve of the passengers were detained whilst the rest were eventually allowed to continue their journey on an early morning Blackpool to Euston service.

Seven months later Paul Carberry, aged 17, was found guilty of murder and wounding another with intent by a jury at Chester Crown Court. The court heard how Carberry had rushed back to his compartment and hurriedly changed clothes to disguise his appearance following the assault. The jail sentence was "during Her Majesty's pleasure" – or indefinite.

On the Friday a British Airways Trident aircraft had to be withdrawn from service and disinfected after a number of London-bound fans had urinated in a gallery during the flight with the toilet occupied.

Fans in London on the Friday afternoon found the fountains at their traditional meeting place of Trafalgar Square turned off and the Eros statue at Piccadilly Circus boarded up. This failed to stop them scaling the basins of the fountains to lark around before leaving a mountain of empty bottles and tins behind when the pubs reopened at 5pm. Thirsty supporters found many of the West End's hostelries closed for the weekend with those permitting entry generally away from the Soho area. The *Press and Journal* told its readers: "Hundreds of Scottish fans were involved in West End disturbances involving fighting and bottle throwing" on the Friday night.

At least the tubes were running on the day of the match – for a time. After a communication cord had been pulled at Willesden Green some fans in the delayed train feared they were going to miss the start of the match and forced the train doors open before walking along the track towards Wembley Park. Concerned for their safety on the electrified lines, London Transport closed the entire underground network in north London causing all match-bound trains to be halted. This resulted in hundreds more joining the march and it was estimated that as many as 2,000 walked along the rail tracks.

There may or may not have been 100,000 Scots inside Wembley but there were certainly that number in London on the Saturday. Those inside now found that fences ringed the terraces which looked likely to prevent any repeat of the pitch invasion during their last visit.

"Is there an Englishman in the house?" joked the stadium announcer before continuing, "Ah, there you are. Good afternoon to you, sir!"

Stein stuck by Wood in goal and named the same side which had beaten Northern Ireland.

Scotland responded to their huge support and dominated the early period. Wark shot narrowly over then a Dalglish corner was cleared by Wilkins on the goal line before a Souness drive was deflected just wide by Phil Neal.

A couple of hundred late arrivals were being escorted around the pitch to one of the lower pens when Scotland went ahead after 20 minutes.

Jordan began the move in his own half before Graham took the ball to the byline then sent a cross to Dalglish at the far post. John Wark must have thought it was his birthday as the Liverpool man cleverly knocked the ball into his path where he really could not miss from two yards. The late arrivals refrained from invading the pitch as Wembley Stadium erupted, leaving those still outside in little doubt as to the score.

Soon afterwards one supporter proved that the new fences were not impregnable by running on to the pitch in what initially appeared to be an attempt to communicate with George Wood. The game was halted as several police officers took off in pursuit with the majority of the crowd first cheering then laughing as the fan evaded their clutches in what might have been a scene from a Keystone Cops comedy. At one point the supporter seemed to be collared then suddenly took off again, leaving one constable flat on his back. Some fans had jeered and Stein was seen to leave the dugout shaking his head in disgust as the intruder, wearing a tartan scarf, was eventually apprehended and led away.

The turning point of the match came soon after when Jordan sent a powerful shot goalwards from 20 yards. Clemence was diving in the direction of the ball when it struck the head of Dave Watson and cannoned towards the opposite corner. Somehow the goalkeeper twisted in mid-air and managed to turn the ball behind for a corner. Clemence's reactions produced a save which was at least the equal of Shilton's late stop from Dalglish in the 1973 fixture but is less well remembered.

In his history of the Scotland v England fixture, *The Auld Enemy*, Dean Hayes says: "It was one of the most remarkable saves ever seen at Wembley."

The thoughts of thousands must have flashed back to 1977 when McQueen rose to meet Dalglish's corner in the same goalmouth in which he had scored two years earlier. But this time there were sighs rather than cheers as the ball drifted wide.

Although it had not all been one-way traffic Stein's men deserved more than the slender one-goal lead which separated the sides as half-time approached. In injury time Keegan found Peter Barnes, who hit a low speculative effort from 20 yards which crept just inside Wood's left-hand post with the goalkeeper looking slow to react.

The terraces were more subdued as the teams left on level terms and it was later pointed out that the equaliser had been scored during time added on for the delay caused by the pitch invader.

If the first half had belonged to Scotland then the second was very much England's with the Scots once again made to rue earlier missed opportunities.

Wood again looked at fault when he fumbled a Wilkins shot allowing Steve Coppell to give England a 63rd-minute lead. Stein's men conceded again several minutes later and it was a goal of undeniable quality. Coppell played a 1-2 with Keegan who then did the same with Brooking on the edge of the box before finishing the move by shooting clinically past the diving Wood. It was 3-1 and the game had been killed.

As the Scottish players left the pitch some fans still held banners aloft singing "We'll Support You Ever More" whilst others at the tunnel end jeered. It was the first sign that the fans were beginning to lose patience after 12 months of indifferent results.

The win gave England the championship with five points. Scotland finished third behind the Welsh with just the two points, acquired in the home match. Eddie Turnbull flew back to Scotland that evening as he had to take a training session with his Hibs players ahead of the Scottish Cup Final second replay on the Monday.

A number of fans from Eyemouth stayed in a hotel at Heathrow Airport. After the match they found themselves mingling with a number of the players they had watched at Wembley, as the Liverpool squad were flying to Israel in the morning for an end-of-season game.

Still marvelling at the save from Jordan at 1-0 and what might have been, Tommy Collin engaged in conversation with Ray Clemence. "I shook his hand and said 'Ray, that save won the game for England today!'"

The goalkeeper's modest response was "Do you really think so?"

As Eddie Gray points out, Clemence was never allowed to forget his error in the 1976 fixture but he probably made amends three years later with far less publicity.

More than 450 Scottish supporters were arrested in London over the course of the weekend on charges ranging from assault, theft, indecent exposure and drunkenness. One coachload of returning fans were stopped by police on the M1 after the proprietors of an off-licence in Finchley Road discovered a substantial amount of alcohol had been stolen whilst some of their party had staged a distraction. Amongst the detained passengers was an army deserter who had been on the run for three years.

The senior vice-president of the National Union of Licensed Victuallers wrote to the Home Office stating that the Scots had vandalised trains, terrified women and children on the underground and caused the closing of numerous public houses. "Why not keep these mindless hooligans in Scotland where they can smash things as they please?" he asked.

Although 450 is a small figure – less than half of one percent – in comparison to the numbers who travelled, there were reports of fans vandalising hotel rooms and leaving unwelcome calling cards in cupboards for chambermaids to clean. The pitch invader was not amongst those who appeared in court as he was merely ejected from the ground. He turned out to be an Englishman, an Evertonian who apparently wanted to shake the hand of George Wood.

In trying to avoid the usual clichéd phrases such as "a small minority of troublemakers spoiled it for the majority" and "the vast majority of fans were well behaved" offered when supporters cause trouble, it is true that many returning fans were surprised at the reports having not personally witnessed any violence. Whilst there may have been 100,000 Scots in London on the Saturday there was nothing like that number of hooligans, the consequences of which would have been total carnage. Scotland fans did not head to London intent on causing vandalism and destruction but the lines between acceptable and unacceptable behaviour became blurred once large amounts of alcohol were introduced to the mix. The events surrounding the fixture became a continuing source of embarrassment for the SFA.

The *Sunday Mail*'s Gavin Goodwin travelled to London a couple of weeks later to seek the views of those who had witnessed the scenes at first hand. His 17 June report was a double-page spread of horror stories. Although there were some who spoke favourably of the Scots, tales included assaults on police officers and of a 16-year-old local being chased by "twenty bottle-throwing Scots for no apparent reason" who was struck by a car then kicked as he lay unconscious in the road. A spokesman for the Transport Police told of "deplorable behaviour with women and children subjected to the disgusting sight of men and youths urinating into beer cans". Many observers cite the pitch invasion of 1977 as the beginning of the end for the fixture but the decline can be traced further back to the 1973 match when there was an increase in trouble including the assault on the underground guard and the attack on Alan Ball.

"The English got pissed off with us after '77," is Stuart Borrowman's view. He had been a regular at Wembley since 1969. "There were things happening that by any stretch of the imagination were not clever and not cute. So I assume that the police said we're not having this and thought we're going to treat them differently. It changed the attitude, it was no longer 'daft boys, let's indulge them'. In '77 it went too far. It went from being an irritation to being something more.

"I remember in 1969 going out to visit my great aunt in Leigh-on-Sea about 30 miles from London and there was this teenage boy with a tartan tammy and scarf being smiled at by people because I would be the only one. But if you're living in north London and your business is being invaded by 10,000 people it's different."

A good analogy would be a football stadium emptying at 4.45 on a Saturday afternoon. For a period the highway code goes out of the window and the spectators make the rules, dictating when the traffic can move again. A similar situation existed throughout the centre of London every two years although it lasted for days rather than minutes. It should of course not be forgotten that the London economy was boosted by thousands of Scottish banknotes when the Scots came to town.

Yet no one who was there in 1979 could have predicted that they were witnessing the last of the great Wembley invasions by the Scots. Although Scottish supporters still outnumbered the home fans during the next two visits, circumstances dictated that neither of those matches sold out.

Scotland had a chance to redeem themselves the following Saturday with a home fixture – against world champions Argentina. This bridged the gap before the trip to Norway for the European Championship qualifier a few days later. The twice-replayed cup final meant Hibs and Rangers played their final league match on the Thursday evening, which eliminated any chance of Bobby Russell joining up with the Scotland squad. Russell, having been one of the stars of the second replay, could with some justification claim that the fixture congestion of 1979 cost him his best chance of an international cap.

The 62,000 crowd fell well short of the predicted sell-out on a beautiful summer afternoon. Rough was reinstated as goalkeeper although Stein introduced Wood for the second half in a bid to boost his confidence. St Mirren full-back Ian Munro made his debut with Frank McGarvey collecting his second cap.

The game followed the same pattern as Wembley with Scotland competing well in the opening period before eventually losing by a score of 3-1. In the opening minutes Burley fired narrowly over from a tight angle before the midfield combined with the forwards in a quite excellent move. The ball was passed from Dalglish in the centre circle to Burley and on to Hartford, before Wark calmly sidestepped Fillol and stroked the ball into the net. Alas the linesman had correctly raised his flag as Wark had been half a yard offside.

The match will always be remembered as the day 18-year-old Diego Maradona came to prominence in his second international appearance. It was he who made the opening goal just after the half-hour mark when he evaded two tackles then released the ball to World Cup hero Leopoldo Luque who sidestepped both Munro and Rough before scoring from 12 yards.

At this stage of the Radio Scotland commentary David Francey was already raving about the "little fellow", even daring to suggest he may be a "new Pele". Shortly before the break the little fellow took off on another run and waltzed past two defenders before his forward pass was desperately cleared by Burley. From the resulting corner Maradona thumped the ball against the post and out of play.

Maradona certainly made a big impression on Asa Hartford. "You couldn't get near him, he was just magnificent. You just knew then that this was a star player. He was quick, strong and you would have needed, I don't know, a sledgehammer to knock him down. My sons got a picture when I'm taking the ball away and he is trying to chase me and I thought – that's not how I remember the game!"

Luque scored again after an hour before Valencia sent Maradona through. The Argentinian teased Wood before squeezing the ball between the goalkeeper and his post from the tightest of angles, displaying all the composure of a veteran.

As with Keegan's goal it was difficult not to admire but the fans were not in a charitable mood that afternoon and turned against the Scottish team with a chant of "What a load of rubbish" as hundreds streamed towards the exits. A frustrated shout of "Argentina! Argentina!" rang out which was widely reported and is audible on the Radio Scotland recording with just under ten minutes of the match left. Jeers can also be heard attempting to drown out the chant followed by "We'll Support You Ever More", indicating a division within the support. The visiting manager Carlos Menotti completely misinterpreted the Argentina chant as a great sporting gesture when speaking with journalists later. After losing possession to Tarantini, Dalglish, of whom so much was always expected, was booed and booed almost each time he touched the ball in the few minutes that remained.

There was a brief late cheer when Passarella headed out as far as Gray, who cleverly lobbed the ball back over the defence where both Dalglish and Graham lurked. Dalglish held back, allowing Graham to slip the ball beyond Fillol for a consolation. Graham was initially reluctant to celebrate, suspecting a possible offside decision.

The players exchanged tops at the end and the visitors, sporting Scotland's blue, waved from the centre circle as the crowd applauded and repeated the chant of "Argentina!"

Having won the World Cup since the 1977 tour game, which had been marred by cynical fouls, Argentina showed they were capable of entertaining football in Glasgow that afternoon.

"They were more 'normal' if you like at Hampden and they beat us easy 3-1," says Asa Hartford. "In Buenos Aires in '77 maybe they were marking out territory so to speak."

Summarising for the radio commentary, Jim Reynolds was pessimistic about the team's prospects in Norway: "For the second time in eight days we've seen a Scotland side collapse in the second half after showing so much early promise. The big question is: who is going to score the goals?"

Fellow summariser Jock Brown was far more upbeat: "I'm not going out there with any great feeling of despondency. I thought there was a lot to be happy about in the performance. Remember we lost to the best side in the world."

For the third successive Saturday Scotland had conceded three goals but more than that it completed 12 months of disappointment since the defeat against Peru in Córdoba. For some, the second-half slump at Wembley had been the last straw – as reflected in the Hampden attendance – and the sight of Scotland being outplayed at home tested the loyalty of even the most dedicated of supporters.

There was little time to reflect as the players flew to Oslo on the Tuesday boosted by the return of the Nottingham Forest trio of Burns, Gemmill and Robertson following the European Cup triumph which had eliminated them from the home series.

Stein deflected criticism of the previous results stressing that a win in the Ulleval Stadium would keep Scotland's European chances alive. He told journalists: "This is a one-off situation – a real cup tie. If we lose we are out. It's as simple as that."

On 7 June, exactly one year since the Iran match, Stein selected seven of the men who had played in Córdoba to start in Oslo. Ian Munro, who had been praised for his debut in difficult circumstances, retained his place.

As in the match at Hampden, Norway gave Scotland a real fright in a breakaway when Aas struck the underside of Rough's crossbar. The loss of a goal at that point may have seen the Scots' heads go down. But luck was with them and they went ahead just two minutes later when a fine run and cross to the far post by Dalglish picked out the lurking Jordan who found the corner of the net.

Boosted by the goal, Scotland scored twice more before the interval to wrap the game up. First Burley passed to Dalglish on the edge of the area. The Liverpool man waltzed past a defender before firing a low drive beyond Jacobsen. Then, as the home defence struggled to recover, Munro's pass evaded all but Robertson who scored his first international goal from close range.

Dalglish watched a shot rebound from the woodwork early in the second half before McQueen completed the scoring a couple of minutes later by heading a Robertson corner in via a goalpost.

The home fans cheered when the tannoy announced that their Under-21 side had taken a 2-1 lead. It was the few hundred Scots standing behind the goal who celebrated the senior team's 4-0 win at full time.

Alex Cameron was certainly satisfied with what he saw, telling *Record* readers: "When the elegant Dalglish and Gemmill got things really going the Scots jogged stylishly to an emphatic win. Dalglish surely knocked his critics for six. He dominated the forward play and his goal was the best in an international in the last 12 months."

Turnbull was in charge of the Under-21 side whose match in Haugesund, 275 miles west of the capital, had kicked off half an hour ahead of the game in Oslo.

In that match, Scotland dominated the first half with a first-time Bannon shot from a McLeod cross, giving them the advantage. They paid the price for missed chances just ahead of the hour mark when Davidsen equalised. Halvorsen then chipped the ball over Thomson nine minutes later which delighted the 1,908 Norwegians watching as well as those in the Ulleval. Norway were just seven minutes from victory when a bad pass-back allowed McLeod to hammer in a left-foot shot to make the final score 2-2.

With the two results gained in Norway keeping qualification hopes alive, season 1978/79 at least ended on a high Note: for Scotland.

Stein felt that wingers could be the key to victory against Austria when they came to Glasgow in October and experimented by fielding Davie Cooper, winning his first cap, and Robertson in a warm-up game against Peru at Hampden in September.

When he released his player pool Stein named Bobby Clark as Scotland's first goalkeeping coach. "I suppose I was officially the goalkeeper coach but since I was still playing Jock possibly saw me as the third goalkeeper," Bobby recalls. "I think the idea came to Jock when Andy Roxburgh invited me down to an SFA managers' course where I did a field session on goalkeeping. I remember Jock took part and was rolling around doing all the exercises."

Jardine, making his first appearance since the Iran game, captained the side with the manager insisting the contest was about preparing for the Austrians' visit. "There is no question of a grudge match. I just want a good performance and it is useful to be able to blood one or two players," he said in response to a Córdoba-related question at the press conference on the eve of the game.

Hartford, the only player to feature all three times Scotland had met Peru, had the 41,035-strong crowd roaring after four minutes. Wark crossed to the far post where the midfielder turned the ball in from close range.

The early goal worked wonders for the team's confidence and Cooper and Hartford both went close. The best chance of all was missed in the 35th minute after Dalglish had been floored by Chumpitaz inside the area. In Gemmill's absence Wark took the penalty but Acasuzo fingertipped it round for a corner just as Quiroga had done with Masson's kick.

A margin of 3-0 would not have flattered Scotland at the interval but there was less urgency thereafter and the South Americans salvaged a draw five minutes from time when, following a scramble, German Leguia beat Rough from 12 yards.

Although he was as disappointed as anyone with the late equaliser, Stein highlighted the overall performance in the *Evening Times*: "There was a lot to be happy about in the way Scotland played. We should have won and we certainly made splendid openings against a Peru side who are South American champions. We showed the pattern we want is emerging."

There was a huge turnout of 67,700 for the Austrians' visit on 17 October in what was considered the most important match since Stein had taken charge 12 months earlier. It really was win or bust as far as Scotland's European Championship prospects were concerned, with the visitors four points ahead in the table but having played two games more.

Alan Rough equalled the goalkeeping record of 28 Scotland appearances established by Bill Brown in 1965 but the evening would not be remembered as one of his best internationals.

Again, Scotland pressed from the start and what Jim Reynolds described as "a glaring penalty" was denied by the Hungarian referee when Dalglish was felled by Pezzey before a blunder silenced the crowd in an isolated breakaway.

Jara sent a harmless-looking ball in the direction of the Scottish goal which Rough shouted for Munro to leave. The crowd then watched in horror as the ball skidded from the goalkeeper's arm and behind him where Krankl nipped in to score five minutes before the break. After a Dalglish header came back from the crossbar the fans sensed they were watching a rerun of an old movie as another night of disappointment seemed likely.

Jardine cut the ball back for Gemmill to equalise spectacularly from 22 yards with a shot which flew high into the net 15 minutes from time. It was a quite stunning finish and, rejuvenated, Scotland poured forward in search of a winner which they never really looked like getting. The draw all but extinguished Scotland's European hopes and they occupied fourth place in the group of five.

Alan Rough accepted full responsibility for the goal before retreating to the pub that he ran in Maryhill, entering the Goal Post just as the *Sportscene* highlights were beginning on the television.

Stein appointed Dundee United manager Jim McLean as his assistant for the trip to Belgium in November which allowed Turnbull to concentrate fully on the Under-21 side.

Bobby Clark recalls that the manager was keen to be involved in all aspects of training. "I remember before the match in Brussels that Jock came and took the goalkeepers. He told me to take part where he basically just gave me shots. It was fun getting to be around Jock and Jim McLean."

Despite the recent setbacks a large travelling support of at least 3,000 were in Brussels with the majority of those fans travelling on the Dover to Ostend ferry in the days leading up to the game.

Eddie Turnbull's side leapfrogged the hosts to top their section with a 1-0 victory in Beveren on the Tuesday thanks to a 40th-minute George McCluskey goal. The game was considered dour at times with debutant Gordon Strachan cursing his luck midway through the first period when his shot was deflected inches wide. Didier Electeur then missed an open goal from two yards for the hosts before Ray Stewart fed McCluskey who beat a full-back with ease then cheekily pushed the ball through the goalkeeper's legs and into the net. The highlight of the second half was a trademark free kick from Morton's Andy Ritchie which flew narrowly wide.

"The lads played it the right way and did Scotland proud," the delighted Turnbull told Hugh Taylor. Stein had watched the match before turning his attention to the tougher task facing his senior squad in the Heysel Stadium the following evening.

The manager kept faith with Rough, and with McQueen injured tried a new central defence of Hansen and Willie Miller with Robertson, Dalglish and Jordan in attack. Just over 14,000 were inside the ground meaning the home support numbered only around 10,000.

"A woeful performance, one of the worst ever on foreign soil," was Alex Cameron's view in Thursday's *Daily Record*. The final scoreline of 2-0 barely reflected the superiority of the Belgians, who were ahead inside seven minutes after Voordeckers laid the ball back for Van Der

Elst to beat Rough. The Hansen–Miller partnership looked fragile as the Belgians controlled the game. Victory was secured seconds after the restart when Gerets's long forward ball was headed down by Ceulemans to Voordeckers whose shot rippled the netting behind Rough.

The timing of the goals, one at the start of each half, could not have been worse but the Belgians were comfortable winners and once again Scotland had failed to qualify for the European Championships with two home matches still to play.

Stein rang the changes for the rearranged return match with the Belgians in mid-December – the game which had been postponed from February. In a change of policy, the SFA decided to offer refunds to those who had bought tickets for the original date up until the day of the game.

When queried by a journalist at Park Gardens over the omission of Hartford, Jordan and Hansen, Stein just said: "I don't see the need to include them this time." The 21-year-old Eamonn Bannon and Roy Aitken, 20, made the step up from the Under-21side with the Aberdeen duo of McLeish and Archibald considered adequate replacements for the match at Tynecastle, where the youngsters required a draw to reach the quarter-finals.

With the Hampden game arguably of lesser importance Stein took charge of the Under-21 fixture which took place one week before Christmas Day.

The declining interest in Scottish international football was reflected in the attendance of 7,486, which was around half the number that had turned up for the last such fixture at the same venue. Those who did attend failed to provide any of the atmosphere of the Czech game but cheered as Scotland established a two-goal half-time lead.

The opener came from the penalty spot after McCluskey had been felled by Vriese which allowed Ray Stewart to score after half an hour. Melrose replaced Russell, who was suffering a knee injury, ten minutes later and he soon found the net, controlling a cross from Stewart on his chest before firing home a right-foot volley.

Thomson saved from Martens but was unable to prevent Lecloux netting the rebound halfway through the second period. The scores were level nine minutes later when Martens scored from 12 yards. Only two fine saves denied the Belgians a winner which would have kept them in with a chance of qualification.

Stein announced that his players were hungry for both a good result and performance at Hampden. The midfield trio of Aitken, Wark and Bannon started, having impressed the manager in the Under-21 match in Lisbon a year earlier. When questioned over the youngsters' inexperience Stein responded that they were "surrounded by experience". Part of that experience was the welcome return of Danny McGrain, who had fought back from his ankle injury and had last played for Scotland against Czechoslovakia two years earlier. In their final match only a win would see the Belgians qualify for the European Championship finals. A draw would leave them locked on 11 points with the Austrians, who had completed their eight fixtures but had the advantage of a far superior goal difference. Just over 25,000 spectators were inside Hampden, around 60 per cent of the number who had purchased tickets for the original date.

McGrain looked as though he had never been away when he took the ball from the middle of the park and found Dalglish, who scooped the ball over. Robertson then watched his shot fly narrowly past as the visitors rode out the early storm before doing what was required of them.

Scotland's decline began when a free kick was conceded to the Belgians in the 80th minute. Rough did well to halt Vandereyckens well-hit shot around the wall. He then blocked Vandenbergh's effort from the rebound but could do nothing as the same player scored at the second attempt.

Within ten minutes Van Der Elst had beaten Rough twice to finish the game as a contest. The loss of three goals during an 11-minute period stunned the crowd, some of whom must have grudgingly admired the clinical finishing of the visitors.

Robertson did find the net in style for Scotland after 55 minutes, as he sent a right-footed free kick from 25 yards into the top corner. That was the end of the scoring with the visitors content to play out time.

The Belgians had been both ruthless and well organised but few really expected them to progress to the final of the European Championships, which they lost by the odd goal in three to West Germany.

Although he clearly had the respect of the players, press and supporters, simmering doubts over Stein's abilities began to surface with each defeat. His record of six losses in 11 matches was not good with two of his three victories achieved against Norway. MacLeod's first 11 matches had produced six wins and two defeats whilst Ormond's record over the same period was much worse with two wins against eight losses. Docherty achieved six wins from 11 with just three defeats and an overall record of seven wins from his 12 games in charge.

Scotland at least completed their section matches with a win – and an impressive one – with a 4-1 victory over Portugal at Hampden the following year. The February weather jinx struck again with the final fixture delayed into March. The weather also postponed the Under-21 game with Portugal which UEFA reluctantly agreed to delete as the result would have had no bearing on the final group placings. In the quarter-finals Scotland's Under-21 side were drawn against England, exiting the tournament on an aggregate score of 2-1.

The final 1970s' meeting of the SFA's Executive and General Purposes Committee took place on 27 December during which matters concerning two of the other home associations were discussed.

The qualifying draw for the 1982 World Cup finals had been made in October and Scotland had been placed in a section alongside Portugal, Sweden, Israel and Northern Ireland. With the number of participants increased by 50 per cent to 24, two teams were guaranteed a place in Spain. The presence of Northern Ireland did increase the pressure on the association to resume playing in the province; there might have been repercussions had the fixture not been fulfilled.

The SFA agreed to test the water for the World Cup tie by travelling to Belfast for the 1980 Home International after certain strict conditions had been agreed. These were designed to discourage supporters from travelling to the match and included the scheduling of the game on a Friday evening, live television coverage in Scotland and the SFA's refusal to accept any tickets.

Article 136 reported on a meeting held with the Football Association "to discuss the widespread misbehaviour of Scotland supporters who had travelled to London on 26 May 1979". The entry includes: "After a lengthy and detailed discussion during which the FA's representatives indicated that, following talks with government and police authorities, it was evident that the future of this fixture was in jeopardy."

The recommendations from that meeting were accepted by the committee, which had concluded that stringent measures were necessary if the fixture was to continue.

It was mutually agreed that the SFA would not accept an allocation of tickets for a match played in England, with the FA rejecting tickets for reverse fixtures. Both bodies also committed to "take every possible measure to ensure tickets were distributed only in the country of the Home Association".

The association's Annual Report was damning of the supporters' behaviour as the secretary recorded: "Many of those who chose to attend Scotland's biannual match at Wembley were quite incapable of conducting themselves in a civilised manner. Drunkenness and violence are the order of the day and this has deteriorated to the extent that the future of the fixture is in serious jeopardy.

"Who could blame the English for choosing not to have this kind of barbarism visited upon them? The saddest feature of this sorry trend is that, traditionally, for the last century, the very best of Scottish people have travelled to London to support their team. Everyone had a good time regardless of the result and the weekend in the south was one of the great institutions of Scottish sport. It is infuriating that the majority have had their enjoyment ruined by the louts who latch on to football's coat-tails."

With regard to matters on the pitch, the same Annual Report, although acknowledging the success of the Under-21 side and the continued emergence of young talent, did not make optimistic reading. Commenting on recent international performances, it included: "It is quite evident that we are scarcely on the crest of a wave at this moment. We have never been much of a threat to anyone when playing away from our own backyard but could usually be relied upon to make life difficult for the best of them in front of our own supporters, and in view of that our 1-3 Hampden defeat at the hands of Belgium was particularly hard to stomach. We were outclassed and it would be folly to suggest otherwise."

As the 1970s passed into history the future was clearly going to be a challenging time for the Scottish international team who had yet to fully exorcise the lingering ghosts of Iran and Peru.

Lucky Man

"I always have had an optimistic attitude and things have always worked out for me," says Robbie Sterry from his Canadian home in the autumn of 2018. "None of my life was ever planned, at least not by me and to say my life has been colourful might be an understatement. Things just seem to flow from one thing to another and I have to invoke the word destiny to much of it."

Anyone studying the details of his epic trip to and from Argentina 40 years ago would have difficulty in disagreeing with that last sentence. His lucky escape in the bombed-bus incident in Peru is the stuff of fiction.

After returning from the World Cup Robbie only remained in Perth for around six months before heading off on his travels again.

He had enjoyed the warmth and hospitality of the Argentinian people so much that he was determined to return to Córdoba where he hoped to resume his relationship with a local girl, Carolina, whom he had first met at a party. Planning a less adventurous route, he made for Canada in early 1979 in search of work, which he hoped would finance the rest of his trip.

"I got picked up hitch-hiking by a couple of guys in British Columbia and they talked me into going to Edmonton where I got a job on a drilling rig where the money was excellent," he recounts. Again, that word destiny seems appropriate.

After four months on the rig Robbie flew to Vancouver from where a Greyhound bus transported him to Florida. Another flight took him back to Lima from where he hitched the 3,300 miles through Chile to Córdoba, arriving in the early part of 1980.

"I was smiling when I walked into the Sorocabana to find the lion rampant still pinned behind the bar with dozens of postcards from all over Scotland surrounding it," Robbie reminisces.

"All the waiters remembered me and the owner told me that prior to the World Cup he was at the point of selling up for a lack of customers. He sold more beer in a month than he had in the past five years and his bar became one of the most popular (post-World Cup) because of our presence during it."

After reuniting with Carol, who could scarcely believe her eyes when he turned up unannounced at her home, he returned to Canada to continue working but went back to Argentina the following year.

The Falklands War put paid to his annual visits and the pair lost touch for a period, during which Robbie was granted Canadian citizenship in 1985. It was whilst he was recovering from a motorcycle accident that he decided to write again and the correspondence to and from Córdoba resumed.

Within four months Carol had travelled to join Robbie in Canada but her visa limited the duration of her stay.

Advice was then sought from the immigration department of the Canadian government on how they could remain together.

"The official was suspicious that this was a marriage of convenience," says Robbie. "So I explained our history together and he told me to marry her and apply for her immigration on 'compassionate and humanitarian grounds'."

Carol happily accepted Robbie's proposal and they were married in 1990. She now runs a modern and contemporary art gallery in Kelowna, British Columbia.

"The 1978 soccer World Cup has changed Robbie's and my life in a great way," she reflects. "We have been together now for 28 years."

"The full story of Carol and I is akin to a romance novel. Many events happened along the way to this union that sometimes beggar belief, but happen they did," Robbie says 40 years after their first meeting.

"My life has been an adventure that never would have happened had I not made that trip in 1978," he says, looking back on the crazy days of Ally's Army. Perhaps the only thing that didn't go well for Robbie was Scotland's failure to win the World Cup. But then that really would have been pushing even his luck too far.

Appendix

Scotland's Full Internationals 1970–79

All televised matches shown in colour unless otherwise stated

18 April 1970 NORTHERN IRELAND 0 SCOTLAND 1 (O'Hare, 58 minutes) (Home International) Windsor Park, Belfast. Attendance: 31,000. NORTHERN IRELAND: Jennings (Tottenham), Craig (Newcastle), Clements (Coventry), Todd (Burnley), Neill (Arsenal, captain), Nicholson (Huddersfield), Campbell (Dundee), Lutton (Wolves), Dougan (Wolves), McMordie (Middlesbrough), Best (Manchester United). Substitutions: O'Kane (Nottingham Forest) for Todd (46 minutes), Dickson (Coleraine) for Campbell (75 minutes). Sent off: Best (64 minutes). SCOTLAND: Clark (Aberdeen), Hay (Celtic), Dickson (Kilmarnock), McLintock (Arsenal, captain), McKinnon (Rangers), Moncur (Newcastle), McLean (Kilmarnock), Carr (Coventry), O'Hare (Derby), Gilzean (Tottenham), Johnston (Rangers). Substitution: Stein (Rangers) for Gilzean (70 minutes). Referee: E. Jennings (England). Broadcast details: BBC no coverage; *Match of the Day* 19.30–21.00 featured delayed coverage of Wales v England only; ITV Network (including STV and Grampian) Home International Championship 22.10–23.10 Highlights of Northern Ireland v Scotland. 19 April STV *The Home International Championship* 14.20-15.20 Main feature was Wales 1 England 1 but also featured a few minutes of Northern Ireland v Scotland. Note: This was the first Scotland international to be televised in colour.

22 April SCOTLAND 0 WALES 0 (Home International) Hampden Park, Glasgow. Attendance: 30,434. SCOTLAND: Cruickshank (Hearts), Callaghan (Dunfermline), Dickson (Kilmarnock), Greig (Rangers, captain), McKinnon (Rangers), Moncur (Newcastle), McLean (Kilmarnock), Hay (Celtic), O'Hare (Derby), Stein (Rangers), Carr (Coventry). Substitution: Lennox (Celtic) for McLean (70 minutes). WALES: Millington (Swansea), Rodrigues (Leicester), Thomas (Swindon), Hennessey (Derby, captain), England (Tottenham), Powell (Sheffield United), Krzywicki (Huddersfield), Durban (Derby), Davies (Southampton), Moore (Charlton), Rees (Nottingham Forest). Referee: D. W. Smith (England). Broadcast details: BBC no coverage; ITV Network 10.40-12.20 *The Home International Championship* delayed coverage of full match shown.

25 April 1970 SCOTLAND 0 ENGLAND 0 (Home International) Hampden Park. Attendance: 137,438. SCOTLAND: Cruickshank (Hearts), Gemmell (Celtic), Dickson (Kilmarnock), Greig (Rangers, captain), McKinnon (Rangers), Moncur (Newcastle), Johnstone (Celtic), Hay (Celtic), Stein (Rangers), O'Hare (Derby), Carr (Coventry). Substitution: Gilzean (Tottenham) for Moncur (82 minutes). ENGLAND: Banks (Stoke), Newton (Everton), Hughes (Liverpool), Stiles (Manchester United), Labone (Everton), Moore (West Ham, captain), Thompson (Liverpool), Ball (Everton), Astle (West Bromwich), Hurst (West Ham), Peters (Tottenham). Substitution: Mullery (Tottenham) for Thompson (58 minutes). Referee: G. Schulenburg (West Germany). Broadcast details: BBC1 *International Match of the Day* 21.15-22.45 Highlights of Scotland v England (in colour) plus Wales v Northern Ireland; ITV Network *The Home International Championship* 19.15-21.00 Delayed coverage of full match (shown in black and white).

11 November 1970 SCOTLAND 1 (O'Hare, 13 minutes) DENMARK 0 (European Championship Qualification Group 5) Hampden Park. Attendance: 24,618. SCOTLAND: Cruickshank (Hearts), Hay (Celtic), Greig (Rangers), Stanton (Hibs), McKinnon (Rangers), Moncur (Newcastle, captain), Johnstone (Celtic), Carr (Coventry), Stein (Rangers), O'Hare (Derby), Johnston (Rangers). Substitutions: Cormack (Nottingham Forest) for O'Hare (75 minutes), Jardine (Rangers) for Hay (78 minutes). DENMARK: Poulsen (Alboorg), Torben Nielsen (B1903), Frederiksen (Hvidovre), Sandvad (AP Academic) Flemming Pedersen (KB Copenhagen), Hansen (Esberg, captain), Outzen (B1909), Nygaard (Fuglenbakken), Olsen (B1901), Keld Pedersen (Koege), Benny Nielsen (Academic Ball Club). Substitution: Thygesen (KB1903) for Olsen (46 minutes). Referee: E. Linemayer (Austria). Broadcast details: BBC1 *Sportsnight With Coleman* 21.20–22.45 Highlights of Scotland v Denmark plus boxing; STV *Scotsport* 23.00-23.40 Highlights of Scotland v Denmark (black and white); Grampian lists *Scotsport* at 23.00-23.45 with highlights but there was no coverage due to failure to reach an agreement with the SFA.

3 February 1971 BELGIUM 3 (McKinnon (own goal), 36 minutes, Van Himst, 55 and 83 (penalty) SCOTLAND 0 (European Championship Qualification Group 5) Stade Sclessin, Liege. Attendance: 13,931. BELGIUM: Piot (Standard), Heylens (Anderlecht), Dewalque (Standard), Plaskie (Anderlecht), Thissen (Standard), Van Moer (Standard),Van Den Daele (FC Bruges), Semmeling (Standard), Depireux (Stanard), Denul (Lierse), Van Himst (Anderlecht, captain). SCOTLAND: Cruickshank (Hearts), Hay (Celtic), Gemmell (Celtic), Greig (Rangers), McKinnon (Rangers), Stanton (Hibs), Moncur (Newcastle, captain), Gemmill (Derby), Cooke (Chelsea), Stein (Rangers), O'Hare (Derby). Substitutions: Green (Blackpool) for Stanton (46 minutes), Forrest (Aberdeen) for Stein (46). Referee: A. Sbardella (Italy). Broadcast details: BBC1 no coverage STV and Grampian *Scotsport* 22.30-23.20 highlights of Belgium v Scotland game (black and white).

21 April 1971 PORTUGAL 2 (Stanton (own goal), 22 minutes, Eusebio, 82) SCOTLAND 0 (European Championship Qualification Group 5) Stadium of Light, Lisbon. Attendance: 35,463. PORTUGAL: Damas (Sporting), Da Silva (Benfica), Coelho (Benfica), Carlos (Sporting, captain), Calisto (Benfica), Rodrigues (Benfica), Peres (Sporting), Simoes (Benfica), Nene (Benfica), Baptista (Benfica), Euesbio (Benfica). Substitutions: Jorge (Benfica) for Baptista (76 minutes), Neves (Sporting) for Nene (86). SCOTLAND: Clark (Aberdeen), Hay (Celtic), Brogan (Celtic), Stanton (Hibs), McKinnon (Rangers), Moncur (Newcastle, captain), Henderson (Rangers), Robb (Aberdeen), Cormack (Nottingham Forest), McCalliog (Wolves), Gilzean (Tottenham). Substitutions: Jarvie (Airdrie) for McCalliog (63 minutes), Green (Blackpool) for Stanton (75). Referee: M. Kitabjian (France). Broadcast details: No BBC coverage; STV *Scotsport* 22.30-23.10 *European Nations Cup including news of Portugal v Scotland*. No Grampian coverage.

15 May 1971 WALES 0 SCOTLAND 0 (Home International) Ninian Park, Cardiff. Attendance: 19,068. WALES: Sprake (Leeds), Rodrigues (Sheffield Wednesday), Thomas (Swindon), James (Blackpool), Roberts (Arsenal), Yorath (Leeds), Phillips (Cardiff), Durban (Derby), Davies (Southampton),Toshack (Liverpool), Reece (Sheffield United). SCOTLAND: Clark (Aberdeen), Hay (Celtic), Brogan (Celtic), Bremner (Leeds), McLintock (Arsenal), Moncur (Newcastle, captain), Lorimer (Leeds), Cormack (Nottingham Forest), Gray (Leeds), Robb (Aberdeen), O'Hare (Derby). Substitution: Greig (Rangers) for Bremner (72 minutes). Referee: J. Taylor (England). Broadcast details: BBC1 *Match of the Day* 22.00-23.30 Highlights of Wales v Scotland and Northern Ireland v England STV and Grampian no coverage. Delayed coverage of complete Northern Ireland v England match shown between 19.15 and 20.55.

18 May 1971 SCOTLAND 0 NORTHERN IRELAND 1 (Greig (own goal), 14 minutes) (Home International) Hampden Park. Attendance: 31,643. SCOTLAND: Clark (Aberdeen), Hay (Celtic), Brogan (Celtic), Greig (Rangers), McLintock (Arsenal),Moncur (Newcastle, captain), Lorimer (Leeds), Green (Blackpool), Gray (Leeds), Curran (Wolves), O'Hare (Derby). Substitutions: Jarvie (Airdrie) for O'Hare (46 minutes), Munro (Wolves)

for McLintock (71). NORTHERN IRELAND: Jennings (Tottenham), Rice (Arsenal), Nelson (Arsenal), O'Kane (Nottingham Forest), Hunter (Blackburn), Nicholson (Huddersfield), Hamilton (Linfield), McMordie (Middlesbrough), Dougan (Wolves), Clements (Coventry), Best (Manchester United). Substitution: Craig for McMordie (67 minutes). Referee: C. THOMAS (Wales). Broadcast details: No BBC coverage; ITV Network. Highlights during *The Home Internationals 1971* 22.30-23.30.

22 May 1971 ENGLAND 3 (Peters, 9 minutes, Chivers, 30 and 40) SCOTLAND 1 (Curran, 11 minutes) (Home International) Wembley Stadium, London. Attendance: 91,469. ENGLAND: Banks (Stoke), Lawler (Liverpool), Cooper (Leeds), Storey (Arsenal), McFarland (Derby), Moore (West Ham, captain), Lee (Manchester City), Ball (Everton), Hurst (West Ham), Chivers (Tottenham), Peters (Tottenham) Substitute: Clarke (Leeds) for Lee (73 minutes). SCOTLAND: Clark (Aberdeen), Greig (Rangers), Brogan (Celtic), Bremner (Leeds), McLintock (Arsenal), Moncur (Newcastle, captain), Johnstone (Celtic), Green (Blackpool), Cormack (Nottingham Forest), Robb (Aberdeen), Curran (Wolves),). Substitutions: Munro (Wolves) for Curran (46 minutes), Jarvie (Airdrie) for Green (82). Referee: J. F. Dorpmans (Holland). Broadcast details: BBC1 Live coverage during *Grandstand* BBC1 12.45-17.45 and *World of Sport* ITV network 12.35-17.40. Highlights shown on BBC1 22.00-23.15 *International Match of the Day* plus Northern Ireland v Wales. Highlights shown the following day 23 May on ITV Network including Grampian but not STV *The Home International Championships* 14.15-15.15.

9 June 1971 DENMARK 1 (Laudrup, 44 minutes) SCOTLAND 0 (European Championship Qualification Group 5) Idraetsparken, Copenhagen. Attendance: 37,682. DENMARK: Sorensen (Morton), Torben Nielsen (B1903), Berg (B1909), Arentoft (Newcastle), Rasmussen (Randers Freja), Bjerre (Racing, captain), Laudrup (B1909), Bjornmose (Werder Bremen), Le Fevre (Borussia Monchengladbach), Benny Nieson (Academic Ball Club), Kristensen (Sparta Rotterdam). Substitutions: Pedersen (Koege) for B Nielsen (46 minutes), Outzen (B1909) for Laudrup (75). SCOTLAND: Clark (Aberdeen), Munro (Wolves), Dickson (Kilmarnock), Stanton (Hibs), McKinnon (Rangers), Moncur (Newcastle, captain), McLean (Kilmarnock), Forsyth (Motherwell), Forrest (Aberdeen), Curran (Wolves), Stein (Rangers). Substitutions: Robb (Aberdeen) for Forsyth (46 minutes), Scott (Dundee) for Forrest (70). Referee: W. Riedel (East Germany). Broadcast details: No UK TV coverage.

14 June 1971 USSR 1 (Yevryuzhikhin, 24 minutes) SCOTLAND 0 (Friendly) Lenin Stadium, Moscow. Attendance: 20,000. USSR: Rudakov (Dynamo Kiev), Istomin (CSKA Moscow), Shesternev (CSKA Moscow), Matvienko (Dynamo Kiev), Kaplichni (CSKA Moscow), Kolotov (Dynamo Kiev), Konkov (Shakhtar Donetsk), Nodia (Dinamo Tbilisi), Fedotov (CSKA Moscow), Shevchenko (Neftci PFK), Yevryuzhikhin (Dynamo Moscow). Substitutions: Khmelntiski (Dynamo Kiev) for Yevryuzhikhin (46 minutes), Dolgov (CSKA Moscow) for Nodija (70). SCOTLAND: Clark (Aberdeen), Brownlie (Hibs), Dickson (Kilmarnock), Munro (Wolves), McKinnon (Rangers), Stanton (Hibs, captain), Watson (Motherwell), Robb (Aberdeen), Scott (Dundee), Forrest (Aberdeen), Stein (Rangers). Substitutions: Curran (Wolves) for Stein (71 minutes). Referee: F. Marschall (Austria). Broadcast details: No UK TV coverage.

13 October 1971 SCOTLAND 2 (O'Hare, 23 minutes, Gemmill, 58) PORTUGAL 1 (Rodrigues, 57) (European Championship Qualification Group 5) Hampden Park. Attendance: 58,612. SCOTLAND: Wilson (Arsenal), Jardine (Rangers), Hay (Celtic), Stanton (Hibs), Colquhoun (Sheffield United), Johnstone (Celtic), Bremner (Leeds, captain), Graham (Arsenal), Cropley (Hibs), Gemmill (Derby), O'Hare (Derby). Substitution: Buchan (Aberdeen) for Colquhoun (60 minutes). PORTUGAL: Damas (Sporting), Da Silva (Benfica), Calo (Sporting), Rodrigues (Benfica), Calisto (Benfica), Graca (Sporting), Goncalves (Porto), Simoes (Benfica), Nene (Benfica), Baptista (Benfica), Eusebio (Benfica, captain). Substitutions: Jorge (Benfica) for Eusebio (46 minutes), Peres (Sporting) for Calo (66). Referee: B. Piotrowicz (Poland). Broadcast details: BBC no

coverage; STV *Scotsport* 23.00-23.30 highlights of Scotland v Portugal (black and white) and England v Switzerland (in colour) Grampian no coverage; Switzerland v England shown 22.30-23.

10 November 1971 SCOTLAND 1 (O'Hare, 6 minutes) BELGIUM 0 (European Championship Qualification Group 5) Pittodrie, Aberdeen. Attendance: 36,500. SCOTLAND: Clark (Aberdeen), Jardine (Rangers), Hay (Celtic), Stanton (Hibs), Buchan (Aberdeen), Johnstone (Celtic), Bremner (Leeds, captain), Cropley (Hibs), Gray (Leeds), Murray (Aberdeen), O'Hare (Derby). Substitutions: Dalglish (Celtic) for Cropley (48 minutes), Hansen (Partick) for Johnstone (79). BELGIUM: Piot (Standard), Heylens (Anderlecht), Dewalque (Standard),Stassart (Racing), Dolmans (Liege), Van Moer (Standard), Van Den Daele (FC Bruges), Semmeling (Standard), Devrindt (Sparta Rotterdam), Van Himst (Anderlecht, captain), Puis (Bruges). Substitutions: Martens (Racing White) for Van Moer 57, Lambert (Bruges) for Puis 69. Referee: E. Bostrom (Sweden). Broadcast details: BBC1 *Sportsnight With Coleman* 22.25-23.10 featured highlights of Scotland v Belgium and England v Switzerland; STV *Scotsport* 23.00-23.00 highlights of Scotland v Belgium; Grampian no coverage.

1 December 1971 HOLLAND 2 (Cruyff, 5 minutes, Hulshoff, 87) SCOTLAND 1 (Graham, 58 minutes) (Friendly) Olympic Stadium, Amsterdam. Attendance: 18,000. HOLLAND: Schrijvers (FC Twente), Venneker (Sparta Rotterdam), Hulshoff (Ajax), Israel (Feyenoord), Kroll (Ajax), Neeskens (Ajax), Van Hanegem (Feyenoord),Wery (Feyenoord), Pahlplatz (FC Twente), Cruyff (Ajax, captain), Keizer (Ajax). Substitutions: Jansen (Feyenoord) for Wery (46 minutes), Muhren (Ajax) for Keizer (46). SCOTLAND: Wilson (Arsenal), Jardine (Rangers), Hay (Celtic), Stanton (Hibs), Colquhoun (Sheffield United), Johnstone (Celtic), Bremner (Leeds, captain), Gemmill (Derby), Gray (Leeds), Graham (Arsenal), Dalglish (Celtic). Substitutions: O'Hare (Derby) for Johnstone (56 minutes), Cormack (Nottingham Forest) for Gray (84). Referee: F. Biwersi (West Germany). Broadcast details: BBC1 *Sportsnight With Coleman* 21.20-22.50 Featured highlights of Greece v England and Holland v Scotland; STV *Scotsport* 23.00-23.Highlights of Holland v Scotland; Grampian no coverage.

26 April 1972 SCOTLAND 2 (O'Hare, 47 minutes, Law, 65) PERU 0 (Friendly) Hampden Park. Attendance: 21,001. SCOTLAND: Hunter (Kilmarnock), Brownlie (Hibs), Donachie (Manchester City), Moncur (Newcastle), Colquhoun (Sheffield United), Morgan (Manchester United), Carr (Coventry), Hartford (West Bromwich), Gemmill (Derby), O'Hare (Derby), Law (Manchester United, captain). PERU: Uribe (Defensor Lima), Manzo (Defensor Lima), Velasquez (Alianza Lima), Chumpitaz (Universitario de Deportes), Trigueros (Defensor Lima), Mifflin (Sporting Cristal), Quesada (Sporting Cristal), Munante (Universitario de Deportes), Cubillas (Alianza Lima), Rojas (Universitario de Deportes), Orbegozo (Sporting Cristal). Substitution: Sotil (Deportivo Municipal) for Rojas (46 minutes). Referee: P. Partridge (England). Broadcast details: BBC1 *Sportsreel* 22.15-22.50 Scotland v Peru Highlights (black and white); STV *Scotsport* 22.45-23.45 colour Highlights of Scotland v Peru plus Derby County v Airdrie (Texaco Cup Final).

20 May 1972 NORTHERN IRELAND 0 SCOTLAND 2 (Law, 86 minutes, Lorimer, 89) (Home International) Hampden Park. Attendance: 39,710. NORTHERN IRELAND: Jennings (Tottenham), Rice (Arsenal), Nelson (Arsenal), Neill (Hull), Hunter (Ipswich), Clements (Sheffield Wednesday), Hegan (Wolves), McMordie (Middlesbrough), Dougan (Wolves), Irvine (Brighton), Jackson (Nottingham Forest). Substitutions: McIlroy (Manchester United) for McMordie (68 minutes), Craig (Newcastle) for Clements (83). SCOTLAND: Clark (Aberdeen), Brownlie (Hibs), Donachie (Manchester City), Bremner (Leeds, captain), McNeill (Celtic), Moncur (Newcastle), Johnstone (Celtic), Gemmill (Derby), O'Hare (Derby), Law (Manchester United), Graham (Arsenal). Substitution: Lorimer (Leeds) for Johnstone (61 minutes). Referee: C. Thomas (Wales). Broadcast details: BBC1 *International Match of the Day* 22.00-23.15 Highlights of Wales v England and Scotland v Northern Ireland; STV and Grampian no coverage.

25 May 1972 SCOTLAND 1 WALES 0 (Lorimer, 72 minutes) (Home International) Hampden Park. Attendance: 21,332. SCOTLAND: Clark (Aberdeen), Buchan (Manchester United), Stanton (Hibs), Bremner (Leeds, captain), McNeill (Celtic), Moncur (Newcastle), Lorimer (Leeds), Gemmill (Derby), O'Hare (Derby), Law (Manchester United, Green (Newcastle). Substitutions: Hartford (West Bromwich) for Gemmill (35 minutes), Macari (Celtic) for O'Hare (56). WALES: Sprake (Leeds), Page (Birmingham), Thomas (Swindon), Hennessey (Derby, captain), England (Tottenham), Yorath (Leeds), Durban (Derby), Wyn Davies (Manchester City), Reece (Sheffield United), Ron Davies (Southampton), Phillips (Cardiff). Substitution: James (Burnley) for Hennessey (74 minutes). Referee: J. Lawther (Northern Ireland). Broadcast details: BBC1 *Sportsreel* 22.35-00.30 Delayed coverage of Rangers v Moscow Dynamo (European Cup Winners' Cup Final) and highlights of Scotland v Wales; STV and Grampian *Scotsport* 22.30-00.44 Delayed coverage of Rangers v Moscow Dynamo (European Cup Winners' Cup Final) and highlights of Scotland v Wales.

27 May SCOTLAND 0 ENGLAND 1 (Ball, 28 minutes) (Home International) Hampden Park. Attendance: 119,325. SCOTLAND: Clark (Aberdeen), Brownlie (Hibs), Donachie (Manchester City), Moncur (Newcastle), McNeill (Celtic), Lorimer (Leeds), Bremner (Leeds, captain), Gemmill (Derby), Hartford (West Bromwich), Macari (Celtic), Law (Manchester United). Substitutions: Johnstone (Celtic) for Gemmill (49 minutes), Green (Newcastle) for Donachie (74). ENGLAND: Banks (Stoke), Madeley (Leeds), Hughes (Liverpool), McFarland (Derby), Moore (West Ham, captain), Ball (Arsenal), Hunter (Leeds), Storey (Arsenal), Bell (Manchester City), Marsh (Manchester City), Chivers (Tottenham). Substitution: MacDonald (Newcastle) for Marsh (84 minutes). Referee: S. Gonella (Italy). Broadcast details: Live coverage during BBC1 *Grandstand* 12.45-17.05 and ITV network *World of Sport* 12.50-17.10; Highlights during *International Match of the Day* BBC1 22.25-23.55 and Sunday 28 May Some ITV regions including Grampian (not STV) *Star Soccer* 14.15-15.15.

29 June 1972 YUGOSLAVIA 2 (Bajević, 61 minutes, Jekovic, 86) SCOTLAND 2 (Macari, 40 and 64 minutes) (Brazil Independence Tournament, Group A) Estadio Governador Magalhaes Pinto, Belo Horizonte. Attendance: 3,500. YUGOSLAVIA: Mešković (Sloboda Tuzla), Krivokuka (Red Star Belgrade), Boskovic (Hadjuk Split), Pavlovic (Red Star Belgrade), Paunovic (Partizan), Katalinski (FK Zeljeznicar Sarajevo), Popivoda (Olimpija), Oblak (Olimpija), Acimovic (Red Star Belgrade), Bajević (Velez Mostar), Dzajic (Red Star Belgrade). Substitutions: Santrac (OFK Belgrade) for Boskovic (38 minutes), Jerković (Hadjuk Split) for Paunovic (46). SCOTLAND: Hunter (Kilmarnock), Forsyth (Partick Thistle), Donachie (Manchester City), Buchan (Manchester United), Colquhoun (Sheffield United), Morgan (Manchester United), Bremner (Leeds, captain), Graham (Arsenal), Hartford (West Bromwich), Macari (Celtic), Law (Manchester United). Substitutions: Hansen (Partick Thistle) for Forsyth (46 minutes), Bone (Norwich) for Law (76). Missed penalty: Morgan (77 minutes). Referee: A. Corezza (Argentina). Broadcast details: No UK TV coverage.

2 July 1972 CZECHOSLOVAKIA 0 SCOTLAND 0 (Brazil Independence Tournament, Group A) Estadio Beiro-Rio, Porto Alegre. Attendance: 15,000. CZECHOSLOVAKIA: Viktor (Dukla Prague), Dobias (Spartak Trnava), Zlocha (Slovan Bratislava), Hagara (Spartak Trnava), Pivarnik (VSS Kosice), Medvid (Slovan Bratislava), Kuna (Spartak Trnava), Pollak (VSS Kosice), Terneny (AC Nitra), Adamec (Spartak Trnava), Kabat (Spartak Trnava). Substitutions: Capkovic (Slovan Bratislava) for Kabat (60 minutes), Hrusecky (Spartak Trnava) for Terneny (70) (Spartak Trnava). SCOTLAND: Clark (Aberdeen), Forsyth (Partick Thistle), Donachie (Manchester City), Buchan (Manchester United), Colquhoun (Sheffield United), Morgan (Manchester United), Bremner (Leeds, captain), Graham (Arsenal), Hartford (West Bromwich), Macari (Celtic), Law (Manchester United). Substitution: Stein (Rangers) for Law (78 minutes). Referee: A. Marques (Brazil). Broadcast details: No UK TV coverage.

5 July 1972 BRAZIL 1 (Jairzinho, 80 minutes) SCOTLAND 0 (Brazil Independence Tournament, Group A) Maracana Stadium, Rio de Janeiro. Attendance: 130,000. BRAZIL: Leao (Palmeiras), Ze Maria (Portuguesa), Brito (Botafogo), Vantuir (Atletico Mineiro), Marco Antonio (Fluminense), Clodoaldo (Santos), Gerson (Sao Paulo), Rivelino (Corinthians), Tostao (Cruzeiro), Leivinha (Palmeiras), Jarzinho (Botafogo). Substitution: Dario (Atletico Mineiro) for Leivinha (63 minutes). SCOTLAND: Clark (Aberdeen), Forsyth (Partick Thistle), Donachie (Manchester City), Buchan (Manchester United), Colquhoun (Sheffield United), Morgan (Manchester United), Bremner (Leeds, captain), Graham (Arsenal), Hartford (West Bromwich), Macari (Celtic), Law (Manchester United). Referee: A. Klein (Israel). Broadcast details: No UK TV coverage. Note: Televised in host country.

18 October 1972 DENMARK 1 (Laudrup, 28 minutes) SCOTLAND 4 (Macari, 17 minutes, Bone, 19, Harper, 80, Morgan, 83) (World Cup Qualification Group 8), Idraetsparken, Copenhagen. Attendance: 31,200. DENMARK: Therkildsen (Odense BK), Nielsen (Mainz), Munk-Jensen (PSV Eindhoven), Rontved (Werder Bremen), Ahlberg (BK Frem), Olsen (DOS Utrecht), Hansen (B1913), Bjornmose (SV Hamburg), Laudrup (Bronshoj), Nielsen (Winterthur), Henning Jennsen (Borussia Mönchengladbach). Substitution: Bent Jensen (Eintracht Braunschweig) for Hansen (68 minutes). SCOTLAND: Clark (Aberdeen), Brownlie (Hibs), Forsyth (Partick Thistle), Buchan (Manchester United), Colquhoun (Sheffield United), Lorimer (Leeds), Bremner (Leeds, captain), Graham (Arsenal), Morgan (Manchester United), Macari (Celtic), Bone (Norwich). Substitutions: Harper (Aberdeen) for Bone (65 minutes), Dalglish (Celtic) for Macari (88). Referee: T Bakhramov (USSR). Broadcast details: Live coverage on BBC1 *Scotland Sportsreel World Cup Special* 18.50-21.00 (black and white) and STV and Grampian *Scotsport World Cup Spec*ial 19.00-21.00 (black and white).

15 November 1972 SCOTLAND 2 (Dalglish, 2 minutes, Lorimer, 48) DENMARK 0 (World Cup Qualification Group 8), Hampden Park. Attendance: 47,109. SCOTLAND: Harvey (Leeds), Brownlie (Hibs), Donachie (Manchester City), Buchan (Manchester United), Colquhoun (Sheffield United), Lorimer (Leeds), Bremner (Leeds, captain), Graham (Arsenal), Morgan (Manchester United), Dalglish (Celtic), Harper (Aberdeen). Substitution: Carr (Coventry) for Dalglish (75 minutes). Missed penalty: Morgan (86 minutes). Sent off: Lorimer (84 minutes). DENMARK: Therkildsen (Odense BK), Ahlberg (BK Frem), Munk-Jensen (PSV Eindhoven), Rontved (Werder Bremen), Hansen (Bayern Munich) Michaelsen (Eintracht Braunschweig), Olsen (DOS Utrecht), Bjerre (RWD Molenbeek), Kristensen (Feyenoord), Jensen (Eintracht Braunschweig), Le Fevre (FC Brugge). Substitutions: Hildebrandt (Hvidovre IF) for Therkildsen (46 minutes), Laudrup ((Bronshoj) for Kristensen (75). Sent off: Ahlberg (84 minutes). Referee: C. Corver (Holland). Broadcast details: Highlights shown during *Sportsnight* BBC1 22.15-23.00 and STV and Grampian *Scotsport World Cup Special* 22.50-23.50 plus Wales v England

14 February 1973 SCOTLAND 0 ENGLAND 5 (Lorimer (own goal), 6 minutes, Clarke, 12 and 85, Channon, 15, Chivers, 76) (SFA Centenary International) Hampden Park. Attendance: 48,470. SCOTLAND: Clark (Aberdeen), Forsyth (Manchester United), Donachie (Manchester City), Bremner (Leeds, captain), Colquhoun (Sheffield United), Buchan (Manchester United), Lorimer (Leeds), Dalglish (Celtic), Macari (Manchester United), Graham (Manchester United), Morgan (Manchester United). Substitution: Stein (Coventry) for Morgan (19 minutes). ENGLAND: Shilton (Leicester), Storey (Arsenal), Hughes (Liverpool), Bell (Manchester City), Madeley (Leeds), Moore (West Ham, captain), Ball (Arsenal), Channon (Southampton), Chivers (Tottenham), Clarke (Leeds), Peters (Tottenham). Referee: R. Wurtz (France). Broadcast details: BBC no coverage ITV Network highlights during *International Football* 22.40-23.40.

12 May 1973 WALES 0 SCOTLAND 2 (Graham, 18 and 80 minutes) (Home International) Racecourse Ground, Wrexham. Attendance: 18,682. WALES: Sprake (Leeds), Rodrigues (Sheffield Wednesday),Thomas (Swindon), Hockey (Norwich), England (Tottenham,

captain), Roberts (Birmingham), James (Burnley), Mahoney (Stoke), Toshack (Liverpool), Yorath (Leeds), Evans (Swansea). Substitutions: Davies (Manchester United) for Yorath (69 minutes), O'Sullivan (Brighton) for Evans (78). SCOTLAND: McCloy (Rangers), McGrain (Celtic), Donachie (Manchester City), Graham (Manchester United), Holton (Manchester United), Johnstone (Rangers), Dalglish (Celtic), Stanton (Hibs, captain), Parlane (Rangers), Hay (Celtic), Morgan (Manchester United). Substitutions: Stein (Coventry) for Parlane (80 minutes), Macari (Manchester United) for Dalglish (84). Referee: J. Lawther (Northern Ireland). Broadcast details: BBC1 *International Match of the Day* 22.00-23.30 Highlights of Northern Ireland v England and Wales v Scotland; STV and Grampian no coverage.

16 May 1973 SCOTLAND 1 (Dalglish, 89 minutes) NORTHERN IRELAND 2 (O'Neill, 3 minutes, Anderson, 17) (Home International) Hampden Park. Attendance: 39,018. SCOTLAND: McCloy (Rangers), McGrain (Celtic), Donachie (Manchester City), Holton (Manchester United), Johnstone (Rangers), Stanton (Hibs, captain), Graham (Manchester United), Hay (Celtic), Morgan (Manchester United), Dalglish (Celtic), Stein (Coventry). Substitutions: Bremner (Leeds) for Stanton (50 minutes), Macari (Manchester United) for Graham (77). NORTHERN IRELAND: Jennings (Tottenham), Rice (Arsenal), Craig (Newcastle), Neill (Hull, captain), Hunter (Ipswich), Clements (Sheffield Wednesday), Hamilton (Ipswich), Jackson (Nottingham Forest), Morgan (Port Vale), O'Neill (Nottingham Forest), Anderson (Manchester United). Substitution: Lutton (West Ham) for Anderson (65 minutes). Referee: K. Burns (England). Broadcast details: Highlights during *Sportsreel* BBC1 22.40-23.10 and ITV Network *International Football* 22.30-23.30.

19 May 1973 ENGLAND 1 (Peters, 55 minutes) SCOTLAND 0 (Home International) Wembley Stadium. Attendance: 95,950. ENGLAND: Shilton (Leicester), Storey (Arsenal), Hughes (Liverpool), Bell (Manchester City), McFarland (Derby), Moore (West Ham, captain), Ball (Arsenal), Channon (Southampton), Chivers (Tottenham), Clarke (Leeds), Peters (Tottenham). SCOTLAND: Hunter (Celtic), Jardine (Rangers), McGrain (Celtic), Bremner (Leeds, captain), Holton (Manchester United), Johnstone (Rangers), Morgan (Manchester United), Macari (Manchester United), Dalglish (Celtic), Hay (Celtic), Lorimer (Leeds). Substitutions: Jordan (Leeds) for Macari (74 minutes), Stein (Coventry) for Lorimer (80). Referee: K. Tschenscher (West Germany). Broadcast details: Live coverage during *Grandstand* BBC1 12.30-17.25 and *World of Sport* ITV network 12.35-17.10; Highlights during *Match of the Day* BBC1 22.10-23.40 plus Northern Ireland v Wales Sunday 20 May; Most ITV regions including STV and Grampian included highlights during *Sportsworld '73* 14.15-15.05.

22 June 1973 SWITZERLAND 1 (Mundschin, 62 minutes) SCOTLAND 0 (Friendly) Wankdorf Stadium, Berne. Attendance: 10,000. SWITZERLAND: Burgener (Lausanne), Mundschin (FC Basel), Valentini (Sion), Ramseier (Basel), Hasler (Basel), Odermatt (Basel), Kuhn (Zurich), Blattler (St Gallen), Balmer (Basel), Luisier (Sion), Demarmels (Basel). Substitutions: Quientin (Sion) for Blattler (25 minutes), Wegmann (Servette) for Ramseier. SCOTLAND: McCloy (Rangers), Jardine (Rangers), McGrain (Celtic), Holton (Manchester United), Johnstone (Rangers), Connelly (Everton), Bremner (Leeds, captain), Hay (Celtic), Morgan (Manchester United), Dalglish (Celtic), Parlane (Rangers). Substitutions: Jordan (Leeds) for Connelly (46 minutes). Referee: A. Verbeke (France). Broadcast details: No UK TV coverage.

30 June 1973 SCOTLAND 0 BRAZIL 1 (Johnstone (own goal), 33 minutes) (SFA Centenary International) Hampden Park. Attendance: 78,181. SCOTLAND: McCloy (Rangers), Jardine (Rangers), McGrain (Celtic), Holton (Manchester United), Johnstone (Rangers), Hay (Celtic), Bremner (Leeds, captain), Morgan (Manchester United), Dalglish (Celtic), Jordan (Leeds), Parlane (Rangers). Substitution: Graham (Manchester United) for Dalglish (70 minutes). BRAZIL: Leao (Palmeiras), Pereira (Palmeiras), Piazza (Cruzeiro), Ze Maria (Corinthians), Marco Antonio (Fluminse), Clodoaldo (Santos), Cesar (Flamengo), Rivelino (Fluminense), Valdomiro (Internacional), Jairzinho (Botafogo),

Dirceu, (Botafogo). Referee: K. Burns (England). Broadcast details: Highlights during *Sportsreel* BBC1 22.40-23.10; No STV or Grampian coverage.

26 September 1973 SCOTLAND 2 (Holton, 40 minutes, Jordan, 75) CZECHOSLOVAKIA 1 (Nehoda, 33 minutes) (World Cup Qualification Group 8), Hampden Park. Attendance: 95,786. SCOTLAND: Hunter (Celtic), Jardine (Rangers), McGrain (Celtic), Hay (Celtic), Holton (Manchester United), Hutchison (Coventry), Bremner (Leeds, captain), Connelly (Celtic), Morgan (Manchester United), Dalglish (Celtic), Law (Manchester City). Substitution: Jordan (Leeds) for Dalglish (63 minutes). CZECHOSLOVAKIA: Viktor (Dukla Prague), Pivarnik (VSS Kosice), Samek (Dukla Prague), Zlocha (Slovan Bratislava), Bendl (Dukla Prague), Bicovsky (FK Teplice), Panenka (Bohemians Prague), Kuna (Spartak Trnava, captain), Adamec (Spartak Trnava), Nehoda (Dukla Prague), Stratil (FK Teplice). Substitutions: Dobias (Spartak Trnava) for Kuna (20 minutes), Capkovic (Slovan Bratislava) for Pananka (77). Referee: H. Oberg (Norway). Broadcast details: BBC no coverage; Live coverage STV and Grampian *World Cup Soccer* 19.35-22.00 . Note: Full match repeated on STV Saturday 29 September from 23.30.

17 October 1973 CZECHOSLOVAKIA 1 (Nehoda (penalty), 17 minutes) SCOTLAND 0 (World Cup Qualification Group 8), Tehelne Pole Stadium, Bratislava. Attendance: 13,668. CZECHOSLOVAKIA: Viktor (Dukla Prague), Pivarnik (VSS Kosice), Samek (Dukla Prague), Dvorak (Dukla Prague), Hagara (Spartak Trnava), Bicovsky (FK Teplice), Pollak (VSS Kosice), Gajdusek (Dukla Prague), Vesely (Slavia Prague), Nehoda (Dukla Prague), Capkovic (Slovan Bratislava). Substitutions: Klement (Banik Ostrava) for Vesele (61 minutes), Panenka (Bohemians Prague) for Capkovic (78). SCOTLAND: Harvey (Leeds), Jardine (Rangers), McGrain (Celtic), Forsyth (Rangers), Blackley (Hibs), Hutchison (Coventry), Hay (Celtic, captain), Morgan (Manchester United), Dalglish (Celtic), Jordan (Leeds), Law (Manchester City). Substitution: Ford (Hearts) for Law (58 minutes). Referee: F. Biwersi (West Germany). Broadcast details: BBC no coverage; Live coverage on STV and Grampian *World Cup Soccer* 16.45-18.50 (black and white).

14 November 1973 SCOTLAND 1 (Holton, 7 minutes) WEST GERMANY 1 (Hoeness, 80 minutes) (SFA Centenary International) Hampden Park. Attendance: 58,235. SCOTLAND: Harvey (Leeds), Jardine (Rangers), McGrain (Celtic), Connelly (Celtic), Holton (Manchester United), Hutchison (Coventry), Bremner (Leeds, captain), Smith (Newcastle), Morgan (Manchester United), Dalglish (Celtic), Law (Manchester City). Substitutions: Lorimer (Leeds) for Smith (81 minutes), Jordan (Leeds) for Law (87). Missed penalty: Bremner (75 minutes). WEST GERMANY: Kleff (Borussia Monchengladbach), Vogts (Borussia Monchengladbach), Hottges (Werder Bremen), Beckenbaeur (Bayern Munich, captain), Weber (FC Cologne), Hoeness (Bayern Munich), Netzer (Real Madrid), Wimmer (Borussia Monchengladbach), Grabowski (Eintracht Frankfurt), Held (Kickers Offenbach), Kremers (Schalke 04). Substitutions: Maier (Bayern Munich) for Kleff (46 minutes), Heynckes (Borussia Monchengladbach) for Kremers (46), Cullman (FC Cologne) for Wimmer (75), Flohe (FC Cologne) for Held (75). Referee: J. Taylor (England). Broadcast details: Highlights included in *Sportsnight* BBC1 21.25-22.45 plus boxing; STV and Grampian no coverage.

27 March 1974 WEST GERMANY 2 (Breitner (penalty), 33 minutes, Grabowski, 35) SCOTLAND 1 (Dalglish, 76 minutes) (Friendly) Waldstadion, Frankfurt. Attendance: 62,000. WEST GERMANY: Maier (Bayern Munich), Vogts (Borussia Monchengladbach), Breitner (Bayern Munich), Schwarzenbeck (Bayern Munich), Beckenbauer (Bayern Munich, captain), Cullman (FC Cologne), Grabowski (Eintracht Frankfurt), Hoeness (Bayern Munich), Muller (Bayern Munich), Wimmer (Borussia Monchengladbach), Herzog (Fortuna Dusseldorf). SCOTLAND: Allan (Dundee), Jardine (Rangers), Schaedler (Hibs), Buchan (Manchester United), Burns (Birmingham), Hutchison (Coventry), Stanton (Hibs), Hay (Celtic, captain), Morgan (Manchester United), Dalglish (Celtic), Law (Manchester City). Substitutions: Ford (Hearts) for Law (59 minutes), Robinson (Dundee) for Burns (59). Referee: P. Schiller (Austria). Broadcast details: No BBC coverage; Highlights on STV and Grampian 22.45-23.45 *Football: West Germany v Scotland*.

11 May 1974 NORTHERN IRELAND: 1 Cassidy (40 minutes) SCOTLAND 0 (Home International) Hampden Park. Attendance: 53,775. NORTHERN IRELAND Jennings (Tottenham), Rice (Arsenal), Nelson (Arsenal), O'Kane (Nottingham Forest), Hunter (Ipswich), Clements (Everton, captain), Hamilton (Ipswich), Cassidy (Newcastle), Morgan (Aston Villa), McIlroy (Manchester United), McGrath (Tottenham). Substitution: Jackson (Nottingham Forest) for Hamilton (48 minutes). SCOTLAND: Harvey (Leeds), Jardine (Rangers), Donachie (Manchester City), Bremner (Leeds, captain), Holton (Manchester United), Buchan (Manchester United), Morgan (Manchester United), Hay (Celtic), Law (Manchester City), Dalglish (Celtic), Hutchison (Coventry). Substitutions: Smith (Newcastle) for Donachie (46 minutes), Jordan (Leeds) for Law (65). Referee: I. P. Jones (Wales). Broadcast details: BBC *Match of the Day* 22.00-23.30 Highlights of Wales v England and Northern Ireland v Scotland; STV and Grampian no coverage.

14 May 1974 SCOTLAND 2 (Dalglish, 24 minutes, Jardine (penalty), 44) WALES 0 (Home International) Hampden Park. Attendance: 41,969. SCOTLAND: Harvey (Leeds), Jardine (Rangers), Hay (Celtic), Bremner (Leeds, captain), Holton (Manchester United), Buchan (Manchester United), Johnstone (Celtic), Dalglish (Celtic), Ford (Hearts), Jordan (Leeds), Hutchison (Coventry). Substitutions: Smith (Newcastle) for Hutchison (6 minutes), McGrain (Celtic) for Buchan (76). WALES: Sprake (Leeds), Thomas (Derby), Page (Birmingham), Mahoney (Stoke), John Roberts (Birmingham), David Roberts (Oxford), Reece (Cardiff), Villars (Cardiff), Yorath (Leeds), Cartwright (Coventry), James (Burnley). Substitution: Smallman (Wrexham) for Reece (46 minutes). Referee: M. Wright (Northern Ireland). Broadcast details: BBC no coverage; ITV Network screened highlights during *International Football: Scotland v Wales* 22.30-23.30.

18 May 1974 SCOTLAND 2 (Pejic (own goal), 4 minutes, Todd (own goal), 30) ENGLAND 0 (Home International) Hampden Park. Attendance: 94,487. SCOTLAND: Harvey (Leeds), Jardine (Rangers), McGrain (Celtic), Bremner (Leeds, captain), Holton (Manchester United), Blackley (Hibs), Johnstone (Celtic), Dalglish (Celtic), Jordan (Leeds), Hay (Celtic), Lorimer (Leeds). ENGLAND: Shilton (Leicester), Nish (Derby), Pejic (Stoke), Hughes (Liverpool, captain), Hunter (Leeds), Todd (Derby), Channon (Southampton), Bell (Manchester City), Worthington (Leicester), Weller (Leicester), Peters (Tottenham). Substitutions: Watson (Sunderland) for Hunter (46 minutes), MacDonald (Newcastle) for Worthington (70). Referee: L. Van Der Kroft (Holland). Broadcast details: Live coverage during *Grandstand* BBC1 12.30-17.30 and *World of Sport* ITV Network 12.30-17.10; Highlights during *International Match of the Day* BBC1 22.00-23.30 plus Wales v Northern Ireland.

1 June 1974 BELGIUM 2 (Henrotay, 23 minutes, Lambert (penalty), 83) SCOTLAND 1 (Johnstone, 41) (Friendly) Klokke Stadium, Bruges. Attendance: 7,769. BELGIUM: Piot (Standard), Van Bist (Anderlecht), Dewalque (Standard), Van Den Daele (Bruges), Martens (Molenbeek), Van Moer (Standard), Verheyen (Anderlecht), Van Herp (Mechelen), Henrotay (Liege), Van Himst (Anderlecht), Lambert (Bruges). Substitutions: Thissen (Liege) for Dewalque (40 minutes), Cools (Bruges) for Henrotay (68). SCOTLAND: Harvey (Leeds), Jardine (Rangers), McGrain (Celtic), Bremner (Leeds, captain), McQueen (Leeds), Blackley (Hibs), Lorimer (Leeds) Johnstone (Celtic), Jordan (Leeds), Dalglish (Celtic), Hay (Celtic). Substitutions: Morgan (Manchester United) for Johnstone (69 minutes), Hutchison (Coventry) for Dalglish (80). Referee: K. Ohmsen (West Germany). Broadcast details: No UK TV coverage. Note: The goals only (in black and white) featured on *World Cup 74: Can Scotland Do It?* on the ITV network on 12 June 21.00-22.00.

6 June 1974 NORWAY 1 (Lund, 19 minutes) SCOTLAND 2 (Jordan, 74 minutes, Dalglish, 86) (Friendly) Ullevaal Stadium. Attendance: 18,432. NORWAY: Karlsen (Dunfermline), Wormdahl (Rosenborg), Birkelund (Skeid), Kordahl (Lyn Oslo), Grondalen (Raufoss), Berg (Bodo Glimt), Johansen (Skeid Oslo), Kvia (Viking), Skuseth (Start Kristiansand), Lund (Lillestrom), Hestad (Molde). Substitution: Thunberg (Skeid Oslo) for Berg (70 minutes). SCOTLAND: Allan (Dundee), Jardine (Rangers), McGrain (Celtic), Bremner (Leeds,

captain), Holton (Manchester United), Buchan (Manchester United), Johnstone (Celtic), Hutchison (Coventry), Jordan (Leeds), Hay (Celtic), Lorimer (Leeds). Substitution: Dalglish (Celtic) for Johnstone (70 minutes). Referee: A. Axelsson (Sweden). Broadcast details: No UK TV coverage. Some footage from this match was shown on ITV's *World of Sport* 12.30-17.05 on 8 June during *World Cup On The Ball*. The goals also featured on *World Cup 74: Can Scotland Do It?* on 12 June on the ITV network 21.00-22.00.

14 June 1974 SCOTLAND 2 (Lorimer, 26 minutes, Jordan, 33) ZAIRE 0 (World Cup finals Group B) Westfalen Stadium, Dortmund. Attendance: 25,800. SCOTLAND: Harvey (Leeds), Jardine (Rangers), McGrain (Celtic), Holton (Manchester United), Blackley (Hibs), Bremner (Leeds, captain), Hay (Celtic), Dalglish (Celtic), Jordan (Leeds), Lorimer (Leeds), Law (Manchester City). Substitution: Hutchison (Coventry) for Dalglish (75 minutes). ZAIRE: Kazadi (Mazembe Lubumbashi), Mwepu (Mazembe Lubumbashi), Mukombo (Mazembe Lubumbashi), Bwanga (Mazembe Lubumbashi), Lobilo (AS Vita Kinshasa), Kilasu (FC Bilima), Mana (Imana Kinshasa), Kidumu (Imana Kinshasa, captain), N'Daye (AS Vita Kinshasa), Mayanga (AS Vita Kinshasa), Kakoko (Imana Kinshasa). Substitutions: Kembo (AS Vita Kinshasa) for Mayanga (64 minutes), Kibonge (AS Vita Kinshasa) for Kidumu (78). Referee: G. Schulenburg (West Germany). Broadcast details: Live coverage BBC1 *World Cup Grandstand* 18.45-21.30 and ITV Network *World Cup 74* 19.00-21.30; Highlights during *World Cup Highlights* BBC1 22.45-23.30 plus East Germany v Australia and West Germany v Chile and *World Cup 74* 00.10-00.45 ITV Network plus East Germany v Australia and West Germany v Chile.

18 June 1974 SCOTLAND 0 BRAZIL 0 (World Cup finals Group B) Waldstadion, Frankfurt. Attendance: 62,000. SCOTLAND: Harvey (Leeds), Jardine (Rangers), McGrain (Celtic), Holton (Manchester United), Buchan (Manchester United), Bremner (Leeds, captain), Hay (Celtic), Dalglish (Celtic), Jordan (Leeds), Lorimer (Leeds), Morgan (Manchester United). BRAZIL: Leao (Palmeiras), Pereira (Palmeiras), Marinho Peres (Santos), Marinho Chagas (Botafogo), Nelinho (Cruzeiro), Piazza (Cruzeiro, captain), Paulo Cesar (Flamengo), Jairzinho (Botafogo), Levinha (Palmeiras), Rivelino (Corinthians), Mirandinha (Sao Paolo). Substitution: Carpegiani (Internacional) for Levinha (65 minutes). Referee: A. Van Gemert (Holland). Broadcast details: Live coverage BBC1 *World Cup Grandstand* 18.45-21.30 and ITV Network *World Cup 74* 18.30-21.30; Highlights during *World Cup Highlights* BBC1 22.30-23.15 plus West Germany v Australia, East Germany v Chile and Yugoslavia v Zaire, and *World Cup 74* ITV 23.00-00.00 plus West Germany v Australia, East Germany v Chile and Yugoslavia v Zaire.

22 June 1974 SCOTLAND 1 (Jordan, 88 minutes) YUGOSLAVIA 1 (Karasi, 82 minutes) (World Cup finals Group B) Waldstadion, Frankfurt. Attendance: 56,000. SCOTLAND: Harvey (Leeds), Jardine (Rangers), McGrain (Celtic), Holton (Manchester United), Buchan (Manchester United), Bremner (Leeds, captain), Hay (Celtic), Dalglish (Celtic), Jordan (Leeds), Lorimer (Leeds), Morgan (Manchester United). Substitution: Hutchison (Coventry) for Dalglish (65 minutes). YUGOSLAVIA: Marić (Velez Mostar), Buljan (Hajduk Split), Hadziabdic (Zeljeznicar Sarajevo), Katalinski (Zeljeznicar Sarajevo), Bogicevuc (Red Star Belgrade), Petkovic (Troyes), Oblak (Hajduk Split), Acimovic (Red Star Belgrade), Surjak (Hajduk Split), Dzajic (Red Star Belgrade, captain), Bajević (Velez Mostar). Substitution: Karasi (Red Star Belgrade) for Bajević (70 minutes). Referee: A. G. Archundia (Mexico). Broadcast details: Live coverage during *World Cup Grandstand* BBC1 13.30-18.20 and *World of Sport* ITV Network 12.30-18.05; Highlights during *World Cup Match of the Day* BBC1 23.50-00.37 plus Brazil v Yugoslavia, Australia v Chile and West Germany v East Germany BBC1 23.50–00.37.

30 October 1974 SCOTLAND 3 (Hutchison (penalty), 34 minutes, Burns, 36, Dalglish, 75) EAST GERMANY 0 (Friendly) Hampden Park. Attendance: 39,445. SCOTLAND: Harvey (Leeds), Jardine (Rangers), Forsyth (Manchester United), Buchan (Manchester United), Holton (Manchester United), Johnstone (Celtic), Souness (Middlesbrough), Hutchison (Coventry), Deans (Celtic), Dalglish (Celtic), Jordan (Leeds). Substitutions:

Burns (Birmingham) for Holton (12 minutes) Johnstone (Rangers) for Dalglish (86). Missed penalty: Jardine (17 minutes). EAST GERMANY:: Croy (Sachsenring Zwickau), Bransch (Carl Zeiss Jena), Kische (Hansa Rostock), Weise (Carl Zeiss Jena), Watzlich (Dynamo Dresden), Kurbjuweit (Carl Zeiss Jena), Haefner (Dynamo Dresden), Lauck (Dynamo Berlin), Kreische (Dynamo Dresden), Sparwasser (Magdeburg), Hoffmann (Magdeburg). Substitutions: Zapf (Magdeburg) for Bransch (38 minutes), Irmscher (Carl Zeiss Jena) for Kurbjuweit (56), Streich (Hansa Rostock) for Lauck (73). Referee: J. Taylor (England). Broadcast details: Highlights during *Sportsreel* BBC1 21.55-22.50; STV and Grampian no coverage.

20 November 1974 SCOTLAND 1 (Bremner, 11 minutes) SPAIN 2 (Castro, 36 and 61 minutes) (European Championship Qualification Group B) Hampden Park. Attendance: 92,100. SCOTLAND: Harvey (Leeds), Jardine (Rangers), Forsyth (Manchester United), Burns (Birmingham), McQueen (Leeds), Johnstone (Celtic), Bremner (Leeds, captain), Souness (Middlesbrough), Hutchison (Coventry), Deans (Celtic), Jordan (Leeds). Substitutions: Dalglish (Celtic) for Hutchison (65 minutes), Lorimer (Leeds) for Deans (65). Missed penalty: Hutchison (20 minutes). SPAIN: Iribar (Athletic Bilbao), Castellanos (Granada), Benito (Real Madrid), Capon (Atletico Madrid), Migueli (Barcelona), Costas (Barcelona), Martinez (Real Madrid), Villar (Athletic Bilbao), Rexach (Barcelona), Planas (Zaragoza), Quini (Gijon). Substitutions: Sol (Valencia) for Migueli (75 minutes). Referee: E. Linemayr (Austria). Broadcast details: Highlights during *International Football* STV and Grampian 23.15-23.45; No BBC coverage.

5 February 1975 SPAIN 1 (Megido, 67 minutes) SCOTLAND 1 (Jordan, 2 minutes) (European Championship Qualification Group B) Luis Casanova Stadium, Valencia. Attendance: 40,952. SPAIN: Iribar (Athletic Bilbao), Benito (Real Madrid), Camacho (Real Madrid), Sol (Valencia), Costas (Barcelona), Claramunt (Valencia), Villar (Athletic Bilbao), Asensi (Barcelona), Rexach (Barcelona), Garate (Atletico Madrid), Quini (Gijon). Substitutions: Megido (Sporting Gijon) for Garate (66 minutes), Migueli (Barcelona) for Costas (70). SCOTLAND: Harvey (Leeds), Jardine (Rangers), McGrain (Celtic), Buchan (Manchester United), McQueen (Leeds), Cooke (Chelsea), Burns (Birmingham), Bremner (Leeds, captain), Hutchison (Coventry), Dalglish (Celtic), Jordan (Leeds). Substitutions: Parlane (Rangers) for Jordan (66 minutes), Wilson (Celtic) for Burns (79). Referee: A. Delcourt (Belgium). Broadcast details: BBC1 *Sportsnight* 21.55-22.45 highlights of Scotland v Spain (black and white); STV and Grampian live coverage during *Football: Spain v Scotland* 19.30-21.30 (black and white).

16 April 1975 SWEDEN 1 (Sjoberg, 44 minutes) SCOTLAND 1 (MacDougall, 86 minutes) (Friendly) Ullevi Stadium, Gothenburg. Attendance: 15,574. SWEDEN: Hagberg (Osters IF), B Andesson (Bayern Munich), Karlsson (Atvidabergs FF), Nordqvist (PSV Eindhoven), Augustsson (Atvidabergs FF), Fredriksson (GAIS Gothenburg), Tortensson (Bayern Munich), Edstrom (PSV Eindhoven), Ahlstrom (Elfsborg), Mattson (Oster), Sjoberg (Malmo). Substitutions: R Andersson (Malmo) for Nordqvist (46 minutes), Linderoth (Osters) for Edstrom (46), Nordahl (Orebro) for Ahlstrom (65). SCOTLAND: Kennedy (Rangers), Jardine (Rangers), McGrain (Celtic), Munro (Wolves), Jackson (Rangers), Robinson (Dundee), Souness (Middlesbrough), Dalglish (Celtic), Macari (Manchester United), Parlane (Rangers), MacDougall (Norwich). Substitutions: Johnstone (Rangers) for Macari (54 minutes), Hughes (Sunderland) for Souness (54). Referee: S. I. Thime (Norway). Broadcast details: No UK TV coverage.

13 May 1975 SCOTLAND 1 (Artur (own goal), 43 minutes) PORTUGAL 0 (Friendly) Hampden Park. Attendance: 34,307. SCOTLAND: Kennedy (Rangers), Jardine (Rangers), McGrain (Celtic), Buchan (Manchester United), McQueen (Leeds), Cooke (Chelsea), Rioch (Derby), Dalglish (Celtic), Hutchison (Coventry), Parlane (Rangers), MacDougall (Norwich). Substitutions: Jackson (Rangers) for Buchan (27 minutes), Macari (Manchester United) for Cooke (77), Duncan (Hibs) for Rioch (77). PORTUGAL: Damas (Sporting), Artur (Benfica), Coelho (Benfica), Alhinho (Sporting), Barros (Benfica), Octavio (Vitoria

FC), Fraguito (Sporting), Oliviera (Porto), Moinhos (Benfica), Alves (Boavista), Nene (Benfica). Substitutions: Pereira (CUF Bareiro) for Alves (66 minutes), Gomes (Porto) for Nene (66), Romeu (Vitoria Guimaraes) for Moinhos (66). Referee: R. Matthewson (England). Broadcast details: Highlights during *International Football: Scotland v Portugal* BBC1 22.15-22.40; STV and Grampian no coverage.

17 May 1975 WALES 2 (Toshack, 28 minutes, Flynn, 35) SCOTLAND 2 (Jackson, 54 minutes, Rioch, 62) (Home International) Ninian Park, Cardiff. Attendance: 23,509. WALES: Davies (Everton),Thomas (Derby), Page (Birmingham, Yorath (Leeds, captain), Roberts (Birmingham), Reece (Cardiff), Mahoney (Stoke), Flynn (Burnley), Phillips (Aston Villa), Toshack (Liverpool), James (Burnley). SCOTLAND: Kennedy (Rangers), Jardine (Rangers, captain), McGrain (Celtic), Jackson (Rangers), McQueen (Leeds), Rioch (Derby), Macari (Manchester United), Duncan (Hibs), Dalglish (Celtic), Parlane (Rangers), MacDougall (Norwich). Substitution: Munro (Wolves) for Jackson (77 minutes). Referee: M. Wright (Northern Ireland). Broadcast details: Highlights shown during *International Match of the Day Special* BBC1 21.45-23.45 plus Northern Ireland v England and heavyweight championship boxing, Sunday 18 May; highlights featured in *Home International Championship* ITV network 14.10-15.10 plus Northern Ireland v England.

20 May 1975 SCOTLAND 3 (MacDougall, 15 minutes, Dalglish, 21, Parlane, 80) NORTHERN IRELAND 0 (Home International) Hampden Park. Attendance: 64,696. SCOTLAND: Kennedy (Rangers), Jardine (Rangers, captain), McGrain (Celtic), Munro (Wolves), McQueen (Leeds), Robinson (Dundee), Rioch (Derby), Dalglish (Celtic), Duncan (Hibs), Parlane (Rangers), MacDougall (Norwich). Substitutions: Conn (Tottenham) for Robinson (76 minutes), Forsyth (Manchester United) for Jardine (89). NORTHERN IRELAND: Jennings (Tottenham), Rice (Arsenal), O'Kane (Nottingham Forest), Nicholl (Aston Villa), Hunter (Ipswich), Clements (Everton, captain), Finney (Sunderland), O'Neill (Nottingham Forest), Spence (Bury), McIlroy (Manchester United), Jackson (Nottingham Forest). Substitutions: Blair (Oldham) for Hunter (83 minutes), Anderson (Swansea) for O'Neill (87). Referee: P. Partridge (England). Broadcast details: No BBC coverage; Highlights during *Home International Football* on ITV Network 22.30-23.30.

24 May 1975 ENGLAND 5 (Francis, 5 and 65 minutes, Beattie, 7, Bell, 40, Johnson, 75) SCOTLAND 1 (Rioch (penalty), 41 minutes) (Home International) Wembley Stadium. Attendance: 98,241. ENGLAND: Clemence (Liverpool), Whitworth (Leicester), Todd (Derby), Beattie (Ipswich), Watson (Sunderland), Ball (Arsenal, captain), Bell (Manchester City), Channon (Southampton), Keegan (Liverpool), Johnston (Ipswich), Francis (QPR). Substitution: Thomas (QPR) for Keegan (85 minutes). SCOTLAND: Kennedy (Rangers), Jardine (Rangers, captain), McGrain (Celtic), Munro (Wolves), McQueen (Leeds), Conn (Tottenham), Rioch (Derby), Dalglish (Celtic), Duncan (Hibs), Parlane (Rangers), MacDougall (Norwich). Substitutions: Hutchison (Coventry) for Duncan (61 minutes), Macari (Manchester United) for MacDougall (71). Referee: R. Glockner (East Germany). Broadcast details: Live coverage during *Grandstand* BBC1 12.30-17.05; No STV or Grampian coverage due to industrial dispute. London Weekend and Westward were the only ITV regions to broadcast live coverage during *World of Sport* 11.30-17.10 Highlights in *International Match of the Day* BBC1 22.50-23.50.

1 June 1975 ROMANIA 1 (Georgescu, 19 minutes) SCOTLAND 1 (McQueen, 89) (European Championship Qualification Group B) 23 August Stadionul, Bucharest. Attendance: 52,203. ROMANIA: Raducanu (SS Bucharest) Cheran (Dinamo Bucharest), Sandu (Dinamo Bucharest), Satmareanu (Dinamo Bucharest), Anghelini (Steaua Bucharest), Dumitru (Steaua Bucharest), Dinu (Dinamo Bucharest, captain), Dobrin (Arges Pitesti), Crisan (Universitatea Craiova), Georgescu (Dinamo Bucharest), Lucescu (Dinamo Bucharest). Substitutions: Balaci (Universitatea Craiova) for Georgescu (37 minutes), Kun (Bihor Oradea) for Dobrin (82). SCOTLAND: Brown (Sheffield United), McGrain (Celtic), Forsyth (Manchester United), Munro (Wolves), McQueen (Leeds,

captain), Miller (Aberdeen), Rioch (Derby), Dalglish (Celtic), Duncan (Hibs), Macari (Manchester United), Parlane (Rangers). Substitutions: Hutchison (Coventry) for Rioch (67 minutes), Robinson (Dundee) for Macari (67). Referee: E. Dilek (Turkey). Broadcast details: live coverage on BBC1 *Football* 16.30-18.15 (black and white); No STV or Grampian coverage. Note: STV had agreement for live coverage but an industrial dispute ensured the channel was completely off the air. BBC Scotland then made late arrangements to cover the match.

3 September 1975 DENMARK 0 SCOTLAND 1 (Harper, 51 minutes) (European Championship Qualification Group B) Idraetsparken, Copenhagen. Attendance: 40,300. DENMARK B: Jensen (Brugges), Mortensen (Frem), Munk-Jensen (AAB), Larsen (Frem), Hansen (Holbaek), Bjerg (FC Wacker Innsbruck), Bjornmose (Hamburg), Nielsen (RWD Molenbeek), Simonsen (Borussia Monchengladbach), H Jensen (AAB), Le Fevre (Brugges), captain). SCOTLAND: Harvey (Leeds), McGrain (Celtic), Forsyth (Manchester United), Buchan (Manchester United), McQueen (Leeds), Lorimer (Leeds), Bremner (Leeds, captain), Rioch (Derby), Hutchison (Coventry), Dalglish (Celtic), Harper (Aberdeen). Substitution: Duncan (Hibs) for Hutchison (71 minutes). Referee: R. Nyhus (Norway). Broadcast details: Highlights during *Sportscene* BBC1 22.05-22.55 (black and white) plus England v Switzerland; STV and Grampian no coverage.

29 October 1975 SCOTLAND 3 (Dalglish, 48 minutes, Rioch, 54, MacDougall, 61) DENMARK 1 (Bastrup, 22 minutes) (European Championship Qualifier Group B) Hampden Park. Attendance: 48,021. SCOTLAND: Harvey (Leeds), McGrain (Celtic), Houston (Manchester United), Greig (Rangers, captain), Jackson (Rangers), Lorimer (Leeds), Hartford (Manchester City), Rioch (Derby), Gemmill (Derby), Dalglish (Celtic), MacDougall (Norwich). Substitution: Parlane (Rangers) for MacDougall (85 minutes). DENMARK: Larsen (Holbaek), Andersen (B1903), Munk-Jensen (AAB, captain), L. Larsen (Frem), N. Hansen (Holbaek), J. Hansen (Bayern Munich), H. Hansen (St Pauli), Nygaard (AZ 67) Sorensen (KB), Bastrup (IHF Aarhus), Kolding (B93 Copenhagen). Substitution: Nielsen (Frederikshavn) for N. Hansen (68 minutes). Referee: R. Nyhus (Norway). Broadcast details: Highlights during *Sportsnight* BBC1 21.25-23.10 plus Czechoslovakia v England; STV and Grampian no coverage.

17 December 1975 SCOTLAND 1 (Rioch, 39 minutes) ROMANIA 1 (Crisan, 74 minutes) (European Championship Qualification Group B) Hampden Park. Attendance: 11,375. SCOTLAND: Cruickshank (Hearts), Brownlie (Hibs), Donachie ((Manchester City), Buchan (Manchester United), Jackson (Rangers), Doyle (Ayr), Hartford (Manchester City), Rioch (Derby), Gemmill (Derby), Dalglish (Celtic), Gray (Aston Villa). Substitution: Lorimer (Leeds) for Doyle (73 minutes), MacDougall (Norwich) for Dalglish (73 minutes). ROMANIA: Raducanu (SS Bucharest), Cheran (Dinamo Bucharest), Sandu (Dinamo Bucharest), Satmareanu (Dinamo Bucharest), Anghelini (Steaua Bucharest), Romila (Politechnica Jasi), Dinu (Dinamo Bucharest, captain), Boloni (Asa Targu Mures), Lucescu (Dinamo Bucharest), Georgescu (Dinamo Bucharest), Iordanescu (Steaua Bucharest). Substitution: Crisan (Universitatea Craiova) for Lucescu (60 minutes). Referee: A, Prokop (East Germany). Broadcast details: Highlights during *Sportscene* BBC1 22.10-23.05 plus show jumping; STV and Grampian no coverage.

7 April 1976 SCOTLAND 1 (Pettigrew, 2 minutes) SWITZERLAND 0 (Friendly) Hampden Park. Attendance: 15,531. SCOTLAND: Rough (Partick Thistle), McGrain (Celtic), F Gray (Leeds), Forsyth (Rangers, captain), Blackley (Hibs), Craig (Newcastle), MacDonald (Rangers), Dalglish (Celtic), Pettigrew (Motherwell), A. Gray (Aston Villa), Johnstone (Rangers). Substitutions: McKean (Rangers) for Pettigrew (46 minutes), Bremner (Hibs) for Dalglish (64). SWITZERLAND: Burgener (Lausanne), Guyot (Servette), Stohler (FC Basel), Bizzini (Servette), Fischbach (FC Zurich), Hasler (FC Basel), Botteron (FC Zurich), Risi (FC Zurich), Elsener (Grasshoppers), Muller (Servette), Jeandupeux (Girondins). Substitutions: Andrey (Servette) for Hasler (53 minutes), Schnyder (Servette) for Elsener (64). Referee: P. Partridge (England). Broadcast details: No TV coverage.

6 May 1976 SCOTLAND 3 (Pettigrew, 38 minutes, Rioch, 44 Gray, 69) WALES 1 (Griffiths (penalty), 61 minutes) (Home International) Hampden Park. Attendance: 25,466. SCOTLAND: Rough (Partick Thistle), McGrain (Celtic), Donachie (Manchester City), Forsyth (Rangers), Jackson (Rangers), Gemmill (Derby, captain), Masson (QPR), Rioch (Derby), E. Gray (Leeds), Pettigrew (Motherwell), Jordan (Leeds). WALES: Lloyd (Wrexham), D. Jones (Norwich), J. Jones (Liverpool), D. Roberts (Hull), J. Roberts (Birmingham), Harris (Leeds), Yorath (Leeds, captain), Griffiths (Wrexham), Curtis (Swansea), O'Sullivan (Brighton), James (Derby). Substitution: Cartwright (Coventry) for Harris (46 minutes). Referee: M. Wright (Northern Ireland). Broadcast details: BBC no coverage; Highlights on *Home International Championship* ITV Network 22.45-23.45.

8 May 1976 NORTHERN IRELAND 0 SCOTLAND 3 (Gemmill, 23 minutes), Masson (47), Dalglish (52) (Home International) Hampden Park. Attendance: 49,897. NORTHERN IRELAND: Jennings (Tottenham), Rice (Arsenal), Scott (York), Nicholl (Manchester United), Hunter (Ipswich), Finney (Sunderland), Hamilton (Everton), Sharkey (Ipswich), Cassidy (Newcastle), McIlroy (Manchester United), Morgan (Brighton). Substitutions: McCreery (Manchester United) for Sharkey (61 minutes), Spence (Bury) for Morgan (85). SCOTLAND: Rough (Partick Thistle), McGrain (Celtic), Donachie (Manchester City), Forsyth (Rangers), Jackson (Rangers), Gemmill (Derby, captain), Masson (QPR), Rioch (Derby), Dalglish (Celtic), Pettigrew (Motherwell), Jordan (Leeds). Substitutions: Hartford (Manchester City) for Rioch (56 minutes), Johnstone (Rangers) for Pettigrew (66). Missed penalty: Rioch (46 minutes). Referee: T. H. C. Reynolds (Wales). Broadcast details: Highlights on *International Match of the Day* BBC1 22.10-23.40 plus Wales v England following day 9 May; Highlights on *Home International Championships* 14.10-15.10 ITV network plus Wales v England.

15 May 1976 SCOTLAND 2 (Masson, 18 minutes, Dalglish, 49) ENGLAND 1 (Channon, 11 minutes) (Home International) Hampden Park. Attendance: 85,165. SCOTLAND: Rough (Partick Thistle), McGrain (Celtic), Donachie (Manchester City), Forsyth (Rangers), Jackson (Rangers), Gemmill (Derby, captain), Masson (QPR), Rioch (Derby), E. Gray (Leeds), Dalglish (Celtic), Jordan (Leeds). Substitution: Johnstone (Rangers) for Gray (79 minutes). ENGLAND: Clemence (Liverpool), Todd (Derby), Mills (Ipswich), Thompson (Liverpool), McFarland (Derby), Kennedy (Liverpool), Keegan (Liverpool), Channon (Southampton), Pearson (Manchester United), Francis (QPR, captain), Taylor (Crystal Palace). Substitutions: Cherry (Leeds) for Pearson (46 minutes), Doyle (Manchester City) for MacFarland (70). Referee: K. Palotai (Hungary). Broadcast details: Live coverage during *Grandstand* BBC1 12.30-17.15 and *World of Sport* ITV Network 12.50-17.05; Highlights in *International Match of the Day* BBC1 22.25-23.15.

8 September 1976 SCOTLAND 6 (Rioch, 7 minutes, Masson (penalty), 16, Dalglish, 23, A. Gray, 44 and 80, E. Gray, 68) FINLAND 0 (Friendly) Hampden Park. Attendance: 16,338. SCOTLAND: Rough (Partick Thistle), McGrain (Celtic), Donachie (Manchester City), Forsyth (Rangers), Buchan (Manchester United), Gemmill (Derby, captain), Masson (QPR), Rioch (Derby), E. Gray (Leeds), Dalglish (Celtic), A. Gray (Aston Villa). Substitution: Harvey (Leeds) for Rough (46 minutes). FINLAND: Alaja (TPS), Heikennen (OTP Oulu), Vihtila (Tampere), Makynen (TPS), Ranta (Valkeakosken Haka), Jantunen (Lahden Reipas), Suomalainen (Kuopion Pallotoverit), Toivola (HJK), Rissanen (Kuipion Palloseura), Dahllund (HJK), Paatelainen (Valkeakosken Haka, captain). Substitutions: Nieminen (HJK) for Paatelainen (39 minutes), Enckleman (TPS) for Alaja (46), Ahonen (VPS) for Heikennen (75). Referee: G. Kew (England). Broadcast details: Highlights during *Sportscene* BBC1 21.55-22.50; no coverage on STV or Grampian.

13 October 1976 CZECHOSLOVAKIA 2 (Panenka, 46 minutes, Petras, 48) SCOTLAND 0 (World Cup Qualification Group 7) Sparta Stadium, Prague. Attendance: 38,000. CZECHOSLOVAKIA: Vencel (Slovan Bratislava), Biros (Slavia Prague), Capkovic (Slovan Bratislava), Ondrus (Slovan Bratislava), Gogh (Slovan Bratislava), Pollak (VSS Kosice), Dobias (Spartak Trnava), Panenka (Bohemians Prague), Masny (Slovan Bratislava),

Nehoda (Dukla Prague), Petras (Inter Bratislava). Substitutions: Kozak (Lokomotiva Kosice) for Gogh (13 minutes), Jurkemik (Inter Bratislava) for Capkovic (68). Sent off: Ondrus (43 minutes). SCOTLAND: Rough (Partick Thistle), McGrain (Celtic), Donachie (Manchester City), Buchan (Manchester United), McQueen (Leeds), Gemmill (Derby, captain), Masson (QPR), Rioch (Derby), Dalglish (Celtic), Jordan (Leeds), Gray (Aston Villa). Substitutions: Burns (Birmingham) for Dalglish (56 minutes), Hartford (Manchester City) for Masson (68). Sent off: Gray (43 minutes). Referee: A. Michelotti (Italy). Broadcast details: Live coverage on BBC1 *World Cup Football* 16.45-18.50 and STV and Grampian *Scotsport Special* 16.45-18.50.

17 November 1976 SCOTLAND 1 (Evans (own goal), 15 minutes) WALES 0 (World Cup Qualification Group 7) Hampden Park. Attendance: 63,233. SCOTLAND: Rough (Partick Thistle), McGrain (Celtic), Donachie (Manchester City), Blackley (Hibs), McQueen (Leeds), Gemmill (Derby, captain), Burns (Birmingham), Rioch (Derby), E Gray (Leeds), Dalglish (Celtic), Jordan (Leeds). Substitution: Hartford (Manchester City) for Rioch (67 minutes), Pettigrew (Motherwell) for Gray (84). WALES: Davies (Everton), Page (Birmingham), J. Jones (Liverpool), Phillips (Aston Villa), Evans (Crystal Palace), Griffiths (Wrexham), Yorath (Leeds, captain), Flynn (Burnley), Thomas (Wrexham), Toshack (Liverpool), James (Derby). Substitution: Curtis (Swansea) for James (74 minutes). Referee: F. Biwersi (West Germany). Broadcast details: Highlights featured during *World Cup Sportscene* BBC1 21.55-22.55 and *Scotsport Special* STV 22.30-23.00; *Scotsport Special* shown on Grampian 23.00-23.30.

27 April 1977 SCOTLAND 3 (Hellstrom (own goal), 30 minutes), Dalglish, 56, Craig 79) SWEDEN 1 (Wendt, 51 minutes) (Friendly) Hampden Park. Attendance: 22,659. SCOTLAND: Rough (Partick Thistle), McGrain (Celtic), Donachie (Manchester City), Forsyth (Rangers), Blackley (Hibs), Glavin (Celtic), Burns (Birmingham), Hartford (Manchester City) Johnston (West Bromwich), Dalglish (Celtic, captain), Pettigrew (Motherwell). Substitutions: Jardine (Rangers) for Glavin (58 minutes), Narey (Dundee United) for Blackley (76), Craig (Celtic) for Burns (76). SWEDEN: Hellstrom (Kaiserlautern), M Andersson (Malmo), B. Andersson (Bayern Munich), Nordqvist (IFK Gothenburg, captain), R. Andersson (Malmo), Larsson (Helmstads), Torstensson (Bayern Munich), Borjesson (IFK Sundsvall), Johansson (Halmstads), Wendt (Tennis Borussia Berlin), Sjoberg (Karlsruher). Substitutions: Borg (Eintracht Braunschweig) for Torstensson (55 minutes), Ljunberg (Malmo) for Borjesson (65), Nordin (IFK Gothenburg) for Johansson (71). Referee: J. Taylor (England). Broadcast details: Highlights during *Sportscene* BBC1 21.35-22.40; STV and Grampian no coverage.

28 May 1977 WALES 0 SCOTLAND 0 (Home International) Racecourse Ground. Attendance: 14,469. WALES: Davies (Everton), R. Thomas (Derby), J. Jones (Liverpool), Phillips (Aston Villa), Evans (Crystal Palace), Sayer (Cardiff), Mahoney (Stoke), Yorath (Coventry, captain), Flynn (Burnley), Deacy (PSV Eindhoven), James (Derby). Substitution: M. Thomas (Swansea) for James (67 minutes). SCOTLAND: Rough (Partick Thistle), McGrain (Celtic), Donachie (Manchester City), Forsyth (Rangers), McQueen (Leeds), Gemmill (Derby), Masson (QPR), Rioch (Everton, captain), Hartford (Manchester City), Dalglish (Celtic), Parlane (Rangers). Substitutions: Johnston (West Bromwich) for Rioch (65 minutes), Burns (Birmingham) for Parlane (74). Referee: M. Moffatt (Northern Ireland). Broadcast details: Highlights during *International Match of the Day* BBC1 22.25-23.50 plus Northern Ireland v England; STV and Grampian no coverage.. Note: some ITV regions broadcast *Sportsworld 77* the following afternoon which included highlights of the match.

1 June 1977 SCOTLAND 3 (Dalglish, 37 and 79 minutes, McQueen, 61) NORTHERN IRELAND 0 (Home International) Hampden Park. Attendance: 44,699. SCOTLAND: Rough (Partick Thistle), McGrain (Celtic), Donachie (Manchester City), Forsyth (Rangers), McQueen (Leeds), Masson (QPR), Rioch (Everton, captain), Hartford (Manchester City), Johnston (West Bromwich), Dalglish (Celtic), Jordan (Leeds). Substitutions: Macari

(Manchester United) for Jordan (69 minutes), Gemmill (Derby) for Johnston (86). NORTHERN IRELAND: Jennings (Tottenham), Nicholl (Manchester United), Rice (Arsenal), Jackson (Manchester United), Hunter (Ipswich, captain), Hamilton (Everton), McCreery (Manchester United), McGrath (Manchester United), McIlroy (Manchester United), O'Neill (Nottingham Forest), Anderson (Swindon). Substitution: Spence (Blackpool) for Anderson (56 minutes). Referee: W. J. Gow (Swansea). Broadcast details: BBC no coverage; Highlights featured on all ITV regions during *Home International Championship* 22.30-23.25.

4 June 1977 ENGLAND 1 (Channon (penalty), 87 minutes), SCOTLAND 2 (McQueen, 43 minutes, Dalglish, 61) (Home International) Wembley Stadium. Attendance: 98,103. ENGLAND: Clemence (Liverpool), Neal (Liverpool), Mills (Ipswich), Hughes (Liverpool, captain), Watson (Manchester City), Greenhoff (Manchester United), Kennedy (Liverpool), Talbot (Ipswich), Channon (Southampton), Francis (Birmingham), Pearson (Manchester United). Substitutions: Cherry (Leeds) for Greenhoff (57 minutes), Tueart (Manchester City) for Kennedy (67). SCOTLAND: Rough (Partick Thistle), McGrain (Celtic), Donachie (Manchester City), Forsyth (Rangers), McQueen (Leeds), Masson (QPR), Rioch (Everton, captain), Hartford (Manchester City), Johnston (West Bromwich), Dalglish (Celtic), Jordan (Leeds). Substitutions: Macari (Manchester United) for Jordan (43 minutes), Gemmill (Derby) for Masson (83). Referee: K. Palotai (Hungary). Broadcast details: Live coverage during *Grandstand* BBC1 12.45-17.05 and *World of Sport* ITV Network 12.30-17.05; Highlights featured during *International Match of the Day* BBC1 22.50-23.40.

15 June 1977 CHILE 2 (Crisoto, 49 and 72 minutes) SCOTLAND 4 (Dalglish, 19 minutes, Macari 30 and 57, Hartford, 37) (Friendly) National Stadium, Santiago. Attendance: 60,000. CHILE: Nef (Colo Colo), Machuca (Union Esponala), Escobar(Union Esponala), Figueroa (Palestino), Quintano (Cruz Azul), Quiroz (Union Esponala), Inostroza (Colo Colo), Soto (Union Esponala), Veliz (Union Esponala), Farias (Union Esponala), Pinto (Colo Colo). Substitutions: Crisoto (Colo Colo) for Soto (37 minutes), Moscoso (Universidad Catolica) for Veliz (79). SCOTLAND: Rough (Partick Thistle), McGrain (Celtic), Donachie (Manchester City), Buchan (Manchester United), Forsyth (Rangers), Masson (QPR), Rioch (Everton, captain), Hartford (Manchester City), Johnston (West Bromwich), Macari (Manchester United), Dalglish (Celtic). Substitutions: Stewart (Kilmarnock) for Rough (46 minutes), Gemmill (Derby) for Rioch (46), Jardine (Rangers) for Hartford (80). Referee: J. Silvagno (Chile). Broadcast details: No UK TV coverage.

18 June 1977 ARGENTINA 1 (Passarella (penalty), 81 minutes) SCOTLAND 1 Masson (penalty), 77 minutes) (Friendly) Boca Juniors Stadium, Buenos Ai4res. Attendance: 57,000. ARGENTINA: Baley (Huracan), Pernia (Boca Juniors), Killer (Racing Club), Passarella (River Plate), Carrascosa (Huracan), Ardiles (Huracan), Gallego (Newells Old Boys), Larrosa (Independiente), Gonzalez (River Plate), Luque (River Plate), Houseman (Huracan). Substitutions: Tarantini (Boca Juniors) for Gonzales (59 minutes), Trossero (Union de Santa Fe) for Larrosa (70). Sent off: Pernia (56 minutes). SCOTLAND: Rough (Partick Thistle), McGrain (Celtic), Donachie (Manchester City), Buchan (Manchester United, captain), Forsyth (Rangers), Masson (QPR), Gemmill (Derby), Hartford (Manchester City), Johnston (West Bromwich), Macari (Manchester United), Dalglish (Celtic). Sent off: Johnston (56 minutes). Referee: R. A. Filho (Brazil). Broadcast details: Live coverage on BBC1 *International Football* 18.50-20.55 (black and white); STV no coverage. Note: planned highlights scheduled for 22.30-23.00 for STV and Grampian cancelled due to financial dispute.

Note: From this point on all televised matches were transmitted in colour.

23 June 1977 BRAZIL 2 (Zico, 70 minutes, Cerezo, 75) SCOTLAND 0 (Friendly) Maracana Stadium, Rio de Janeiro. Attendance: 60,763. BRAZIL: Leao (Palmeiras), Ze Maria (Corinthians), Marinho (Fluminense), Pereira (Atletico Madrid), Edinho (Fluminense), Isidoro (Atletico Mineiro), Cerezo (Atletico Mineiro), Rivelino (Fluminense), Paulo

Cesar (Fluminense), Gil (Fluminense), Reinaldo (Atletico Mineiro). Substitution: Zico (Flamengo) for Gil (46 minutes). SCOTLAND: Rough (Partick Thistle), McGrain (Celtic), Donachie (Manchester City), Buchan (Manchester United), Forsyth (Rangers), Masson (QPR), Rioch (Everton, captain), Gemmill (Derby), Hartford (Manchester City), Johnston (West Bromwich), Dalglish (Celtic). Substitution: Jardine (Rangers) for Johnston (61 minutes). Referee: O. Scolfaro (Brazil). Broadcast details: Live coverage on STV and Grampian *International Football* 12.45-03.15; Highlights on BBC1 *Sportscene Special* 19.30–20.30.

7 September 1977 EAST GERMANY 1 (Schade, 59 minutes) SCOTLAND 0 (Friendly) World Youth Stadium, East Berlin. Attendance: 50,000. EAST GERMANY: Croy (Sachsenring Zwickau), Dorner (Dynamo Dresden), Kische (Hansa Rostock), Weise (Carl Zeiss Jena), Weber (Dynamo Dresden), Hafner (Dynamo Dresden), Schade (Dynamo Dresden), Lindemann (Carl Zeiss Jena), Heidler (Dynamo Dresden), Sparwasser (FC Magdeburg), Streich (FC Magdeburg). Substitutions: Kotte (Dynamo Dresden) for Sparwasser (46 minutes), Hoffman (FC Magdeburg) for Streich (46). Missed penalty: Dorner (74 minutes). SCOTLAND: Stewart (Leeds), McGrain (Celtic), Donachie (Manchester City), Buchan (Manchester United), McQueen (Leeds), Masson (QPR, captain), Hartford (Manchester City), Macari (Manchester United), Johnston (West Bromwich), Dalglish (Liverpool), Jordan (Leeds). Substitution: Graham (Leeds) for Johnston (59 minutes), Gemmill (Derby) for Hartford (65). Referee: M. Horbas (Czechoslovakia). Broadcast details: No UK TV coverage; STV had an agreement to show highlights but a dispute between the SFA and the broadcasters cancelled the coverage.

21 September 1977 SCOTLAND 3 (Jordan, 19 minutes, Hartford, 35, Dalglish, 54) CZECHOSLOVAKIA 1 (Gajdusek, 80 minutes) (World Cup Qualification Group 7) Hampden Park. Attendance: 83,675. SCOTLAND: Rough (Partick Thistle), Jardine (Rangers), McGrain (Celtic), Forsyth (Rangers), McQueen (Leeds), Masson (QPR), Rioch (Everton, captain), Hartford (Manchester City), Johnston (West Bromwich), Dalglish (Liverpool), Jordan (Leeds). CZECHOSLOVAKIA: Michalik (OKD Ostrava), Paurik (Slavia Prague), Capkovic (Dukla Prague), Dvorak (Zbrojovko Brno), Gogh (Slovan Bratislava), Dobias (Bohemians Prague), Pollak (Dukla Bystrica, captain), Moder (Lokomotiv Kosice), Gajdusek (Dukla Prague), Masny (Slovan Bratislava), Nehoda (Dukla Prague). Substitutions: Knapp (OKD Ostrava) for Moder (46 minutes), Gallis (Slovan Bratislava) for Dobias (69). Referee: F. Rion (Belgium). Broadcast details: Live coverage on STV and Grampian in *Scotsport World Cup Special* 19.50-22.00; BBC no coverage.

12 October 1977 WALES 0 SCOTLAND 2 (Masson (penalty), 79 minutes, Dalglish, 87) (World Cup Qualification Group 7) Anfield, Liverpool. Attendance: 50,800. WALES: Davies (Wrexham), R. Thomas (Derby), J. Jones (Liverpool), Phillips (Aston Villa), D. Jones (Norwich), Sayer (Cardiff), Mahoney (Middlesbrough), Yorath (Coventry, captain), Flynn (Burnley), M. Thomas (Wrexham), Toshack (Liverpool). Substitution: Deacy (PSV Eindhoven) for Sayer (75 minutes). SCOTLAND: Rough (Partick Thistle), Jardine (Rangers), Donachie (Manchester City), Forsyth (Rangers), McQueen (Leeds), Masson (QPR, captain), Hartford (Manchester City), Macari (Manchester United), Johnston (West Bromwich), Dalglish (Liverpool), Jordan (Leeds). Substitution: Buchan (Manchester United) for Jardine (57 minutes). Referee: R. Wurtz (France). Broadcast details: Live coverage on BBC1 *World Cup Sportscene* 19.25-21.15; Highlights STV *Scotsport Special* 22.30-23.00; Grampian no coverage.

22 February 1978 SCOTLAND 2 (Gemmill (penalty), 41 minutes, Wallace, 85) BULGARIA 1 (Mladenov, 8 minutes) (Friendly) Hampden Park. Attendance: 59,524. SCOTLAND: Blyth (Coventry), Kennedy (Aberdeen), Donachie (Manchester City), Miller (Aberdeen), McQueen (Manchester United), Gemmill (Nottingham Forest, captain), Souness (Liverpool), Hartford (Manchester City), Macari (Manchester United), Dalglish (Liverpool), Jordan (Manchester United). Substitutions: Wallace (Coventry) for Dalglish (65 minutes), Johnstone (Rangers) for Jordan (65). BULGARIA: Staikov (Levski Sofia),

Appendix

Nikolov (Levski Sofia), Enchev (Levski Sofia), Bonev (Lokomotiv Sofia), Iliev (Slavia Sofia), Kasherov (PFC Beroe), Ivanov (Trakia Plovdiv), Slavkov (Trakia Plovdiv), Zdravkov (Lokomotiv Sofia), Jeliazkov (Slavia Sofia, captain), Mladenov (Beroe Stara Zagora). Substitution: Tishanski (Levski Sofia) for Slakov (68 minutes). Referee: P. Partridge (England). Broadcast details: Highlights during *Sportscene* BBC1 21.55-23.10 plus boxing; No STV or Grampian coverage.

13 May 1978 NORTHERN IRELAND 1 (O'Neill, 26 minutes) SCOTLAND 1 (Johnstone, 36 minutes) (Home International) Hampden Park. Attendance: 64,433. NORTHERN IRELAND: Platt (Middlesbrough), J Nicholl (Manchester United), Scott (York), B Hamilton (Millwall), C Nicholl (Southampton), McCreery (Manchester United), McIlroy (Manchester United), O'Neill (Nottingham Forest), McGrath (Manchester United), Anderson (Peterborough), Armstrong (Tottenham). Substitutions: W. Hamilton (QPR) for McGrath (63 minutes), Cochrane (Burnley) for Anderson (77). SCOTLAND: Rough (Partick Thistle), Jardine (Rangers), Buchan (Manchester United), Forsyth (Rangers), McQueen (Leeds), Masson (QPR) Rioch (Derby, captain), Gemmill (Nottingham Forest), Robertson (Nottingham Forest), Jordan (Manchester United), Johnstone (Rangers). Substitutions: Burns (Nottingham Forest) for Buchan (37 minutes), Dalglish (Liverpool) for Jordan (46). Referee: W. J. Gow (Wales). Broadcast details: Highlights during *International Sportscene* BBC1 22.20-23.50 plus Wales v England. No STV or Grampian coverage.

17 May 1978 SCOTLAND 1 (Johnstone, 12 minutes), WALES 1 (Donachie (own goal), 89 minutes) (Home International) Hampden Park. Attendance: 70,241. SCOTLAND: Blyth (Coventry), Kennedy (Aberdeen), Donachie (Manchester City), Burns (Nottingham Forest), McQueen (Leeds), Gemmill (Nottingham Forest, captain), Souness (Liverpool), Hartford (Manchester City), Johnston (West Bromwich), Dalglish (Liverpool), Johnstone (Rangers). Substitutions: Forsyth (Rangers) for McQueen (32 minutes), Robertson (Nottingham Forest) for Johnston (85). WALES: Davies (Wrexham), Page (Birmingham), Jones (Liverpool), Phillips (Aston Villa), Roberts (Hull), Harris (Leeds), Mahoney (Middlesbrough), Yorath (Coventry, captain), Flynn (Burnley), Dwyer (Cardiff), Curtis (Swansea). Substitution: Deacy (PSV Eindhoven) for Page (76 minutes). Missed penalty: Flynn (86 minutes). Referee: M. Wright (Northern Ireland). Broadcast details: Highlights during *Home International Football* throughout the ITV Network 22.45-23.45; No BBC coverage.

20 May 1978 SCOTLAND 0 ENGLAND 1 (Coppell, 83 minutes) (Home International) Hampden Park. Attendance: 88,319. SCOTLAND: Rough (Partick Thistle), Kennedy (Aberdeen), Donachie (Manchester City), Forsyth (Rangers), Burns (Nottingham Forest), Masson (Derby), Rioch (Derby, captain), Hartford (Manchester City), Johnston (West Bromwich), Dalglish (Liverpool), Jordan (Manchester United). Substitutions: Souness (Liverpool) for Rioch (74 minutes), Gemmill (Nottingham Forest) for Masson (74). ENGLAND: Clemence (Liverpool), Neal (Liverpool), Mills (Ipswich), Hughes (Liverpool, captain), Watson (Manchester City) , Coppell (Manchester United), Currie (Leeds), Wilkins (Chelsea), Barnes (Manchester City), Mariner (Ipswich), Francis (Birmingham). Substitutions: Greenhoff (Manchester United) for Hughes (73), Brooking (West Ham) for Mariner (76). Referee: G. Konrath (France). Broadcast details: Live coverage during *Grandstand* BBC1 12.30-17.30 and *World of Sport* ITV Network 12.00-17.05; Highlights during *International Sportscene* BBC1 22.15-23.15.

3 June 1978 PERU 3 (Cueto, 43 minutes, Cubillas, 72 and 75) SCOTLAND 1 (Jordan 15 minutes) (World Cup finals Group 4) Chateau Carreras Stadium, Cordoba. Attendance: 37,792. SCOTLAND: Rough (Partick Thistle), Kennedy (Aberdeen), Buchan (Manchester United), Forsyth (Rangers), Burns (Nottingham Forest), Masson (Derby), Rioch (Derby, captain), Hartford (Manchester City), Johnston (West Bromwich), Dalglish (Liverpool), Jordan (Manchester United). Substitutions: Macari (Manchester United) for Rioch (70 minutes), Gemmill (Nottingham Forest) for Masson (70). Missed penalty: Masson (63 minutes). PERU: Quiroga (Sporting Cristal), Duarte (Alianza Lima), Manzo (Deportivo

Municipal), Chumpitaz (Sporting Cristal, captain), Diaz (Sporting Cristal), Velazquez (Alianza Lima), Munante (UNAM), Cueto (Alianza Lima), Cubillas (Alianza Lima), Oblitas (Sporting Cristal), La Rosa (Alianza Lima). Substitutions: Sotil (Alianza Lima) for La Rosa (63 minutes), Rojas (Sporting Cristal) for Cueto (83). Referee: U. Eriksson (Sweden). Broadcast details: Live coverage during *World Cup Grandstand* BBC1 20.20-23.00 and *World Cup '78* ITV Network 20.15-23.00; Highlights included the following day 4 June in *World Cup '78* ITV Network 14.15-15.15.

7 June 1978 IRAN 1 (Danaifar, 77 minutes) SCOTLAND 1 (Eskandarian (own goal), 43 minutes) (World Cup finals Group 4) Chateau Carreras Stadium, Cordoba. Attendance: 7,938. SCOTLAND: Rough (Partick Thistle), Jardine (Rangers), Donachie (Manchester City), Buchan (Manchester United), Burns (Nottingham Forest), Hartford (Manchester City), Gemmill (Nottingham Forest, captain), Dalglish (Liverpool), Jordan (Manchester United), Macari (Manchester United), Robertson (Nottingham Forest),. Substitutions: Forsyth (Rangers) for Buchan (57 minutes), Harper (Aberdeen) for Dalglish (73). IRAN: Hejazi (Shahbaz), Nazari (Tadj), Eskandarian (Tadj), Kazerani (Pas), Danaifar (Tadj), Parvin (Persepolis, captain), Ghassempour (Shahbaz), Sadeghi (Pas), Djahani (Malavan), Faraki (Pas), Abdollahi (Shahbaz). Substitutions: Rowshan (Tadj) for Faraki (83 minutes), Nayebagha (Homa) for Danaifar. Referee: Y. N'Diaye (Senegal). Broadcast details: Live coverage during *World Cup Grandstand* BBC1 20.20-23.05 and *World Cup '78* ITV Network 20.15-23.00.

11 June 1978 HOLLAND 2 (Rensenbrink (penalty) 34 minutes, Rep, 71 minutes) SCOTLAND 3 (Dalglish, 44 minutes, Gemmill (penalty), 46 and 68) (World Cup finals Group 4) San Martin Stadium, Mendoza. Attendance: 35,130. HOLLAND: Jongbloed (Roda Kerkrade), Suurbier (Shalke 04), Rijsbergen (Feyenoord), Poortvliet (PSV Eindhoven), Krol (Ajax, captain), Jansen (Feyenoord), Neeskens (Barcelona), R. Van De Kerkhof (PSV Eindhoven), Rensenbrink (Anderlecht), W. Van De Kerkhof (PSV Eindhoven), Rep (SC Bastia). Substitutions: Boskamp (Racing Molanbeek) for Neeskens (10 minutes), Wildschut (FC Twente) for Rijsbergen (44). SCOTLAND: Rough (Partick Thistle), Kennedy (Aberdeen), Donachie (Manchester City), Buchan (Manchester United), Forsyth (Rangers), Gemmill (Nottingham Forest), Rioch (Derby, captain), Souness (Liverpool), Hartford (Manchester City), Dalglish (Liverpool), Jordan (Manchester United). Referee: E. Linemayr (Austria). Broadcast details: Live coverage during *World Cup Grandstand* BBC1 20.15-23.00 and *World Cup '78* ITV Network 20.15-23.15.

20 September 1978 AUSTRIA 3 (Pezzey, 27 minutes, Schachner, 48, Kreuz, 64) SCOTLAND 2 (McQueen, 65 minutes, Gray, 77) (European Championship Qualification Group 2) Prater Stadium, Vienna. Attendance: 62,281. AUSTRIA: Fuchsbichler (Voest Linz), Sara (Austria Memphis), Obermayer (Austria Memphis), Strasser (Admira Wacker), Pezzey (Eintracht Frankfurt), Weber (Rapid Vienna), Jara (Duisburg), Prohaska (Austria Memphis), Schachner (Austria Memphis), Kreuz (Voest Linz), Krankl (Barcelona). Substitution: Oberacher (Wacker Innsbruck) for Prohaska (87 minutes). SCOTLAND: Rough (Partick Thistle), Kennedy (Aberdeen), Donachie (Manchester City), Buchan (Manchester United), McQueen (Manchester United), Gemmill (Nottingham Forest, captain), Souness (Liverpool), Hartford (Manchester City), Dalglish (Liverpool), Jordan (Manchester United), Gray (Aston Villa). Substitution: Graham (Leeds) for Jordan (61 minutes). Referee: A. Michelotti (Italy). Broadcast details: Live coverage during *European Sportscene* BBC1 18.45-21.00; STV and Grampian no coverage.

25 October 1978 SCOTLAND 3 (Dalglish, 30 and 82 minutes, Gemmill (penalty), 87) NORWAY 2 (Aas, 3 minutes, Okland, 64) (European Championship Qualification Group 2) Hampden Park. Attendance: 65,372. SCOTLAND: Stewart (Middlesbrough), Donachie (Manchester City), F. Gray (Leeds), Buchan (Manchester United), McQueen (Manchester United), Gemmill (Nottingham Forest, captain), Souness (Liverpool), Hartford (Manchester City), Graham (Leeds), Dalglish (Liverpool), A. Gray (Aston

Villa). NORWAY: Jacobsen (Bryne), Pedersen (Start), Birkelund (Lillestrom), Grondalen (Rosenborg), Aas (Moss), Kordahl (Lillestrom), Johansen (Skeid), Mathisen (Start), T. Jacobsen (Hamarkameratene), Okland (Bryne), Thoresen (FC Twente). Substitutions: Hansen (Rosenborg) for T. Jacobsen (37 minutes), Karlsen (Bran) for Pedersen (86). Referee: V. Christov (Czechoslovkia). Broadcast details: Highlights during *Midweek Sports Special* STV and Grampian 22.40-00.25 plus World Gymnastics Championships; BBC no coverage.

29 November 1978 PORTUGAL 1 (Alberto, 29 minutes) SCOTLAND 0 (European Championship Qualification Group 2) Stadium of Light, Lisbon. Attendance: 70,000. PORTUGAL: Bento (Benfica), Artur (Sporting), Coelho (Benfica), Alhinho (Benfica), Alberto (Benfica), Pietra (Benfica), Oliveira (Porto), Alves (Benfica), Costa (Porto), Nene (Benfica), Gomes (Porto). Substitutions: Sheu (Benfica) for Costa (46 minutes), Eurico (Benfica)for Oliveira (82). SCOTLAND: Rough (Partick Thistle), Kennedy (Aberdeen), Gray (Leeds), Narey (Dundee United), McQueen (Manchester United), Buchan (Manchester United), Gemmill (Nottingham Forest, captain), Hartford (Manchester City), Robertson (Nottingham Forest), Dalglish (Liverpool), Jordan (Manchester United). Substitutions: Donachie (Manchester City) for Gray (65 minutes), Wallace (Coventry) for Jordan (78). Referee: E. Dolflinger (Switzerland). Broadcast details: Live coverage during *Sportscene Special* on BBC1 21.25-23.15; No STV or Grampian coverage.

19 May 1979 WALES 3 (Toshack, 28, 35 and 75 minutes) SCOTLAND 0 (Home International) Ninian Park. Attendance: 20,371. WALES: Davies (Wrexham), Stevenson (Leeds), Jones (Wrexham), Phillips (Swansea), Dwyer (Cardiff), James (Swansea), Mahoney (Middlesbrough), Yorath (Coventry, captain), Flynn (Leeds), Curtis (Leeds), Toshack (Swansea). Substitution: Nicholas (Crystal Palace) for Yorath (89 minutes). SCOTLAND: Rough (Partick Thistle), Burley (Ipswich), Gray (Leeds), Hansen (Liverpool), Hegarty (Dundee United), Wark (Ipswich), Hartford (Manchester City), Souness (Liverpool), Graham (Leeds), Dalglish (Liverpool, captain), Wallace (Coventry). Substitution: Jordan (Manchester United) for Wallace (55 minutes). Referee: P. Partridge (England). Broadcast details: Highlights during *International Match of the Day* BBC1 22.00-23.10 plus Northern Ireland v England; STV and Grampian no coverage.

22 May 1979 SCOTLAND 1 (Graham, 76 minutes) NORTHERN IRELAND 0 (Home International) Hampden Park. Attendance: 28,524. SCOTLAND: Wood (Everton), Burley (Ipswich), Gray (Leeds), Hegarty (Dundee United), McQueen (Manchester United), Wark (Ipswich), Souness (Liverpool), Hartford (Manchester City), Graham (Leeds), Dalglish (Liverpool, captain), Jordan (Manchester United). Substitutions: Narey (Dundee United) for Wark (46 minutes), McGarvey (Liverpool) for Graham (89). NORTHERN IRELAND: Jennings (Arsenal), Rice (Arsenal), Nelson (Arsenal), J. Nicholl (Manchester United), Hunter (Ipswich), Moreland (Derby), Hamilton (Swindon, captain), McIlroy (Manchester United), Sloan (Manchester United), Spence (Blackpool), Armstrong (Tottenham). Substitutions: Scott (Aldershot) for Moreland (62 minutes), Caskey (Derby) for Spence (77). Referee: C. Thomas (Wales). Broadcast details: No TV coverage. ITV Network contracted to show exclusive highlights 22.30-23.40 but match not recorded due to industrial action by STV staff.

26 May 1979 ENGLAND 3 (Barnes, 44 minutes, Coppell, 63, Keegan, 70) SCOTLAND 1 (Wark, 20 minutes) (Home International) Wembley Stadium. Attendance: 100,000. ENGLAND: Clemence (Liverpool), Neal (Liverpool), Mills (Ipswich), Thompson (Liverpool), Watson (Manchester City), Coppell (Manchester United), Wilkins (Chelsea), Brooking (West Ham), Barnes (Manchester City), Keegan (Hamburg), Latchford (Everton). SCOTLAND: Wood (Everton), Burley (Ipswich), Gray (Leeds), Hegarty (Dundee United), McQueen (Manchester United), Wark (Ipswich), Souness (Liverpool), Hartford (Manchester City), Graham (Leeds), Dalglish (Liverpool, captain), Jordan (Manchester United). Referee: A. Garrido (Portugal). Broadcast details: Live coverage

during *Grandstand* BBC1 12.30-17.20 and *World of Sport* ITV Network 12.30-17.05; Highlights featured in *Sportscene* BBC1 22.15-23.15.

2 June 1979 SCOTLAND 1 (Graham, 85 minutes) ARGENTINA 3 (Luque, 33 and 60 minutes, Maradona, 70) (Friendly) Hampden Park. Attendance: 61,918. SCOTLAND: Rough (Partick Thistle), Burley (Ipswich), Munro (St Mirren), Hansen (Liverpool), Hegarty (Dundee United), Narey (Dundee United), Wark (Ipswich), Hartford (Manchester City), Graham (Leeds), Dalglish (Liverpool, captain), McGarvey (Liverpool). Substitutions: Wood (Everton) for Rough (46 minutes), Gray (Leeds) for Hartford (70 minutes). ARGENTINA: Fillol (Quilmes), Olguin (San Lorenzo), Tarantini (Talleres de Cordoba), Villaverde (Independiente), Passarella (River Plate), Barbas (US Lecce), Gallego (Newells Old Boys), Maradona (Argentinos Juniors), Valencia (Talleres de Cordoba), Houseman (Huracan), Luque (River Plate). Substitutions: Trossero (Independiente) for Villaverde (21 minutes), Outes (Independiente) for Houseman (56). Referee: P. Partridge (England). Broadcast details: No TV coverage.

7 June 1979 NORWAY 0 SCOTLAND 4 (Jordan, 32 minutes, Dalglish, 39, Robertson, 43, McQueen, 55) (European Championship Qualification Group 2) Ulleval Stadium, Oslo. Attendance: 17,269. NORWAY: Jacobsen (Bryne), Pedersen (Start), Karlsen (Brann), Grondalen (Rosenborg), Aas (Moss), Kordahl (Lillestrom), Albertsen (Den Haag), Thunberg (Start), Mathisen (Start), Okland (Bryne), Thoresen (FC Twente). Substitutions: Hansen (Rosenborg) for Pedersen (67 minutes), Svendsen (Viking Stavanger) for Thunberg (75). SCOTLAND: Rough (Partick Thistle), Burley (Ipswich), Munro (St Mirren), Burns (Nottingham Forest), McQueen (Manchester United), Graham (Leeds), Gemmill (Nottingham Forest, captain), Hartford (Manchester City), Robertson (Nottingham Forest), Dalglish (Liverpool), Jordan (Manchester United). Substitutions: Hegarty (Dundee United) for Burley (46 minutes), Wark (Ipswich) for Hegarty (70). Referee: I. Nielsen (Denmark). Broadcast details: Live coverage on STV and Grampian *Norway v Scotland* 18.55-20.45; No BBC coverage.

12 September 1979 SCOTLAND 1 (Hartford, 4 minutes) PERU 1 (Leguia, 85 minutes) (Friendly) Hampden Park. Attendance: 41,035. SCOTLAND: Rough (Partick Thistle), Jardine (Rangers, captain), Munro (St Mirren), Burns (Nottingham Forest), McQueen (Manchester United), Cooper (Rangers), Wark (Ipswich), Souness (Liverpool), Hartford (Everton), Robertson (Nottingham Forest), Dalglish (Liverpool). Substitutions: Aitken (Celtic) for Wark (71 minutes), Graham (Leeds) for Cooper (71). Missed penalty: Wark (35 minutes). PERU: Acasuzo (Universitario), Gastulo (Universitario), Olaechea (Alianza Lima), Chumpitaz (Sporting Cristal, captain), Diaz (Sporting Cristal), Mosquera (Sporting Cristal), Velasquez (Independiente Medellín), Cueto (Atletico Nacional), Leguia (Universitario), Labarthe (Palestino), La Rosa (Atletico Nacional). Substitution: Ravello (Alianza Lima) for Labarthe (46 minutes). Referee: G. Courtney (England). Broadcast details: No TV coverage. Entire ITV network on strike during this period otherwise STV may have shown recorded highlights.

17 October 1979 SCOTLAND 1 (Gemmill, 75 minutes) AUSTRIA 1 (Krankl, 40 minutes) (European Championship Qualification Group 2) Hampden Park. Attendance: 67,700. SCOTLAND: Rough (Partick Thistle), Jardine (Rangers), Munro (St Mirren), Burns (Nottingham Forest), McQueen (Manchester United), Graham (Leeds), Wark (Ipswich), Souness (Liverpool), Gemmill (Nottingham Forest, captain), Robertson (Nottingham Forest), Dalglish (Liverpool). Substitution: Cooper (Rangers) for Graham (61 minutes). AUSTRIA: Koncilia (Anderlecht), Sara (Austria Vienna), Mirnegg (MSV Duisburg), Hattenberger (Stuttgart), Pezzey (Eintracht Frankfurt), Weber (Rapid Vienna), Jara (MSV Duisburg), Prohaska (Austria Vienna), Schachner (Austria Vienna), Kreuz (Voest Linz), Krankl (Barcelona). Substitutions: Steinkogler (Grazer AK) for Schachner (80 minutes), Hintermaier (Nuremberg) for Krankl (89). Referee: K. Palotai (Hungary). Broadcast details: Highlights during *International Sportscene* BBC1 22.10-23.00 No STV or Grampian coverage.

21 November 1979 BELGIUM 2 (Van der Elst, 7 minutes, Voordeckers, 46) SCOTLAND 0 (European Championship Qualification Group 2) Heysel Stadium, Brussels. Attendance: 14,289. BELGIUM: Custers (Antwerp), Gerets (Standard Liege), Millecamps (SV Waregem), Meeuws (Bruges), Renquin (Standard Liege), Cools (Beerschot VAC, captain), Van Moer (Beringen), Vandereycken (Bruges), Van der Elst (Anderlecht), Ceulemans (Bruges), Voordeckers (Standard Liege). Substitution: Verheyen (Lokeren) for Van Moer (66 minutes). SCOTLAND: Rough (Partick Thistle), Jardine (Rangers, captain), Munro (St Mirren), Hansen (Liverpool), Miller (Aberdeen), Wark (Ipswich), Souness (Liverpool), Hartford (Everton), Robertson (Nottingham Forest), Dalglish (Liverpool), Jordan (Manchester United). Substitutions: Gray (Nottingham Forest) for Munro, 61 minutes, Provan (Celtic) for Jordan, (61 minutes). Referee: E. Zade (USSR). Broadcast details: Live coverage during *International Sportscene* BBC1 18.55-21.00. STV and Grampian no coverage.

19 December 1979 SCOTLAND 1 (Robertson, 55 minutes) BELGIUM 3 (Vanderbergh, 18 minutes, Van der Elst, 23 and 29) (European Championship Qualification Group 2) Hampden Park. Attendance: 25,389. SCOTLAND: Rough (Partick Thistle), Jardine (Rangers, captain), McGrain (Celtic), Burns (Nottingham Forest), McQueen (Manchester United), Bannon (Dundee United), Aitken (Celtic), Wark (Ipswich), Robertson (Nottingham Forest), Dalglish (Liverpool), Johnstone (Rangers). Substitution: Provan (Celtic) for Bannon, (46 minutes). BELGIUM: Custers (Antwerp), Gerets (Standard Liege), Millecamps (SV Waregem), Meeuws (Bruges), Martens (RWD Molenbeek), Cools (Beerschot VAC, captain), Van Moer (Beringen), Vandereycken (Bruges), Van der Elst (Anderlecht), Ceulemans (Bruges), Vandenbergh (Lierse SV). Substitutions: Plessers (Standard Liege) for Van Moer (49 minutes), Dardenne (Lokeren) for Vandenbergh (73). Referee: H. Aldinger (West Germany). Broadcast details: Highlights during *Scotsport* STV 23.00-00.00; no coverage on Grampian or BBC.

Scottish League International Matches Played 1970–79

All details complete except accurate substitution times for one player each in 19/04/76 and 01/11/78 fixtures; @ indicates approximate time.

Note: For Inter League matches involving Northern Ireland during the period the team are referred to as the Irish League whilst the League of Ireland are the representative side from the Irish Republic.

18 March 1970 FOOTBALL LEAGUE 3 (Astle, 16 and 72 minutes, Rogers, 24) SCOTTISH LEAGUE 2 (Cormack, 57 minutes, Graham, 76) Highfield Road, Coventry. Attendance: 26,693. FOOTBALL LEAGUE: Stepney (Manchester United), Smith (Sheffield Wednesday), Hughes (Liverpool), Newton, (Nottingham Forest), McFarland (Derby), Todd (Sunderland), Coates (Burnley), Kidd (Manchester United), Astle (West Bromwich Albion), Harvey (Everton), Rogers (Swindon). Substitutions: Glazier (Coventry) for Stepney (46 minutes) Peters (West Ham) for Kidd (50 minutes). SCOTTISH LEAGUE: McCrae (Motherwell), Callaghan (Dunfermline), Dickson (Kilmarnock), McKinnon (Rangers), Smith (Rangers), Stanton (Hibs), Cormack (Hibs), Greig (Rangers, captain), McLean (Kilmarnock), Hall (St Johnstone), Johnston (Rangers). Substitutions: Graham (Hibs) for Hall (58 minutes). Referee: G. Hill (Leicester). Broadcast details: No TV coverage.

2 September 1970 SCOTTISH LEAGUE 1 LEAGUE OF IRELAND 0 (Connelly, 63 minutes) Celtic Park. Attendance: 7,654. SCOTTISH LEAGUE: Cruickshank (Hearts), Hay (Celtic), Dickson (Kilmarnock), Stanton (Hibs, captain), McKinnon (Rangers), Henry (Dundee United), Johnstone (Celtic), Connelly (Celtic), Hood (Celtic), Graham (Hibs), Duncan (Hibs). Substitutions: McLean (Kilmarnock) for Duncan (78 minutes). LEAGUE OF IRELAND: Thomas (Waterford), Bryan (Waterford), Brennan (Waterford, captain), O'Mahoney (Limerick), Finucane (Limerick), Dunning (Shelbourne), McGeoch (Waterford), Lawlor (Shamrock Rovers), Hale (Waterford), Minnock (Athlone), Mathews (Waterford). Referee: J. Callaghan (Glasgow). Broadcast details: No TV coverage.

17 March 1971 SCOTTISH LEAGUE 0 FOOTBALL LEAGUE 1 (Coates, 6 minutes) Hampden Park. Attendance: 17,657. SCOTTISH LEAGUE: Clark (Aberdeen), Hay (Celtic), Dickson (Kilmarnock), Forsyth (Motherwell), McKinnon (Rangers, captain), Brogan (Celtic), McLean (Kilmarnock), Callaghan (Celtic), Robb (Aberdeen), Jarvie (Airdrie), Ford (Hearts),. Substitution: Connelly (Celtic) for Forsyth (64 minutes). FOOTBALL LEAGUE: Jackson (Crystal Palace), Reaney (Leeds), Parkin (Wolves), Hollins (Chelsea), McFarland (Derby), Bobby Moore (West Ham, captain), Coates (Burnley), Brown (West Bromwich Albion), Hurst (West Ham), O'Neill (Southampton), Ian Moore (Nottingham Forest). Referee: W. Anderson (East Kilbride). Broadcast details: STV featured highlights during *Scotsport Special* 22.30–23.15; No Grampian coverage; No BBC coverage.

15 March 1972 FOOTBALL LEAGUE 3 (Currie 14 and 55 minutes, Doyle, 24) SCOTTISH LEAGUE 2 (McQuade, 52 minutes, Stein, 71) Ayresome Park, Middlesbrough. Attendance: 19,996. FOOTBALL LEAGUE: Clemence (Liverpool), Lawler (Liverpool), Nish (Leicester), Doyle (Manchester City), Blockley (Coventry), Moore (West Ham, captain), Hughes (Liverpool), Hurst (West Ham), MacDonald (Newcastle), Currie (Sheffield United), Wagstaffe (Wolves). SCOTTISH LEAGUE: Hunter (Kilmarnock), Brownlie (Hibs), Forsyth (Partick Thistle), Jardine (Rangers, captain), Connelly (Celtic), Blackley (Hibs), McQuade (Partick Thistle), Phillip (Dundee), Stein (Rangers), Hay (Celtic), Ford (Hearts). Substitution: Graham (Aberdeen) for Jardine (60minutes). Referee: P. Partridge (Middlesbrough). Broadcast details: Highlights during *Sportsnight* BBC1 22.10–22.55; No STV or Grampian coverage.

27 March 1973 SCOTTISH LEAGUE 2 (J. Duncan, 38 and 44 minutes) FOOTBALL LEAGUE 2 (Channon, 19 and 78 minutes) Hampden Park. Attendance: 18,548. SCOTTISH LEAGUE: McCloy (Rangers), Jardine (Rangers), McGrain (Celtic), Connelly (Celtic), Johnstone (Rangers), Hay (Celtic), McLean (Rangers), Stanton (Hibs, captain), Parlane (Rangers), J. Duncan (Dundee), A. Duncan (Hibs). FOOTBALL LEAGUE: Shilton (Leicester), Mills (Ipswich), Nish (Derby), Kendall (Everton), McFarland (Derby), Moore (West Ham, captain), Weller (Leicester), Channon (Southampton), Worthington (Leicester), Richards (Wolves), Bell (Manchester City). Referee: A. MacKenzie (Larbert). Broadcast details: No TV coverage.

20 March 1974 FOOTBALL LEAGUE 5 (Bell, 12 minutes, Brown (own goal), 25, Tueart (penalty), 51, Brooking, 70, Bowles, 84) SCOTTISH LEAGUE 0 Maine Road, Manchester. Attendance: 11,471. FOOTBALL LEAGUE: Clemence (Liverpool), Storey (Arsenal), Nish (Derby), Dobson (Burnley), McFarland (Derby), Todd (Derby), Bowles (QPR), Bell (Manchester City, captain), Latchford (Everton), Brooking (West Ham), Tueart (Manchester City). Substitution: Hector (Derby) for Latchford (26 minutes). SCOTTISH LEAGUE: Stewart (Kilmarnock), Hermiston (Aberdeen), Wallace (Dunfermline), Copland (Dundee United), Fleming (Ayr), Miller (Motherwell), Brown (Hearts), Parlane (Rangers), Ford (Hearts), Robb (Aberdeen), Prentice (Hearts). Substitution: Johnstone (Rangers) for Robb (51 minutes). Referee: A. W. S. Jones (Ormskirk). Broadcast details: No TV coverage.

17 March 1976 SCOTTISH LEAGUE 0 FOOTBALL LEAGUE 1 (Cherry, 3 minutes) Hampden Park. Attendance: 8,874. SCOTTISH LEAGUE: Stewart (Kilmarnock), Rolland (Dundee United), Jackson (Rangers, captain), Forsyth (Rangers), Wark (Motherwell), Bremner (Hibs), Miller (Aberdeen), MacDonald (Rangers), McKean (Rangers), Craig (Partick Thistle), Duncan (Hibs). Substitutions: Dickson (Queen of the South) for Craig (12 minutes), Greig (Rangers) for Rolland (84 minutes). FOOTBALL LEAGUE: Shilton (Stoke), Cherry (Leeds), Mills (Ipswich), Doyle (Manchester City), McFarland (Derby, captain), Dodd (Stoke), Wilkins (Chelsea), Channon (Southampton), Greenhoff (Stoke), Currie (Sheffield United), Tueart (Manchester City). Referee: W. J. Mullan (Dalkeith). Broadcast details: No TV coverage.

19 April 1976 HIGHLAND LEAGUE 0 SCOTTISH LEAGUE 3 (Craig, 69 minutes, Barr, 84, Craig, 86) Borough Briggs, Elgin. Attendance: 2,188. HIGHLAND SELECT: Gray (Keith), Cochran (Nairn), Fraser (Inverness Thistle), Dalgarno (Keith), Nicol (Elgin), Seaton (Ross County), C. Duncan (Inverness Thistle), I. Duncan (Keith), Urquhart (Ross County), Hunter (Fraserburgh), MacKintosh (Inverness Caledonian). Substitutions: Cowie (Brora) for Urquhart (65 minutes), Black (Inverness Thistle) for Seaton (70). SCOTTISH LEAGUE: Stewart (Kilmarnock), Kennedy (Falkirk), Kellachan (Partick Thistle), D'Arcy (Montrose), Clark (East Fife), Shirra (Falkirk), Johnstone (Montrose), Smith (Kilmarnock), Craig (Partick Thistle), Cooper (Clydebank), McCulloch (Kilmarnock). Substitutions: Barr (Montrose) for McCulloch (unspecified time during second half), McNaughton (Queen's Park) for Smith (53). Referee: W. D. Reid (Aberdeen). Broadcast details: No TV coverage.

26 April 1978 ITALY B 1 (Pruzo, 60 minutes) SCOTTISH LEAGUE 1 (Somner, 64 minutes) Stadio Communale, Verona. Attendance: 10,000. ITALY B: Conti (Roma), Cucurrado (Juventus), Cabirini (Juventus), Oriali (Inter Milan), Belugoi (Bologna), Manfredonia (Lazio), Rossi (Laneossi Vicenza), Pecci (Torino), Pruzzo (Genoa), Pin (Napoli), Novellino (Perugia). Substitutions: Sala (Torino) for Oriali (46 minutes), Bordon (Sampdoria) for Conti (46 minutes). SCOTTISH LEAGUE: Stewart (Kilmarnock), Sinclair (Dumbarton), Whittaker (Partick Thistle), Stevens (Motherwell), Clarke (Kilmarnock), Fitzpatrick (St Mirren), McGarvey (St Mirren), Pettigrew (Motherwell), Somner (Partick Thistle), Cramond (Ayr), Provan (Kilmarnock). Substitution: MacLeod (Dumbarton) for Cramond (75 minutes). Referee: A. Brummeir (Austria). Broadcast details: No UK TV coverage. Note: TV highlights shown in Italy later same evening.

1 November 1978 SCOTTISH LEAGUE 1 (Pettigrew, 73 minutes) IRISH LEAGUE 1 (Armstrong, 20 minutes) Fir Park, Motherwell. Attendance: 4,427. SCOTTISH LEAGUE:

Rough (Partick Thistle), Narey (Dundee United), Burns (Celtic), Stevens (Motherwell), Hegarty (Dundee United), Thomson (Morton), Houston (Partick Thistle), Bannon (Hearts), Pettigrew (Motherwell), McAdam (Celtic), Marinello (Motherwell). Substitution: Redford (Dundee) for Marinello (@87 minutes) Somner (Partick Thistle) for McAdam (70 minutes). IRISH LEAGUE: Barclay (Linfield), Kennedy (Ards), Cromie (Ards), Walsh (Glentoran), Rafferty (Linfield), Cleary (Portadown), Sloan (Ballymena), Dornan (Linfield), Armstrong (Ards), Dickson (Coleraine), Murray (Linfield). Referee: I. M. D. Foote (Glasgow). Broadcast details: No TV coverage.

Scotland Under-23 Matches Played 1970–76

All details complete except six substitution times which are approximate and listed with @. Names of two visiting team substitutes were unnanounced in 10/01/72 fixture as detailed in that entry. Club for one Romanian player in 16/12/75 fixture unavailable.

14 January 1970 SCOTLAND 1 (O'Hare, 86 minutes) WALES 1 (Krzywicki, 11 minutes) Pittodrie. Attendance: 15,349. SCOTLAND: Stewart (Ayr), Clunie (Hearts), Wilson (West Bromwich), Blackley (Hibs, captain), Thomson (Hearts), Campbell (Charlton), Lorimer (Leeds), Carr (Coventry), O'Hare (Derby), Robb (Aberdeen), Hartford (West Bromwich). Substitutions: Harper (Aberdeen) for Hartford (64 minutes), Munro (Wolves) for Campbell (73). WALES: Lloyd (Southend), Pearson (Southport), Thomas (Swindon, captain), Davis (Wrexham), Morgan (Cardiff), Yorath (Leeds), Krzywicki (West Bromwich), Page (Birmingham), Price (Peterborough), Jones (Bristol Rovers), Hawkins (Shrewsbury). Referee: N. C. H. Burtenshaw (Great Yarmouth). Broadcast details: No TV coverage.

4 March 1970 ENGLAND 3 (Osgood 24 and 54 minutes, Kidd, 59) SCOTLAND 1 (Todd (own goal), 60) Roker Park, Sunderland (ABANDONED after 62 minutes due to snow). Attendance: 12,885. ENGLAND: Shilton (Leicester), Smith (Sheffield Wednesday), Parkin (Wolves), Todd (Sunderland), McFarland (Derby), Nish (Leicester), Hudson (Everton), Husband (Chelsea), Osgood (Chelsea), Kidd (Manchester City), Thomas (Burnley). Substitution: Royle (Manchester City) for Osgood (56 minutes). SCOTLAND: Hughes (Chelsea), Clunie (Hearts), Dickson (Kilmarnock), Blackley (Hibs, captain), Thomson (Hearts), Munro (Wolves), McLean (Kilmarnock), Connelly (Celtic), O'Hare (Derby), Gemmill (Preston), Johnston (Rangers). Substitution: Marinello (Arsenal) for Connelly (56 minutes). Referee: C. Thomas (Wales). Broadcast details: No TV coverage.

13 January 1971 WALES 1 (Price, 67 minutes) SCOTLAND 0 Vetch Field, Swansea. Attendance: 9,037. WALES: D. Davies (Everton), Roberts (Bristol Rovers), Derrett (Cardiff), Prince (Bristol Rovers), Davis (Wrexham), Thomas (Swansea), Hughes (Blackpool), Price (Peterborough), Phillips (Cardiff), Jones (Bristol Rovers), C. Davies (Charlton). Substitution: Screen (Swansea) for Derrett (88 minutes). SCOTLAND: MacRae (Motherwell), Hay (Celtic), Hermiston (Aberdeen), Kelly (Arsenal), Munro (Wolves), Buchan (Aberdeen, captain), Hartford (West Bromwich), Carr (Coventry), Harper (Aberdeen), Connolly (St Johnstone), Hutchison (Blackpool). Substitutions: Oliver (Hearts) for Hermiston (46 minutes), Jardine (Rangers) for Hay (53). Referee: D. W. Smith (England). Broadcast details: No TV coverage.

24 February 1971 SCOTLAND 2 (Kelly, 28 minutes, Robb, 36) ENGLAND 2 (Lloyd, 55 minutes and Currie, 80) Hampden Park. Attendance: 13,839. SCOTLAND: MacRae (Motherwell), Jardine (Rangers), Hay (Celtic), Blackley (Hibs, captain), Connelly (Celtic), Kelly (Arsenal), Young (Ayr), Forsyth (Motherwell), Robb (Aberdeen), Jarvie (Airdrie), Duncan (Hibs). Substitution: Hunter (Kilmarnock) for MacRae (20 minutes). Missed

Appearing centered: *Appendix*

penalty: Blackley (5 minutes). ENGLAND: Clemence (Liverpool), Parkin (Wolves), Robson (Derby), Todd (Derby, captain), Lloyd (Liverpool), Nish (Leicester), Piper (Portsmouth), Hudson (Chelsea), Hutchinson (Chelsea), Channon (Southampton), Currie (Sheffield United). Referee: M. Wright (Portadown). Broadcast details: BBC1 Highlights during *Sportsnight with Coleman* 21.20-22.45; STV Highlights during *Scotsport* 22.30-23.15; no coverage on Grampian.

10 January 1972 SCOTLAND UNDER-23s 1 (Donachie, 18 minutes) WEST GERMAN OLYMPIC XI 0 Hampden Park. Attendance: 5,903. SCOTLAND: Hewitt (Dundee), Hansen (Partick Thistle), Donachie (Manchester City), Kelly (Arsenal), Phillip (Dundee), Buchan (Aberdeen, captain), Brown (Leicester), Jardine (Rangers), Dalglish (Celtic), Steele (Dundee), Connolly (St Johnstone). Substitution: McQuade (Partick Thistle) for Steele (65 minutes). WEST GERMANY: Bradler (VFL Bochum), Baltes (Fortuna Dusseldorf), Bleidick (Borussia Monchengladbach), Mietz (Borrusia Dortmund), Haebermann (Eintracht Braunschweig), Bitz (Kaiserlautern), Kalb (Eintracht Frankfurt), Hoeness (Bayern Munich), Wunder (MSV Duisburg), Nickel (Eintracht Frankfurt), Stegmayer (Nuremberg). Substitutions: Unspecified replacements for Bitz (46 minutes), Stegmayer (77). Note: *Daily Express* match report records that both West German substitutes were "unnamed and unnumbered". Referee: T. Marshall (Glasgow). Broadcast details: No TV coverage.

19 January 1972 SCOTLAND UNDER-23s 5 (Wilson, 17 minutes and 84, Bone, 58, Young 64, Somner, 88) SCOTTISH PROFESSIONAL YOUTHS 2 (McLauchlan 18, Burns 70) Firhill, Glasgow. Attendance: 2,800. SCOTLAND: Rough (Partick Thistle), McEwan (Hibs), Forsyth (Partick Thistle), Glavin (Partick Thistle), Young (Aberdeen), McQueen (St Mirren), Wilson (Celtic), Macari (Celtic), Somner (Falkirk), Henry (Dundee United), Lambie (Dundee). Substitutions: Bone (Partick Thistle) for Macari (46 minutes), McDonald (Clydebank) for Rough (46 minutes). SCOTTISH PROFESSIONAL YOUTHS: Stewart (Kilmarnock), Fillipi (Ayr), Riddle (Bristol Rovers), McLaughlan (Celtic), Anderson (Morton), Cannon (Crystal Palace), Brody (Chelsea), McCartney (West Bromwich), Burns (Birmingham), Hamilton (Sunderland), McLauchlan (Preston). Substitutions: Britton (Chelsea) for McLauchlan (70 minutes). Referee: I. D. Foote (Glasgow). Broadcast details: STV Highlights during *Scotsport* 23.00-23.30; no coverage on BBC or Grampian.

26 January 1972 SCOTLAND 2 (Jardine, 61 minutes, McQuade, 83) WALES 0 Pittodrie. Attendance: 15,000. SCOTLAND: Hunter (Kilmarnock), Brownlie (Hibs), Donachie (Manchester City), Jardine (Rangers, captain), Young (Aberdeen), Buchan (Aberdeen), McGovern (Derby), Macari (Celtic), Bone (Partick Thistle), Dalglish (Celtic), Cropley (Hibs),. Substitutions: McQuade (Partick Thistle) for McGovern (77 minutes), Brown (Leicester) for Dalglish (84 minutes). WALES: Parton (Burnley), Roberts (Bristol Rovers), Collins (Portsmouth), Prince (Bristol Rovers), Aizlewood (Newport), Yorath (Leeds, captain), Phillips (Cardiff City), Gwyther (Swansea), Llewlyn (West Ham), O'Sullivan (Brighton), James (Burnley). Substitution: Davies (Charlton) for Phillips (@ 80 minutes). Referee: J. Lawther (Bangor). Broadcast details: Highlights during BBC1 *Sportsreel* 23.15–23.30 and STV *Scotsport* 23.10–23.40 plus Airdrie v Derby (Texaco Cup Final, first leg); no coverage on Grampian.

16 February 1972 ENGLAND 2 (Channon, 39 and 68 minutes) SCOTLAND 2 (Dalglish, 38 and 74 minutes) Baseball Ground, Derby. Attendance: 18,176. ENGLAND: Parkes (QPR), Mills (Ipswich), Robson (Derby), Hudson (Chelsea), Booth (Manchester City), Blockley (Coventry, captain), Thomas (Burnley), Channon (Southampton), MacDonald (Newcastle), Keegan (Liverpool), Currie (Sheffield United). SCOTLAND: Hunter (Kilmarnock), Brownley (Hibs), Donachie (Manchester City), Jardine (Rangers, captain), Connelly (Celtic), Buchan (Aberdeen), Carr (Coventry), Macari (Celtic), Dalglish (Celtic), Bone (Partick Thistle), Hartford (West Bromwich). Referee: T. H. C. Reynolds (Swansea). Broadcast details: BBC1 Highlights during *Sportsnight With Coleman* 21.20-22.45; No STV or Grampian coverage.

20 November 1972 SCOTLAND UNDER-23s 1 (Carruthers, 10 minutes) SCOTTISH PROFESSIONAL YOUTHS 2 (Finnieston, 50, Smith, 83) Easter Road, Edinburgh. Attendance: 1,076. SCOTLAND: McArthur (Hibs), Hayes (Morton), Ralston (Partick Thistle), Sullivan (Clyde), Anderson (Morton), Clarke (East Fife), Doyle (Ayr), Carruthers (Hearts), McAdam (Dumbarton), Honeyman (East Fife), Lynch (Hearts). Substitutions: Jim Brown (Hearts) for Honeyman (39 minutes), Stewart (Kilmarnock) for McArthur (46 minutes), Dave McNichol (Dunfermline) for Doyle (46), McGregor (Ayr) for Carruthers (46), Craig (Partick Thistle) for Ralston (46). PROFESSIONAL YOUTHS: Blyth (Coventry), McLachlan (St Mirren), Roberts (Shrewsbury), Anderson (Dundee), McDonald (Celtic), McLaughlin (Celtic), Calderwood (Birmingham), Smith (Kilmarnock), Mackie (Dunfermline), Ritchie (Celtic), Gray (Leeds). Substitutions: John Brown (Partick Thistle) for Blyth (46 minutes), Forsyth (Dundee United) for McDonald (46), Finnieston (Chelsea) for Mackie (46), Hotson (St Johnstone) for Gray (late second half), Willie McNichol (Rangers) for Ritchie (late second half). Referee: E. H. Pringle (Edinburgh). Broadcast details: No TV coverage.

13 February 1973 SCOTLAND 1 (Bone, 25 minutes) ENGLAND 2 (Whymark, 46, Barrowclough, 51) Rugby Park, Kilmarnock. Attendance: 6,000. SCOTLAND: Rough (Partick Thistle), Kennedy (Falkirk), McGrain (Celtic), Phillip (Crystal Palace), Young (Aberdeen), Hartford (West Bromwich, captain), Doyle (Ayr), McCluskey (Celtic), Alderson (Coventry), Bone (Norwich), Cropley (Hibs). Substitutions: Parlane (Rangers) for Cropley (66 minutes). ENGLAND: Stevenson (Burnley), McDowell (West Ham), Pejic (Stoke), Mortimer (Coventry), Blockley (Arsenal), Beattie (Ipswich), Barrowclough (Newcastle), Perryman (Tottenham), Richards (Wolves), Whymark (Ipswich), Currie (Sheffield United, captain). Referee: H. Wilson (Belfast). Broadcast details: No TV coverage.

14 March 1973 WALES 1 (James, 65 minutes) SCOTLAND 2 (Dalglish, 6 minutes, Hartford, 89) Vetch Field, Swansea. Attendance: 2,439. WALES: J. Phillips (Chelsea), P. Roberts (Bristol Rovers), Edwards (Chester), D. Roberts (Oxford), Aizlewood (Newport), Jones (Bournemouth), L. Phillips (Cardiff), James (Burnley), Showers (Cardiff), Smallman (Wrexham), O'Sullivan (Brighton). Substitution: Hubbard (Swindon) for Jones (46 minutes). SCOTLAND: Stewart (Kilmarnock), Kennedy (Falkirk), McGrain (Celtic), Anderson (Morton), Holton (Manchester United), Hartford (West Bromwich, captain), Doyle (Ayr), McGovern (Derby), Parlane (Rangers), Dalglish (Celtic), Connolly (Everton). Substitutions: McCulloch (Cardiff) for Parlane (63), McCluskey (Celtic) for McGovern (80 minutes). Referee: R. Mathewson (England). Broadcast details: No TV coverage.

27 February 1974 SCOTLAND 3 (Parlane (penalty), 33 minutes, Robinson, 80, Pearson, 89) WALES 0 Pittodrie. Attendance: 5,951. SCOTLAND: Stewart (Kilmarnock), Forsyth (Manchester United, captain), Wallace (Dunfermline), Robinson (Dundee), Johnstone (Rangers), Burns (Birmingham), Parlane (Rangers), Kelly (Arsenal), Pearson (St Johnstone), Cropley (Hibs), Prentice (Hearts). Substitutions: Brown (Chesterfield) for Stewart (36 minutes), Doyle for Prentice (61). WALES: Phillips (Chelsea), Dwyer (Cardiff), J. Jones (Wrexham), Griffiths (Manchester United), Evans (QPR), D. Jones (Bournemouth), Cartwright (Coventry), Villars (Cardiff), Showers (Cardiff), Smallman (Wrexham), Johnson (Crystal Palace). Referee: R. McFadden (Londonderry). Broadcast details: No TV coverage.

13 March 1974 ENGLAND 2 (Mills, 17 minutes, Latchford, 48) SCOTLAND 0 St James' Park, Newcastle. Attendance: 4,511. ENGLAND: Stevenson (Burnley), McDowell (West Ham), Gillard (QPR), Francis (QPR), Taylor (West Ham), Madren (Middlesbrough), Powell (Wolves), Mills (Middlesbrough), Latchford (Everton), Perryman (Tottenham), Hudson (Stoke). SCOTLAND: Stewart (Kilmarnock), Miller (Aberdeen), Calderwood (Birmingham), Johnstone (Rangers), MacDonald (St Johnstone), Gray (Leeds), Souness (Middlesbrough), Bruce (Newcastle), Pearson (St Johnstone), Craig (Sheffield Wednesday, captain), Gillies (Bristol City). Substitutions: Brown (Chesterfield) for Stewart (46 minutes), Gow (Bristol City) for Calderwood (51), Lamb (Preston) for Bruce (70). Referee:

J. D. Williams (Wrexham). Broadcast details: Highlights during *Sportsreel* BBC1 21.25-22.50; No STV or Grampian coverage.

18 December 1974 SCOTLAND 0 ENGLAND 3 (Tueart, 33 and 49 minutes, Whitworth, 86) Pittodrie. Attendance: 14,141. SCOTLAND: Stewart (Kilmarnock), Bremner (Hibs), Miller (Aberdeen), MacDonald (St Johnstone), Burley (Ipswich), Sullivan (Clyde), Johnstone (Rangers, captain), McCluskey (Celtic), Parlane (Rangers), Gray (Dundee United), Graham (Aberdeen). Substitutions: Brown (Sheffield United) for Stewart (54 minutes), Purdie (Aberdeen) for Sullivan (54). ENGLAND: Day (West Ham), Whitworth (Leicester), Gillard (QPR), Perryman (Tottenham), Lyons (Everton), Dodd (Stoke), B Powell (Wolves), Hankin (Burnley), Boyer (Norwich), S Powell (Derby), Tueart (Manchester City). Referee: E. Smyton (Northern Ireland). Broadcast details: No TV coverage.

25 February 1975 WALES 2 (Smallman, 27 minutes, James (penalty), 70) SCOTLAND 0 Vetch Field, Swansea. Attendance: 3,383 WALES: Phillips (Chelsea), Dwyer (Cardiff), Innes (Wrexham), Aitken (Bristol Rovers), Roberts (Oxford), Flynn (Burnley), Cartwright (Coventry), Emmanuel (Birmingham), Showers (Cardiff), Smallman (Wrexham), James (Burnley). SCOTLAND: Stewart Kennedy (Rangers), Stuart Kennedy (Falkirk), McCluskey (Celtic), McDougall (Rangers), Young (Aberdeen), Miller (Aberdeen), Parlane (Rangers), Bremner (Hibs), Gray (Dundee United), Craig (Newcastle, captain), Smith (Kilmarnock). Substitutions: Sullivan (Clyde) for McDougall (46 minutes), Pearson (Everton) for Gray (46). Referee: G. C. Kew (Leeds). Broadcast details: No TV coverage.

16 April 1975 SWEDEN 1 (Sjostrom, 55 minutes) SCOTLAND 2 (Craig, 41 and 65 (penalty)) Gamla Ullevi Stadium, Gothenburg. Attendance: 1,000. SWEDEN: Sevestedt (GAIS Gothenburg), Werner (Hammarby), Alund (Hammarby), Arvidsson (Osters IF), Borg (Orebro SK), Andersson (IFK Norrkoping), Samuelsson (Djurgardens), Nillson (Landskrona Bols), Gronhagen (GIF Sundsvall), Sjostrom (IFK Gothenburg), Dalqvist (AIK). SCOTLAND: Rough (Partick Thistle), Burley (Ipswich), Houston (Manchester United), Miller (Aberdeen), Hansen (Partick Thistle), Bremner (Hibs), Graham (Aberdeen), Craig (Newcastle, captain), Pearson (Everton), Pettigrew (Motherwell), Smith (Kilmarnock). Substitution: Brown (Sheffield United) for Rough (46 minutes). Referee: E. Pedersen (Denmark). Broadcast details: No TV coverage.

19 May 1975 SCOTLAND UNDER-23s 3 (Craig, 12 minutes, Conn, 15, Forsyth, 27) LEEDS UNITED 2 (Lorimer, 8 and 30) Hampden Park. Attendance: 9,978. SCOTLAND: Rough (Partick Thistle), Forsyth (Manchester United), S. Houston (Manchester United), McCluskey (Celtic), Young (Aberdeen), Narey (Dundee United), Conn (Tottenham), Pettigrew (Motherwell), Pearson (Everton), Gray (Dundee United), Craig (Newcastle, captain). Substitutions: Miller (Aberdeen) for McCluskey (46 minutes), Gordon Smith (St Johnstone) for Pettigrew (57), Gordon Smith (Kilmarnock) for Gray (75), B. Houston (Partick Thistle) for Forsyth (81). LEEDS: Harvey, Reaney, F. Gray, Bremner, Madeley, Hunter, Lorimer, Clarke, Jordan, Yorath, E. Gray. Substitutions: Letheran for Harvey (46 minutes), Cherry for Reaney (46), McKenzie for Jordan (46), Hampton for Frank Gray (76). Referee: R. H. Davidsson (Airdrie). Broadcast details: No TV coverage.

31 May 1975 ROMANIA 1 (Bolania, 65 minutes) SCOTLAND 2 (Young, 34 minutes, Pettigrew, 75) (European Championship Qualification Group B) 1 Mai Stadium, Pitesti. Attendance: 10,000. ROMANIA: Moraru (Steaua Bucharest), Zamfir (Arges Pitesti), Grigoras (Rapid Bucharest), Marin (Rapid Bucharest), Hajnal (Targu-Mures), Dumitru (Steaua Bucharest), Beldeanu (FCM Resita), Raducanu (Steaua Bucharest), Troi (Arges Pitesti), Boloni (Targu-Mures), Radu (Arges Pitesti). Substitutions: Multescu (Jiul Petrosani) for Dumitru (67 minutes), Nasatase (Steaua Bucharest) for Radu (75). SCOTLAND: Rough (Partick Thistle), Smith (St Johnstone), Houston (Manchester United), McCluskey (Celtic), Young (Aberdeen), Narey (Dundee United), Conn (Tottenham), Pettigrew (Motherwell), Pearson (Everton), Gray (Dundee United), Craig (Newcastle, captain). Substitutions: Graham (Aberdeen) for Conn (75 minutes), Smith (Kilmarnock) for Pettigrew (77). Referee: A. Ivanov (USSR). Broadcast details: No UK TV coverage.

2 September 1975 DENMARK 0 SCOTLAND 1 (Bremner, 28 minutes) (European Championship Qualification Group B) Frederikshaven Stadium, Frederikshaven. Attendance: 5,685. DENMARK: Kjaer (Esbjerg) Hojgaard (KB), Hansen (Frem), Sorensen (Velje), Andersen (B1903), Lorentzen (B1903), Rasmussen (Naestved), Christensen (Naestved), Bastrup (Aarhus), Petersen (Copenhagen Boldklub), Skov (OB). Substitution: Bertelsen (Esjberg) for Christensen (62 minutes), Nielsen (B1903) for Skov (81 minutes). SCOTLAND: Rough (Partick Thistle), Smith (St Johnstone), Frank Gray (Leeds), Narey (Dundee United), Young (Aberdeen), McCluskey (Celtic), Pearson (Everton), Bremner (Hibs), Pettigrew (Motherwell), J. Craig (Partick Thistle), T. Craig (Newcastle, captain). Substitution: Graham (Aberdeen) for Pettigrew (79 minutes). Referee: K. Scheurell (East Germany). Broadcast details: No UK TV coverage.

28 October 1975 SCOTLAND 4 (A. Gray, 11, 32 and 74 minutes, Prentice, 75) DENMARK 1 (Hansen, 45) (European Championship Qualification Group B) Easter Road. Attendance: 16,441. SCOTLAND: Rough (Partick Thistle), G. Smith (St Johnstone), F. Gray (Leeds), Narey (Dundee United), MacDonald (Celtic), Miller (Aberdeen), Conn (Tottenham), Bremner (Hibs), Pettigrew (Motherwell), A. Gray (Aston Villa), Craig (Newcastle, captain). Substitution: Prentice (Hearts) for Narey (64 minutes). DENMARK: Poulsen (B1903), Hojgaard (KB), P. H. Hansen (Frem), Sorensen (Vejle), Steffensen (AAB), Lorentzen (B1903), Bertelsen (Esjberg), Nielsen (B1903), J. Hansen (Kastrup), Arnesen (Fremad Amager), Skov (OB). Substitution: Pedersen (Koge Boldklub) for Skov (@ 60 minutes). Referee: L. A. Bjorck (Sweden). Broadcast details: No TV coverage.

16 December 1975 SCOTLAND 4 (Pettigrew, 35 and 50 minutes, Bremner, 63, Craig, 83 (penalty)) ROMANIA 0 (European Championship Qualification Group B) Brockville Park, Falkirk. Attendance: 8,419. SCOTLAND: Rough (Partick Thistle), Smith (St Johnstone), F Gray (Leeds), Bremner (Hibs), Hansen (Partick Thistle), Miller (Aberdeen), Conn (Tottenham), Pettigrew (Motherwell), J. Craig (Partick Thistle), T. Craig (Newcastle, captain), Prentice (Hearts). Substitution: Smith (Kilmarnock) for Conn (76 minutes) ROMANIA: Moraru (Steaua Bucharest), Poraczky (Universitatea Cluj), Ciocan (CLUB UNKNOWN), Dobrau (Dynamo Bucharest), Purima (Universitatea Craiova), Keiser (Olimpia Satu-Mare), Gligore (Asa Targu Mures), Muresan (Universitatea Cluj), Troi (Steaua Bucharest), Raducanu (Steaua Bucharest), Vrinceanu (Dynamo Bucharest). Substitutions: Atodiresi (FCM Resita) for Vrinceanu (46 minutes), Stefan (Dynamo Bucharest) for Moraru (53 minutes). Referee: M. Vautrot (France). Broadcast details: No TV coverage.

February 4 1976 WALES 2 (Thomas, 81 minutes, Deacy, 88 minutes (penalty)) SCOTLAND 3 (Craig, 20 minutes, Pettigrew, 44, Pettigrew, 62) Racecourse Ground, Wrexham. Attendance: 2,222. WALES: Letheran (Leeds), Dwyer (Cardiff), Jones (Liverpool), Johnson (Crystal Palace), Aizlewood (Newport), Williams (Bristol Rovers), Cartwright (Coventry), Lewis (Grimsby), Deacy (PSV Eindhoven), O'Sullivan (Brighton), Harris (Leeds). Substitutions: Thomas (Wrexham) for Cartwright (@57 minutes), Aitken (Bristol Rovers) for Williams (@57), Curtis (Swansea) for Lewis (77). SCOTLAND: Rough (Partick Thistle), Brownlie (Hibs), McLelland (Aberdeen), Miller (Aberdeen), McVie (Motherwell), T. Craig (Newcastle, captain), Johnstone (Rangers), Bremner (Hibs), Pettigrew (Motherwell), J. Craig (Partick Thistle), Prentice (Hearts). Substitutions: Stewart (Kilmarnock) for Rough (46 minutes), Gordon Smith (Kilmarnock) for Prentice (46), Hansen (Partick Thistle) for McVie (64), Joe Smith (Aberdeen) for Johnstone (75). Missed penalty: Craig (62 minutes). Referee: J. A. Hunting (Leicester). Broadcast details: No TV coverage.

18 February 1976 HOLLAND 2 (Van Deinsten, 48 minutes, Kist, 71) SCOTLAND 0 (European Championship Quarter-Final, First Leg) NAC Stadium, Breda. Attendance: 14,000. HOLLAND: Ruiter (Anderlecht), Antz (Go Ahead Eagles), Rijsbergen (Feyenoord, captain), Kraay (PSV Eindhoven), Everse (Feyenoord), Peters (NEC), Van de Kerkhof (PSV Eindhoven), Lubse (PSV Eindhoven), Kist (AZ 67), Jansen (Feyenoord), Van Deinsten

(Go Ahead Eagles). SCOTLAND: Rough (Partick Thistle), Brownlie (Hibs), McLelland (Aberdeen), Miller (Aberdeen, captain), McVie (Motherwell), Souness (Middlesbrough), Burns (Birmingham), Bremner (Hibs), Craig (Partick Thistle), Dalglish (Celtic), Johnstone (Rangers). Substitution: Narey (Dundee United) for McVie (75 minutes). Referee: L. Nielsen (Denmark). Broadcast details: Highlights included in *Sportscene* BBC1 21.25-22.45; No STV or Grampian coverage.

March 24 1976 SCOTLAND 2 (Johnstone, 15 minutes, Jackson, 30) HOLLAND 0 (European Championship Quarter-Final, Second Leg) After extra time, aggregate score 2-2 (Holland won 4-3 on penalties). Penalties: SCOTLAND: Miller (Scored), Jordan (Missed), Brownlie (Scored), F. Gray (Scored), Craig (Missed). HOLLAND: Nanninga (Scored), Van Rijnsoever (Scored), Meutstege (Missed), Van Deinsen (Scored), Kila (Scored) Easter Road. Attendance: 32,583. SCOTLAND: Rough (Partick Thistle), Brownlie (Hibs), F. Gray (Leeds), Jackson (Rangers), Miller (Aberdeen), T. Craig (Newcastle, captain), Bremner (Hibs), Pettigrew (Motherwell), Jordan (Leeds), Smith (Kilmarnock), Johnstone (Rangers). Substitution: Dickson (Queen of the South) for Smith (46 minutes). HOLLAND: Schellekens (NEC), Meutstege (Sparta), Lacroi (MVV), Balkenstein (Sparta), Everse (Feyenoord), Kila (The Hague), Lubse (PSV Eindhoven), Hovenkamp (AZ 67), Kist (AZ67), Nanninga (Roda JC), Van Deinsen (Go Ahead Eagles). Referee: K. Ohmsen (West Germany). Broadcast details: No TV coverage.

Scotland Under-21 International Matches played 1970–79

All details complete except during 1977 Toulon tournament where four substitiute times are
unavailable and one Hungarian player's club unidentified.

9 October 1976 KILMARNOCK 0 SCOTLAND UNDER-21s 3 (Wark, 9 minutes, McNiven, 56, Burley, 62) Rugby Park. Attendance: 2,859. KILMARNOCK: A. McCulloch, Maxwell, Robertson, Murdoch, Clarke, McDicken, McLean, I. McCulloch, Fallis, Sheed, Smith. Substitutions: Fleming for Smith (60 minutes), Ward for McDicken (70). SCOTLAND: Clark (Aberdeen), Burley (Ipswich), Stanton (Celtic, captain), Aitken (Celtic), Albiston (Manchester United), Wark (Ipswich), Narey (Dundee United), Burns (Celtic), Provan (Kilmarnock), Wallace (Coventry), Sturrock (Dundee United). Substitutions: McNiven (Leeds) for Wallace (29 minutes), Paterson (Manchester United) for Aitken (56), Muir (Hibs) for Wark (70). Referee: D. Syme (Glasgow). Broadcast details: No TV coverage.

12 October 1976 CZECHOSLOVAKIA 0 SCOTLAND 0 (European Under-21 Championship Group 6) Stadion Mesta Plzne, Pilsen. Attendance: 6,000. CZECHOSLOVAKIA: Macak (Banik Ostrava), Fiala (Dukla Prague), Duda (MFK Frydek- Mistek), Novak (Dukla Prague), Prokes (Bohemians), Hudec (Inter Bratislava), Gasparik (Spartak Trnava), Pokluda (Sklo Union Teplice), Farkas (Lokomitiva Kosice), Herda (Slavia Prague), Nemec (Slovan Bratislava). Substitution: Pelc (Dukla Prague) for Nenec (58 minutes). SCOTLAND: Clark (Aberdeen), Burley (Ipswich), Albiston (Manchester United), Stanton (Celtic, captain), Aitken (Celtic), Burns (Celtic), Cooper (Clydebank), Wark (Ipswich), McNiven (Leeds), Narey (Dundee United), Sturrock (Dundee United). Substitutions: Provan (Kilmarnock) for McNiven (60 minutes), Muir (Hibs) for Narey (84). Referee: H. Latzin (Austria). Broadcast details: No UK TV coverage.

9 February 1977 SCOTLAND 3 (Sturrock, 4 minutes, Wark, 52, McNiven, 88) WALES 2 (Deacy, 20 minutes, Sayer, 86) Easter Road. Attendance: 4,538. SCOTLAND: Clark (Aberdeen, captain), Burley (Ipswich), Albiston (Manchester United), Ross (Arsenal), Reid (St Mirren), Aitken (Celtic), Cooper (Clydebank), Wark (Ipswich), Parlane (Rangers), Burns (Celtic), Sturrock (Dundee United). Substitutions: McNiven (Leeds) for Sturrock (46 minutes), Fitzpatrick (St Mirren) for Ross (71). WALES: Letheran (Leeds), Tibbott (Ipswich), Stevenson (Leeds), Bater (Bristol Rovers), Cegieski (Wrexham), Hughes (West Bromwich), Sayer (Cardiff), Giles

(Cardiff), James (Swansea), Deacy (PSV Eindhoven), Edwards (Chester). Substitution: Harris (Leeds) for James (71). Referee: T. R. Kyle (Glasgow). Broadcast details: No UK TV coverage.

30 March 1977 SWITZERLAND 2 (Decastel, 71 minutes, Zappa, 84) SCOTLAND 0 (European Under-21 Championship Group 6) Wankdorf Stadium, Berne. Attendance: 500. SWITZERLAND: Engel (Servette), In-Albon (FC Sion), Mast (Young Boys), Casanova (FC Lugano), Dumont (CS Chenois), Askeret (Winterthur), Von Wartburg (FC Basel), Scheiwiler (FC Zurich, captain), Maisaen (FC Basel), Decastel (Neuchatel Xamax), Schonenberger (FC Basel). Substitutions: Zappa (Lugano) for Schonenberger (59 minutes), Luthi (FC Biel) for Ackeret (84). SCOTLAND: Clark (Aberdeen), Burley (Ipswich), Albiston (Manchester United), Wark (Ipswich), Reid (St Mirren), Narey (Dundee United), Cooper (Clydebank), Hartford (Manchester City, captain), Sturrock (Dundee United), Aitken (Celtic), Melrose (Partick Thistle). Substitutions: McNiven (Leeds) for Melrose (64) Fitzpatrick (St Mirren) for Reid (71). Referee: R. Vigliani (France). Broadcast details: No UK TV coverage.

27 April 1977 ENGLAND 1 (Cunningham, 50 minutes) SCOTLAND 0 Bramall Lane, Sheffield. Attendance: 8,934. ENGLAND: Bradshaw (Blackburn), Daniel (Hull), Peach (Southampton), Sims (Leicester), Futcher (Luton), Owen (Manchester City), Cunningham (West Bromwich), Williams (Southampton), Bertschin (Ipswich), Reid (Bolton), Barnes (Manchester City). SCOTLAND: Ferguson (Hamilton), Sinclair (Dumbarton), Burns (Celtic), Fitzpatrick (St Mirren), Reid (St Mirren), Stevens (Motherwell), McGarvey (St Mirren), Watson (Rangers), Sturrock (Dundee United), Craig (Newcastle, captain), Cooper (Clydebank). Substitutions: Thomson (Partick Thistle) for Ferguson (46 minutes) Robertson (Rangers) for McGarvey (65). Referee: G. C. Kew (Middlesbrough Thistle). Broadcast details: No TV coverage.

12 June 1977 SCOTLAND 0 HUNGARY 1 (Fuko, 33 minutes) Stade Scaglia, La Seyne. Attendance: 5,000. SCOTLAND: Thomson (Partick Thistle), Burley (Ipswich), Albiston (Manchester United), Wark (Ipswich), Hansen (Liverpool), Narey (Dundee United), Sturrock (Dundee United), Aitken (Celtic), Craig (Celtic), Watson (Rangers), Payne (Dundee United). Substitutions: Wallace (Coventry) for Aitken (52 minutes), Burns (Celtic) for Watson (time unknown). HUNGARY: Kiss (Tatabanya Banyasz), Major (MTK Budapest), Gellert (MTK Budapest), Adams (club unknown), Hamori (Kossuth KFSE), Becsei (Vasas), Fuko (DVTK), Tar (Szombathelyi Haladas), Hegyi (Ujpest Dozsa), Szabo (Dorogi Banyasz), Borostyan (Diosgyori VTK). Referee: M. Van Langenhove (Belgium). Broadcast details: No UK TV coverage.

14 June 1977 SCOTLAND 4 (Wallace, 14 and 60 minutes, Craig 49, McGarvey, 67) PORTUGAL 3 (Fonesca, 31 minutes, Gomes, 35 and 86) Stade de Bon Recontre, Toulon. Attendance: 5,000. SCOTLAND: Thomson (Partick Thistle), Burley (Ipswich), Albiston (Manchester United), Wark (Ipswich), Hansen (Liverpool), Narey (Dundee United), Sturrock (Dundee United), Fitzpatrick (St Mirren), Craig (Celtic), Wallace (Coventry), Payne (Dundee United). Substitution: McGarvey (St Mirren) for Sturrock (46 minutes) Burns (Celtic) for Payne (time unknown). PORTUGAL: Jorge (Postinon), Teixeira (Porto), Eduardo (Maritimo), Alberto (Benfica), Vilaca (Braga), Isidro (Belenenses), Barao (Sporting), Frasco (Leixoes), Gomes (V Set), Fonesca (Montijo), Garces (B Mar). Referee: M. Van Langenhove (Belgium). Broadcast details: No UK TV coverage.

16 June 1977 FRANCE 1 (Soler, 86 minutes) SCOTLAND 0 Stade de Bon Recontre, Toulon. Attendance: 20,000. FRANCE: De Rocco (Olympique Lyon), Paillot (Olympique Lyon), Mahut (Troyes), Renaut (PSG), Pilorget (PSG), Justier (PSG), Martinez (Olympique Lyon), Jeannol (Nancy), Soler (Sochaux, captain), Flores (Olimpique Marseille), Francoice (Lens). SCOTLAND: Thomson (Partick Thistle), Burley (Ipswich), Albiston (Manchester United), Hansen (Liverpool), Aitken (Celtic) Fitzpatrick (St Mirren), McGarvey (St Mirren), Wallace (Coventry), Craig (Celtic), Watson (Rangers), Wark (Ipswich). Substitutions: Burns (Celtic) for Watson (time unknown), Payne (Dundee United) for Craig (time unknown). Referee: S. Serafino (Italy). Broadcast details: No UK TV coverage.

19 June 1977 SCOTLAND 2 (Wark, 12 and 75 minutes) ITALY 2 (Bozzi, 25 minutes and Rondon, 73) 5th/6th-Place Play Off Italy won 3-0 on penalties. Penalties: SCOTLAND Wark (Missed), Hansen (Missed), Aitken (Missed) ITALY Bodini (Missed), Donati (Scored), Brilli (Scored),

Rondon (Scored) Toulon. Attendance: 13,000. SCOTLAND: Thomson (Partick Thistle), Burley (Ipswich), Albiston (Manchester United), Wark (Ipswich), Hansen (Liverpool), Narey (Dundee United), Sturrock (Dundee United), Aitken (Celtic), Wallace (Coventry), Fitzpatrick (St Mirren), Payne (Dundee United). Substitutions: Sinclair (Dumbarton) for Albiston (46 minutes), McGarvey (St Mirren) for Sturrock (46 minutes). ITALY: Bodini (Cremonese), Bonini (Bellaria), Tesser (Treviso), Brio (Pistoiese), Prandelli (Cremonese), Pasinato (Treviso), Pileggi (Alessandria), Bozzi (Benevento), Donati (Benacense), Rondon (Bolzano), Brilli (Licorno). Sent off: Prandelli (First half for 5 minute period in sin bin). Referee: M. Van Langenhove (Belgium). Broadcast details: No UK TV coverage.

7 September 1977 SCOTLAND 3 (Wallace, 26 and 70 minutes, Cooper, 64) SWITZERLAND 1 Brigger, 26 minutes) (European Under-21 Championship Group 6) Ibrox. Attendance: 3,866. SCOTLAND: Stewart (Kilmarnock), Burley (Ipswich), Albiston (Manchester United), Miller (Aberdeen), Narey (Dundee United), Fitzpatrick (St Mirren, captain), Sturrock (Dundee United), Payne (Dundee United), Wallace (Coventry), Burns (Celtic), Cooper (Rangers). Substitution: Watson (Rangers) for Burns (57 minutes). Missed penalty: Narey (29 minutes). SWITZERLAND: Berbig (Grasshoppers), Baur (FC Zurich), Gretier (FC Vevey Sports), Zappa (Lugano), In-Albon (FC Sion), Tanner (FC Basel), Wehrli (Winterthur), Scheiwiler (FC Zurich, captain), Brigger (Sion), Decastel (Neuchatel Xamax), Schonenberger (FC Basel). Substitutions: Luthi (FC Biel) for Gretler (74 minutes), Mast (Young Boys) for Brigger (80). Referee: J. Lorimer (Belfast). Broadcast details: No TV coverage.

20 September 1977 SCOTLAND 2 (Burley, 39 minutes, Sturrock, 42) CZECHOSLOVAKIA 1 (Kroupa, 26 minutes) (European Under-21 Championship Group 6) Tynecastle. Attendance: 14,015. SCOTLAND: Stewart (Kilmarnock), Burley (Ipswich), Albiston (Manchester United), Miller (Aberdeen), Narey (Dundee United), Fitzpatrick (St Mirren, captain), Sturrock (Dundee United), Payne (Dundee United), McGarvey (Celtic), Aitken (Celtic), Cooper (Rangers). CZECHOSLOVAKIA: Macek (Banik Ostrava), Hudec (Inter Bratislava), Fiala (Dukla Prague), Ondrus (Dukla Banska Bystrica), Siladi (Dukla Banska Bystrica), Berger (Viktoria Plzen), Brezik (Inter Bratislava), Janecka (Zbrojovka Brno), Kroupa (Zbrojovka Brno), Herda (Slavia Prague), Pelc (Dukla Prague). Referee: J. Peeters (Belgium). Broadcast details: No TV coverage.

8 February 1978 WALES 1 (James, 33 minutes) SCOTLAND 0 Sealand Road, Chester. Attendance: 2,454. WALES: Kendall (Tottenham), Nicholas (Crystal Palace), Stevenson (Leeds), Hughes (West Bromwich), Pontin (Cardiff), Thomas (Wrexham, captain), Nardiello (Coventry), Giles (Cardiff), Edwards (Chester), Clarke (Manchester United), James (Swansea). Substitution: Davies (Norwich) for Thomas (88 minutes). SCOTLAND: Thomson (Partick Thistle), Brazil (Hibs), Casey (Celtic), Wark (Ipswich, captain), McLeish (Aberdeen), Aitken (Celtic), Payne (Dundee United), Russell (Rangers), Dodds (Dundee United), Smith (Rangers), McNab (Tottenham). Substitution: Orr (Morton) for Casey (63 minutes). Referee: R. Bridges (Wales). Broadcast details: No TV coverage.

17 September 1978 SCOTLAND UNDER-21s 3 (Melrose, 11 minutes, Orr, 66, MacLeod, 68) USA 1 (Russell, 46 minutes) Pittodrie. Attendance: 5,993. SCOTLAND: Thomson (St Mirren), Sneddon (Celtic), Gillespie (Coventry), Orr (Morton), McLeish (Aberdeen), MacLeod (Dumbarton), Melrose (Partick Thistle), Jardine (Kilmarnock), McCluskey (Celtic), Bannon (Hearts, captain), Lindsay (Motherwell). Substitutions: McNicholl (Luton) for McLeish (46 minutes), Mitchell (Queen of the South) for Jardine (46), Redford (Dundee) for Lindsay (64), Leighton (Aberdeen) for Thomson (69). USA: Brcic (New York Cosmos), Pollihan (Rochester Lancers), Myernick (Dallas Tornadoes), Droege (Rochester Lancers), Fowles (Fort Lauderdale Strikers), Davis (New York Cosmos), Russell (Houston Hurricanes), Bandov (Tampa Bay Rowdies), Trost (California Surf), Nanchoff (Colorado Caribous), Etherington (New York Cosmos). Substitutions: Villa (Minnesota Kicks) for Trost (56 minutes), George Nanchoff (Fort Lauderdale Strikers) for Etherington (64), McAlister (Seattle Sounders) for Fowles (67). Referee: R. B. Valentine (Dundee). Broadcast

details: STV and Grampian *Scotsport* 15.50-17.20 featured live second-half coverage plus highlights of Leeds v Tottenham; No BBC coverage.

24 October 1978 SCOTLAND 5 (Stewart, 37 minutes, McCluskey, 49 and 65, McLeod, 53 Wark, 69) NORWAY 1 (Jacobsen, 84 minutes) (European Under-21 Championship Group 2) Easter Road. Attendance: 9,858. SCOTLAND: Thomson (St Mirren), Narey (Dundee United), McNicholl (Brentford), Orr (Morton), Stewart (Dundee United), Bannon (Hearts), Wark (Ipswich), Aitken (Celtic), McCluskey (Celtic), A. McLeod (Hibs, captain), Melrose (Partick Thistle). Substitutions: M. MacLeod (Dumbarton) for Wark (73 minutes), Redford (Dundee) for Melrose (73). NORWAY: Haugvaldstad (Viking), Inversen (Bryne), Fjaelberg (Sola), Gran (Lyn Oslo), Giske (Kristiansund), Anderson (Start), Myhre (Start), Kojedal (Hamar), Davidsen (Frigg), Jacobsen (Hamry), Refvik (Viking). Substitutions: Pedersen (Brann) for Fjaelberg (73 minutes), Asia (Hamkam) for Anderson (73). Referee: G. Haraldsson (Iceland). Broadcast details: No TV coverage.

28 November 1978 PORTUGAL 0 SCOTLAND 3 (McCluskey, 54 minutes, McLeod (penalty) 62 and 86) (European Under-21 Championship Group 2) Restelo Stadium, Lisbon. Attendance: 1,000. PORTUGAL: Martins (Barreirense), Olavo (Maritimo), Silva (V Setubal), Alinho (Belenenses, captain) Tobica (Farense), Pereirinha (Benfica), Manuel (Barreirense), Antonio (Estoril), Jorge (Benfica), Fontes (Braga), Folha (Leixoes). Substitutions: Moutinho (Portimonense) for Tobica (58 minutes), Freire (Sporting) for Manuel (74). SCOTLAND: J. Stewart (Middlesbrough), R. Stewart (Dundee United), Dawson (Rangers), Wark (Ipswich), McNicholl (Brentford), Orr (Morton), McCluskey (Celtic), Bannon (Hearts), A. McLeod (Hibs, captain), Aitken (Celtic), Melrose (Partick Thistle). Substitution: M. MacLeod (Celtic) for Melrose (84 minutes). Referee: G. Carrion (Spain). Broadcast details: No UK TV coverage. Note: Shown live on Portuguese TV.

7 June 1979 NORWAY 2 (Davidsen, 59 minutes, Halvorsen, 68) SCOTLAND 2 (Bannon, 16 minutes, A McLeod, 83) (European Under-21 Championship Group 2) Haugesund Stadium. Attendance: 1,908. NORWAY: Eggen (Nessegutten), Asia (Hamkam), Gran (Valerengen), Herlovsen (Frederikstad), Brevik (Steinkjer IFK), Kojedal (Hamar), Davidsen (Frigg), Myhre (Start), Kortgaard (Mjondalen), Halvorsen (Pors Grenland), Brandhaug (Strindheim). SCOTLAND: Thompson (St Mirren), Stewart (Dundee United), Dawson (Rangers), Aitken (Celtic), McNicholl (Brentford), Orr (Morton), Brazil (Ipswich), Bannon (Chelsea), A. McLeod (Hibs, captain), M. MacLeod (Celtic), Melrose (Partick Thistle). Substitution: Abercrombie (St Mirren) for Murdo MacLeod (80 minutes). Referee: J. F. Svenson (Sweden). Broadcast details: No UK TV coverage.

20 November 1979 BELGIUM 0 SCOTLAND 1 (McCluskey, 40 minutes) (European Under-21 Championship Group 2) Freethiel Stadium, Beveren. Attendance: 2,500. BELGIUM: Preud'homme (Standard Liege), Devriese (Molenbeek), Ipermans (Antwerp), De Greed (Beringen), Mariman (Antwerp), Cluytens (Beveren), Plessers (Standard Liege), Mommens (Lokeren, Captain), Electeur (Anderlecht), Snelders (Antwerp), Dardenne (Lokeren). Substitution: Lecloux (FC Liegeois) for Plessers (79 minutes). SCOTLAND: Thompson (St Mirren), Stewart (Dundee United), Dawson (Rangers), Orr (Morton), McNicholl (Brentford), Aitken (Celtic, Captain), Strachan (Aberdeen), Bannon (Chelsea), McCluskey (Celtic), Brazil (Ipswich), Ritchie (Morton). Referee: J. Baumaan (Switzerland). Broadcast details: No UK TV coverage.

18 December 1979 SCOTLAND 2 (Stewart (penalty), 30 minutes, Melrose, 44) BELGIUM 2 (Lecloux, 68 minutes, Martens, 78) (European Under-21 Championship Group 2) Tynecastle. Attendance: 7,486. SCOTLAND: Thomson (St Mirren), Stewart (West Ham, Captain), Dawson (Rangers), McLeish (Aberdeen), McNicholl (Brentford), Fulton (St Mirren), McCluskey (Celtic), Russell (Rangers), Archibald (Aberdeen), MacLeod (Celtic), Brazil (Ipswich). Substitutions: Melrose (Partick Thistle) for Russell (40 minutes), Tolmie (Morton) for Brazil (67). BELGIUM: Preud'homme (Standard Liege), DeVriese (RWD Molenbeek), De Wolf (RWD Molenbeek), De Greef (Beringen), Mariman (Antwerp),

Ipermans (Antwerp), Snelders (Antwerp), Mommens (Lokeren), Bosch (Lierse SK), Lecloux (FC Liegeois), Martens (Anderlecht). Substitution: Claes (Mechelen) for Impermaans (60–67 minutes). Referee: P. Jansen (Denmark). Broadcast details: No TV coverage.

Other Matches

27 January 1971 RANGERS/CELTIC SELECT 1 (Best, 29 minutes) SCOTLAND 2 (Gemmill, 10 minutes, Lorimer, 84) Ibrox Disaster Benefit Match Hampden Park. Attendance: 81,405. OLD FIRM SELECT: Bonetti (Chelsea), Jardine (Rangers), Greig (Rangers), Murdoch (Celtic), McNeill (Celtic), Small (Rangers), Henderson (Rangers), Hughes (Celtic), Charlton (Manchester United), Johnston (Rangers), Best (Manchester United). SCOTLAND XI: Cruickshank (Hearts), Hay (Celtic), Gemmell (Celtic), Stanton (Hibs), McKinnon (Rangers), Moncur (Newcastle, Captain), Lorimer (Leeds), Gemmill (Derby), Stein (Rangers), O'Hare (Derby), Cooke (Chelsea). Substitution: Craig(Celtic) for McKinnon (46 minutes), McLean (Kilmarnock) for O'Hare (86). Referee: W. Anderson (East Kilbride). Broadcast details: BBC1 *Ibrox Disaster Charity Football Highlights* 22.45-23.15; STV's *Scotsport* 23.00-23.40 also featured highlights; No Grampian coverage.

22 March 1976 GREAT BRITAIN XI 3 (Perryman, Greaves, Ball) SCOTLAND XI 2 (Hunter, Lorimer) Alan Mullery Testimonial Match, Craven Cottage, London. Attendance: 9,300 no goal times available, half-time score was 2-2. GREAT BRITAIN: Mellor (Fulham), Hollins (QPR), Lampard (West Ham), Mullery (Fulham), A. Hunter (Ipswich), Moore (Fulham), Ball (Arsenal), Taylor (West Ham), Chivers (Tottenham), Greaves (Brentwood), Perryman (Tottenham). SCOTLAND: Harvey (Leeds), Burley (Ipswich), Cooper (Middlesbrough), Young (Tottenham), McLintock (QPR), Cordova (Roma), Lorimer (Leeds), Souness (Middlesbrough), Masson (QPR), Hutchison (Coventry), N. Hunter (Leeds). Referee: J. Taylor (Wolverhampton). Broadcast details: No TV coverage.

16 April 1978 RANGERS 5 (Johnstone, 1 minute, Greig, 60 and 80, Russell, 63 and 74) SCOTLAND XI 0 John Greig Testimonial Match, Ibrox Stadium. Attendance: 65,000. RANGERS: McCloy, Jardine, Greig, Forsyth, Jackson, MacDonald, McLean, Russell, Johnstone, Smith, Cooper. Substitutions: Watson for MacDonald (46 minutes), Strickland for McLean (46). SCOTLAND: Blyth (Coventry), Brownlie (Hibs), Whitaker (Partick Thistle), Masson (Derby), McQueen (Manchester United), Rioch (Derby), Robertson (Nottingham Forest), Wallace (Coventry), Jordan (Manchester United), Hartford (Manchester City), Gemmill (Nottingham Forest). Referee: I. Foote (Glasgow). Broadcast details: No TV coverage.

19 April 1978 HIGHLAND LEAGUE SELECT 2 (Urquhart, 43 minutes, MacKintosh, 65) SCOTLAND XI 2 (Sneddon, 78 minutes, Cramond, 85) Kingmills Park, Inverness. Attendance: 4,301. HIGHLAND SELECT: Gray (Keith), Bruce (Buckie Thistle), Buchan (Elgin City), Considine (Huntly), Cochrane (Nairn County), Corbett (Inverness Caledonian), McKay (Ross County), Duncan (Inverness Thistle), Urquhart (Inverness Caledonian), MacKintosh (Inverness Caledonian), Wilson (Elgin City). Substitutions: Winton for McKay (89 minutes). SCOTLAND: Stewart (Kilmarnock), Sneddon (Celtic), Aitken (Celtic), Stevens (Motherwell), Reid (St Mirren), McMaster (Aberdeen), Bannon (Hearts), Fitzpatrick (St Mirren), McGarvey (St Mirren), Provan (Kilmarnock), McCluskey (Celtic). Substitutions: Clarke (Kilmarnock) for Reid (20 minutes), Cramond (Ayr) for Provan (46). Referee: W. P. Knowles (Inverurie). Broadcast details: No TV coverage.

Recommended Bibliography

Bale, B, *Bremner!* (London, Andre Deutsch, 1998)

Gordon, Richard, *Scotland '74* (Edinburgh: Black and White, 2014)

Harrison, P, *Keep Fighting: The Billy Bremner Story* (Edinburgh, Black and White, 2017)

McColl, G, *'78 How a Nation Lost the World Cup* (London: Headline, 2008)

Macpherson, A, *Adventures in the Golden Age: Scotland in the World Cup Finals* (Edinburgh: Black and White, 2018)

Rostron, P, *Peter Lorimer: Leeds and Scotland Hero* (Edinburgh, Mainstream, 2005)

Wilson, M, *Don't Cry For Me Argentina* (Edinburgh: Mainstream, 1998)